AGAINST TOLERATION

'In three Caribbean colonies, laws prohibiting Spiritual Baptist worship were enacted between 1912 and 1927, approved by the Colonial Office despite Britain's commitment to religious toleration. This deeply researched and powerfully argued book explains why and how Britain betrayed its own fundamental principles and violated the human and religious rights of Caribbean people.'

Bridget Brereton
Emerita Professor of History, The UWI, Trinidad & Tobago

AGAINST TOLERATION

Britain's Persecution of the Spiritual Baptists

Claudius K. Fergus

IAN RANDLE PUBLISHERS
Kingston • Miami
www.ianrandlepublishers.com

First published in Jamaica, 2024 by
Ian Randle Publishers
16 Herb McKenley Drive
Box 686
Kingston 6
www.ianrandlepublishers.com

© 2024, Claudius K. Fergus

National Library of Jamaica Cataloguing-In-Publication Data

   Name: Fergus, Claudius K., author.
   Title: Against Toleration : Britain's persecution of the Spiritual
      Baptists / Claudius K. Fergus.
Description: Kingston, Jamaica : Ian Randle Publishers, 2024.
   | Includes bibliographical references.
Identifiers: ISBN 9789768339027 (hbk). | ISBN 9789768339034
   (pbk).
   Subjects: LCSH : Spiritual Baptists – West Indies, British. |
      Religious tolerance – Great Britain – Baptists. | Toleration –
      Religious aspects – Baptists. | Prohibition – Religious aspects. |
      Black people – West Indies, British – Religion. | Christian sect –
      West Indies, British.
   Classification: DDC 286 -- dc23.

Cover Illustration by Al Alexander

Cover and Book Design by Ian Randle Publishers
Printed and Bound in the United States of America

Dedication

I dedicate this study to my maternal grandmother, Elverlee Bouville, a member of the Spiritual Baptist faith, who transitioned in 1950, one year before the repeal of the Shouters Prohibition Ordinance of 1917. I also dedicate this study to my maternal aunt, Christiana Bouville who followed in her mother's footsteps and became a Spiritual Baptist itinerant preacher; also, to my father, Cecil Fergus, a shepherd in the faith.

Contents

Preface

*'Since the beginning of Christianity converts of African
descent were present.'**

This study began in 2010 with a focus on Trinidad and Tobago. The topic soon shifted from the received narrative of Spiritual Baptist resistance against prohibition to the constitutionality of the Shouters' Prohibition Ordinance, 1917. With the realisation that the Trinidad and Tobago law was a near replica of the Shakerism Prohibition Ordinance of St Vincent enacted five years earlier, it became increasingly evident that the prohibition of the Shouters could not be properly understood independent of a detailed study of the socio-political and cultural environment in St Vincent and the background of the men at the Colonial Office who reviewed the anti-Shakerism legislation and recommended its assent to the secretary of state for the Colonies.

Having prior knowledge of some of the major milestones along the nearly two-hundred-year journey of conscience in the British Empire from the enactment of the Toleration Act, 1689 to the ubiquitous Places of Worship Registration Act (PWRA), 1855, I was intrigued that the colonial legislatures in three colonies not only passed prohibition ordinances against the Spiritual Baptists between 1912 and 1927 but more so, that those laws received gubernatorial and royal sanction

---

* Olayemi O.T. Fatusi, 'The Retransmission of Evangelical Christianity in Nigeria: The Legacy and Lessons from Bishop Samuel Ajayi Crowther's Life and Ministry (1810–1891),' *Southwestern Journal of Theology* (2019): https:// swbtsv7.s3.amazonaws.com/media/Theology_Journal/61.2/61.2_The_ Retransmission_of_Evangelical_Christianity_in_Nigeria_Fatusi.pdf.

despite officials of the Colonial Office making a *prima facie* case against the St Vincent government for violating the laws of conscience more than once; moreover, the metropolitan watchdogs at the Colonial Office acknowledged that St Vincent's administrator had blatantly violated a century's old royal admonition to colonial governors against legislating matters of religious rights without first seeking a review from the Colonial Office. Painstaking research unravelled a web of political intrigues and compromises at the highest levels of colonial administration. The revelations support demands for reparatory justice for the victims of this inhumane chapter in modern Caribbean history in which imperial churches were primary collaborators and agents. Frantz Fanon states, 'The Church in the colonies is the White people's Church, the foreigner's Church. She does not call the natives to God's ways but to the ways of the White man, of the master, of the oppressor.'[1] According to Fanon, the 'logical conclusion' of this socialisation is that it turns the colonised 'into an animal' with the elites even adopting 'zoological terms' to describe the traditional culture of the colonised.[2] Fanon could well have been writing about Spiritual Baptists and the demonisation and dehumanisation to which the elites subjected them.

Religious toleration was an epic journey for civil rights campaigners in the United Kingdom and its colonies. By the late nineteenth century, constitutional protection of the right of conscience had become so ubiquitous that any religious denomination confessing its faith in Biblical Jesus and the Christian Trinity and any religious denomination professing a deity could not be outlawed without the sinister political influences that the administrator of St Vincent wielded in Parliament and the Colonial Office.

The work explores aspects of the origin and doctrinal character of the Spiritual Baptist that have never been explored before or inadequately explored and which add context to the hostility of colonial elites toward the religion. Freed from the administrative control of White church leaders, the African American Baptist Church transitioned into various expressions of African Caribbean credobaptism, the first of such institutions in the region.

Although Grenada was a third colony of prohibition, the study does not engage in the politics of repression or the legal-political struggle in that colony to repeal the ordinance. Grenada is worthy of inclusion, but the author lacked the resources to do so in this study; only the legislation is addressed and combined with the chapter on the Shouters' Prohibition Ordinance. On the other hand, Jamaica is important to this study although a bill to proscribe Revival Zion failed to get the nod of the governor. Jamaica was one of the earliest sites of free African Baptists in the Caribbean. The pioneers of the Jamaican Baptist Church faced legal discrimination during the lifetime of its founders but did not suffer the absolute prohibition imposed on the Spiritual Baptists. The defeat of Jamaica's prohibition bill in 1903 provides historical context for evaluating the success of prohibition in the selected colonies.

Research for this study was carried out in the National Archives and Legal Affairs Department of St Vincent and the Grenadines – a special appreciation to Ms Cashena Allen-Foster of the SVGNA; the British Library and Public Records Office in London, UK; the Alma Jordan Library of The University of the West Indies and the National Archives of Trinidad and Tobago. Online sources supplied vital primary materials, including rare books, especially Google Books, Questia Online Library (now defunct), *The Baptist Magazine*, the *New York Times*, Florida International University newspaper archives, JSTOR, and the latest, the Internet Archive, an online borrowing platform that hold many Google Books. Unfortunately, many online sources forego pagination, even if they are digitised copies of the original printed texts; the same applies to Kindle versions of published books. For invaluable insights into the Spiritual Baptist as a living faith, I am indebted to many through formal and informal interviews, including Stacy Clarke and Stella Bouville of Trinidad and Veda Edwards of St Vincent. Invitations to lecture by the Spiritual Baptist leadership stimulated further research on the movement. I am also indebted to Al Alexander of Trinidad for his contribution to the cover design as well as to Taiwo Agnes Olemoh of Ghana for comparative lived experiences of the Aladura Church of Nigeria. I wish to thank the unknown readers of the manuscript for their reviews and comments. And finally, I am particularly grateful to the publisher, Ian Randle, for his patience, inspiration, guidance, and encouragement, and to his team of editors for their expertise and diligence at every stage in preparing the manuscript for the press.

Keywords: *Spiritual Baptists, Shouters, Penitents, Converted, prohibition, British constitution, St Vincent, Trinidad.*

Notes

1. See Frantz Fanon, *The Wretched of the Earth*, trans. Constance Farrington (New York: Grove Press, 1968), 42.
2. Ibid., 42.

Acknowledgements

Research for this study was carried out in the National Archives and Legal Affairs Department of St Vincent and the Grenadines – a special appreciation to Ms Cashena Allen-Foster of the SVGNA; the British Library and Public Records Office in London, UK; the Alma Jordan Library of The University of the West Indies and the National Archives of Trinidad and Tobago. Online sources supplied vital primary materials, including rare books, especially Google Books, Questia Online Library (now defunct), The Baptist Magazine, the New York Times, Florida International University newspaper archives, JSTOR, and the latest, the Internet Archive, an online borrowing platform with many Google Books. Unfortunately, many online sources forego pagination, even if they are digitised copies of the original printed texts; the same applies to Kindle versions of published books. For invaluable insights into the Spiritual Baptist as a living faith, I am indebted to many through formal and informal interviews, including Stacy Clarke and Stella Bouville of Trinidad and Veda Edwards of St Vincent. Invitations to lecture by the Spiritual Baptist leadership stimulated further research on the movement. I am also indebted to Al Alexander of Trinidad for his contribution to the cover design and Taiwo Agnes Olemoh of Ghana for comparative lived experiences of the Aladura Church of Nigeria. I wish to thank the unknown readers of the manuscript for their reviews and comments. And finally, I am particularly grateful to the publisher, Ian Randle, for his patience, inspiration, guidance, and encouragement, and to his team of editors for their expertise and diligence at every stage in preparing the manuscript for the press.

Introduction

*'These then, were the primary and universal rights – "independent of all human grant, not derived from any compact" – and of these the most sacred and incontestable was the right of private conscience in matters of religion.'**

Having examined the first century of Dissenters' struggle for equality since the passing of the Toleration Act 1689, Alan Saunders concurs with leading scholars on the interplay of religion, social contract and enlightenment and concludes, 'Laws that circumscribed the exercise of conscience were thus inconsistent with the very founding principles of the state.'[1] Britain's assent to ordinances to proscribe the Spiritual Baptists was one of the most extreme violations of human rights in the Caribbean since the abolition of chattel slavery. Several colonial governments adopted prohibition to compensate for the failure of formal education and imperial evangelism to diminish the attraction of Africanised Christianity. The successful passage of prohibition ordinances that clearly violated the religious toleration laws of Britain was made possible by an alliance of desperate colonial elites within the 'recognised' Christian denominations, colonial media and local governments and their cohorts in the Colonial Office. Questions of the constitutionality of prohibition and the circumstances that allowed for its royal assent and endurance are deserving of special attention in the annals of transmarine jurisdiction of British laws of conscience and human rights in general. Equally, the story of Spiritual Baptist resistance against multiple agents and allies of State violence

---

* Alan Saunders, 'The State as Highwayman: From Candour to Rights,' in *Enlightenment and Religion: Rational Dissent in Eighteenth Century Britain*, ed., Knud Haakonssen (Cambridge, UK: Cambridge University Press, 2006), 243.

justifies the elevation of the Spiritual Baptist community to centre-stage of the saga of cultural-political resistance by anti-colonialists in the first half of the twentieth century and beyond.

The history of Spiritual Baptism in the Caribbean did not begin with the politics of prohibition but knowledge of the movement prior to prohibition is sketchy. Whereas Jamaica's census captured Bedwardism as a religion from the early twentieth century, Spiritual Baptists in the colonies of persecution were not officially recognised until after repeal of the prohibition ordinance.[2] Knowledge of Spiritual Baptism exploded exponentially as it became the object of prohibitionists' ire. This assertion applies equally to the several other spirited forms of Africanised Christianity operating primarily within oral frameworks and independent of European-controlled churches. Prohibition of Christian denominations in the Caribbean began in the eighteenth century. This phase included Jamaica's Ethiopian Baptist Church founded by George Liele, commonly known as the Native Baptist Church. Jamaica also initiated the renewed attack on Africanised Christianity in the twentieth century with its attempt to proscribe Revivalist Zion in 1903. Failing in their main objective, the government settled for the less provocative compromise of regulating 'shouting.'[3] Shortly afterwards, the Spiritual Baptists of St Vincent, Trinidad and Tobago, and Grenada faced several decades of State persecution following the successful passage of prohibition ordinances.[4]

At the time of prohibition, adherents of the Spiritual Baptist faith were labelled 'Shouters' in Trinidad and Tobago and 'Shakers' in St Vincent and Grenada, both ascriptions disparaging their form of worship that featured loud, spontaneous shouting, hand-clapping, doption, call-and-response, jumping, dancing, and shaking while catching the spirit. Several attempts were made to change these identities after prohibition and several more had existed long before prohibition. Because of the paucity of sources, scholars cannot be certain that the various nineteenth-century appellations identify a singular group or movement in any colony, thus making it impossible to determine the precise origins and evolution of the denomination.

Review of the Literature

There is a large body of literature on the Spiritual Baptists. Based on anthropological research conducted in 1939 by Herskovits and Herskovits, Trinidad Village is of seminal importance because it includes a study of the Spiritual Baptists of Toco, a remote, rural community, at the height of the prohibition era. Herskovits and Herskovits debunked the negative stereotypes propagated by colonial elites to justify prohibition, stating emphatically, 'the Shouters must be given a place of prominence in any consideration of the religious life of Trinidad.'[5]

Up to 1951, when the Shouters' Prohibition Ordinance was repealed, many people conflated Shouterism with Shangoism (Orisha). The popular term Shango-Baptist aided in perpetuating this error well into the post-colonial period. Accordingly, many wrongly believed that the prohibition ordinance had also banned Shango worship and even the Rada, a Dahomeyan-originated sect in Port of Spain. On the contrary, prohibition exclusively targeted the Spiritual Baptists.

The end of prohibition was the beginning of new trends in embracing the rich cultural matrices of African cultural retentions and syncretism. What the Herskovitses did for the Spiritual Baptists, local anthropologist, Andrew Carr, did for the Rada.[6] The essay, 'A Rada Community in Trinidad,' came just four years after the repeal. However, the vast majority of works on the Spiritual Baptists and traditional African religions, which help in a better understanding of the former, emerged during the post-colonial period. The first known recognition of the Spiritual Baptists in a conventional history text is that of Eric Williams's *History of the People of Trinidad and Tobago*, published in 1962. Because of the role of the Spiritual Baptists in his rise to political office, Williams could not ignore them in the history text that he wrote as gift to the people of the new-born nation.

Among the foreign pioneers in the early post-repeal environment was George Eaton Simpson with a comparative study of the Shango (Orisha) of Trinidad and Nigeria, published in 1962.[7] Other foreign pioneers included Charles Gullick and Jeannette Henney focussing on St Vincent.[8] Most of the earliest post-colonial, specialised studies are anthropological and sociological, produced from field studies. These scholars were mainly White foreigners whose interest in Spiritual Baptism was that of a socially marginalised, lower-class sect. These works provide invaluable insights into the cosmology, structure, membership, rituals and practices of the faith, but many are tinged with cultural and religious biases that reflect the Euro-American, imperial-Christian worldview of the researchers.

The Black Power movement that swept across the Caribbean from 1969 gave Black people greater confidence and pride in their African ancestral traditions. This re-evaluation is reflected in the emergence of literary works by more local scholars investigating and celebrating African traditional religious survivals, particularly the Orisha (formerly known as Shango), and the Rada (Vodou) as well as African elements in Spiritual Baptism.[9] In this era, Spiritual Baptists went beyond testifying to foreign anthropologists to writing of their historical roots in Africa, the Merikin migration of early nineteenth century, as well as the uniqueness of their beliefs and practices. Merikins like John Milton Hackshaw were also writing their own histories.[10] Local writers emphasise resistance to prohibition, resilience in the face of adversity and ultimate triumph, narratives that continue to dominate their literary output to this day.[11] One of the few works of fiction on the faith is the celebrated 1980 novel, *The Wine of Astonishment* by Earl Lovelace, which brings to life the trauma and triumph of the Spiritual Baptist community during the prohibition era.[12]

As the twentieth century drew to a close, there was an explosion of literature on the Spiritual Baptists in the Caribbean and beyond. The anthropological foundation had inspired scholars to engage the subject from more historical perspectives. One of the pioneers in this genre is Peter Brewer with a study of the evolution of the Merikin Baptist Church in the nineteenth century.[13] Biographical studies such as C. M. Jacobs' *Joy Comes in the Morning* also began to emerge celebrating the leaders of the resistance movement, who were also great institution-builders. Beside the pioneering research in St Vincent by Jeannette Henney in the 1960s and Charles Gullick in the 1970s, little attention had been paid to the Spiritual Baptists. In the early 1990s, the first in-depth study was that of Edward Cox, in a paper presented to a conference of the Caribbean Studies Association (CSA).

Cultural anthropologist Maarit Forde, native of Finland, is a believer or convert to the faith. Her essay, 'The Spiritual Baptist Religion,' is a thorough study of the origin, development, cosmology and persecution of the Spiritual Baptists of Trinidad and Tobago.[14] The most comprehensive, concise, historical account of the Spiritual Baptists of St Vincent is Adrian Fraser's *From Shakers to Spiritual Baptists.* Unlike, Forde's essay, Fraser's study is strictly historical: it does not engage the ritual, cosmological or organisational structure of the denomination as Forde's essay and presents no findings from personal observations or interactions with members of the faith.[15]

Anthropologists and sociologists did not question the unconstitutionality and injustice of prohibition. Cox's paper was the first thorough examination of the prohibition ordinance and the political environment that created it but although he treats with the complicity of officials in the Colonial Office, he does not explain how the Ordinance survived those hurdles to enter the statute books.[16] Fraser also engaged the politics of prohibition but focussed mostly on the advocacy of George McIntosh and his associates in the Legislative Council. The current study is the first to expose the network of political, familial and collegial connections that the administrator of St Vincent had exploited to ensure that his ordinance receive the assent of the British government and survived without amendment until the year of his death. It is also the first in-depth comparative of the emergence of Spiritual Baptism and the politics of prohibition in St Vincent and Trinidad and Tobago.

The Evolution of Spiritual Baptist Identity and Nomenclatures

African converts to Methodism and Baptism in North America incorporated 'shouting,' 'jumping' and 'dancing' as expressions of worship but they were not unique. An English sect, The United Society of Believers in Christ's Second Coming, popularly known as the 'Shakers,' originated in the mid-eighteenth, century and soon spread to North America. Members of the White Metropolitan Church Association (MCA) of late nineteenth-century Chicago were called the 'Holy Jumpers,' a name that also spread into the Caribbean. Edward Cox argues, 'There is really nothing to tie the Shakers to British and American Shakers.'[17] Doubtlessly, the Shakers, Shouters and Holy Jumpers in the Caribbean 'evolved their own structures,' as Cox contends, but the colonial elites certainly borrowed the foreign nomenclatures and ascribed them to the regional phenomena. These names were pejorative in Britain and North America; they were also pejorative in the Caribbean.

The Shakers of St Vincent have been associated with an array of sobriquets beginning with 'The Converted,' the earliest known label for an African-initiated Christian sect in the island. The name first appeared in 1810 in the 'Report' of Dr Thomas Coke, co-founder of the Methodist Church and pioneer-missionary in the Caribbean and North America.[18] Shakers maintained the 'Converted' label into the twentieth century and many still identify as such. Since the Methodists had started their first mission on the island in 1787, and because there was no formal African Baptist church or chapel, the name 'Converted' may well have been a reference to newly converted enslaved Methodists within the colony's Methodist communion. This interpretation remains valid notwithstanding that another group of enslaved African Baptists from North America had been brought to the island four years earlier and enslaved on the Grand Sable plantation off the north-windward coast. Those forced migrants were refugees from the War of American Independence, contemporaries of the better-known groups that founded the Baptist Church in The Bahamas and Jamaica in late-eighteenth century.

By the 1840's, the name 'Wilderness People' appears for the first time in the written records, describing congregants at prayer meetings that conformed closely to Converted and 'Shaker' liturgy of the latter-nineteenth century.[19] Other sobriquets that described proto-Shaker movements included 'The Penitents,' 'The New Light,' 'The Believers,' 'Baptists,' 'Jumpers,' 'Holy Jumpers,' 'Tieheads,' 'Clap Hands,' 'The Barefoot religion' and 'A Pentecostal Sect.'[20] Because the terms

Shouters and Shakers were inscribed in the prohibition ordinances, they cannot be completely avoided in this study, although the terms 'Converted' and 'Penitent' are often preferred for St Vincent.

The term 'Converted' also applied to members of the Spiritual Baptist faith in Trinidad and may have been indicative of Shaker migrants from St Vincent in the late nineteenth century or Shaker emigrés who fled to escape persecution after the passage of the Shakers Prohibition Ordinance in 1912.[21] It was one of the earliest identities deployed to challenge the prohibition ordinance of 1917, as seen in the name, Mt Tabor Spiritual Converted Church, founded in the early 1920s by Leader William James from Antigua.[22]

Shakers and Shouters shared two other nineteenth-century nomenclatures, 'Candle-light Baptist' and 'Wayside Baptist.' In both instances, descriptions are revealing of the birth of the denomination in North American plantation slavery. Wayside-preaching was a legacy of African-American Baptist exhorters who acted upon dreams and visions in which they were divinely commanded to evangelise.[23] White Evangelical missionaries often sanctioned candlelight preachers as well as organised their preaching schedules. Thomas Coke affirmed that he published candle-light preaching events in St Eustatius for his Black assistant, Harry, because enslaved hearers 'can attend better at that time.'[24] Africans independently continued night-time preaching and evangelising for several decades after emancipation in many colonies, including St Vincent, Trinidad and Jamaica; prohibition did not stop this practice.[25]

Trinidad and Tobago's 1917 prohibition ordinance specifically identified the target group as 'Shouters.' In order to circumvent the ordinance, adherents of the faith in Trinidad adopted the name Spiritual Baptist. Before assuming the Spiritual label, attempts had been made to identify as Independent Baptists who were recognised by government and therefore not subject to prohibition.[26] Both strategies failed to convince presiding magistrates. Independent Baptists were dissenters from the Merikin Church, emerging as a separate denomination in the late-nineteenth century after refusing to join the Baptist Union.[27] The affirmation of being 'Baptist' was a tacit claim to recognition and respectability as members of the universal Baptist Church. The 'Spiritual' handle affirmed the inherent spirituality of indigenous African cultures and its application to daily living. It also implicitly proclaimed the Holy-Spirit experience ('catching the power') and spiritual journeying during the mourning or 'moanin' rite as fundamental tenets of the faith. Equally important, the rebranding emphatically rejected the negative stereotypes of the Shouters as 'savages' and Shouterism as 'barbarism' and 'paganism,' as inscribed in the ordinance. The adoption of the name Spiritual Baptist was not complemented by a repudiation of 'shouting' but rather syncretised the practice with attaining 'spiritual ecstasy' of communion with the Holy Spirit.[28] The unwillingness of the Colonial Office to soften the most draconian measures of the ordinance finally broke the unity of the Spiritual Baptists in the 1940s which saw the creation of two umbrella bodies, one claiming to represent the Spiritual Baptists and the other to represent the Shouters. Interestingly, in the post-repeal era, Spiritual Baptists reclaimed the 'Shouters' identity, appending it to the 'Spiritual,' as in Spiritual (Shouter) Baptist.

Thomas Coke was perceptive of the true nature of African Methodist worship in Virginia. A few years after the War of Independence, he recorded that they 'pray and praise aloud in a most astonishing manner.'[29] This was a salutary admission that synchronised loudness by a Black congregation during worship was astonishing for most Englishmen; nevertheless, it was Christian. Herskovits and Herskovits succinctly resolved the dialectic by explaining that 'the "spirit" is said to enter their bodies and fill them with joy, causing them to shake, to dance, and otherwise to express their worship in the complex rites associated with the term to "shout."'[30]

The Shakers of Grenada and St Vincent later adopted the Spiritual Baptist identity for similar reasons as their counterparts in Trinidad.[31] After appearing to acknowledge the newly minted 'Spiritual Baptists' as a legitimate religious sect, the government of St Vincent rejected the name and also refused to recognise a parallel identity, Pilgrim Christians, claiming that Shakers in disguise were still Shakers and thus proscribed by statute.[32] Other African-Caribbean Christian sects, including Bedwardism, *Pukumina* and Revival Zion in Jamaica, and Jordanites in Guyana, whose emergence paralleled that of the Shouters and Shakers, did not adopt a name-change, largely because prohibition did not become law in those colonies in the early twentieth century. Nevertheless, as Spiritual Baptist Archbishop Oba Douglas explains, these movements properly belong to the same branch of Christianity, for, 'apart from a few differences, they all have the same general trait, "entertainment" of the Holy Spirit, "shakings" and talking in tongues;' Douglas reaffirmed that this trait did not disqualify such congregations as Christians, but rather, 'It is the Christianity of Africans in the New World ....'[33]

Going beyond Douglas, this study affirms that the Spiritual Baptists were a unique branch of Christianity. African Christian churches that carried the 'Baptist' label in Trinidad and Tobago prior to 1917 were excluded from the Shouters' Prohibition Ordinance. Some of those churches were protected by virtue of their affiliation with the Baptist Union; others, because they were Independent Baptists. The literature on African Baptists in the Caribbean suggests that there were at least two main theological divisions: while most congregations adopted shouting in their liturgy or worship, only the congregations that emerged from mid-nineteenth century had adopted mourning and manifesting in tongues; but the chief distinction was mourning, more commonly verbalised as 'moanin' and often in the orthography of believers. As indicated earlier, there were religious shouters in England, the United States of America and many parts of the Caribbean, but no Euro-American or Afro-American denomination practiced mourning. Mourning was the African element that posed the most serious challenge to colonial Christianity. Roman Catholicism created a seven-sacramental system centred on clerical agency; Lutheranism produced the dual sacramental system centred on the priesthood of the believer, which all Euro-American Protestants adopted; African Baptists in the Caribbean retained the American Protestant tradition but one branch later added a third element, mourning, with equal sacramental value: the journey of the initiate through spiritual landscapes that prepared a true convert for leadership roles in the Church.

Weaponising the Marriage Licence against Spiritual Baptist Independence

Before prohibition, Spiritual Baptism was a movement of conscience, but not yet an independent denomination. Their progress toward independence was hampered by systemic racism. A new church, regardless of its denomination, did not need official governmental recognition. Yet, the mechanism of granting or refusing marriage licences to new pastors seriously undermined the status and legitimacy of such churches. While Spiritual Baptist Leaders and Mothers suffered no legal liability for administering baptism, they needed a special licence to be marriage officers. This is not to say that they could not have conducted 'traditional African marriages;' such marriages, however, had lost their cultural currency under the terrors of chattel slavery and clerical and State prejudices after emancipation.

Under colonial patriarchy, statutory marriage had implications for inheritance and the social status of church members. Registrars did not allow a man to be identified as 'father' on a birth certificate, unless he was married to the mother. Children of unmarried mothers were branded 'bastards' and suffered multiple legal encumbrances. Unmarried mothers did not have the same rights as their married counterparts to government employment in the civil service and teaching profession. Without the right to conduct statutory marriage, Spiritual Baptist Leaders wisely exhorted their members to remain affiliated to the 'recognised' Churches of their choice. This explains why 90 per cent of 'Converted' in St Vincent were allegedly members of the Methodist Church at the time of Prohibition.[34] A similar phenomenon was observed in Trinidad among the Spiritual Baptists.[35] Paradoxically, state officials cited this apparent allegiance of Spiritual Baptists to 'recognised' denominations as evidence to reject the claim that Shakerism and Shouterism were true religions.

Intra-denominationalism was not unusual for new religious movements before claiming independence from the parent body. Such, for example, was the early history of Methodism, when it was justifiably called Wesleyanism, a movement within the Church of England. The pioneers of Wesleyanism were clergymen still serving the Anglican communion until the death of the movement's founder in 1791. This relationship also extended to the colonies. On his second visit to Grenada in 1793, Thomas Coke attended Mass and preached a sermon in the Established Church in St Georges on a Sunday morning.[36] Interestingly, in The Bahamas pastors of the British Baptist Missionary Society (BMS) sometimes preached in African Baptist churches.[37]

African-American Baptist and African-American Methodist Churches in the Caribbean had a long history of hostility from colonial elites, but these institutions represented much less an existential threat to Euro-Christian cultural-intellectual hegemony than the Spiritual Baptists. The Spiritual Baptists were the first Black, working-class entity to successfully transcend the barriers of White supremacism that secured cultural hegemony and control of financial institutions for the elites. Not surprisingly, government's censorship of radical media in St Vincent and Trinidad and Tobago in the wake of the First World War did not help the cause of the Spiritual Baptists as evidenced in the sharp increase in arrests of 'Penitents' and a steep increase in fines and length of incarceration.

Prohibition of the Spiritual Baptists is a velvet stain on the British constitution that the current generation must acknowledge. Although prohibitionists had invoked the law on public nuisance to justify proscription, officials in the Colonial Office who reviewed the first successful prohibition ordinance could not in good conscience uphold the colonial government's rationale. Yet, they succumbed to professional camaraderie and personal friendship with the architect of that ordinance, Charles Oliphant Murray, to compromise the integrity of the Colonial Office as watchdog for the religious rights of subjects in overseas colonies. Prohibition set back the Spiritual Baptists several decades of potential growth and development and left stigmas which continue to impact the public's perception of the denomination.

Notes

1. Alan Saunders, 'The State as Highwayman: From Candour to Rights,' in *Enlightenment and Religion: Rational Dissent in Eighteenth Century Britain*, ed. Knud Haakonssen (Cambridge: Cambridge University Press, 2006), 243.

2. See Veront M. Satchell, 'Bedwardism,' in *The Encyclopedia of Caribbean Religions* 1 (A–L), ed. Patrick Taylor and Frederick Ivor Case (Chicago: University of Illinois Press, 2013),118. The exception is Grenada, which has not yet repealed its prohibition law.

3. *Jamaica Laws 1909–1913: Law 31 of 1911, CO 139/111; also, Jamaica 1911* 3 (June–Aug.), CO 137/685, 140.

4. For St Vincent, see Law 13 of 1912, CO 262/26; for Trinidad and Tobago, see *Trinidad and Tobago Authenticated Ordinances 1917–1918*: No. 27 of 1917, CO 297/22; for Grenada, see *Grenada Authenticated Ordinances 1925-1928*: Law No. 11 of 1927, CO 103/26. For comparison with the Jamaica compromise, see Law 31 of 1911, CO 139/111.

5. Melville J. Herskovits and Frances S. Herskovits, *Trinidad Village* (New York: Alfred A. Knopf, 1947), 172.

6. Andrew Carr, 'A Rada Community in Trinidad,' *Caribbean Quarterly* 3, no. 1 (1955), 36–54.

7. George Eaton Simpson, 'The Shango Cult in Nigeria and in Trinidad,' *American Anthropologist* 64, no. 6 (Dec. 1962), 1204–19, https://www.jstor.org/stable/667846.

8. See for example, George Eaton, Simpson, 'Baptismal "Mourning," and "Building" Ceremonies of the Shouters of Trinidad,' *The Journal of American Folklore* 79, no. 314 (October–December 1966), 537–50, https://www.jstor.org/stable/538219. Charles Gullick, 'The Shakers of St Vincent: A Symbolic Focus for Discourses,' in *New Trends and Developments in African Religions,* ed. Peter B. Clarke, 87–104 (Westport, CT: 1998). Stephen Glazier, 'Contested Rituals of the African Diaspora,' in *New Trends and Developments in African Religions*, ed. Peter B. Clarke 105–120 (Westport, CT: 1998). George Eaton Simpson, *Black Religions in the New World* (New York: Columbia University Press, 1978).

9. David Trotman, 'The Yoruba and Orisha Worship in Trinidad and British Guiana: 1838–1870,' *African Studies Review*, 3 no. 2 (Sept. 1976), 1–17, www.jstor.org/stable/523560. J. D. Elder, 'The Yoruba Ancestor Cult in Gasparillo: (Its Structure, Organisation and Function in Community Life),' *Caribbean Quarterly* 16, no. 3 (Sept. 1970): 5–20. A. B. Huggins, *The Saga of the Companies* (Princes Town, Trinidad: Twin Lock), 1978. John McNish Weiss, *The Merikens: Free Black American Settlers in Trinidad 1815–1816* (1995; London: McNish & Weiss, 2008; Weiss was a White Englishman married to a descendant of the Merikins, Althea McNish.

10. John Milton Hacksaw, *The Baptist Denomination: A Concise History Commemorating One Hundred and Seventy-Five Years (1816–1991) of the Establishment of the 'Company Villages' and the BAPTIST FAITH in Trinidad and Tobago* (NP: Amphy & Bashana Jackson Memorial Society, 1992).

11. Ashram L. Stapleton, *The Birth and Growth of the Baptist Church in Trinidad and Tobago and the Caribbean* (Trinidad: A. L. Stapleton, 1983). Patricia Stephens, *The Spiritual Baptist Faith: African New World Religious Identity, History & Testimony* (London: Karnak House, 1999). Hazel Ann De Peza, *My Faith: Spiritual Baptist Christian* (Maitland, FL: Xulon Press, 2007).

12. A. B. Huggins, *The Saga of the Companies* (Princes Town, Trinidad: Twin Lock, 1978). Earl Lovelace, *The Wine of Astonishment* (Oxford, UK: Heinemann, 1982). Peter Brewer, 'The Baptist Churches of South Trinidad and their Missionaries, 1815–1892' (Mtheo Diss., University of Glasgow, 1988). Stephen D. Glazier, *Marching the Pilgrims Home: A Study of the Spiritual Baptists of Trinidad* (Salem, WI: Sheffield, 1991). Wallace Wayne Zane, 'Journeys to the Spiritual Lands: Ritual Experience in Converted (Spiritual Baptist) Churches in St Vincent and Brooklyn,' later published under the title, *Journeys to the Spiritual Lands: The Natural History of a West Indian Religion* (New York: Oxford University Press, 1999). C. M. Jacobs, *Joy Comes in the Morning: Elton George Griffith and the Shouter Baptists* (Trinidad: Caribbean Historical Society, 1996).

13. Peter Brewer, 'The Baptist Churches of South Trinidad and their Missionaries, 1815–1892' (Mtheo Diss., University of Glasgow, 1988).

14. Maarit Forde, 'The Spiritual Baptist Religion,' *Caribbean Quarterly: A Journal of Caribbean Culture*, 65, no. 2 (2019): 212–40, https://doi.org/1 0.1080/00086495.2019.1606991.

15. Adrian Fraser, *From Shakers to Spiritual Baptists: The Struggle for Survival of the Shakers of St Vincent and the Grenadines* (Kingstown, St Vincent: Kings-SVG Publishers, 2011).

16. Edward L. Cox, 'Religious Intolerance and Persecution: The Case of the Shakers in St Vincent, 1900–1934' (Paper presented to the 18th annual conference of the Caribbean Studies Association, May 1993), https://ufdcimages.uflib.ufl.edu/CA/00/40/01/21/00/0001/pdf.pdf.

17. Edward Cox, cited by Adrian Fraser, 'George McIntosh and the Spiritual Baptists,' *Searchlight*, March 13, 2008, https://www.searchlight.vc/dr-fraser/2008, accessed March 20, 2022.

18. Thomas Coke, *A History of the West Indies Containing the Natural, Civil and Ecclesiastical History of Each Island: with an Account of the Missions* 2 (London: 1810), 281–82.

19. Sheena Boa, 'Colour, Class and Gender in Post-Emancipation St Vincent, 1834–1884' (PhD Diss., University of Warwick, 1998), 259.

20. Wallace Wayne Zane, 'Journeys to the Spiritual Lands: Ritual Experience in Converted (Spiritual Baptist) Churches in St Vincent

and Brooklyn,' (PhD Diss., University College of Los Angeles, 1987), 238–39; Fraser, *From Shakers to Spiritual Baptists*, 11–13; Boa, *'Colour, Class and Gender,'* 261-62.

21.   See Herskovits and Herskovits, *Trinidad Village*, 204.

22.   Forde, 'The Spiritual Baptist Religion,' 234.

23.   See Sylvia R. Frey and Betty Wood, *Come Shouting to Zion: African American Protestantism in the American South and British Caribbean to 1830* (Chapel Hill, NC: University of North Carolina Press, 1998), 124–25, https://www.questia.com, accessed May 20, 2013.

24.   John Neal, '"In the beginning:" Gender, Ethnicity and the Methodist Missionary Enterprise,' 5, available at http://www.methodistheritage.org.uk/missionary-history-neal-in-the-beginning-2011.pdf, accessed, March 1, 2020.

25.   Hackshaw, *The Baptist Denomination*, 77–78; also, *Personal Interview*, testimony of Stella Bouville, 2017.

26.   See 'Shouters Meeting Interrupted by Police,' January 23, 1918, *Port of Spain Gazette*, TTNA, 8.

27.   See Brewer, 'The Baptist Churches of South Trinidad,' 298.

28.   See Frey and Wood, *Come Shouting to Zion*, 123.

29.   Cited in Frey and Wood, *Come Shouting to Zion*, 124.

30.   Herskovits and Herskovits, *Trinidad Village*, 1947, 167.

31.   Rev. V. Hobert & A. Eubanks to A. V. King (Acting-Government Secretary), November 29, 1950, SVGNA, CR-SMP-GA-62/39/49 (31).

32.   Fraser, *From Shakers to Spiritual Baptists*, 81–82.

33.   Kim Johnson, 'Born Again in Living Waters,' http://www.raceandhistory.com/historicalviews/africanspirit.htm, accessed March 26, 2010. To the Jamaica list, George Eaton Simpson, adds the '"Convince," in "Baptismal 'Mourning," and "Building" Ceremonies of the Shouters of Trinidad,' *The Journal of American Folklore* 79, no. 314 (October–December 1966), 538, https://www.jstor.org/stable/538219; and Stephen D. Glazier adds the 'Spirit Baptists,' in 'Adumbrations of Dread: Spiritual Baptists at the Dawn of the Millennium,' *Journal of Ritual Studies* 15, no. 1 (2001), 17, https://www.jstor.org/stable/44368584.

34.   Fraser, *From Shakers to Spiritual Baptists*, 11.

35.   'Report from the *Mirror*,' April 23, 1906, CO 321/269.

36.   George G. Findlay and William W. Holdsworth, *The History of The Wesleyan Methodist Missionary Society* (London: Epsworth Press, 1921), 65; 73. Google Books.

37.   See Peter Brewer, 'British Baptist Missionaries and Baptist Work in the Bahamas,' *The Baptist Quarterly* 32, no. 6 (1988), 298, https://biblicalstudies.org.uk, accessed May 25, 2022.

Acronymns and Abbreviations

BL:	British Library
BMS:	Baptist Missionary Society
BNA:	British National Archives
CCU:	Colonial Church Union
CMS:	Church Missionary Society
CO:	Colonial Office
EAL:	Eight Army of Liberation
HIA:	*History in Action* (journal)
JAH:	*Journal of African History*
JCH:	*Journal of Caribbean History*
JIAI:	*Journal of the International African Institute*
JNH:	*Journal of Negro History*
JP:	Justice of the Peace
MCA:	Metropolitan Church Association
NYT:	*New York Times*
PNM:	Peoples National Movement
PPG:	Political Progress Group
PPP:	People's Political Party
PWRA:	Places of Worship Registration Act
S. of S.:	Secretary of State (for the Colonies)
SOAS:	School of Asian and African Studies
SPG:	Society for the Propagation of the Gospel
SVGAG:	St Vincent and the Grenadines Attorney General's Office

SVGNA: St Vincent and the Grenadines National Archives
TTNA: Trinidad and Tobago National Archives
UF: United Front (political party)
UNIA-ACL: Universal Negro Improvement Association and African
            Communities League
UWI/AJL: The University of the West Indies/Alma Jordan Library
            branch
UWRPU: United Workers and Rate Payers Union
WIESBF: West Indian Evangelical Spiritual Baptist Faith
WMMS: Wesleyan Methodist Missionary Society.

CHAPTER 1

The Rise of African Caribbean Christianity

*'Religion is the deification of culture; and the gods look like the people talking about it.'**

Slavery was the first system of domination in the Caribbean to attempt the complete control of the minds and bodies of Africans. The Emancipation Act 1833 (3 & 4 Will. 4) was the first of a cluster of laws and regulations to deepen this control after the slavery era.[1] In the enforcement of those laws, colonial governments aggressively deployed the militia, the police, the magistracy and the prison. These agencies of oppression were reasonably successful in thwarting the aspirations of Africans for self-esteem, self-realisation, and economic emancipation. Underlying this mainly economic strategy was a long-term agenda to construct an Anglo-Saxon, cultural-intellectual hegemony in the region utilising mainly religion during slavery and a combination of religion and education after slavery. Although the colonial elites never relented, the oppressed masses successfully developed their own armoury in this epic culture-war. The pushback most feared by the colonials was African spirituality and African-Christian church organisations.

Minna Salami conceptualises seven aspects of 'African spirituality.' Of the sixth aspect she says, '[I]t is about resistance.' Having traced African-centred religious systems from as early as Kemet or Ancient Egypt, she concludes that African spirituality 'developed into a means of strategically resisting persecution and abuse as much as a means

---

* Yosef Ben Jochannan, 'Dr Yosef Ben-Jochannan & George Simmons (1987)/ African Origins,' *Reelblack One,* https://www.youtube.com/watch?app=desktop&v =kRFf6CYzm_g, (Alabama: University of Montevallo, 1987), accessed February 2, 2023.

to sacred belonging.'[2] Spiritual Baptism falls within this narrative of belonging in exile and resistance to White supremacy.[3]

The North American Cradle of the African Caribbean Baptist Church

The formative stage of this narrative in North America is a corollary to the Age of Revolutions in the western hemisphere featuring the American Revolution, the French Revolution, the Haitian Revolution, the Hispanic American Revolution and the Industrial Revolution.[4] It was against this backdrop that the first African-led Christian Churches emerged in the hemisphere: among them, the First Baptist Church in Savannah, Georgia, 1778; the African Episcopal Church of St Thomas, 1792; the Bethel African Methodist Church, 1794; and the Lombard Street Presbyterian Church, 1810.[5] The Spiritual Baptist faith is indigenous to the Caribbean, but it draws its doctrines, theology and liturgy from three continents: Africa, Europe and North America. Translating, transforming, and syncretising the immigrant beliefs and practices into Spiritual Baptism was a complex process involving multiple streams of migration, intra-migration and re-migration. Because the genesis church was Baptist founded by Africans of North America, the preeminent role of African-American Christianity will be explored in this chapter.

The first independent African-Christian congregations in the western Atlantic are testaments to enslaved and formerly enslaved Africans' reactions to American Revivalism from mid-eighteenth century and their rejection of mental slavery in Virginia, Georgia and South Carolina, the largest plantation colonies in British North America. There, within the bosom of slavery, Black preachers created the first African American Baptist and African Methodist Episcopal (AME) Churches. African Baptists pioneered the way. At first, enslaved people and free Blacks enjoyed a measure of privilege within plantation-based Baptist churches; many became preachers, some of whom were ordained full pastors and allowed independence over all-Black congregations.[6] Shortly after the War of Independence, White Baptists began to fall in line with the national ideology of racial segregation, which led to the alienation of enslaved converts during worship. Determined to circumvent this prejudice, enslaved converts resorted to independent and often clandestine prayer meetings during which they could express their emotions with highly spirited or corybantic fervour. Most Black preachers were unschooled; so were many White preachers.[7] Notwithstanding their deficit in formal education, Black preachers distinguished themselves 'by their enterprising zeal and unwearied perseverance.'[8]

Hymnals, Hermeneutics, and Emancipatory Theology

Bonded and manumitted evangelists did not shy away from coding messages of secular liberation that would ordinarily be considered seditious or even blasphemous by defenders of slavery including Eurocentric dogmatists. Central to survival in such a high-risk environment, Black Christian leaders integrated extemporaneous work songs as sacred music, later to be called Negro Spirituals, which often included subversive content supportive of self-liberation but solidly grounded in Biblical events, personalities, landscapes and poetic imagery.[9] Some of the more common motifs of resistance drawn from the *Bible* included the Exodus, Mt Zion, River Jordan, and Moses.[10] Jordanites of Guyana, Revival Zion of Jamaica, and multiple other churches with 'Zion' titles speak to the transcendence of these motifs.

Africans from both official and subaltern Baptist communions in the northern plantation colonies were the pioneers of the African Baptist Church in Canada, the Caribbean and Sierra Leone in West Africa. Unlike those in Canada and Sierra Leone, the first missions in the Caribbean were also circumscribed by slavery; but unlike the American model, the Caribbean Baptist Church was never chaperoned by White clergymen: this was incontestably so for the duration of the slavery period in Trinidad and for most of the slavery period in Jamaica and The Bahamas. The arrival of English Baptist missionaries in Jamaica in 1814, The Bahamas in 1833, and Trinidad in 1843 threatened but failed to destroy the independence of the Black Churches. Notwithstanding their self-emancipation and unique styles of worship, the African Baptist Church in North America and the Caribbean belongs historically and doctrinally to the English Baptist communion. The 'constitution' of the early English Baptists as expressed in the 1660 manifesto, 'A Brief Confession of Declaration of Faith,' created a culture of leadership that was liberal, even by today's standards. Although the Declaration of Faith coincided with the dawn of Britain's Sugar Revolution and mass enslavement of Africans in its Caribbean plantations, and although the document was silent on slave holding, enslavement and slave trading, the manifesto entrenched one of the earliest European declarations of freedom of conscience as a universal right by acclaiming, 'that all men should have the free liberty of their own Consciences in matters of Religion, or Worship, without the least oppression or persecution ....'[11] It is primarily this liberalism that explains why the Baptist Church was the most attractive to Africans who voluntarily converted to Christianity.

The 1660 Declaration of Faith allowed morally upright men 'brought up in the School of Christ's Church,' who demonstrated that they were 'considerably gifted by God's Spirit' the right to 'preach to the World,' after approval by the Church.[12] To prepare them formally 'for the work of the Ministry,' Deacons must be 'faithful men, chosen by the Church, and ordained by Prayer and Laying of Hands.'[13] The Declaration elevated naturally gifted persons above those who 'are only brought up in the Schools of humane learning, to the attaining humane arts, and variety of languages, with many vain curiosities of speech,'[14] a clear reference to Episcopal churches.

English Baptists' repudiation of elitist ordination practised by the Church of England carried over into the Baptist Church in colonial North America. Unlettered preachers abounded; many were elevated to the pastorate without formal education or even formal ordination. Albert Newman acknowledges the resilience of this situation over many centuries: 'At the beginning of the nineteenth century the number of Baptist ministers that could with due regard to the meaning of words be called well educated could be counted on one's fingers.'[15] Gifted Black exhorters and preachers skilled in extemporaneous hermeneutics exploited this liberal environment and often attracted influential Whites to their sermons.[16]

The Congregational structure of Baptist Church organisation was also important to the establishment, survival, dynamism and expansion of the faith by Africans in the Caribbean. In North America, Africans ordained by Whites in Baptist, Episcopalian, and Presbyterian churches were empowered to establish new congregations and ordain new pastors.[17] In The Bahamas and Jamaica, new converts of the African American pioneers as well as rivals of the founding fathers spread across each colony establishing churches under their own authority just as they had done in North America.[18] This 'multiplication by division' remains a hallmark of Black Baptism in the Caribbean; but the phenomenon was not unique to the region. Newman affirms,

> That without a creed recognized as authoritative and binding, without ecclesiastical courts for the enforcement of uniformity in doctrine and practice on churches and ministers, and with the completest independence of individual Baptist churches, there is as much in common as there is among five million Baptists of America, is one of the marvels of church history.[19]

Unfortunately, BMS missionaries who arrived decades after the establishment of the 'Native Baptists,' tried to subdue Black Baptist leaders rather than treat them as equals in pioneering the faith.

Pioneer African-American Missionaries in the Caribbean

The most influential African-Americans to emerge from the short-lived pre-Revolution Baptist liberalism in North America were destined to leave their largest historical footprints in other parts of the world. They included leaders such as Amos, Frank Spence, Prince William, and Sharper Morris all of whom migrated to The Bahamas and became the pioneers of the Baptist Church in that colony.[20] Africans from this communion were taken to Trinidad as part of the intra-regional forced migration of labour following Britain's abolition of her Atlantic slave trade in 1808;[21] some of these Bahamians featured in the establishment of the first African Baptists in the island.

More famous than the Bahamians were George Liele and David George. Liele was the pioneer-missionary and founding father of the Baptist Church in Jamaica, which later gave birth to *Pukumina*,

Bedwardism, and Revival Zion. Liele was born to enslaved parents in Virginia but won his freedom as a preacher in Georgia.[22] He and David George were pioneer pastors at the First African Baptist Church (originally named First Coloured Church) in Silver Buff, South Carolina, established by a Mr Palmer during the early 1770s.[23] After the evacuation of Savannah by the Patriots in 1778, Liele reorganised the fledgling congregation into the first 'Negro Baptist Church' in the colony, the oldest independent Black Christian Church in North America.[24] George was originally baptised by a White minister in South Carolina, where he developed into a competent preacher. He was re-baptised by Liele in Georgia and became his right-hand man in the new church.[25] Another of Liele's celebrated convert, Andrew Bryan, remained in Georgia after the war to lead the new church.[26] Despite the absence of a regulating authority, African Christian churches in North America and the Caribbean constituted a single communion of New World African-inspired Christianity.[27]

In 1782, Liele apprenticed himself to loyalist officer, Colonel Kirkland, and fled the United States for Jamaica to escape potential re-enslavement after the war.[28] In Jamaica, he attached himself to the governor for two years during which time he had earned sufficient money to amortise his indenture.[29] After receiving his certificate of full freedom from the governor, he immediately embarked upon building the first Baptist congregation in the island, self-identified as 'Anabaptist,' the principal doctrine of which is credobaptism or believers' baptism, instituted in the Confessions of Faith during the seventeenth-century.[30] Inspired by his favourite biblical text, 'Except a man be born again of water and of the Spirit, he cannot enter into the Kingdom of God,' Liele conducted 'baptism in living water.' Article 3 in his self-authored covenant mandated his pastoral brethren that baptism must take place 'in a river, or a place where there is much water.'[31] This practice became a hallmark of Spiritual Baptism.

Beginning with just four members, Liele's church grew to hundreds by the close of the century.[32] One of his most significant converts in the island was Moses Baker, a fellow immigrant from North America. After some difficulties, Liele secured the confidence and financial backing of enslavers, including members of Jamaica's House of Assembly.[33] From then on, the Church spread rapidly, with Baker the principal evangelist in western Jamaica. Two of Liele's other African American converts, George Vineyard and John Gilbert, evangelised other regions of the island.[34] Liele's Church structure comprised 'deacons and elders ... and teachers of small congregation in the town and country' functioning under his covenant of twenty-one Articles of Faith. In recognising the importance of literacy, Liele built a 'free school,' setting an example for Baker and other clerics of his Church to emulate.[35] In time, Liele became unofficial Patriarch of African Baptism in the Caribbean. He earned the title by maintaining regular correspondence with Black Baptist pastors in The Bahamas and Canada as well as the Baptist Missionary Society in London.[36]

By the close of the century, many Myal practitioners had become converts in Liele's Church.[37] Liele's appeal to them to repudiate 'obeah' and witchcraft was cosmologically consistent with Myalism, which enslaved Africans had come to consider an antidote to obeah and witchcraft.[38] The resulting infusion of Myal spirituality and practices transformed the immigrant African American Baptist Church into Jamaica's Native Baptist Church. Liele must have been conscious that the syncretism of Myalism and American Baptist had created a new branch of Christianity, for he coined the term 'Ethiopian Baptist' to describe his members and named his church the Ethiopian Baptist Church.[39] The name might have derived from his awareness of the new Scientific Racism that classified humanity into 'races' one of which was '*Homo ethiopicus*' or Ethiopian man. Liele might also have independently adopted the name from the Bible as other early Pan-Africanists of his generation had done. Whatever the reason, the name emphatically established Liele's Church as an independent denomination proud to be African.

The crossover from Myal to Baptist was not difficult. Jamaica's Myalism originated in the Congo River basin of Central West Africa.[40] Many Kongolese had pre-transatlantic experience with Christianity, which they successfully infused with traditional Kongolese rites, esotery, and iconography. One example of this syncretism was the

Kongolese demand for salt as a condition for baptism.[41] Moravian missionaries observed a similar syncretism in the Danish colonies, where newly arrived Kongolese often sought specialists among the enslaved population to baptise them by 'pouring water over the head of the neophyte, placing salt in his mouth, and praying over him in the Koongo language.'[42] This Kongolese element did not impact the church in The Bahamas the same way as in Jamaica, St Vincent, Trinidad, and Grenada and primarily accounts for the difference in attitude by colonial elites and foreign missionaries toward African baptism in the Caribbean.

Another element that facilitated the movement of Myalists into Liele's Ethiopian Church was the extension of the practice of immersion common to most Baptist churches into a canon of baptism by living water, mainly in the sea or the river.[43] The 1689 Baptist Confession of Faith stipulated, 'Immersion, or dipping of the person in water, is necessary for this ordinance to be administered properly.'[44] The injunction did not include the state of the water. Immersion in living water was not uncommon in West and Central Africa. The practice survived the Middle Passage, reconstituted in the Caribbean as Mami Wata (Water Mama or *Mama L'eau* in French-speaking colonies).[45] There was something poetic and triumphal about baptism by immersion in living water for African-Caribbean Baptists: living water had carried them into bondage; living water was emancipating them from psychological, intellectual and cultural enslavement.

The Nova Scotia Connection in the Construction of the African-Caribbean Baptist Church

Not all African-American war evacuees were taken to the Caribbean. A large number migrated to Nova Scotia taking the African-American Baptist Church with them. Birchwood, the biggest and most important of the new settlements in Nova Scotia would come to play a complex role in the history of Spiritual Baptism in the Caribbean, but mainly through its diaspora in Sierra Leone. To date there is little to no scholarship on this circular connection. Nevertheless, David George looms large in this intra-Atlantic narrative.[46] Like Liele, David George was ordained a minister of the faith and became the pastor of Silver Buff Baptist Church in South Carolina before escaping to British-occupied Georgia during the War of Independence.[47] Like many others, George fled from the US when the British evacuated. After a few years in Canada, he re-migrated to Sierra Leone with his family in 1792.[48] At the time, Sierra Leone was a struggling, experimental colony in the hands of White entrepreneurial abolitionists headed by Lieut. John Clarkson, brother of well-known abolitionist, Thomas Clarkson. Altogether, some 1,200 African-Americans in Canada made the voyage with George. A significant number of the passengers were Baptists; most were members of George's congregation.[49] In Freetown, George founded the First Baptist Church in Africa, now identified as Regent Road Baptist Church.[50] Although never investigated, David George's church may have had some influence on the development of the Spiritual Baptist faith in Trinidad and St Vincent through indentured 'Liberated' Africans who migrated from Sierra Leone in the mid-nineteenth century. Some of these migrants were Baptists, although the influence of George's church was overshadowed by a second wave of Baptists from London, despatched by the Baptist Missionary Society (BMS) as early as 1795.[51] Whether directly from George's church or indirectly through the BMS, the Sierra Leonean dynamic in the evolution of Shakerism and Shouterism remains valid.

The Imperial Missionary Challenge and Post-emancipation African Immigration

The theory of Christianisation as a force for subduing the revolutionary inclination of enslaved Africans in the Caribbean gained momentum after the large-scale insurgency in Jamaica in 1760, culminating in the formation of a multiplicity of metropolitan-based missionary societies in the 1790s and early 1800s. The earliest was the BMS, founded in 1792, followed by the London Missionary Society (LMS) in 1795 and the Anglican Church Missionary Society (CMS) in 1799. The original name of the BMS, 'Particular Baptist Society for the Propagation of the Gospel amongst the Heathen,' evidences its vanguard role alongside later missionary societies in furthering British cultural imperialism around the world.

After many years of Liele's pleas for metropolitan support, the BMS, commonly called London Baptists in the Caribbean, began a new enterprise in Jamaica from 1814 with three missionaries. Liele was still alive and well. The Ethiopian Baptist Church did not yield authority to the Whites and continued to operate under its own identity. This distinction was most evident in December 1831 when Native Baptists, under enslaved Deacon Samuel Sharp's leadership, unleashed the most formidable challenge to the slavery system by way of the Christmas Rebellion, also popularly known as the Baptist War of 1831–32.[52] The independence of the Native Church was confirmed when the three London missionaries left the island shortly after the insurgency and did not return until full emancipation was achieved in 1838. Although proprietors attacked the English Baptists, evidence extracted by Court Martial established no alliance between these two branches of the Baptist Church.

In post-emancipation Jamaica, Native Baptists interfaced more strongly with home-grown Myalism than before, but the most significant change came after 1840. Between 1841 and 1867, some ten thousand new Africans were shipped to Jamaica from Sierra Leone and St Helena.[53] These had been freed from slave ships violating the treaties of abolition of their respective countries.[54] Demographically the Sierra Leone diaspora was overwhelmingly Igbo and Yoruba; the St Helena Diaspora was overwhelmingly Bakongo and Mbundu, originating mainly from the ports of Luanda, Benguela, Ambriz, Cabinda, and the Congo River.[55] The diaspora from St Helena brought with them the *Kumina* religious phenomenon, a form of ancestral worship, with the living dead as ancestors, that is, the dead in personal memory.[56] During the mid-century Jamaican Revival, *Kumina* devotees transformed the older Myal-Baptist syncretism into two new Christian religious expressions, *Pukumina* and Revival Zion.[57] The Liberated African diaspora had similar impacts on the African Christianity in St Vincent and Trinidad, which will be addressed in the next chapter.

Notes

1.   The main body of laws were Master and Servant ordinances, vagrancy laws and tenancy-rent laws linked to wages; see O. Nigel Bolland, 'Systems of Domination after Slavery: The Control of Land and Labor in the British West Indies after 1838,' *Comparative Studies in Society and History* 23, no. 4 (1981), 594–98, https://www.jstor.org/stable/178395.

2.   Minna Salami, 'What Most People don't know about African Spirituality,' https://www.blackwomenarelove.com/stories/2019/7/12what-most-people-don't-know-about-african-spirituality, accessed May 7, 2020.

3.   John W. Cromwell, 'First Negro Churches in the District of Columbia,' *JNN* 7, no. 1 (Jan. 1922), 65. The same conclusion is made about the Jordanites of Guyana by Judith Roback, 'The White-Robed Army: Cultural Nationalism and a Religious Movement in Guyana' (PhD Diss., McGill University, Montreal, 1973), 1.

4.   David Brion Davis, *The Problem of Slavery in the Age of Revolution* (Ithaca, NY: Cornell University Press, 1975). Davis wrongly omitted Haiti from his conceptualisation of this Age.

5.   Walter H. Brooks, 'The Evolution of the Negro Baptist Church,' *Journal of Negro History* 7, no. 1 (January1922), 15, https://www.jstor.org/stable/2713578, accessed February 7, 2020; Kenneth J. Ross, 'The Church on Lombard Street,' *Presbyterian Historical Society* 23 (Mar. 2017), https://www/history.pcusa.org/blog/2017/03/church-lombard-street. Not all sources agree on a specific date.

6.   Brooks, 'The Evolution of the Negro Baptist Church,' 12.

7.   John T. Christian, 'The Baptists of Virginia,' *Baptist History Homepage*, http://baptisthistoryhomepage.com/Virginia.baptist.jtchristian.html. The illiterate White pastorate greatly expanded in the early years of the nineteenth century: see Albert H. Newman, 'Recent Changes in the Theology of Baptists,' *The American Journal of Theology* 10, no. 4 (October1906), 593.

8.   Christian, 'The Baptists of Virginia.'

9.   B. Maharry, 'The History of Negro Spirituals and Folk Music,' *Black Music Scholar*, https://blackmusicscholar.com/negro-spirituals-and-folk-music-kalia-simms-and-betanya-maharry/, accessed June 20, 2020. Anon., 'Songs of Slave Resistance,' California State University Northridge (CSUN) Library, https://library.csun/SCA/Peek-in-the-Stocks/slave-resistance, posted February 23, 2016, accessed February 24, 2020.

10.   Anon., 'Slave Songs of Resistance,' CSUN Library, February 23, 2016, https://www.library.csun.edu, accessed March 23, 2020.

11.   Article xxiv, *A Brief Confession or Declaration of Faith (London: 1660)*, http://www.reformedreader.org/ccc/tsc.htm, accessed February 21, 2020.

12.   Article v, *A Brief Confession or Declaration of Faith.*

13.   Article xix, *A Brief Confession.*

14.   Article v, *A Brief Confession.*

15. Newman, 'Theology of Baptists,' 593.

16. See G. G. Finlay and W. W. Holdsworth, *The History of the Wesleyan Methodist Missionary Society 2* (London: Epsworth Press, 1921), 40; Frey and Wood, *Shouting to Zion*, 124–25; Brooks, 'Negro Baptist Church,' 12.

17. See Brooks, 'Negro Baptist Church,' 16.

18. Frey and Wood, *Shouting to Zion*, 124.

19. Newman, 'Theology of Baptists,' 609.

20. Harold R. James, 'Back to Africa,' in *African American Experience in World Missions: A Call Beyond Community*, eds. Vaughn J. Watson and Robert J. Stephens (Pasadena, CA: William Carey Library, 2002), 83, Google Books. Anon., 'The History,' *Bahamas Baptist Union of Churches*, https://bahamasbaptistunion.org/.

21. See Eric Williams, 'The British West Indian Slave Trade After its Abolition in 1807,' *JNH* 27, no. 2 (April 1942), 178; 187, https://www.jstor.org/stable/2714732.

22. Carter G. Woodson, *The History of the Negro Church* (Washington, DC: Associated Press, 1921), 43–44. Anon., 'Liele, George,' Encyclopedia.com, https://www.encyclopedia.com/environment/encyclopedias-almanacs-transcripts-and-maps/liele-george, accessed April 19, 2020; also, Liele et al., 'Letters,' 73.

23. Woodson, *History of the Negro Church*, 41–42; Christopher Fyfe, ed., *'Our Children are Free and Happy:' Letters from Black Settlers in Africa in the 1790s* (Edinburgh: Edinburgh University Press, 1991), 4, https://www.questia.com.

24. Woodson, *History of the Negro Church*, 42–43. Walter H. Brooks, 'The Silver Bluff Church: The History of Negro Baptist Churches in America,' *The Reformed Reader* (1910), https://www.reformedreader.org/history/negrobaptistchurches.htm.

25. Anon. 'Liele, George,' Encyclopedia.com.

26. Woodson, *History*, 44–45.

27. See Frey and Wood, *Shouting to Zion*, 131.

28. Woodson, *History*, 44; Liele et al., *'Letters,'* 71; John Hayes, 'African American Baptists,' *New Georgia Encyclopedia*, 2006, https://www.georgiaencyclopedia.org/articles/arts-culture/african-american-baptists, accessed on May 7, 2020.

29. Woodson, *History of the Negro Church*, 45; Liele et al., 'Letters,' 71.

30. '17th Century Baptist Confession of Faith,' http://www.vor.org/rbdisk/baptistconf.htm, accessed April 30, 2020. There were two Confessions: The First London Baptist Confession of Faith, 1644, and the Second London Baptist Confession of Faith, 1677.

31. Ernest A. Payne, 'Baptist Work in Jamaica Before the Arrival of the Missionaries,' *The Baptist Quarterly* 7, no. 1 (1934), 24.

32. Liele, et al., 'Letters,' 71.

33. Ibid., 74.

34. Frey and Wood, *Shouting to Zion*, 131.

35. Woodson, *History of the Negro Church*, 46.

36. See Liele et al., 'Letters,' 72; John W. Davis, 'George Liele and Andrew Ryan, Pioneer Negro Baptist Preachers,' *JNH* 3 no. 2 (April 1918), 120.

37. Paul H. Williams, 'The Evolution of Myalism, Part 2,' *The Gleaner*, May 30, 2015, https://jamaica-gleaner.com/article/news/20150530/evolution-myalism-part2, accessed on April 22, 2021.

38. Williams, 'Myalism.'

39. Noel Leo Erskine, 'George Liele: Liberated Slave and African American Baptist Missionary to Jamaica,' *Missiology: An International Review* 50, no. 1 (2022), 27, https://journals.sage.pub.com/doi/pdf/10.1177/00918296211043527, accessed August 11, 2023; James Anthony Noel, 'Liele, George,' https://www.encyclopedia.com/environment/encyclopedias-almanaccs-transcripts-and-maps/liele-george, updated March 8, 2020.

40. Emanuela Guano, 'Revival Zion: An Afro-Christian Religion in Jamaica,' *Anthropos* 89 (1994), 517, https://www.jstor.org/stable/40463021.

41. Ann Hilton, *Kingdom of Kongo* (Oxford: Clarendon Press, 1985), 98. Google Book. Hilton explained that the kiKongo term for Christian baptism was *ncuria mmungia*, which carried the same meaning as 'to eat salt.' Maureen Warner-Lewis, *Central Africa in the Caribbean: Transcending Time, Transforming Cultures (Bridgetown, Barbados: University of the West Indies Press, 2003), 102; 215, accessed at* www.questia.com.

42. Warner-Lewis, *Central Africa in the Caribbean*, 185.

43. See Payne, 'Baptist Work in Jamaica,' 21; Liele et al., 'Letters,' 72.

44. Par. 4, *The 1689 Baptist Confession of Faith*, https://www.the1689confession.com/1689, accessed February 2020. The document is also known as *The Second London Baptist Confession*.

45. Kim Johnson, 'Born Again in Living Waters,' *TriniView*, May 17, 1992, http://www.triniview.com/TnT/baptists.html.

46. Other significant figures included Moses Wilkinson and Boston King who founded the first Methodist Church in Sierra Leone in 1792: see Fyfe, *Letters from Black Settlers*, 4–5. The Countess of Huntingdon's Connection, an affiliate of Methodism, was also established in Sierra Leone at this time by African refugee preachers on the 1792 voyage from Nova Scotia. The two most prominent figures in this sphere were Cato Perkins and John Marrant, the accredited missionary who expanded the Huntingdonians/Connection from England to Nova Scotia.

47. Fyfe, *Letters from Black Settlers*, 4; Adrian Hastings, *The Church in Africa, 1450–1950* (Oxford: Clarendon Press, 1996), 176.

48. For Africans such as Ottobah Cugoano and Thomas Peters whose advocacy convinced the British government and British anti-slave trade society to support George's emigration, see Hastings, *The Church in Africa*, 180; Peter Fryer, *Staying Power: The History of Black People in Britain* (London, Pluto Press, 1984), 202.

49. Homepage, 'Regent Road Baptist Church,' https://regentroadbaptistchurch.webs.com/history.htm, accessed May 22, 2019.

50.   See *The Baptist Magazine*, 21 (London: 1798), 96.

51. Arthur T. Porter, 'Religious Affiliation in Freetown, Sierra Leone,' *Journal of the International African Institute* 23, no. 1 (January 1953), 6, https://www.jstor.org/stable/1156028.

52. See Richard Hart, *Slaves Who Abolished Slavery: Blacks in Rebellion* (Kingston, Jamaica: University of the West Indies Press, 2002), 244–311. The Baptist War had a decisive impact on the British government's decision to draft a Bill for immediate, general emancipation the following year.

53. Arlene Munro, 'The Immigration of Africans into the British Caribbean,' *Stabroek News*, June 20, 2002, https://www.landofsixpeoples.com/news02/ns206206.htm, accessed February 20, 2020. Beginning in 1834, the number is 11,391, but may have included other places of origin; see Tony Martin, *Caribbean History: From Pre-Colonial Origins to the Present* (Boston, MA: Pearson, 2012), 221.

54. Daniel Domingues da Silva et al., 'The Diaspora Liberated from Slave Ships in the Nineteenth Century,' *Journal of African History* 55 no. 3 (November 2014), 352.

55. Da Silva et al., 'Liberated from Slave Ships,' 352.

56. See Bandele Agyemang Davy, 'Kumina in Rural Southeastern Jamaica: Beyond Resistance to Antithetical-Hegemonic-Subsumption,' *Africology: The Journal of Pan-African Studies*, 11, no. 7 (May 2018), 49.

57. Nathaniel Samuel Murrell, *Afro-Caribbean Religions: An Introduction to the Historical, Cultural and Sacred Traditions* (Philadelphia: PA, Temple University Press, 2010), 259. Jean Besson and Barry Chevannes, 'The Continuity-Creativity Debate: The Case of Revival,' *New West Indian Guide* 70, no 3/4 (1996), 215–16, https://www.jstor.org/stable/41819777.

CHAPTER 2

The Rise of the Spiritual Baptist Faith

'The African initiatory traditions bring death to life as the entry into a spiritual route.'*

The African diaspora in the greater Caribbean created new languages, all interconnected; new musical genres, all interconnected; new religions, all interconnected. Each is a synthesis of many historical, cultural, and cosmological elements. All were forged from resistance to oppression and diverse struggles to humanise their environment according to their own circumstances. The Spiritual Baptist religion is one of these creations. One of the earliest anthropo-historical explanation for the origin and character of Spiritual Baptism was that of Herskovits and Herskovits. Although the co-authors acknowledged the 'sect' as authentic religion, they were reluctant to classify it as a Christian denomination; instead, they concluded that it was 'African worship' akin to 'the Shango cult' that 'had been shaped and reinterpreted to fit into the pattern of European worship.'[1] This explanation is classical, racist stereotyping of Africans as imitators and borrowers of European culture.

The Emergence and Evolution of Spiritual Baptism in Trinidad

In his *History of Trinidad and Tobago*, Eric Williams authoritatively declares, 'the shouters and the shango, the latter the God of the Yoruba people, have come to Trinidad straight from Africa.'[2] Since

---

* Didier Mupaya Kapiten, 'Vivre sa Mort dans les traditions initiatives d'Afrique Noire: Une Voie d'approche au mystère de la croix,' *Théologiques* 19, no. 1 (2011): 163-80, https://wwwerudit.org/en/journals/theologi/1900-v1-n1-theologi0443/1014186ar.pdf.

Williams's statement is characteristically axiomatic, the reader has no choice but to conclude that Shouterism and Shangoism were African cultural exports, thus reinforcing the Herskovitses' misconception.

Williams explicitly assigns these religions to Africans who arrived 'during the slavery period;'[3] he does not consider, however, those Africans who came to the island as free settlers during that period nor does he give credence to a provenance of Shouterism in the twice-captured, post-emancipation, indentured Yoruba, a popular perception among contemporary Spiritual Baptists. However, there is no simple or single answer to the origin of this denomination. In an early paper on the subject, David Trotman observes that the post-emancipation Yoruba diaspora in Trinidad could not singularly account for the rise of the Spiritual Baptist. He argues that British Guiana (now Guyana) had received a significantly higher number of Yoruba migrants than Trinidad over the same period, yet there was no Spiritual Baptist or Orisha practice in that colony during the nineteenth century.[4] Trotman's argument still holds, even if we consider the Jordanites who trace their beginnings to Joseph MacLaren of Grenada. MacLaren arrived in Guyana in 1895, abandoned Anglicanism and launched a career as an independent preacher practising adult baptism by immersion in living water.[5] There is no evidence for MacLaren being Yoruba.

Early scholars on the origin of Shouterism as a distinct denomination in Trinidad overwhelmingly concur that the faith was introduced by African Baptist settlers from North America, whose descendants are known as the Merikins. This study aligns with the scholarship that challenges this school of thought. In 1802, the British government initiated a policy of settling the newly ceded island with small landholders, including discharged soldiers from various wars. African American veterans were the first significant group of discharged soldiers under this scheme.[6] These veterans comprised the core of the six hundred maroons from plantations extending from Chesapeake to Georgia, who volunteered to fight for the British as the Corps of Colonial Marines in the closing months of the second Anglo-American War, 1812–14.[7] Their preference for military service under the British flag was one of two options under Vice-Admiral Alexander Cochrane's 'Proclamation' to enslaved Africans enticing them to escape slavery.[8]

After the war, the Six Companies of Colonial Marines rejected an offer of reassignment to the Fourth West India Regiment, a Black standing army garrisoned in Bermuda. Instead, they invoked the second option in Cochrane's Proclamation: to become 'Free Settlers' in unnamed British colonies.[9] The choice of Trinidad was determined by imperial policy. In 1816, most of the ex-Marines arrived in the colony, some with their spouses and children, 574 altogether.[10] They were settled on grants of Crown lands in the Naparima forest of southern Trinidad forming the Company Villages, which extend from New Grant to Moruga. There they became known as 'The Americans' (Africanised into 'The Merikins' much later) and distinguished from the veterans of the West India Regiments settled in the northeast of the island under similar conditions and known as 'The West Indians.'[11] According to Peter Brewer, 'The great majority of the settlers were Baptists' whose worship was characterised by 'jumping, shouting and shaking.'[12] But they were not the Shouters targeted for proscription in the early twentieth century. 'Shouterism' is a post-slavery phenomenon. Governor Ralph Woodford who oversaw the settlement of the Merikins identified the principal religion of the group as Anabaptist,[13] the same identity claimed by George Liele in Jamaica. Almost certainly they were members of the Church founded by Liele and George in pre-Independence United States of America. About two hundred of the newly arrived Merikins were Methodists and about twenty were Muslims.[14]

The Merikin Baptists came with their preachers and exhorters and quickly created the last significant communion of the African American Baptist Church in the Caribbean. One of their most outstanding and literate pastors was William Hamilton who served as pastor of the church at Fifth Company.[15] Hamilton was already an accomplished preacher-exhorter before he became a maroon to fight with Admiral Alexander Cochrane in the Anglo-American War of 1812–14.[16] He worked as a teacher in Indian Walk and Savannah Grande. He also likely acted as a BMS missionary in his later life, because none was named for that station.[17] Hamilton was the George Liele of Trinidad by training others for the clergy and inviting the BMS to the island to assist the Merikin Baptist Church.[18] The sixteen acres of land granted to each disbanded Colonial Marine was made in accordance with the principles established for 'coloureds' in Spain's Cedula of Population of 1783, by which Catholic immigrants were enticed to the island as cultivators. The grant, however, was considerably less than the 100 acres offered to White veterans after the Battle of Waterloo.[19] Nevertheless, within a short time, the Merikins became a prosperous peasantry, placing the African Baptist Church upon a solid economic foundation. The Merikin Church nurtured many other strands of African Protestantism in the island as the century progressed making it the most successful pre-emancipation institution in the island pioneered and controlled by Africans.

Some West India Regiment settlers in northeast Trinidad were Muslims.[20] There were no known Baptist converts among them. The most likely reason for this difference is that the recruits had been acquired directly from slave ships, purchased from auction blocks, or levied from plantations not yet impacted by evangelists.[21] The comparison underscores the significance of the African-American diaspora to the spread of the Baptist faith in the colony. One of the earliest BMS missionaries in Trinidad, John Law, evangelised members of the West India Regiment, some of whom were forcefully conscripted from among the liberated Africans in Sierra Leone;[22] but the history of the Baptist Church among them is yet to be written.

By 1823, the population of Merikins had increased to 883.[23] This dramatic growth may have been the result of single veterans starting families; however, other factors were also at play, principally the settlement of newly arrived women: in 1817, fifty-three women liberated from a French slaver were settled among the Merikins; these were followed by another group of sixty women from Antigua who were also distributed among the Merikins.[24] In 1821, ninety-five African-American refugees formerly settled in Nova Scotia arrived in the island and received land grants in Naparima, Merikin country.[25] Many of them were Baptists. Furthermore, as early as 1815, 205 'civilians' from Bermuda had arrived in the island, of which fifty-two were given Crown lands in Naparima; the rest were placed in Laventille in east Port of Spain, San Fernando and Caroni.[26] The Bermudans were also mainly an African-American diaspora many of whom belonged to the Baptist Church founded by Liele and expanded by Amos and others in Bahamas.[27] They were some of the pioneers of what became Yoruba Village, in which Belmont and Laventille would emerge as the stronghold of Shouterism in north-western Trinidad.

The arrival of the Merikins coincided with efforts of Wesleyan Methodists to establish a foothold in the colony. The first Wesleyan Methodist missionary, Thomas Talboys, arrived in 1810 and immediately aroused the hostility of the White slavocracy. The Cabildo or City Council reacted acrimoniously to protect the strange Catholic-Anglican hegemony that preserved the illiteracy of the enslaved population. By 1815, the Methodists and the Cabildo were locked in battle over the Toleration Act, but by 1818, the Trinidad government capitulated after receiving the declaration by the Colonial Office that Methodists were protected under the original Toleration Act, 1689, as well as several amending Acts.[28]

The resolution of the conflict was timely for the Merikins because it is doubtful that Black Baptists would have been more welcomed as evangelists to the enslaved population. One thing that favoured the Merikins politically was that they had no direct connection to the abolitionist movement in England or elsewhere and, therefore, could not be perceived as their agents. Furthermore, although the BMS had recently established a mission in Jamaica, that organisation did not have a track record in advocacy for abolition of the slave trade or slavery. Another advantage the Merikins had over the Methodist missionaries was that some Merikins worked as hired labourers on sugar plantations in addition to being self-employed farmers.[29] Whereas the Methodists engaged the enslaved population through formal meetings and chapel worship, the Merikins' close contacts with enslaved labourers provided continuous opportunities for informal proselytising. It is also highly likely that the Merikins would have established relations with Baptist converts from the Bahamas, who continued to trickle into Trinidad

– many by recruiters' deception – to alleviate the naturally declining enslaved population. Such cultural exchanges were equally subversive, but less noticeable, because Africans were masters of oral pedagogy, a tool that yielded little or no evidence of subversion. Up to the prohibition, extempore was the characteristic mode of composing and delivering sermons, prayers, and hymns.

Whereas the African Baptist Church of Jamaica was an evangelical enterprise, its equivalent in Trinidad was a settler congregation from the very outset; and whereas the dominant congregation in Jamaica was enslaved, the dominant congregation in Trinidad was free and had not experienced slavery in the island. These differences are critical to understanding why Jamaica's Native Baptists had to negotiate with an already established Myal culture and why in Trinidad, the Merikins had little or no doctrinal challenges until the influx of Liberated Africans and the arrival of BMS missionaries well after Emancipation.

Merikin Baptists' negotiation with native African cultures may be deduced from the beliefs and practices of Spiritual Baptists, as no documentary evidence exists to shed light on the subject. Yoruba culture was influential but not as decisive as Bakongo in the making of Spiritual Baptism. Just as occurred in Jamaica, the rite of credobaptism attracted Yorubas to Merikin baptisms; invariably, these sites were the rivers or coastal waters, both of which were translatable to Osun, one of the most popular orishas of Yorubaland, especially of the Ijesha kingdom from which many of the Liberated Yoruba in Trinidad originated.[30] Having twice survived forced journeys across thousands of miles in the Atlantic Ocean, the faith of Yoruba and other Liberated Africans would have been doubly reinforced in their respective water deities.[31] Another element in the Yoruba attraction to Spiritual Baptists was spirit possession, a common element in many African religions.

Little or nothing is known of the Igbo influence on Trinidad's Spiritual Baptists, although Igbos were demographically well represented during the slavery era and indentured Igbos equalled the Yoruba in the post-slavery era.[32] Liberated Igbos also had a variety of powerful water deities of both sexes, such as Njaba, Orimili, Idemeli also called Mami Wata (Mother of Waters), and Imo Mmri.[33] It should also be noted that many Liberated Igbos, Yorubas, and other ethnic minorities from the Gulf of Guinea had become Christians in Sierra Leone and assimilated into the African American Christian diaspora of the late-eighteenth century.[34] Charles Kingsley observed that they all belonged 'nominally to some denomination of Christianity: but their lives are more influenced by their belief in Obeah.'[35] The reference to obeah is generic but it suggests the resilience of African spirituality that remained embedded in Spiritual Baptism.

Many scholars allude to a significant migration of Vincentian Penitent refugees to Belmont and Laventille in the years immediately following the Shakers' Prohibition Ordinance, 1912.[36] The impact of this migration, however, is mired in contemporary political propaganda. Its magnification conveniently fuelled the scare tactic of the Trinidad and Tobago government to justify replicating St Vincent's prohibition ordinance and deploying it against the Shouters. Although the Shouters could not possibly have originated from this migration, a Vincentian factor in the earliest public awareness of the Shouters cannot be ruled out absolutely. The first record of a distinctive Shouters sect in Trinidad coincided with the era of permanent and seasonal migration into Trinidad by thousands of Vincentians from mid-nineteenth century, some of whom were known to be Penitents or Converted.[37] The Vincentian migration began much earlier than claimed by John Hackshaw.[38] Joseph Spinelli shows that between 1844 and 1881, the population of St Vincent experienced a natural increase of over forty-thousand, yet the net increase was a mere 7,413, which supports a relatively large, permanent emigration. According to Spinelli, most of the Black Vincentian emigrants 'were either in temporary or permanent residence in Trinidad.'[39] Emigration was fuelled by the rapid decline of the sugar industry, the biggest employer of wage labour. By 1862 the number of sugar estates in St Vincent had declined by almost 50 per cent since the end of chattel slavery.[40] Between 1881 and 1911, the complete collapse of the sugar industry, exacerbated by other factors, created unprecedented levels of unemployment. Accordingly, the estimated net emigration for the period was 15,667, of which

Trinidad received a substantial share.[41] Because some of the largest sugar plantations in St Vincent were strongholds of Penitentism, it is to be expected that Trinidad absorbed much more than labour from that colony. Indeed, Vincentians collaborated with other Caribbean migrants to establish the first Moravian Church in Trinidad by 1880.[42] The African foundation of this Church inspired Tubal Uriah Butler, a Spiritual Baptist from Grenada, to coin the term, Moravian Baptist Church, to escape the prohibition ordinance. Notwithstanding this constant stream of Vincentians into Trinidad, the most glaring anomaly in the St Vincent factor is that the existing literature does not recognise a Baptist Church in St Vincent prior to the mid-twentieth century. However, the lack of literature on the subject as well as the absence of a formal Baptist 'Church' do not rule out the presence of African Baptists, as addressed later in this chapter.

Trinidad-born Australian anthropologist, Kenneth Anthony Lum, was one of the earliest scholars to promote a provenance for Shouterism in Penitentism based on the account of Trinidad's Viola Gopaul-Whittington, a Spiritual Baptist. Lum shared Whittington's view that the faith originated in Antigua whence it spread to St Vincent and Grenada and finally to Trinidad.[43] One Sister Lyddeatte, described as 'High Priestess' of Penitentism, 'a missionary from Antigua,' was imprisoned in 1921 for practising 'Shakerism' in St Vincent.[44] According to Whittington, the original proponents of the faith in Antigua were formerly of 'the Orisha cult' and because of persecution they fled to St Vincent.[45] An Antiguan connection in the rise of the Spiritual Baptists is useful for the interplay of diasporic forces and cultures that fed into the construction of the faith. Whittington narrated that her grandfather, Emmanuel Gopaul, son of an Indian-born indentured labourer, told her that the faith originated in Antigua in 1870.[46] Wittington claimed that her native Indian great-grandfather, 'an indentured slave,' had taken Facitae, 'a runaway African Yoruba slave' for his wife.[47] The faith was allegedly founded by the Antiguans following a transcendental experience that involved revelations of the mysteries of Ancient Egypt, including its speech and hieroglyphs.[48]

According to Whittington, the faith reached Trinidad at the beginning of the twentieth century. She claims that the first church was established in Point Fortin, the second in Laventille and the third in Lopinot Road, Arouca.[49] After the death of Emmanuel's father, Facitae is said to have 'opened a Palais' in Arouca 'with other slaves' and practised the Orisha faith.[50] Lum, who admits that he knew nothing of the Spiritual Baptists before embarking on his doctoral dissertation in 1986, does not critique this narrative, although he later gives a more traditional survey of scholarly literature on the history of the faith. Still, it needs to be noted that Whittington's account is seriously flawed. The name 'Shakers' was used in St Vincent well before 1870; the status of Emmanuel's father as 'an indentured slave' is confusing; so, too, is the claim that he married a maroon, since slavery had ended before the beginning of Indian immigration; even if Facitae was a former runaway, it is highly unlikely that she was still alive at the beginning of the twentieth century, more so, to set up a palais 'with other African slaves.'[51] Furthermore, an Orisha palais does not establish a Spiritual Baptist presence. If there is any value in this narrative it is the intersection of Spiritual Baptism with Orisha and Hinduism in its formative years and the early use of 'Kabbalist' markings used in mourning rites.[52] Also, it lends credibility to the attraction of Indians to Spiritual Baptism during the indentureship period. Indeed, Indians were also charged under the Shouters' Prohibition Ordinance.[53]

The injection of new African cultural content into the Merikin Baptist Church came from multiple sources over several decades. The flow of captured Africans into Trinidad certainly did not stop after Britain's abolition of her Atlantic slave trade. Among the new demographic were Africans rescued from slave ships by the British navy between 1808 and 1866. Some two hundred recaptives disembarked in the island directly from slave ships; between 1834 and 1849, over four thousand were removed from Cuba to Trinidad.[54] Between 1841 and 1867, about 36,120 other liberated captives, including some of their offspring, were taken from Sierra Leone and the south Atlantic Island, St Helena, to the Caribbean as indentured labourers. Of the almost nine thousand that disembarked in Trinidad, just over 3,500 had started their journey in Sierra Leone and almost 3,400 from St Helena.[55] From 1844 to 1861, between 1,036 and 1,068 Liberated Africans arrived in St Vincent.[56] In the period 1836 to 1863, some 2,709 Liberated Africans disembarked in Grenada.[57] The primary religious impact of the new African immigrants was the transformation of African American Baptism into Spiritual (Shouter) Baptism, the most formidable arsenal in the culture-war between colonials and Africans in these colonies.

A recent study, using registered personal names of a large sample of the total liberated captives that embarked from ports in the Bight of Benin and disembarked in Sierra Leone, reveals that over 95 per cent were Yoruba speakers; in a similarly large sample of liberated captives disembarked from the Bight of Biafra, 88 per cent were Igbo.[58] It is further estimated that some 60 per cent of those who were forced into indentureship in Trinidad from Sierra Leone were Yoruba and Igbo. It goes without saying that similar proportions of the unfortunates from Cuba also must have been Yoruba and Igbo.[59]

Evangelists of the African-American Baptist and Methodist Churches in Sierra Leone were active in the earliest Liberated African settlements. Within a few years, the CMS, the principal umbrella for Anglican evangelism overseas, had overtaken the African-Americans as the dominant evangelising force but up to the 1830s some of the preachers in the European missionary churches were 'original settlers' and Liberated Africans attended daily service 'in great numbers.'[60] Writing in 1863, Robert Clarke, a British surgeon resident in Freetown, affirmed that Christian chapels proliferated 'in every part of the town;' furthermore, the Wesleyan chapels were managed predominantly by 'native preachers.'[61] By the 1840s, the combined Christianisation project had already achieved outstanding results, as evidenced in the return of some Yoruba to evangelise their own homeland.[62] Most of the native Africans were formally educated; some were graduates of Fourah Bay College.[63] This means that a considerable number of the Liberated Africans indentured in the Caribbean after 1840 had prior experience with African-led or European-led Protestantism and Western education.[64] In addition, between 1839 and 1847, over one thousand, three hundred African Americans from both 'free' and slave-owning states were recruited for indentured labour in Trinidad.[65] These recruits would have found a congenial religious climate within the native Baptist communion in the colony.

A critical examination of the relevant migrant streams into Trinidad supports the conclusion that Shouterism is a syncretism of the Merikin Church with mainly Kongolese and Yoruba religious traditions and clerical structures, some of which may have been influenced by Vincentian migrants. Two contemporary sources recognise Third Company for special consideration. One is the 1907 *Annual Report of the Baptist Missionary Society*, which identified only three Baptist Churches that were not in the Union: one was Third Company; the others were Momga and St Julien's, both in the heartland of the Merikin district.[66] The BMS Report did not advance any reason for the defiance of the trio but one may surmise from an investigative article in The *Mirror*, published the previous year, that it was a case of cultural-doctrinal resistance. The *Mirror* reporter claimed that a Church at Third Company 'is the headquarters of shouterism in Trinidad.'[67] We must treat this conclusion with circumspection, since the reporter did not define Shouterism. Nevertheless, the Merikin Baptists labelled 'Disobedients' by BMS missionaries were associated with the three non-conforming churches that rejected affiliation with the London BMS and self-identified as Independent Baptists, not Shouters.[68] They would later form a coalition with the local Baptist Union,[69] which immunised them from the prohibition ordinance of 1917.

The primary distinction between Spiritual Baptism and Merikin Baptism was the rite of mourning.[70] More likely than not, mourning (popularly pronounced 'moanin') is a Caribbean translation of a distinct Kongolese-Bantu rite of 'living one's own death.' This Kongolese esoteric called *Kumina* was first evident in Myalism in Jamaica during slavery, as discussed in the previous chapter. Myalists ritualised death through dance and trance from which they were revived or reborn in the same dance routine.[71] When Myalists were enslaved, these ceremonies had to be clandestine and necessarily of short duration. *Kumina* was also evident in St Vincent during slavery.[72]

In the post-slavery period, greater freedom allowed for longer periods of mourning, extending over three days and sometimes lasting as much as an entire week or more. In St Vincent, the rite of mourning was associated with the Wilderness People in the mid-nineteenth century.[73] Based on the testimony of Maria Jones of Trinidad, a formerly enslaved autobiographer, Liberated African converts transliterated *Kumina* into the Baptist sacrament of baptism as being 'buried with Christ' and being reborn as a new Christian.[74] Jones was born in Africa and experienced the terrors of the barracoon and the bowel of a slave ship. Mourning was a trial of faith unlike any other experience to which Christian congregants were subjected as a rite of passage to become a full-fledged member of the community of converted; it was also a test of worthiness for holding religious office or performing clerical roles. Such was the centrality of this experience that the Shakers of St Vincent self-identified as 'The Converted' and 'Penitents.'

Evidently, the final syncretism of *Kumina* with African-Caribbean Christianity occurred during the Great Revival of the mid-nineteenth century, following the significantly large migration of Kongolese indentured workers into the Caribbean. In Jamaica, the new synthesis was *Pukumina* (Pocomania) and Revival Zion.[75] Merikin Baptists also came under the influence of African-American revivalism in this period.[76] The revivalist movement of the 1860s, coupled with the relatively large migration of Kikongo and Kimbundu peoples from St Helena into Trinidad, may have deepened the schism within the Merikin Church leading to the birth of Shouterism: the pastor of the Fourth Company church, Trinidad-born Charles Webb, communicated to the BMS that he had successfully 'kept out the "wild and fanatical notions" which had entered the other churches.'[77] This assertion speaks to a religious phenomenon previously unknown to local Baptist liturgy. The newly arrived Africans were also confidently establishing their own independent chapels. In the same decade, William Hamilton Gamble, a Trinidad-born BMS missionary, reported the existence of 'a "small church" in southern Trinidad "chiefly composed of Africans."'[78] According to Roseanne Adderley, these 'Africans' were natives of Africa.[79] The small chapel was completely independent.

Adderley does not impute a *Kumina* connection, but still concludes that such new independent churches were the real genesis of Spiritual Baptism.[80] It is not to be assumed that these chapels were run by neophytes: in Sierra Leone, native preachers in the era of indentured immigration were 'trumpeting forth the glad tidings of the gospel' with 'wordy eloquence,'[81] reminiscent of the pioneer Black preachers and exhorters in the US in the last quarter of the eighteenth century. They had also maintained the styles of worship of the African American Church, adapting their hymns to profane music, in sharp contrast to the CMS and Wesleyan Methodist Missionary Society (WMMS) churches, where the service was 'conducted with much decorum.'[82] These preachers would not have found 'employment' consistent with their talent, style and calling in the few Wesleyan churches in Trinidad or in the fewer churches of the BMS and would have been spurned by Roman Catholic and Anglican clergy. The solution was to gravitate to the Merikin Baptists or establish their own churches.

Foreign missionaries had little influence on the Merikin Church or other African–led churches. The earliest recorded assault began in 1826 when one Revd Tucker set up a primary school exclusively to instruct the children of Merikins.[83] The strongest cultural assault that the Merikins faced came after slavery. The BMS arrived in Trinidad in 1843 and began to set up vanguard chapels for a strategic assault on African Christianity and African spirituality in the island.[84] They first moved into Belmont, on the outskirts of Port of Spain, an early stronghold of liberated and emancipated Africans who practised their own versions of Christianity or retained their African religions and spiritual traditions. During the rest of the decade the BMS established chapels in all the Merikin districts.[85] The first BMS missionaries, George Cowen and Robin Law, were exasperated over the slow growth of the Trinidad mission: Cowen described the island as 'this wilderness' and 'this dark place' where 'harvest time had not yet appeared;' Law wrote that after three years, he had baptised only 'three individuals' to add to the 'little church' in Belmont.[86]

The irreconcilability of the two canons of Baptism culminated in the 1860s' revolt by African Baptists against BMS authoritarianism.

Charles Webb reported to the BMS:

> At First Company (now Mount Elvin) there had been
> a secession; at Sixth Company the church had closed
> for several weeks following the disciplining of a leader;
> at Third Company there was a fear that the missionary
> would override the local leadership. Only one church had
> remained at peace.[87]

That was Fourth Company. A major consequence of the conflict was that the six churches of the Company Villages formed themselves into a Union 'some time before 1866.'[88] The Union was established 'for the control of the "unruly spirits" who would not submit to the discipline of their own church. The Union also had the sole power to licence a preacher.'[89] After the BMS left the colony in 1892, the remaining churches that they had formerly controlled joined the Baptist Union.

By the end of the nineteenth century, Shouterism as a religion was already fully developed and known by that name throughout Trinidad, although members of the faith rejected the identity.[90] In Tunapuna, Teacher Fanam and his successor, Pastor Pierre, were well-known Shouters before the turn of the century.[91] Teacher Joseph Bailey, born around 1890, the first Baptist leader to be prosecuted under the Prohibition Ordinance, testified that he knew only one religion that his mother and father practiced.[92] He did not put a name to the religion of his parents but he was charged with practising Shouterism. His claim that their form of worship was 'not shouting, but praying in the name of the Lord' was his way of affirming that followers of the faith had the sole right to define their form of worship, not those who despised and persecuted them.

The Origin and Evolution of Spiritual Baptism in St Vincent

Some Spiritual Baptists in St Vincent in the 1990s testified to American anthropologist, Wallace Zane, that Shakerism originated in colonial slavery; some of the respondents also credited John Wesley as progenitor of the faith.[93] These two claims are not mutually exclusive, since Wesleyan proselytisation began during the slavery era.[94] The problem with oral testimony such as transmitted to Zane is the potential for 'distortions,' as explained by Jan Vansina, an early researcher into African oral tradition.[95] The long legislative and legal battles for recognition in St Vincent would have provided much fodder for interference or distortion.

Whether Penitentism began during slavery or upon emancipation is debatable, but it certainly poses fundamental questions as to the actual progenitors of the movement.[96] If the tag 'Converted negroes' used by Dr Thomas Coke in 1810 was not a loose label for enslaved Methodist converts, it is highly likely that he would have communicated that fact.[97] The Converted at the time of Dr Coke's visit may have indulged in shaking and other corybantic behaviour but they were not doctrinally Shakers of the late-nineteenth century. According to Coke, Black Methodists in plantation North America also engaged in loud, ecstatic, congregational singing and praying, call-and-answer liturgy, and wayside- and candlelight-preaching.[98] Black Baptists worshipped in a similar manner. By the 1840s, therefore, independent prayer houses in St Vincent could have been either Methodist or Baptist in origin or both.

By the early 1840s, a 'prayer house' was to be found on every plantation. This is evidence of widespread institution-building by the newly freed and an assertion of their right of conscience. Nevertheless, it seems certain that by 1846 a new movement, the Wilderness People, had emerged on the Calder estate on the south-windward coast.[99] Significantly, this new consciousness manifested just two years from the beginning of Liberated African indenture. Because of the regular tracking of the Wilderness group by Methodist and Anglican clergy as well as political authorities, the evolution of Shakerism is much better documented than the evolution of Shouterism.

The prayer house was ideally suited to the Methodist 'class' system of evangelising; it was also the nursery of Spiritual Baptism. The class system facilitated the emergence of African spiritual leaders who retained considerable independence while serving as 'class Leaders' who easily progressed to 'lay Preachers' and Exhorters.[100] Thomas Coke testified to the critical role of lay preachers, calling them 'one of the main arms of Methodism.'[101] Coke also acknowledged these grass-root networks as the true agents of Methodism: 'As in North American colonies, so in the West Indies, Methodism originated as a self-sown plant; for a quarter of a century it subsisted through the sole agency of lay Preachers and Class Leaders.'[102] This is the structure that produced a Black Harry, one of the foremost preachers on the island of St Eustatius in the late-eighteenth century.[103] Harry had such 'natural eloquence' that even the governor attended his sermons.[104]

It is important to recognise that the core of the first lay preachers were free Africans, including mixed races. According to pioneer English missionary, William Hammet, incursions into the plantations only happened with the consent of estate managers but more importantly, at 'the request' of converted, urban, free Blacks, and mixed-race persons.[105] John Baxter, pioneer missionary to Antigua, denied 'his own entanglement with … the slave plantation.'[106] Such entanglement could easily invite a charge of sedition. Freed Blacks, on the other hand, had familial and other relationship ties with the enslaved on the plantations. The class system was a master strategy for creating staunch believers: free Black Methodists could soften planters' resistance to evangelising the enslaved more readily than if they were White missionaries. Furthermore, free Blacks were the first cohort of catechists, lay preachers, and exhorters – Black allies and agents in the spread of missionary Christianity.

The Kingstown Council Ordinance of June 1807 is the first documented evidence of Africanised Christianity in St Vincent. The ordinance was the last desperate attempt to neutralise Methodist missionaries in the island. It identified forbidden places of worship as 'houses, negro-houses, huts, and the yards thereunto appertaining, and also in divers lands and by-places within this city and parish.'[107] These sites are less indicative of missionary penetration than the pervasive undercurrent of Black Protestant sectarianism. A critical reading of the Ordinance reveals that those subaltern places of worship were already under transformation toward a Penitent style of worship. The island's lawmakers imputed that worshippers and exhorters were engaged in 'indecent and unseemly noises, gesticulation, and behaviours …

to the disrepute of religion itself,' they added that one consequence of such form of worship was that participants became 'actually deranged' driven to this state by 'the fanaticism' of preachers.[108] When decoded, it is evident that enslaved preachers were the pioneers of corybantic Christianity in the colony. The alleged disrepute of religion obviously has meaning only in the context of European orthodoxy: the gesticulations must have included hand and body movements consistent with Africans engaged in group worship, while derangement was simply an unsatisfactory transliteration of a misunderstood phenomenon of trance and spirit possession, intrinsic to traditional African liturgy. In a related Africanised Methodist environment, Thomas Coke reported similar collective deep trances during which many worshippers 'fell down as if they were dead, and some of them remained in a stupor for four hours,'[109] the same experience of *Kumina* practitioners. The religious expressions condemned in the ordinance are indicative of a much earlier period than previously known for an African-Vincentian transformation of Methodism into a new way of worshipping.

The authority-structure and roles or offices of secret societies among enslaved Africans as well as the Methodist system of ranking into 'rulers, elders, leaders and helpers' were foundational to the ranking system of Spiritual Baptists, which expanded into some twenty-two ranks by the end of the nineteenth century.[110] Many of these roles evolved to service the physical and spiritual needs of initiates undergoing mourning. By the turn of the century, expressions such as 'on the knee,' 'pointing,' 'travelling,' 'working the spirit,' and 'riding Zion's donkey' to describe aspects of Penitent worship and the rite of mourning were already in vogue throughout the island.[111] Uniformity of standards was achieved through the constant interchange of preachers and other aides 'to assist at meetings.'[112]

Just as in the economic sphere, where the newly freed people pursued land ownership and other independent economic activities while providing plantation labour, so in the religious sphere, they maintained independent prayer groups while continuing to attend Wesleyan and Anglican chapels.[113] Up to Prohibition, this situation did not change: besides the two oldest Protestant Churches, Penitents could also be found in the Presbyterian Church.[114] Penitent members of the Methodist Church were not there because of old loyalties, but because Methodist stations employed African exhorters whose preaching was compatible with the spiritual dynamics of Penitent prayer meetings. In 1846, there were seven missionaries and five exhorters servicing the two principal circuits, Biabou and Kingstown.[115] With over six thousand members in the whole island at that time, it is more likely than not that African exhorters would have had regular preaching assignments, perhaps independent of the English missionaries.[116]

A policy of mass expulsions of Penitents or Wilderness People from Methodist and Anglican churches began in 1849.[117] Expulsion fuelled rapid expansion of independent Black Dissenters. One factor in this dispersion was the new African diaspora of Liberated Africans. As early as 1852 many of the new immigrants from Escape sugar estate close to Calder in the parish of St George were worshipping in Penitent prayer-houses.[118] By the late 1850s, the nucleus of Penitentism had shifted from the southern windward to Charlotte Parish such that by 1880, villages in the vicinity of Grand Sable and Mt Bentinck were Penitent villages.[119] Interestingly, it was during the 1850s, when the BaKongo factor began to influence the Converted, Penitent, and Wilderness People that the name 'Shakers' appears in the historical record of St Vincent for the first time and when 'mourning' was first associated with conversion in a Christian sect.[120] By this time, it was already evident from the negative stereotyping of the Penitent and calls for legal action against them that they had become a force to be reckoned with, both within the Methodist communion and the wider society. Apparently, the ascription 'Shakers' was not accepted without dissent because by 1856 the Wilderness People or one of their offspring had reasserted their identity as 'The Penitents' and 'The New Light.'[121] The new identities might not necessarily have indicated disunity but rather regional independence or a home-grown aspect of congregationalism common to the Baptist faith.

The first, White-led Baptist church in St Vincent was established only in 1947.[122] This does not rule out an earlier Baptist presence in the colony. Sheena Boa indicates that 'North American Baptist preachers' visited St Vincent from time to time prior to emancipation.

Unfortunately, she presents no documented evidence of their ethnicity or nationality, except for one particular 'African Canadian preacher' known as 'Mr Edwards' who apparently was a guest on Calder estate in the mid-1840s.[123] Further evidence of Baptist evangelism comes from one Mr Francies, a BMS missionary in Jacmel, Haiti. In a letter to the BMS in 1846 he averred, 'There is greater hope of raising up a native ministry than in Jamaica or St Vincent's.'[124] Francies's letter coincided with Edwards' sojourn in St Vincent. No reason was advanced for the near hopelessness of Baptist evangelism in that locality. Baptist missionaries also found conditions in Jacmel extremely challenging. Although native 'inquirers' attended meetings in the low hundreds, very few wanted to be baptised. Inquirers and converts were ridiculed by friends and families for deserting the Catholic Church. There was also the constant threat of yellow fever, with Francies himself falling to the disease shortly after writing the referenced letter.[125] St Vincent lacked the epidemiological terrors of Haiti; the island also lacked the hegemony of Roman Catholicism; and the Anglican Church had less of a hold on the working class than the Wesleyan.

Without a Baptist connection, the emergence of 'Shakers' by late-nineteenth century would more closely parallel African-initiated churches in Africa that separated from European missionary Protestantism or Catholicism, such as occurred in the Kingdom of Kongo in the sixteenth century, and much later, in Sierra Leone, Nigeria, Cameroon, and South Africa. According to received historical knowledge, the parent Church of the Shakers was the Methodist; perhaps one could say, a godparent was the Church of England. Yet, there is no explanation how Penitentism evolved from Methodism and Anglicanism, with their doctrine of infant baptism by way of sprinkling, to credobaptism by way of immersion in living water and the rite of mourning.

Except for a few perfunctory statements, the silence on a Baptist factor in the historiography of Shakerism makes St Vincent the broken link in the chain of African Baptist communion in the Caribbean extending from The Bahamas to Trinidad and Guyana. Nevertheless, it is possible to mend this faulty academic link. The first and most important element is the African-American connection and the agency of Colonel Thomas Brown (Browne), a wealthy Georgian planter, who fought for the British in the War of American Independence. On the eve of the war, Georgia was almost 50 per cent 'Black;' South Carolina and Virginia shared a similar demographic.[126] Georgia also shares with South Carolina historical recognition of having the first African-American Baptist churches in colonial North America, where Black Preachers exuberantly evangelised enslaved Africans. In 1782, Brown evacuated to Florida. Two years later, he re-migrated to The Bahamas, where he developed a large cotton-growing business. In 1805–06, Brown migrated to St Vincent with a complement of six hundred and forty-three Africans who were with him in The Bahamas and whom he re-enslaved on his estate called Grand Sable in the parish of Charlotte on the Windward coast; his was 'the largest single estate' in the colony, comprising some 1,600 acres.[127] It would be mindboggling if there were no Baptist converts among the African-Bahamians on Grand Sable.

Although the available evidence on Brown's labourers in The Bahamas is sketchy, it points to an American origin contemporaneous with Liele and other Baptist refugees mentioned earlier. Brown once boasted that he had 'armed, clothed and disciplined … all of his Negro men during the whole of the last war and never had a cause to repent of the trust in their fidelity.'[128] These men may have been conscripted into the Carolina King's Rangers commanded by Brown or served in the East Florida Rangers, also under Brown's command.[129] It is inconceivable that Brown would have demonstrated such confidence in the loyalty of newly landed native Africans by sending them in a boat armed with cannons and under their own command to intercept a French frigate cruising off Abaco Island.[130] Brown also offered Britain one hundred of his enslaved fighters for the defence of Jamaica during the Haitian Revolution and the Second Maroon War in the 1790s.[131] Such an offer suggests that those men indeed had prior military experience known to Brown or had even distinguished themselves in battle; that they were familiar with gun technology; and that they probably constituted a company of militia garrisoned on Brown's estate on Abaco Island.[132] The legal status of the Black rangers in Abaco is not known but many had won their freedom for their valour and loyalty while in Florida.[133] Brown's allotment of one acre of land to each of these rangers in Abaco may well have been token appeasement for a broken promise of freedom made to them by Admiral Lord Dunmore in Carolina. Nevertheless, their transfer to St Vincent led to their re-enslavement.

As an enslaved people under Brown, a High Church Anglican, it is understandable why the Black Baptists on Grand Sable did not build physical churches or specialised prayer houses. Brown's son and grandson became Anglican clergymen and lived on Grand Sable as heirs to the estate.[134] Nevertheless, the enslaved African-American Bahamians on Grand Sable could have maintained their Baptist faith even without the opportunity to establish a physical church structure, as occurred in The Bahamas, Jamaica and Trinidad. The geographic spread of this diaspora in the post-emancipation villages on the fringe of Grand Sable and on Mt Bentinck, located next to Grand Sable, coincide with the earliest strongholds of Shakerism.[135]

The precursors of Penitentism could not independently develop connections with credo-baptismal organisations from outside the colony because of slavery. The sojourn of an African-Canadian Baptist minister on Calder estate in the early 1840s might reasonably account for the introduction of credobaptism and immersion to the Wilderness sect.[136] The Spiritual Baptists' denial of Edwards' influence, however, gives credence to itinerant preachers, some of whom may have been from The Bahamas BMS stations, as well as pre-existing pockets of Baptists among the survivals of Brown's coerced Bahamian diaspora. In 1838, prior to the end of the Apprenticeship, Baptist cleric Joseph Burton of Nassau wrote, 'The missionaries labouring in The Bahamas had discovered the spiritual wants of St Vincent, Cuba, and St Domingo.'[137] This is the most concrete affirmation that Black Baptist missionaries had attempted to evangelise St Vincent during slavery. Interestingly, Burton noted, 'In St Vincent there were five hundred Baptists, who for the last four or five years had given up the administration of baptism, because they knew not who were to be baptised.'[138] Notably, he called them Baptists, not hearers, and estimated a number close to that of the Africans brought by Brown. Burton's report, therefore, is evidence of a much earlier beginning of African Baptists in St Vincent, most likely, the African-American-Bahamian migrants at Grand Sable. Burton noted, 'The most delightful results had arisen from the labours of the missionaries, and many of the natives had, since their conversion, been as successful preachers of the gospel as the missionaries themselves.'[139] The report also indicates that the wide distribution of Methodist prayer houses must have included a significant number of Baptists.

The second dynamic in the Baptist conundrum in St Vincent is in- and out-migrations in the post-slavery era. Indentured Africans who embarked from St Helena had no prior engagements with Baptists or Methodists. Although the Anglican Church on the island was established in the late-eighteenth century, the extent of evangelising among the liberated Africans is uncertain. This does not rule out personal experience with Christianity. Beginning in the early-sixteenth century, the Kingdom of Kongo had established Roman Catholicism as the national religion. Mass baptisms continued for over a century. Within a short time, many aspects of the imported version of Catholicism were Kongoised using Kikongo terms such as *'kimpasi,'* which approximates Christian baptism; *'nganga,'* the term for native priest or healer, which came to describe European clergymen; and *'Nzambi,'* the Creator, was transliterated into *'Nyambi,'* the Creator in biblical 'Genesis.' It goes without saying that since the Church lasted well into the eighteenth century, many Kongolese trafficked into the European-Atlantic slavery system must have been Catholic, and no more nominally so than enslaved Africans baptised upon arrival in plantation colonies.[140] Edward Long, a Jamaican assemblyman, planter and historian-anthropologist of mid-eighteenth-century Jamaica, recognised Black saints in Catholic churches.[141] A Catholic church in Trinidad, not far from the Company Villages of the Merikins, also has a Black saint dating back at least to the second half of the nineteenth century. Referred to as the 'Black virgin,' she is most likely a representation of the Virgin Mary. Since the 1890s, she has been worshipped jointly by Christians and Hindus who refer to her as

Sopari Mai (Mother of Siparia) and equate her with the goddesses Kali, Durga, and Lakshmi.[142] Elements of Bakongo retentions in St Vincent are evident in the names of plants and cuisine such as jibe yam (juba in Trinidad); in the name Juba (Spring Village) on the Leeward coast; and in place names like Congo Valley, adjacent to Grand Sable. In Trinidad, the Bakongo also impacted the landscape as seen in toponyms such as Congo Block in Moruga, Congo Kunuk near Princes Town and in several northern enclaves.[143] The southern sites are all near the Company Villages of the Merikins.

The Kongolese initiation rite of *Kumina* or living one's own death, was already being manifested through 'trance and dance' during slavery.[144] When no longer under the severe restrictions of slavery, Penitents made trance and dance a central feature of their religion.[145] Expansion of Penitentism to North Leeward was rapid. Sheena Boa notes the similarity in liturgy of a sect at Chateaubelair on the North Leeward coast with what obtained on the Windward side of the island as early as 1841, prior to the new Africans. That they were 'jumping and contorting their bodies to receive messages from the Holy Spirit' is consistent with the Wilderness People's form of worship, although it does not confirm that this practice by itself was of Kongolese origin.[146] From the mid-nineteenth century, the arrival of Liberated Africans from St Helena reinforced *Kumina* in St Vincent. It is important to note that Chateaubelair is directly west of the Grand Sable-Mount Bentinck complex, connected by a footpath that was maintained well into the second half of the twentieth century. English explorer-writer, Charles Day, walked this path in the late 1840s setting out from the Waterloo estate on the east coast to Chateaubelair on the west coast, the trek lasting some seven hours. Interestingly his guide was an African boy ten years of age.[147] Despite the rugged, mountainous terrain the boy's mastery of this footpath establishes that cultural influences could have flowed just as easily in either direction; indeed, by the end of the nineteenth century, Chateaubelair had become a stronghold of Penitentism.

A practitioner of the sect at Chateaubelair testified that messages from the Holy Spirit 'could only be received when they were lying on their backs.'[148] In another instance, informers who had spied on a mourning rite confirmed to Dr Christian W. Branch, author of a damning article on the Penitents in *The Monist* journal, that initiates in the mourning house 'lie flat on their backs' at night.'[149] It is evident from Branch's article that the word mourning had become part of St Vincent's vernacular by the turn of the century. The dorsal position of initiates is also intrinsic to the template of mourning in Trinidad up to the present day: a coffin is drawn on the floor of a mourning house and the initiate must lie in it blindfolded over a period of several days.[150]

The Ontology of Mourning (Moanin')

Haitian Vodou provides a model for comparison and validation of Penitent mourning as a Kongolese–inspired rite of passage. In both religions, the most sacred space is the mourning ground: in Vodou, the mourning rite is called *kanzo* and the mourning ground the *djevo*, the place 'where the candidate is reborn, taught the secrets of the Religion, and remade.'[151] The term 'mourning ground' is exclusively used in Trinidad but in St Vincent, it is also called the Penance House.[152] Both *kanzo* and mourning entail seclusion of the candidates, which could take two weeks in Haiti, the same in St Vincent, and Trinidad and Tobago, although some mourning rites may extend to up to three weeks.[153] During seclusion, the candidates in Vodou and Spiritual Baptist traditions receive special baths: in Haiti, 'the baths are symbolic of the death of the candidates.' They 'mark the spiritual death of the person who will later be reborn as a Hounsi, Houngan or Mambo,' the three highest ranks in Vodou.[154] The *hounsi* or *serviteur* becomes the wife or husband of a *lwa* or deity and relates to the *lwa* as horse and rider; when a *lwa* appears during worship, it manifests in the *hounsi* through spirit possession. A Houngan is a High Priest; a Mambo is a High Priestess. Among Spiritual Baptists, the candidates are reborn with the spiritual wherewithal to assume one of the twenty-two ranks or leadership positions in the Church, such as Teacher, Nurse, Captain, Prover, Shepherd, and Pointer. The highest positions are Leader, the equivalent of the Houngan, and Mother, the equivalent of the Mambo. Most, if not all these ranks were already institutionalised by the beginning of the twentieth century. Within the *djevo*, Vodounsi (worshippers) draw *veves*, comprising geometric lines drawn with a mixture of cornmeal and rum; similar lines are drawn on walls, doorways and the floor of shrines of Spiritual Baptists.[155] Herskovits's first impression was that the drawings paralleled those of Haitian vodou but later cast doubt on this interpretation.[156]

The assumption that these line drawings are Kabbalistic and have a provenance primarily in European thought[157] fails to consider that similar drawings were made by a major Igbo secret society, and spiritual specialists of Dahomey (the modern Republic of Benin) and Kongo, the major cultural spheres that define the 'Rada' *lwa* and the 'Petro' *lwa* respectively, the two major sub-pantheons of Vodou.[158] Revd J. K. Macgregor, a missionary serving in Southern Nigeria in the early nineteenth century, who was a pioneer of European knowledge of the Igbo Nsibidi writing system, acclaimed,

> That the existence of a script is unknown to Europeans must not, however, be taken as conclusive evidence that the script does not exist, for the natives have a strange but natural desire to hide as much as they can from prying eyes of the European who has too often but learned what they held precious only to scoff at them.[159]

Some *veves* remarkably resemble characters in the Nsibidi alphabet of the Ekpe secret society of the Igbo, a major source of enslaved people in the Caribbean and one of the major ethnicities of Liberated Africans transported to the Caribbean in the post-emancipation era as indentured labourers.[160] Scholars have traced some of these writings in the *Abakua* society of Cuba. Applications of similar drawing in the *Palo Monte* sect of Cuba and the *Umbanda* sect of Brazil give further credence to a Central African or West African origin.[161] These practices were adopted and reinforced by Rada practitioners because of their spiritual relatability.

In both Vodou and Spiritual Baptism, candidates are subjected to severe deprivation during the initiation rite: light is shut out from the candidates' eyes using several layers of bandages to simulate the complete darkness of the grave or underworld; even after completing the ceremony, initiates keep the 'bands' on for nine days and continue other restrictions for up to several weeks.[162] One informant in Toco, Trinidad, told Herskovits that 'long time ago' some 'Converted' followers were not baptised before mourning. The informant, however, acknowledged that it was a 'dangerous' thing to do: 'On their way (to Glory) they saw too many things. It hurt them sometimes too much after they got back.'[163] In Haiti, *Vodounsi* (*Vodouisants*) are baptised after emerging from the *djevo* on the final day.[164]

The analogy of coffin and grave goes beyond mythology for the African diaspora. The rite of mourning is psychologically rooted in the slave-ship experience. The slave ship was a death ship: captives were regularly taken out dead and cast overboard; historians estimate that between 17 per cent and 25 per cent of captives lost their lives on board slave ships.[165] The hole of a slave ship was pitch–black, like the darkness of the grave. Eric Williams affirms that each captive 'had less room than a man in a coffin.'[166] Before being placed in a ship, captives were kept in pitch–dark dungeons and basements to familiarise them with the darkness they were to endure for months before arriving at the auction blocks in the Americas. This author has experienced both the great dungeons of Ghana's castles and a lesser known but arguably more terrifying barracoon in Agbodrafo, Togo, where the darkness of the enclosure was absolute and the height no more than one and a half metres, the same as the deck of a slave ship. That was a main purpose of the dungeons of the great walled castles of Senegal and Ghana and smaller barracoons all along the Atlantic coast from Senegal to Angola. All Africans who were rescued by naval squadrons or survived the Atlantic crossing could relate to the phenomenon of living one's death, whether from Kongo or elsewhere. Spiritual Baptists canonised this experience. In response to which, the same imperial government that inflicted unspeakable horrors on them persecuted them for several decades for evolving what was more than a religion: it was psychosomatic therapy.

Notes

1.   Herskovits and Herskovits, *Trinidad Village*, vi.

2.   Eric Williams, *History of Trinidad and Tobago* (New York: Frederick A. Praeger, 1962), 39; Zane, 'Journeys to the Spiritual Lands,' 244.

3.   Williams, *History*, 39.

4.   David Trotman, 'The Yoruba and Orisha Worship,' 1.

5.   Judith Roback, 'The White-Robed Army: Cultural Nationalism and a Religious Movement in Guyana' (PhD diss., McGill University, Montreal, 1973), 6. Peter Halder, 'The Jordanites,' *Guyana Then and Now* (October 2011), https://guyanathenandnow.wordpress.com/2011/10/04/the-jordanites/, accessed February 2020. The name Jordanites comes from another architect of the movement, Elder Nathaniel Jordan who revived the church of MacLaren in 1917.

6.   K. O. Laurence, 'The Settlement of Free Negroes in Trinidad Before Emancipation,' *Caribbean Quarterly* 9, no.1 (1963); Claudius Fergus, *Revolutionary Emancipation: Slavery and Abolitionism in the British West Indies* (Baton Rouge: Louisiana State University Press, 2013), 114–15.

7.   One of the earliest published views on the Merikins as veterans of the War of Independence is Huggins, *Saga of the Companies*, 3–5. They were not migrants from the War of Independence, as many historians conclude.

8.   For Cochrane's proclamation, see 'Alexander Cochrane: A Proclamation,' https://www.battlefields.org/learn/primary-sources/alexander-cochrane-proclamation.

9.   'Cochrane: A Proclamation.'

10.   Anthony de Verteuil, *The Black Earth of South Naparima* (Port of Spain, Trinidad: Litho Press, 2009), 190.

11.   Laurence, 'Free Negroes,' 27; Bridget Brereton, *A History of Modern Trinidad 1783–1962* (Kingston, Jamaica: Heinemann, 1981), 68–69.

12.   Peter Brewer, 'Baptists of Trinidad (1815–1900),' *Missionary Herald: The Monthly Magazine of the Baptist Missionary Society* (January 1976), 5.

13.   Peter Brewer, 'The Baptist Churches of South Trinidad and their Missionaries, 1815–1892' (MTh diss., University of Glasgow, 1988), 71; 81–82. Five 'Anabaptist preachers' were identified in an 1825 report.

14.   Brewer, 'Baptist Churches,' 81–82.

15.   Ibid., 5.

16.   Ibid., n. 62, 283.

17.   See Elyah Hooke, *The Year-Book of Missions: Containing a Comprehensive Account of Missionary Societies, British, Continental and American With a Particular Survey of Stations in Geographical Order* (London: 1847), 322. Google Books.

18.   Brewer, 'Baptist Churches,' 81.

19. Gertrude Carmichael, *The History of the West Indian Islands of Trinidad and Tobago 1498–1900* (London: Alvin Redman, 1961), 135. None accepted the offer.

20. Brereton, *Modern Trinidad*, 69.

21. Fergus, *Revolutionary Emancipation*, 82–83.

22. Brewer, 'Baptist Churches,' 278. It was customary for the British navy to conscript the most able-bodied Africans freed from slave ships.

23. De Verteuil, *Black Earth*, 193; six less is mentioned by Brewer, in 'Baptist Churches,' 71.

24. Brewer, 'Baptist Churches,' 64.

25. De Verteuil, *Black Earth*, 188.

26. Ibid., 188–92; Carmichael cites only fifty, *Trinidad and Tobago*, 136. Brewer, 'Baptist Missionaries,' 60–64.

27. See Gene Allen Smith, '"Sons of Freedom": African Americans Fighting the War of 1812,' *Tennessee Historical Society* 71, no. 3 (Fall 2012), 212; Brewer, 'Baptist Missionaries,' 295.

28. Fergus, *Revolutionary Emancipation*, 136–39.

29. Ibid., 116.

30. Maureen Warner-Lewis, *Trinidad Yoruba: From Mother Tongue to Memory* (Kingston, Jamaica: University of the West Indies Press, 1997), 24; 183.

31. See Joseph M. Murphy and Mei-Mei Sanford, *Osun Across the Waters: A Yoruba Goddess in Africa and the Americas* (Bloomington, IN: Indiana University Press, 2001), 2–6. Mother Superior Elaine Griffith proclaimed, 'When I go to the sea I see my mother,' cited in Johnson, 'Born Again in Living Waters.'

32. Warner-Lewis, *Trinidad Yoruba*, 34–35; Maureen Warner Lewis, *Guinea's Other Suns: The African Dynamic in Trinidad Culture* (Dover, MA: Majority Press), 14–16. Daniel da Silva et al., 'The Diaspora Liberated from Slave Ships in the Nineteenth Century,' *JAH*, 55, no. 3 (November 2014), 352.

33. See Ukpuru, 'Igbo Water Divinities: Historical Images of the Igbo, their Neighbours and Beyond,' https://ukpuru.tumblr.com/post/157318196557/igbo-water-divinities, accessed March 24, 2020); Lawrence N. Okwuosa, Nkechi G. Onuh, Chinyere T. Nwagoa and Favour C. Uroko, 'The Disappearing Mammy Water Myth and Crisis of Values in Oguta, South-Eastern Nigeria,' *HTS Theological Studies* 73, no. 3 (2017), https://dx.doi.org/10.4102/hts.v3i3.4555, accessed October 24, 2022.

34. Charles William Knight, 'A History of Expansion of Evangelical Christianity in Nigeria' (PhD Diss., Southern Baptist Theological Seminary, Louisville, KY, 1951), 33.

35. Charles Kingsley, *At Last: A Christmas in the West Indies* (London: Macmillan, 1871), 249.

36. Hackshaw, *The Baptist Denomination*, 78; Zane, 'Journeys to the Spiritual Lands,' 242.

37. 'The Shakers in Town,' *Port of Spain Gazette*, July 4, 1894, TTNA & UWI/AJL; Zane, *Spiritual Lands*, 242.

38. Hackshaw, *Baptist Denomination*, 78.

39. Joseph Spinelli, *Land Use and Population in St Vincent, 1763–1960: A Contribution to the Study of the Patterns and Demographic Change in a Small West Island* (Gainesville, FL: University of Florida, 1973), 235–36.

40. Spinelli, 'Land Use,' 113.

41. Ibid., 237–38.

42. See Bishop Oliver Maynard, 'History of the Moravian Church in Trinidad, 1885–1915,' https://trinidadmorabians.webs.com/ourhistory.htm, accessed January 26, 2021.

43. Viola Gopaul-Whittington, *History of the Spiritual Baptist & WRITINGS* (St James, Trinidad: Printing Plus, [1983]), 9–10; cited in Lum, *Praising His Name*, 29; Herskovits and Herskovits, *Trinidad Village*, 199, also alluded to a St Vincent provenance for the Shouters.

44. Cox, 'Religious Intolerance,' 18.

45. Gopaul-Whittington, *Spiritual Baptist*, 9.

46. Lum, *Praising His Name*, Kindle, location 678 and 688.

47. Gopaul-Whittington, *Spiritual Baptist*, vii.

48. Lum, *Praising His Name*, Kindle, location 688 and 701; Gopaul-Whittington, *Spiritual Baptist*, v.

49. Lum, *Praising His Name*, Kindle, location 715.

50. Gopaul-Whittington, *Spiritual Baptist*, viii.

51. Lum, *Praising His Name*, 29.

52. White American anthropologists assign a Kabbalah origin to the chalk marking done by Spiritual Baptists. This conclusion is challenged in chapter 8 of this study.

53. *Port of Spain Gazette*. 'Keeping a Shouters' Meeting – Persecution Collapses,' July 15, 1918, UWI/AJL, 13.

54. Da Silva et al., 'The Diaspora,' 357.

55. K. O. Laurence cites 8,854 individuals for the period 1842 to 1867: see *A Question of Labour: Immigration into Trinidad and British Guiana, 1875–1917* (Kingston, Jamaica: Ian Randle Publishers, 1994), 2; Warner Lewis, *Guinea's Other Suns*, 12–14; *Martin, Caribbean History*, 221.

56. See Munro, 'Immigration of Africans;' Spinelli, 'Land Use,' 233; the ethnic breakdown is unknown to this author. Martin, *Caribbean History*, 221.

57. Shantel George, 'Diaspora Consciousness, Historical Memory and Culture in Liberated African Villages in Grenada, 1850s–2014,' in *Liberated Africans and the Abolition of the Slave Trade, 1807–1896*, edited by Richard Anderson and Henry Lovejoy, 369 (New York: University of

Rochester Press, 2020). Da Silva et al., 'The Diaspora,' 369. Martin, *Caribbean History*, 221. Martin reports 2,406: see *Caribbean History*, 221.

58. Da Silva et al., 'The Diaspora,' 352.

59. Ibid., 357.

60. Mary Church, *Sierra Leone or The Liberated Africans in a Series of Letters from a Young Lady to her Sister in 1833 and 34* (London: 1835), http://www.sierra-leone.org/Books/Sierra%20Leone%20or%20the%20Liberated%20 Africans.pdf, Mary to Bertha, 2nd and 4th Letters.

61. Knight, 'Evangelical Christianity,' 15–16.

62. Ibid.,' 44–51; Las, Newman, 'A West Indian Contribution to Christian Mission in Africa: The Career of Jackson Fuller (1845–1888),' *Transformation* 18, no. 4 (October 2001). David Killingray, 'The Black Atlantic Missionary Movement and Africa, 1780s–1920s,' *Journal of Religion in Africa* 33, no. 1 (2003), 3–7. A minority of the missionaries were Africans from the Caribbean.

63. Arthur T. Porter, 'Religious Affiliation in Freetown, Sierra Leone,' *JIAI* 23, no. 1 (January 1953): 9.

64. Warner-Lewis, *Guinea's Other Suns*, 13.

65. Martin, *Caribbean History*, 222; K.O. Laurence, 'The Evolution of Long-Term Labour Contracts in Trinidad and British Guiana 1834–1863,' in *Caribbean Freedom: Society and Economy from Emancipation to the Present*, eds. Hilary Beckles and Verene Shepherd (Kingston, Jamaica: Ian Randle Publishers, 1993), 142–42.

66. *115th Annual Report of the Baptist Missionary Society, to March 1907* (London: BMS, 1907), 110.

67. CO 321/269. 'Report from *The Mirror*,' April 23, 1906, enclosed in Murray to Cameron, October 12, 1912.

68. Kenneth Anthony Lum, *Praising His Name in the Dance: Spirit Possession in the Spiritual Baptist Faith and Orisha Work in Trinidad, West Indies* (Amsterdam: Harwood Academic Publishers, 2000), Kindle version, location 784, location 772; Hackshaw, *The Baptist Denominations*, 68.

69. Lum, *Praising His Name*, location 783.

70. Lum confirms that mourning 'is not found among the London, Independent or Merikin Baptists;' see Lum, *Praising His Name*, location 784.

71. Monica Schuler, Mary Karasch, Richard Price and Edward Kamau Brathwaite, 'Afro-American Slave Culture [with commentary], *Historical Reflections* 6, no. 1 (Summer 1979), 130, https://www.jstor.org/stable/41330420; Leslie R. James, 'Pocomania,' in *African American Religious Cultures 1*, eds. Anthony B. Pinn and Stephen C. Finley, 321 (Santa Barbara, CA: ABC-CLIO, 2009).

72. Findlay and Holdsworth, *History of the Wesleyan Methodist Missionary Society*, n. 1, 40.

73. See Boa, 'Colour, Class and Gender,' 259–260.

74. See Brinsley Samaroo, 'Maria Jones of Africa, St Vincent and Trinidad,' in *Gendering the African Diaspora: Women, Culture and Historical Change in the Caribbean and Nigerian Hinterland*, eds. Judith A. Byfield, LaRay Denzer and Anthea Morison, 139 (Bloomington, IN: 2010).

75. See Murrell, *Afro-Caribbean Religions*, 259; *Lara Putnam, Radical Moves: Caribbean Migrants and the Politics of Race in the Jazz Age* (Chapel Hill, NC: University of North Carolina Press, 2013), 53–54; Emanuela Guano, 'Revival Zion: An Afro-Christian Religion in Jamaica,' *Anthropos* 89 (1994): 518–19.

76. Brewer, 'Baptists of Trinidad,' 6.

77. Ibid., 7.

78. Roseanne Marion Adderley, *'New Negroes from Africa': Slave Trade Abolition and Free African Settlement in the Nineteenth-Century Caribbean* (Bloomington, IN: Indiana University Press, 2006), 179.

79. Adderley, *New Negroes*, 179.

80. Ibid.

81. Robert Clarke, 'Sketches of the Colony of Serra Leone and its Inhabitants,' in *Transactions of the Ethnological Society of London ll* (London: 1863), 333–34.

82. Clarke, 'Sketches of the Colony of Serra Leone,' 334.

83. Brewer, 'Baptist Missionaries,' 71.

84. *115th Annual Report of the Baptist Missionary Society*, 110.

85. Ibid.

86. 'The Missionary Herald' for April 1846 (London: 1846), in *The Baptist Magazine* 38 (April 1846), 250.

87. Brewer, 'Baptists of Trinidad,' 6–7.

88. Ibid., 7.

89. Ibid.

90. See *Port of Spain Gazette*, 'The 'Shouters' at Tunapuna,' October 26, 1898, TTNA, 4.

91. Lum, *Praising His Name*, 32.

92. 'A Shouters' Meeting: Batch of Defendants at Chaguanas – Obstinate Fellow Fined – First Case Under Prohibitive Ordinance,' *Trinidad Guardian*, January 9, 1918, 7. [UWI/AJL].

93. Zane, 'Spiritual Lands,' 236–37.

94. Ibid., 237.

95. See Jan Vansina, 'Once Upon a Time: Oral Traditions as History in Africa,' *Daedalus* 100, no. 2 (Spring 1971), 444, 459.

96. Zane, 'Journeys to the Spiritual Lands,' 336–37.

97. Coke, *History of the West Indies:* 269, 283; Zane, 'Journeys to the Spiritual Lands,' 237.

98. See Frey and Wood, *Come Shouting to Zion*, 124.

99. Adrian Fraser, *From Shakers to Spiritual Baptists*, 11; Boa, 'Colour, Class and Gender,' 259.

100. Findlay and Holdsworth, *Missionary Society*, 32–37.
101. Ibid., 70.
102. Ibid., 37.
103. Ibid., 35–45.
104. Ibid., 35.
105. Jeffrey Cox, *The British Missionary Enterprise Since 1700* (New York: Routledge, 2008), 67. Google Books.
106. Findlay and Holdsworth, *Missionary Society*, 67.
107. Ibid., 15.
108. Ibid.
109. Ibid., n. 1, 40.
110. Richard Worthington Smith, 'Slavery and Christianity in the British West Indies,' *Church History* 19, no. 3 (September 1950): 185, https://www.jstor.org/stable/3161292.
111. C. W. Branch, 'The Endemic Religious Insanity of the Island of St Vincent,' *The Monist* 17, no. 2 (April 1907), enclosed in CO 321/243, Crewe to Crowe, September 6, 1908, 301. The article is also available at https://www.jstor.org/stable/27900040.
112. Branch, 'Religious Insanity,' 299–304.
113. See Boa, 'Colour, Class and Gender,' 260.
114. Branch, 'Religious Insanity,' 300.
115. *Baptist Missionary Magazine* 27 (1847),
116. Ibid.
117. See Boa, 'Colour, Class and Gender,' 260–61.
118. Ibid., 264.
119. Ibid., 261–62.
120. Ibid., 262.
121. Ibid., 261.
122. The founders of the Church were two Virginians, Eugene and Hilda McMillan, of the Baptist Mid-Missions, https://www.bmm.org/serve/where-we-serve/st-vincent, accessed June 30, 2022.
123. Boa, 'Colour, Class and Gender,' 258–59.
124. *The Baptist Magazine* 38 (1846), 656.
125. Ibid.
126. Michael Lee Lanning, *African Americans in the Revolutionary War* (New York: Kensington, 2000), 'Appendix D,' 198.
127. See Spinelli, *Land Use, 65; Dr Charlene Kozy, 'Revealing Thomas Brown,' in Times of the Islands,* https://www.timespub.tc/2010/02/revealing-thomas-brown/. The well-known Black Point Tunnel to shuttle hogsheads of sugar was built by Brown's enslaved Africans.
128. Kozy, 'Revealing Thomas Brown.' Brown rendered his name with the final 'e' while residing in St Vincent.
129. See J. Leitch Wright, Jr., 'Blacks in British East Florida,' *The Florida Historical Quarterly* 54, no. 4 (April 1976): 434–37; J. H. Siebert, 'East Florida as a Refuge of Southern Royalists, 1774–1785,' *American*

Antiquarian Society, https://www.americanantiquariansociety.org/4480
6786.pdf.

130. Joan Marilyn Leggett, 'Thomas 'Burnfoot' Brown,' https://www.
geni.com/people/Thomas-Burnfoot-Brown/6000000000945545016,
accessed March 26, 2020.

131. Leggett, 'Thomas 'Burnfoot' Brown.'

132. Ibid.

133. Wright, Jr., 'Blacks in British East Florida,' 436.

134. 'Revd Alexander Thomas Browne,' *Centre for the Study of the Legacies of
British Slavery*, https://www.ucl.ac.uk/lbs/person/view/2146630473,
accessed May 30, 2020.

135. Fraser, *From Shakers to Spiritual Baptists*, 11.

136. Boa, 'Colour, Class and Gender,' 259.

137. *Missionary Herald* 234 (June 1838), in *The Baptist Magazine* 30 (1838), 272.

138. Ibid.

139. *The Baptist Magazine* 30 (1838), 272.

140. John Thornton, 'The Development of an African Catholic Church in
the Kingdom of Kongo, 1491–1750,' *Journal of African History* 25, no. 2
(1984): 147–48.

141. Edward Long, *History of Jamaica* 2 (London: Frank Cass, 1979), 429–30.

142. K. O. Laurence, *A Question of Labour: Indentured Immigration into Trinidad
and British Guiana 1875–1917* (Kingston, Jamaica: Ian Randle Publishers,
1993), 267; Keith McNeal, 'Miracle Mother: Siparee Mai, La Divina
Pastora,' *Caribbean Beat*, 54, https://www.caribbean-beat.com/issue-54/
siparee-mai-miracle-mother#axzz84YgVHfjW.

143. Charles William Day, *Five Years Residence in the West Indies 1* (London:
1852), 116; Murrell, *Afro-Caribbean Religions, 259, Warner-Lewis, Guinea's
Other Suns,* 36; Warner-Lewis, *Central Africa in the Caribbean: Transcending
Time, Transforming Cultures* (Bridgetown, Barbados: University of the
West Indies Press, 2003), 64.

144. Kapitien, 'Vivre sa Mort.' Edward Long of Jamaica provided the first
descriptions of this ritual: see Monica Schuler, 'Afro-American Slave
Culture,' *Historical Reflections* 6, no. 1 (Summer 1979), 130. Long, *History
of Jamaica* 2, 416–17; Orlando Patterson, *The Sociology of Slavery: An
Analysis of the Origins, Development and Structure of a Negro Slavery in Jamaica*
(Vancouver, BC: Fairleigh Dickinson University Press, 1969), 186–87.

145. See Boa, 'Colour, Class and Gender,' 265.

146. Ibid., 269.

147. Day, *Five Years*, 138–39.

148. Boa, 'Colour, Class and Gender,' 269.

149. Branch, 'Religious Insanity,' 301.

150. Personal interview of Stacy Clarke of Trinidad, who completed the
mourning rite in 2019; Personal interview of Stella Bouville of Trinidad,
whose mother, a Spiritual Baptist, transitioned one year prior to Repeal.

151. 'The Kanzo Ceremony.'

152. Branch, 'Endemic Religious Insanity,' 301. The term 'secret chamber' for the mourning ground in Trinidad was used by Simpson but he did not confirm if the term was used by the sect: see Simpson, 'Baptismal "Mourning," and "Building,"' 243.

153. Glazier, 'Adumbrations,' 21; Simpson, 'Baptismal "Mourning," and "Building,"' 543, 545.

154. Admin, 'The Kanzo Ceremony: Initiation into Haitian Vodou,' http://www.voudoureligion.com/2011/04/the-kanzo-ceremony/, accessed March 15, 2020.

155. Branch, 'Religious Insanity,' 303; case of Theophilus Ottley of Laventille in *Port of Spain Gazette*, 'Keeping a Shouters' Meeting: Prosecution Collapses,' July 15, 1920, TTNA, 13.

156. See Alexander Rocklin, 'Imagining Religions in a Trinidad Village: The Africanity of the Spiritual Baptist Movement and the Politics of Comparing Religions,' *New West Indian Guide* 86, no. 1/2, (2012), 67–68, https://www.jstor.org/stable/41850694.

157. James Houk, 'The Role of the Kabbalah in Afro-Caribbean Religion in Trinidad,' *Caribbean Quarterly*, 39, no. 3/4 (September–December 1993): 42–55, https://www.jstor.org/stable/40653859. See also Glazier, 'Adumbrations,' 18–20.

158. Michel S. Laguerre, *Voodoo and Politics in Haiti* (New York: St. Martin Press, 1989), 22.

159. J. K. Macgregor, 'Some Notes on Nsibidi,' *The Journal of Royal Anthropological Institute of Great Britain and Ireland* 39 (January–June 1909), 209, https://www.jstor.org/stable/2843292.

160. See Macgregor, 'Some Notes on Nsibidi,' 209–19; E[lphinstone] Dayrell, 'Some Nsibidi Signs,' *Man* 10 (1910), https://www.jstor.org/stable/2787339; Elphinstone Dayrell, 'Further Notes on Nsibidi Signs with Their Meanings from the Ikom District of Southern Nigeria,' *The Journal of Royal Anthropological Institute of Great Britain and Ireland* 41 (July-December 1911), 521–40, https://www.jstor.org/stable/2843186; in 1964 African American Professor, M.D.W. Jeffreys authenticated Nsibidi as a writing system but made a few corrections to Dayrell's interpretation of some of its characters: see M. D. W. Jeffreys, 'Corrections: Man 1910, 67 (Nsibidi Writing),' *Man* 64 (September–October 1964), 155, https://www.jstor.org/stable/2797708.

161. See Katarina Kerestetzi, 'Making a Nganga, Begetting God. Materiality and Belief in the Afro-Cuban Religion Palo Monte,' *Ricerche di Storia Sociale e Religiosa*, Nuova Serie 87 (January–December 2015), 157, https://www.researchgate.net/publication/335293064; Patti Wigington, 'Umbanda Religion: History and Beliefs' (November 2019), https://www.learnreligions.com/umbanda-religion-4777681, accessed June 23, 2021.

162. 'The Kanzo Ceremony;' Zane, *Spiritual Lands,* 147.
163. Herskovits and Herskovits, *Trinidad Village,* 204. Personal interview. Testimony of Stella Bouville, 2016.
164. 'The Kanzo Ceremony.'
165. Fergus, *Revolutionary Emancipation,* 7.
166. Eric Williams, *Capitalism and Slavery* (London: Andre Deutsch, 1964), 34–35.

CHAPTER 3

The Epic Journey of Religious Toleration

'When we discuss the practice of tolerance we are talking about
more than personal attitudes; we are talking about the exercise
of power.'*

At the dawn of Western Europe's overseas expansion, most, if not all, of Western Christendom had a shared policy of intolerance for multi-confessionalism. In this regard, Africans had a longer tradition in religious cosmopolitanism than their European colonisers. In Ethiopia, Muslims, Jews, and 'pagans' were accommodated under a Coptic Christian monarchy. Although political and economic rivalry was intense after the destructive jihad of Ahmad al-Ghazi (El Gran) in the sixteenth century, the monarchy did not proscribe Islam.[1] Instead, Ethiopia became more profoundly multicultural to such an extent that some wives of Solomonid Kings were practising Muslims.[2] In Ancient Ghana, rulers professing Malinke faiths welcomed Muslims, allowed them to practise their faith free from interference, and even appointed them notaries and ministers of state.[3] The traditional 'animist' Bori cult of Kanem-Bornu in modern-day northern Nigeria continued to flourish under native Islamic rulers and was even patronised by Muslims for esoteric services; indeed, some Bori priests were Muslims.[4] In south-western Nigeria, Muslims lived without persecution in Oyo, the military capital of the Yoruba Empire. Furthermore, European Christians lived among many coastal peoples without fear of religious persecution.

---

* Bernard Dov Cooperman, Legislating Christian Identity & Negotiating Christian Status, Lecture 7, 'Practising Tolerance in a Religious Society,' 12 Oct. 2014, available at https://www.naturalmoney.org/practisingtoleance.htm#0202, accessed 2 Jan. 2023.

European Overseas Imperialism and the Export of Religious Intolerance

The European practice of enforcing the religion of a monarch upon all the subjects of the realm was taken to foreign lands from the beginning of the Atlantic imperial project in the fifteenth-century. For Europe, conversion was consistently deployed as a weapon for commercial and strategic advantage to such an extent that the first one hundred and fifty years of imperial expansion largely equated with Iberian-driven Catholicisation. The Oba (King) of Benin famously rejected Portuguese pressure to baptise him in the late fifteenth century. In retaliation, the Portuguese terminated trade with the Kingdom of Benin.[5] The Portuguese had tasted success in baptising political leaders in West Africa prior to their entry into Benin.[6] South of the Equator the Portuguese were more successful. Nzinga a Nkuwu, the first King of Kongo to meet the European imperialists, consented to baptism. Although the King remained patriarch of the traditional religion, his son and successor, Mvemba Nzinga (Afonso I), on accession to the throne, became the new Ezana of Africa. During his reign he laid the foundation for Roman Catholicism as the national religion through an alliance of native and foreign clergy and the establishment of schools.[7] From the early sixteenth century, Portuguese inability to control the domestic policy of Kongo led to their denunciation of Kongolese Christianity, violating their own Patronato (Concordat) with the Kingdom. Despite Papal recognition for rebranded Kongolese Christianity, the Portuguese persistently sought to destabilise Kongo because of their inability to control the politics of the kingdom.[8] In retaliation, they abandoned Kongo to set up an enclave in Angola.

Portuguese missionaries returned to Benin in 1515 and started a mission and a school in the Oba's palace.[9] That mission was aborted two years later upon the death of the Oba. The Portuguese emphasis on establishing Christianity collided with every Oba's primary interest in firearms which the Portuguese were forbidden to trade.[10] The missionary enterprise yielded little success by the 1540s when the Portuguese abandoned evangelising in Benin and re-established among the Warri in the Niger Delta, where their churches flourished for over two hundred years.[11] Not until the 1640s would new efforts be made; this time by Capuchin missionaries from Spain.[12] During the seventeenth century, the Oba instructed that all Christian churches be converted to shrines of traditional deities.[13] Despite the protracted variance of interests between Benin and Portugal, the Oba of Benin did not institute persecutory measures against Portuguese missionaries or traders. European evangelising in Benin left pockets of Christianity which may have filtered into the Caribbean via the European slave trade and even after Emancipation, thus impacting the African-Caribbean interpretation of Christianity.

The Portuguese also flexed their imperial muscles against Ethiopia, a Coptic Christian Empire. For assisting Emperor Galawdewos to put down a destructive Muslim *jihad* in the 1540s, the Portuguese demanded that the Emperor accept Roman Catholicism. He steadfastly refused and put restrictions on the Portuguese.[14] Fifty years later, Emperor Susenyos I officially surrendered to foreign pressure and adopted Roman Catholicism as the new imperial religion. However, after the Jesuits demanded the abandonment of Coptic 'errors' for 'orthodox' Roman Catholicism, and after years of popular uprisings to retain the Coptic faith, Susenyos flipped, purged the empire of Popism, restored the Coptic Church and expelled the Jesuit missionaries.[15]

Unlike Africans in their sovereign states, Africans in captivity in European colonies in the Americas generally lost the right to negotiate or the ability to protect their right of conscience. They were not alone. Very early in the Spanish conquest of the Caribbean, the Catholic Church deployed 'The Requirement' (*El Requirimiento)* against native monarchs and the Inquisition against converts. The Requirement of 1513 was the absolute instrument of totalitarian theocracy. Spanish invaders read it to native rulers on first contact threatening them if they failed to submit instantly to the authority of King and Pope:

> I certify to you that, with the help of God, we shall
> powerfully enter your country, and shall make war against
> you in all ways and manners that we can, and shall subject
> you to the yoke and obedience of the Church and of
> their Highness; we shall take you and your wives and your
> children, and shall make slaves of them.[16]

Spaniards in the Americas were also intolerant of Protestants, Jews, and Muslims. Prior to 1518, a royal decree had also prohibited Africans who practised traditional religions, Judaism, or Islam from entering the American colonies.[17]

Freedom of conscience was an alien concept to the English when they became overseas colonisers. Indeed, English governments were more obstinately intolerant of multi-confessionalism than most countries in Europe, including Italy, Spain, Holland, and France.[18] In 1598, France's King Henry IV promulgated the Edict of Nantes, which legally recognised the Protestants or Huguenots, while preserving the primacy of the Catholic Church.[19] In 1685, France reversed its policy of accommodation of Protestants and launched a new era of intolerance and persecution with the revocation of its Edit of Nantes. As a colonial power, religious intolerance was extended to the enslaved class.

In England, Dissenters from the Church of England risked severe penalties and prejudices because of their faith. Some, like the Quakers and Puritans, found freedom in America. English philosopher John Locke's 'Fundamental Constitution' of 1669 for South Carolina that 'guaranteed freedom of religion to Black slaves provided that they remained slaves.'[20] Other dissenter-dominated colonies, Maryland and Rhode Island also took different paths to religious toleration and became models of religious toleration for Britain well before 1689; others continued the practice of religious intolerance, and in many instances, with greater severity than the English Crown.

The Birthing of English Religious Toleration

England's 'Glorious Revolution' of 1688 brought a Calvinist King to the throne and freed Parliament from its traditional role of handmaid of the Crown. One of the most urgent tasks of the new Parliament was to pass the first Toleration Act, which received the assent of the King in May 1689. The Act has been overrated as one of the most consequential pieces of legislation in the history of civil rights in England. It took more than three hundred years and myriad amendments to get to universal religious freedom. The legislators, however, had made no pretence about the limited application of the benefits of the 1689 law, 'An Act for Exempting their Majesties' Protestant Subjects from the Church of England, from the Penalties of Certain Laws.' The Act guaranteed freedom of worship to Protestant dissenters but it did not confer equality with the Church of England, which retained its political and civil primacy at home and abroad. Protestant dissenters continued to be subject to immense state prejudices under the Corporation Act of 1661 and Test Act of 1673. The Test Act required all subjects of the Crown to take the oath of sovereignty and allegiance, to deny the Catholic doctrine of transubstantiation and to receive the Lord's Supper in the Church of England in order to hold any public office or gain acceptance in Oxford University or Cambridge University.[21] The Act preserved all the legal disabilities against 'papists or popish recusants' (Roman Catholics) and anyone who denied the doctrine of the Trinity (Unitarian Protestants, Jews, Muslims, atheists, and other non-Christians).[22] Six months after the passage of the Toleration Act, Parliament enacted its first Bill of Rights, which denied a Catholic the possibility of becoming Monarch of England, deeming such a Prince the gravest threat to national security.[23] To date, discrimination continues against Roman Catholics. Yet, it was the modicum of protection guaranteed by the Toleration Act that frustrated every attempt to proscribe the Spiritual Baptists up to 1912 and which ultimately restored their freedom several decades later.

Of the three dissenting Protestant faiths competing for the minds of Africans in eighteenth-century Caribbean, Moravians and Baptists were named beneficiaries of the Act; the third denomination, the Wesleyans, later known as Methodists, did not yet exist. Wesleyan Methodism emerged as a new religion out of the Church of England in mid-eighteenth century. Many of the early members preached without ordination; others ordained their associates.[24] Although Methodists were the main targets of prohibition legislation in Caribbean colonies during slavery, they consistently received the protection of the Crown as a dissenting beneficiary of the Toleration Act. Emancipation brought an end to the clash of conscience between Methodists and

Anglican oligarchs and the beginning of an alliance against African Christianity. Notwithstanding that the pioneers of African Christianity in the Caribbean had followed a similar line of separation from colonial denominations as those denominations had done from parent faiths, Caribbean oligarchs understood that freedom of conscience for Africans would dangerously loosen their control over the masses. As Bernard Cooperman states, religious toleration is 'about the exercise of power.'[25] In the Caribbean, this power was essentially deployed to preserve White supremacy.

Immediately after the proclamation of the Toleration Act, English philosopher, John Locke, published a widely read commentary, *Epistola de Tolerantia* (A Letter Concerning Toleration), which appealed to the Crown to push the boundaries of religious liberty even further. He asserted, 'neither Pagan nor Mohametan nor Jew ought to be excluded from the civil rights of the commonwealth because of his religion.'[26] Locke further stated, 'not even Americans, subjected unto a Christian prince, are to be punished either in body or goods for not embracing our Faith and Worship.'[27] England was not ready for Locke: most of the rights he advocated were granted only in the nineteenth century. Locke, however, was a child of religion and remained adamant that Atheists were not worthy of toleration.[28]

The first colonial challenge to the seminal Toleration Act of relevance to the Caribbean came from the Leeward Islands whose legislature passed an Act in 1749 admitting Roman Catholics to 'equal political rights,' but the Act was disallowed.[29] In 1793, the Grenada Assembly passed an Act to establish the Roman Catholic Church on equal footing with the Church of England and provide each parish church £200 per annum; the ordinance also 'absolutely' prohibited Dissenting preachers 'of any denomination whatever from exercising the function of ministry' in the colony. In violation, preachers would be treated as 'rogues and vagabonds.'[30]

In 1752, Presbyterian pastor, Samuel Davies of Virginia, wrote to the bishop of London for clarification on the transmarine applicability of the 1689 law. In response, England's attorney general affirmed that the Toleration Act also extended to the colonies. This intervention, however, did not bring an end to the persecution of non-Christian Europeans and non-European Christians in the colony. In the Caribbean, colonists were more dangerously exposed to slave insurrections than in North America. Two years after the Attorney General's affirmation, two absentee Jamaican planters took advantage of his guarantee of protection and enticed Moravian missionaries with a substantial grant of land to evangelise their enslaved labour force.[31]

In 1773, Protestant dissenters petitioned Parliament to exempt them from subscription to the Articles of Religion, 1562, the constitution of the Church of England, and 'to entitle them to the full benefit of the Act of Toleration.'[32] The preamble of the Articles forbade preachers and teachers at all levels of the education system from disputing or discussing any of the Articles on pain of severe penalties. When a Bill to give effect to the petition was laid in the House of Commons, the Bench of Bishops inserted an amendment to exclude Muslims, Deists and Pagans from qualifying as dissenters. According to Bishop Beilby Porteus, future bishop of London, one of the principal reasons for the illiberal position of the Bishops Bench was 'when any one applies for liberty to preach and teach, the state has a right to know what the leading principles of his religion are, in order to be assured nothing injurious to civil society, or to the established form of government.'[33] Not everyone in the Commons shared the prejudice of the Bishops Bench. Liberal MP, John Wilkes, advocated for 'unlimited universal toleration' and expressed a desire 'to see pagodas, mosques, and temples of the sun, rising up in the neighbourhood of our finest gothic cathedrals.'[34] The Bill, however, was defeated in the House of Lords.[35]

Porteus supported the abolition of Britain's Atlantic slave trade but like most White abolitionists of his day he was no emancipator. As bishop of London from 1787, Porteus played an influential role in the religious life of Africans during slavery, the legacy of which continued long after Emancipation. Porteus was interested in projects to control the minds of Africans. It was under his tenure that the Church of England began to play a more forthright role in overseas evangelism through the CMS and the British and Foreign Bible Society. In 1788, the Court of Chancery provided him with funding to execute his 'plan' for converting enslaved Africans to the Christian faith.[36] He shared the belief of many leading abolitionists that Christianisation had the potential to curb Africans' desire for freedom through marronage and insurrection. He shared the belief of leading abolitionists that Christianisation had the potential to curb Africans' desire for freedom through marronage and insurrection. For this purpose, in 1794, he established 'The Society for the Conversion and Religious Instruction and Education of the Negro slaves in the British West Indian Islands.' The Society's major contribution in that regard was the publication of *The Slave Bible* also known as *The Negro Bible* in 1807, which omitted or manipulated any content that might be exploited as liberation theology. The official name of the book is *Select Parts of the Holy Bible for Use of the Negro Slaves in the British West India Islands.*[37] It begins with 'Genesis' after which it goes directly to chapter nineteen of 'Exodus,' a preamble to the Ten Commandments of chapter twenty. The omitted chapters of 'Exodus' pitted Moses who could easily be seen as a metaphor for the enslaved masses against Pharaoh who could just as well be seen as a metaphor for the enslavers: it is the Jewish story of triumph over slavery but could also be interpreted as a dialectic of plantation relations in the shadow of the Haitian Revolution.[38] *The Negro Bible* was worse than statutory prohibition of conscience: its author implicitly denied Africans the right to practice their traditional faiths as well as the right to their independent interpretation of the official King James version of the *Bible* used by all Protestant churches. Porteus justified his violation of the Christian scriptures: 'With the view of rendering the Scriptures more generally useful to the negroes' by making 'a selection of such parts, both Old and New Testament as appeared to him best adapted to their understandings and condition.'[39] Porteus would have been more truthful if he had said that the intention behind his personalised *Bible* was to make the 'negro' more useful to the planters and the imperial economy.

Beginning in 1765, Sir William Blackstone, one of England's foremost jurists, published his four-volume *Commentaries on the Laws of England*, which remained a blueprint for constitutionalism on both sides of the Atlantic, especially on matters concerning civil liberties.

Blackstone hubristically opined that England was 'the only country "in the universe, in which political or civil liberty is the very end and scope of the constitution."'[40] In Book four he addressed the right of conscience as enshrined in 1 William and Mary (Wm & M.), affirming the continuing validity of the key clause: 'All persons, who will approve themselves no papists or oppugners of the Trinity, are at full liberty to act as their consciences shall direct them, in the matter of religious worship.'[41]

The laws of England prohibited practices deemed a threat to public order, but Blackstone assured that the Toleration Act provided immunity to congregations and pastors from the whims of political authorities and protected their right to worship according to conscience. This protection extended to any prayer meeting or dissenter denomination. On this score Blackstone affirmed:

> If any person shall wilfully, maliciously, or contemptuously disturb any congregation, assembled in any church or permitted meeting-house, or shall misuse any preacher or teacher there, he shall (by virtue of the same statute 1 W. & M.) be bound over to the sessions of the peace and forfeit twenty pounds.[42]

From this explanation, the Toleration Act obviously did not provide water-tight immunity from malicious agents of the state intent on abusing their power to harass dissenting Protestants. For a meeting house to qualify as 'permitted' it had to have the certification of the respective regulating authority. In the colonies, this power was often exercised arbitrarily by governors and town councillors who, invariably, belonged to the High Church of England. Despite Blackstone's assurances, Parliament passed the Places of Worship Act 1812 (52 Geo. 3 c. 155), which prohibited the assembly of twenty or more Protestants for religious worship unless the place of worship was duly registered as prescribed in the Toleration Act 1689.[43] If assembled in a private dwelling, members of the immediate family and servants were not to be included in the count. The penalty for violating the Act ranged between 20s. and £20 at the discretion of the magistrate.

The Progress of Toleration in the Age of the Industrial Revolution

Britain's industrial revolution and its consequential urbanisation aided the abolition of the slave trade, slavery, mercantilism and religious persecution. In 1812, a 'Toleration Bill' introduced by Secretary for Foreign Affairs, Lord Castlereagh, stopped short of recognising 'religious liberty to its fullest extent.'[44] On the third reading of the Bill, the prime minister, Earl of Liverpool, expressed the hope that the progress made 'would continue till the great work of religious freedoms received its final consummation;' he was convinced 'that the strength of the Established Church rested in the freedom of religious opinions.'[45] The following year, the Trinity Act, 1813 advanced Liverpool's hope by extending the benefits of Toleration to Unitarians. Although the reference to Unitarians under the Toleration Act, 1689 was to Unitarian Christians, it is under the protection of the Trinity Act that the first African Muslims in Trinidad were able to practice their faith free of persecution from the colonial government. Indeed, in 2013 Muslims in England celebrated the bicentenary of religious freedom under the Trinity Act. The Test Act was repealed in 1828; Catholic Emancipation came the following year by way of The Catholic Relief Act, which still prohibited members of the faith from publicly displaying religious images. Despite these radical changes, colonial oligarchs made no progress toward freedom of conscience for Africans who practised ancestral African religions.

The mid-1850s saw the enactment of Britain's most far-reaching laws on conscience, the Places of Worship Registration Act, 1855 (18 & 19 Vict., c. 81) and the Liberty of Religious Worship Act, 1855 (18 & 19 Vict., c. 86). In debating the Liberty of Religious Worship Bill, Lord Shaftsbury defended the right to hold prayer meetings without permission of a regulating authority as stipulated in Article 19 of the Toleration Act, 1689. He argued that the Pastoral Aid Society of the Church of England had been evangelising in schoolrooms and cottages with packed audiences and that the vast majority of times these meetings 'were positively illegal, for they were almost uniformly commenced by singing and praying, and were consequently "religious meetings," under the definition of the Act and contrary to law.'[46] He reiterated that he 'did not believe any lawyer would venture to say that if a meeting was opened simply with the Lord's Prayer that would not be an act of religious worship which, under the existing law, would render such meeting illegal.'[47] The Act did justice to Shaftsbury's argument. Article 1 assured, 'And no person permitting any such Congregation to meet as herein mentioned in any Place occupied by him shall be liable to any Penalty for so doing.'[48] These places included private dwellings even if not purpose-built or appropriated for religious worship. This Act presented a major challenge to the prohibitionists of St Vincent: how to get around acknowledging Shakerism as anything other than religion while admitting that all their meetings began with conventional Methodist prayers and hymns and conducted mostly in purpose-built Prayer Houses.

> Article 19 of the first Toleration Act (1 Wm & M.) ended with a proviso that no congregation or assembly for religious worship shall be permitted or allowed by this Act, until the place of such meeting shall be certified to the Bishop of the diocese, or the Archdeacon of that archdeaconry, or to the Justice of the Peace.[49]

These certifiers were all resolute gatekeepers of Anglicanism and ultimately denied freedom of conscience to the vast majority of people comprising the 'subjects' of the British Empire around the globe. The Article also had deep ramifications for Non-Conformist missionaries of the eighteenth and nineteenth centuries, more so, for African and African-Christian sects. It was finally repealed in 1855 under the Places of Worship Registration Act.

The PWRA, 1855 was a consolidated Toleration Act. It expanded the Protestant Dissenters Act, 1852 (15 & 16 Vict., c. 36), which effectively repealed section 18 of Act 1 Wm & M., eliminating the arbitrary exercise of certification from governors and Town Councils.[50] Instead, it put religious leaders in direct contact with the Registrar General, a post duplicated in all colonies. The Act explicitly extended protection to the places of worship of all religious organisations in the empire, whose followers worshipped a supernatural being; it also obligated the Registrar General to certify those places of worship upon proper notification. Article 2 states in part:

> Every place of meeting for religious worship of Protestant Dissenters or other Protestants, and of Persons professing the Roman Catholic Religion…and every Place of Meeting for Religious worship of Persons professing the Jewish religion…and every Place of meeting for religious worship of *any other Body or Denomination of Persons*, may be certified in writing to the Registrar General of Births, Deaths, and Marriages in England.[51]

Under 'Schedule A (d)' the Act exhaustively identified the beneficiaries of the Act as Protestant Dissenters, Independents, Particular Baptists, Wesleyan Methodists, Roman Catholics, Jews, and 'any other religious denomination of, or religious appellation adopted by, the persons on whose behalf the building is certified.'[52]

If emancipation were about humanity and justice, colonial governors would have extended the same benefits of protection that they gave to the new denominations entering the colonies to home-grown Christian and other faiths. This was not done. Instead, the state became a facilitator and agency of persecution of these Black religious movements. For example, in 1908, a leader of a Penitent group in New Adelphi in St Vincent applied for permission to erect a Praise-House on his property. The land commissioner denied the request although acknowledging that the local laws did not prohibit such a structure on a residential lot.[53]

The rest of the nineteenth century saw a rapid collapse of most of the pillars of religious intolerance. This development was a catalyst for the spread of new sects across English-ruled colonies, confident of official welcome or immunity from invasion of their places of worship by police. The Jews Relief Act 1858 extended the rights granted under the Religious Disabilities Act, 1846 to allow Jews to take their seats in Parliament without subscription to the Christian-confession oath and laying of hand on the *Bible*.[54] Discrimination against recusants of the Church of England seeking higher office was repealed in 1871 under the Promissory Oaths Act (34 & 35 Vict., c. 48); the Universities Test Act, 1871 (34 & 35 Vict., c. 26) freed prospective professors and students seeking entry to the universities of Cambridge, Oxford, and Durham from oath-taking and compulsory attendance at Anglican worship within these campuses. Prior to 1888, atheists or secularists in Parliament had to take the oath of allegiance to the Queen; only Quakers had been exempted by making an affirmation. The passage of The Oaths Act, 1888 allowed atheists and others professing faiths not previously recognised in British law to take a secular affirmation rather than the customary religious oath as the condition for taking their seat in Parliament.[55] Outside Parliament, however, persons remained liable to fines and imprisonment under the law of blasphemy. Parliament grudgingly granted freedom of conscience to atheists only in 2008 when the law of blasphemy was finally repealed under the Criminal Justice and Immigration Act.[56] The Scottish Parliament followed suit in 2021.[57]

Colonial Oligarchs' Defiance of Imperial Toleration Laws

The 1689 Act of Toleration was invoked in the colony of Virginia in 1699, after the arrival of the first Baptists. Up to the Revolution, Baptists in Virginia were often persecuted for 'unlawful' or 'unlicensed' preaching.[58] Thus, pioneers of African American Christianity were already personally familiar with the persecution of White Baptists in North America.[59] In Jamaica, Liele was 'persecuted' early in his ministry. Using the metaphor 'Israel' for his enslaved brethren, he preached to them from the 'Book of Romans' praying that God would save Israel. He was charged for sedition, placed in irons and put in the stocks while awaiting trial. Fortunately, he was acquitted because no witness came to testify against him.[60] To seek relief, he successfully petitioned the legislature to grant him 'liberty' and sanction his activities.[61] Moses Baker faced similar charges of sedition on several occasions.[62] In retrospect, such charges appear frivolous, but they manifested one of the many loopholes in the Toleration Act that would be used repeatedly in the Caribbean to try and silence dissenters and undermine the legitimacy of their Church organisations. The Toleration Act criminalised preaching outside of a place certified for that purpose by a bishop, archdeacon or justice of the peace.

Interestingly, with all their legal disabilities, Roman Catholic clergy did not have to obtain similar licences to preach or erect places of worship.

Persecution of African Christians was informed by politics and racism. Many colonial elites shared the view expressed by English traveller, Charles Day, that emancipation was an error of imperial policy and that Africans, 'however useful as mere slaves, are not at all to be advocated as a free labouring population.'[63] This attitude supported repressive policies against African land ownership and freedom of conscience, two of the greatest pillars of freedom. Colonial governments denied Africans the right to practise their own brand of reformed Christianity consistent with their spiritual needs as Africans, unless it was subordinated to foreign patronage or control. This was inconsistent with the welcome and recognition given to White-led reformed Protestant spin-offs in the nineteenth century, such as the United Brethren, founded in 1800 in Pennsylvania; the Seventh Day Adventists, founded in 1863 in Michigan; and the Salvation Army, founded in 1865 in London. The only foreign African-founded churches acknowledged as 'Christian' carried White Protestant appellations, the most popular being 'Baptist,' as in First African Baptist Church; and 'Methodist,' as in African Methodist Episcopal Church. The AME Church was established in Trinidad in 1883 and was not subjected to State persecution or harassment.

Until 1812, Toleration Acts offered constitutional protection only for White Christian-led Protestant Churches. In the Caribbean, religious intolerance of African traditional religions was almost absolute. In colonies ruled by Roman Catholic monarchs, Africans were baptised on arrival and taught a few prayers, but denied access to the *Bible*. Illiteracy was enforced so absolutely that Muslims remained in constant danger.[64] Africans baptised in the Catholic Church could not be exhorters or catechists, even when there was a dire shortage of clergy. They were denied the sacrament of Holy Communion, which deprived them of the status of full Catholics and effectively blocked their path to ordination.[65] In colonies ruled by Protestant oligarchs, baptism of Africans was rarely conducted. Even the Society for the

Propagation of the Gospel (SPG) in Barbados, the first Anglican body mandated to evangelise enslaved persons, was more interested in profit-making than proselytising.

The year 1732 was a turning point when the Moravians began to evangelise the enslaved in the Danish colonies. The Moravians gradually broke the stranglehold of the Church of England in Antigua and Jamaica from mid-eighteenth century. They were followed by Wesleyan-Methodists in several colonies shortly after, and by African Baptists in Jamaica and the Bahamas before the close of the century. Although Moravians and Methodists also enslaved Africans and intensely indoctrinated them into subservience, they appointed them to important instructional and doctrinal positions such as deacon, catechist, class leader, lay preacher and exhorter. These converts exploited their roles to engage in resistance theology, promoting ideas of freedom and reversals of master-slave stereotypes, just as they had done in North America. For example, Jamaican Baptist pioneer Moses Baker's favourite text was 'Except a man be born of water and the Spirit, he cannot enter the Kingdom of God,' (John 3:5).[66] This was a passionate call for conversion as well as a discreet repudiation of White supremacy, especially White soteriology. Jamaica's slavocracy was not insensitive to the subliminal messages of subaltern theology as seen in the colony's earliest prohibition laws that shielded White colonials from 'the dangers threatening Jamaica from the injecting of the Negroes with revolutionary ideas.'[67]

The reference to revolution after 1791 centred on Haiti but Jamaica had a longer history of home-grown revolutionary emancipationism that triggered its first law against conscience, 'An Act to Remedy the Evils arising from Irregular Assemblies of Slaves 1760, 1 Geo. Lll c. 22,' passed in 1760 in response to the Tacky-led war of emancipation. This beginning is often overlooked in the literature on religious persecution in the island, largely because the targets were not Christians but practitioners of 'obeiah.'[68] Obeah was not precisely defined in colonial law but was unquestionably a combination of African religions, magic, spiritual science, and esoterica. Jamaica's plantocracy had the greatest reason to fear Obeah, having witnessed its deadly capabilities in the Tacky insurgency of 1760.

The persecution of Obeah professors and their clients was intimately connected to the persecution of African Christians. The legislature moved promptly after the rebellion to make the practice of obeah the same as the practice of witchcraft, punishable by death or transportation.[69] In preparation for emancipation, the Vagrancy Act 1833 continued the criminalisation of Obeah into post-slavery. A revised Vagrancy Act of 1839 maintained the equation of Obeah with vagrancy.[70] According to Sarah Nicolazzo, by this time, Obeah was conceived as 'an economic threat;' she also asserts that the elements of racism and economics were 'inseparable' in the colonisers' perception of Obeah.[71]

The text of Jamaica's Obeah law of 1760 easily allowed for its application to all traditional African religions. After the Tacky War, colonists labelled Myal leaders 'professors of obi.'[72] Jamaica's Obeah Act 1854 deemed 'Obeah' the same as 'Myalism' and raised it to the level of a felony punishable by flogging.[73] The persecution of Mayalists coincided with the influx of new Africans and the renewed infusion of Myalism into the Native Baptist Church. Several anti-obeah laws followed right down to the end of the nineteenth century, climaxing with the Obeah Act, 1898, which reaffirmed that Obeah and Myalism were one and the same.[74] The punishment for accused persons found guilty of violation of this law varied according to age and sex. Men and women were liable to a maximum of twelve months imprisonment with or without hard labour; adult males above sixteen years of age were flogged to a maximum of sixteen strokes; younger male teens to a maximum of twelve strokes and male children between ten and twelve years old, six lashes. The law did not explain how such young children might practise Obeah. Most other British colonies followed a similar path. It goes without saying that the colonialists' perception of Obeah influenced their negative reactions to Revival Zion, *Pukumina* and Spiritual Baptist.

During the 1790s, circumstances in the metropole favoured proselytisation but circumstances in the Caribbean screamed for caution – on the one hand, the imperial government embraced the policy of amelioration of slavery through Christianisation; on the other hand, the Haitian Revolution and related emancipationist wars threatened Britain's sovereignty in several colonies. The first English troops deployed to Haiti went from Jamaica, under the command of Governor Adam Williamson.[75] Jamaica's experience of the Tacky war of 1760 and the island's proximity to Haiti would remain a significant factor in official attitudes to missionaries up to the end of chattel slavery.

Methodist proselytising in St Vincent commenced in 1787 with the visit of Superintendent Dr Thomas Coke. The mission grew rapidly with the cooperation of many influential planters and by 1793, about one thousand enslaved Africans were baptised and 'multitudes more attended the preaching of the word.'[76] But 1793 was a landmark for a completely different reason. Coke was dismayed to learn that 'religious persecution was established by law' in the island. The reference was to an Ordinance banning itinerant missionaries from preaching without first obtaining a licence.[77] Shortly after its proclamation the resident missionary, Mr Matthew Lumb, was imprisoned for preaching in violation of the law.[78] The new law, however, was not about regulating preaching; it was outright prohibition of Methodism under the guise of licensing. Dr Coke operated an 'itinerant plan' whereby he constantly shuffled his missionaries from island to island for only short stints. Knowing this, the St Vincent legislature put in place a measure that a person would only be eligible for a licence 'who had actually resided twelve months in the island.'[79] The ordinance prescribed extreme punishments. For a first offence, a fine of 10 johannes ($£$18) or imprisonment of thirty to ninety days; for a second offence, corporal punishment, the severity to be determined by the magistrate, in addition to banishment; for a third offence, death, should the offender return from banishment.[80] This Act made St Vincent 'the field of battle for religious liberty.'[81] Coke testified that the law was 'enacted in a clandestine kind of manner, and hurried into existence by a few intolerant individuals.'[82] In retrospect, it was a playbook for Administrator Gideon Murray's Shakers' Prohibition Bill in 1912, which was also hurried into existence by a few conniving officials. The 1793 law achieved its main objective: as soon as Lumb completed his sentence, he departed the island.[83] Months later, a delegation of

Methodists headed by Coke met with Henry Dundas, the secretary for war and the Colonies, to make their case for toleration in the Caribbean. Dundas duly informed Coke that the King in Council agreed to 'disannul' the colonial law.[84] To celebrate the achievement, Coke sent two new missionaries to St Vincent the following year.

The prohibition laws against dissenters in Jamaica were prompted by the early success of Methodist proselytising. Prohibition, however, was not really against Methodism as a religion, but against enslaved Africans becoming Methodists. The same laws did not sanction Roman Catholicism, which was expressly excluded from the benefits of Toleration. The legislative attack on Methodism was a desperate expediency to deprive the enslaved of the idiom of evangelical Protestantism as revolutionary ideology. Prior to 1800, it was primarily the missionaries who faced political obstacles and state persecution; after 1800, more and more enslaved Christian converts were directly targeted for criminal prosecution.

By the turn of the century, Methodism had begun to prosper again in Jamaica but not for long. Soon after, there was an upsurge in hostility toward all dissenters. Coke explained the reason for the change as 'the secret cause.'[85] According to one Peter Samuel, the real reason for the new situation was because 'the conversion of some females of colour who used to be the easy prey of licentious men exasperated the enemies of religion, many of whom were armed with wealth, place, and power.'[86] These converted women were residents of Kingston and Morant Bay. Their powerful former clients allegedly sponsored 'the rabble' to interrupt the meetings of the missionaries. Instead of charging the mischief-makers, the police arrested the missionaries and charged them for being 'public nuisances.' Having lost the case, the persecutors decided to adopt 'the St Vincent plan of operating through the local legislature.'[87] Accordingly, a prohibition bill was signed into law on Christmas Day, 1802.[88]

Coke lamented that the ordinance fell like a thunder bolt upon Jamaican Methodism.[89] The Jamaican law was less draconian than St Vincent's, but equally restrictive of both missionary work and the practice of Sectarianism. Under the Act, any preacher 'not duly qualified and authorised' according to the laws of Jamaica and England was liable to be charged as 'a rogue and vagabond.'[90] The penalties for violating the law varied according to race and status. If the offender were an enslaved preacher, the liability for each offence was one month's imprisonment with hard labour; if he were a free Black or Coloured, the first offence carried the same liability, but for any further infringement, the liability was six months' imprisonment with hard labour. Both were tried summarily in a magistrate's court. If the offender were a White preacher, he would be afforded a trial by jury in the Assizes. On conviction, the extent of the punishment was dependent on the will of the court but, unlike the law in St Vincent, capital punishment was ruled out.[91]

The Jamaican lawmakers clearly intended to crush the dissenters. A prime target was John Williams of Morant Bay, 'a coloured local preacher of talent and power and a man of remarkable character.'[92] Williams was careful to avoid preaching in public; nevertheless, he was the first to be imprisoned under the new law, because 'he had sung and prayed with a few friends in his own house.'[93] Senior missionaries who arrived from England with their certificates of ordination in addition to 'a licence signed by the Lord Mayor of London' should have secured their protection under the Toleration Act, 1689 but the authorities disregarded those credentials and still charged them for preaching without a locally issued licence. The courts, dominated by planting interests, ruled against them. One of the unfortunate missionaries was Daniel Campbell who left the island after completing his jail sentence.[94]

It should not be forgotten that 1802 witnessed the greatest test for slavery in the Caribbean when Napoleon Bonaparte deployed tens of thousands of troops to reinstate slavery in France's colonies, which had all benefitted from a general emancipation decree enacted by the French National Convention in 1794. Haiti became the major theatre of war after the arrival of thirty five thousand elite troops under the command of General Le Clerc, Napoleon's brother-in-law. During all of 1803, Haiti fought for its survival as a free nation culminating with the defeat of France in December of that year. Jamaica's proximity to

Haiti presented real security concerns for the slavocracy. The planters could not have forgotten Tacky's war of 1760 or the recent uprising of the Maroons during the early years of the Haitian Revolution. The planters' judges were not ashamed to justify upholding charges of preaching to the enlaved because of 'the dangers threatening Jamaica from the infecting of the Negroes with revolutionary ideas' emanating from Haiti.[95]

Without disregarding the slavocracy's politics of security, the King in Council gave priority to the Toleration Act and disallowed the Jamaica Act in 1804.[96] This injunction did not stop the Jamaican legislators. Two new prohibition laws were passed in 1807, the first by the Common Council of Kingston; the second by the House of Assembly a few months later. Both institutions comprised the great planters and merchants of the colony. Ordinances passed by the Common Council had application only within the boundaries of the city and parish of Kingston; on the other hand, laws passed in the House of Assembly had colony-wide application.

The Council's bill, 'For preventing the profanation of religious rites and false worshipping of God, under the pretence of preaching and teaching, by illiterate, ignorant, and ill-disposed persons, and of the mischief consequent thereupon,' was unassumingly steeped in racial and class prejudice. Several clauses in the Ordinance mirrored the St Vincent ordinance of 1793. The law identified forbidden places of dissenter worship as 'houses, negro-houses, huts, and the yards thereunto appertaining.'[97] By then planters understood the strength of Methodism lay more with the enslaved than the foreign missionaries; in many of the places mentioned Christian worship was conducted independent of foreign missionaries and had the potential to become cells of revolutionary thought and action. The Ordinance authorised the court to be the principal guardian of recognised religion: 'The first and most serious duty of all magistrates and bodies politic, to uphold and encourage the due, proper, and solemn exercise of religion and worshipping of God.'[98]

The law required that a person would be allowed to preach only if duly authorised, qualified and licensed according to the laws of Britain and Jamaica. The Council gave itself sole authority to determine the competence of an applicant for a licence to preach. The licence stated in what places worship was allowed. All the unauthorised places of worship were stomping grounds for African exhorters and preachers. If preachers obeyed the restrictions of the licence, it would effectively rule out proselytising and prayer meetings on plantations and even the singing of psalms privately at home. The law also subjected enslaved exhorters and unlicensed free Black and Coloured preachers to legal liabilities if they engaged in religious activities anywhere.[99] As in St Vincent's vetoed ordinance, punishment was racially differentiated. A White person guilty of breaking this law was liable to a fine not exceeding £100, or imprisonment in the common jail, not exceeding three months, or both; for a free Black or Coloured person, it was the same fine and length of incarceration, but in the workhouse; for an enslaved offender, the law prescribed imprisonment and hard labour in the workhouse not exceeding six months, and whipping, not exceeding thirty-nine stripes. The Ordinance tactically restricted missionary contact with the enslaved to between 6:00 a.m. and sunset, the main hours of forced labour.[100] One missionary was arrested fifteen minutes after sunset and imprisoned for practising the singing of a Psalm with a group of enslaved persons. This Ordinance set a new precedent for religious persecution in imposing legal liabilities on any 'owner, possessor, or occupier of any out-house, yard, or other place whatsoever' for facilitating prayer meetings or the singing of hymns.

In November 1807, the Jamaican House of Assembly passed its own prohibition Act as an amendment to the Consolidated Slave Law. The vested interest that controlled the Kingston Council also controlled the island's Legislative Assembly. Not surprisingly, the Assemblymen simply copied the Council's ordinance and expanded its application to the entire colony. Ostensibly, the Legislature was simply carrying out the mandate of the imperial government to expeditiously enact amelioration of slavery laws that would help sustain and naturally grow the enslaved population considering the passage of the general Abolition of the Slave Trade Act earlier that year. For abolitionists, amelioration of slavery was key to the success of abolition of the slave trade; and Christianisation was key to the success of amelioration. Thus, the framers of the law ensured that the title reflected the imperial mandate, 'a law for the protection, subsisting, clothing, and for the better order and government of slaves, and for other purposes.'[101]

True to the official amelioration agenda, Article 1 of the Act mandated enslavers to endeavour to instruct the enslaved in the principles of Christianity, but only 'as much as in them lies.' Article 2 was the bombshell: instruction was to be 'confined to the doctrines of the Established Church.' To allow for no disambiguation, the article stated unequivocally 'that no Methodist Missionary, or other sectary, or preacher, shall presume to instruct our slaves, or to receive them into their houses, chapels, or conventicles, of any sort or description.' If Bishop Porteus had his way, the only religious instruction would be based on his *Slave Bible*.

The courts of Jamaica offered no relief to the persecuted, because they were essentially planters' courts. In early 1808, four White missionaries, Messrs Bradnock, William Gilgrass, Knowlan, and Wiggins, appeared before a magistrate's court. When ordered not to preach without a licence, they responded that they were already licensed, 'according to the laws of England.'[102] They were obviously stunned with the magistrate's response: 'What are the laws of England to us? What have we to do with them?'[103] Accordingly, Knowlan requested a local licence, to which the magistrate replied, 'Indeed you will not get one.'[104] The next step was to appeal to the Quarterly Session, the higher court. That court dismissed Wiggins' application and simply scoffed at Braddock's licence, which carried the signature of the Lord Mayor of London.

Jewish slave masters in Jamaica also persecuted African-Christians for their faith. Jews appropriated to themselves the authority of magistrates and gaolers. One Jew 'laid down' a female Methodist on the ground and sentenced her to thirty-nine lashes, to be remitted if she promised not to return to the chapel. In defiance, the woman replied, 'Massa, me must pray,' after which the flogging began. After nine strokes, a 'gentleman' intervened. Upon hearing that she was being punished for worshipping God, he ordered her prompt release.[105] Another Jew enslaver sentenced a 'young Black man' to thirty-nine lashes the same day that he was baptised.[106]

The Methodists' last resort was an appeal to the Crown. With the weight of the Annual Methodist Conference behind him, Coke applied to the Privy Council for relief from the Jamaica Act in March 1808, but up to August, the Act had not yet arrived at the Privy Council.[107] In the meantime, Coke, who was secretary of the Conference, submitted a memorial to the Committee of Council for Trade and Foreign Relations pleading with them not to allow the Act to receive the King's assent.[108] The decision took several months in coming. In April 1809, Lord Bathurst wrote to Coke informing him that the Act was disallowed by the King in Council.[109] This time the British government accompanied the veto with seminal instructions to colonial governors to 'refer all laws dealing with religious matters to Britain for royal scrutiny and assent.'[110] Even after knowledge of the King's annulment reached Jamaica, persecution of the dissenters continued because the governor, the Duke of Manchester, claimed that 'he had not received any official instruction from His Majesty's Council.'[111] The Crown's admonition implicitly included prohibition ordinances and regulations of Town Councils. Apparently, the Kingston councillors also did not receive the admonition of the King or simply chose not to comply. Toward the end of the year, the missionaries reported that the Council was still invoking the Ordinance 'to silence the Methodist preachers.'[112] The missionaries, therefore, decided to apply 'for a licence, under the Toleration Act, as is customary in England.'[113] After a lengthy hearing, the court 'unanimously refused the prayer of the petition!'[114]

The period of imperial-mandated Amelioration (1823–34) provided an unexpected opportunity for the Jamaican House of Assembly to revive prohibition. In 1823, the Parliament of Britain passed an amelioration of slavery motion and mandated the executive to enforce it. Action followed immediately in the three Crown Colonies, Trinidad, St Lucia, and Demerara (British Guiana). Governors in all other colonies were mandated to legislate new slave codes incorporating specific amelioration guidelines.[115] News of the imperial mandate triggered slave uprisings and plots in several colonies. In Demerara, the Methodists were accused of instigating unrests and their principal missionary, John Smith, was arrested, tried and sentenced to death.[116]

The lawmakers of Jamaica passed an amelioration bill in 1826, 'The Jamaica Consolidated Slave Law,' but inserted an article to silence the Methodists and other dissenters. The law put no restrictions on the Church of England, the Roman Catholic Church, or Judaism; but it forbade dissenters 'to hold any meeting for slaves after sunset,' claiming that nightly meetings facilitated plotting of insurrection.[117] Secretary of state for the Colonies, William Huskisson, disallowed the entire law because of the article that brazenly violated the Toleration Act.[118] Jamaica's last attempt to circumvent the Toleration Act during slavery came in 1829 as a clause in a new Slave Code, which prohibited 'preaching and teaching by a slave.'[119] For yet another time, the Crown proved an effective watchdog and defender of the constitution by refusing to sanction the 1829 law.[120] The veto, however, came too late to save Sam Swiney, an enslaved Baptist deacon in BMS missionary William Knibb's church. Swiney was arrested while praying and charged before the court for 'preaching and teaching' without a licence. He was found guilty, sentenced to hard labour and whipped.[121]

The final showdown between conscience and the plantocracy in Jamaica came in the aftermath of the 1831–32 Christmas uprising popularly known as the Baptist War. The leader of the uprising was Samuel Sharpe, a Native Baptist deacon. Not seeking the cover of legislation, the state, assisted by civil society, launched an all-out offensive to drive dissenting missionaries from the island. An alliance of Anglican clergy, Jews, and Church of Scotland vigilantes founded the Colonial Church Union (CCU), which Tony Martin described as an 'antinonconformist terrorist' organisation, akin to the infamous Klu Klux Klan in the US.[122] A few months after its formation, CCU members invaded the home of an enslaved person where a group of worshippers was engaged in Good Friday prayers. The CCU thugs put the worshippers in leg shackles, stripped them naked and flogged them with the dreaded cart whip, each worshipper receiving forty-five strokes. The CCU terrorised several other Black and coloured dissenters simply for attending nonconformist churches.[123] Missionary and Native Baptist churches were torn down, and others burnt; some clergymen were tarred and feathered.[124] Samuel Sharpe and hundreds of other Black Jamaicans, many of them Baptists, were executed judicially, or murdered by mobs and soldiers. William Knibb and two other foreign Baptist missionaries were arrested and fled to England upon their release.[125]

In Trinidad, the Roman Catholic Church enjoyed establishment status with the Church of England, as in Dominica. Unlike Dominica, however, the situation in Trinidad enjoyed royal sanction arising from the 1797 'Articles of Capitulation.' The Trinidad governor was the colonial head of the Anglican Church as well as Patron of the Roman Catholic Church, having inherited the authority by right of Conquest. In 1801, the British government issued 'Instructions' to Trinidad's first governor, Colonel Thomas Picton, which protected the rights of dissenters and Evangelicals.[126] Nevertheless, according to Vincent Leahy, establishment of the Catholic Church could only be preserved with an Act of Parliament, which was not pursued.[127]

A small congregation of 'free Coloureds' from Grenada were the only Dissenters before the arrival of the first English missionary, Thomas Talboys, in 1809.[128] Expansion was satisfactory but not as spectacular as in St Vincent two decades earlier, yet Talboys faced similar obstacles as Lumb in that colony. Governor Thomas Hislop did not trust the free coloureds whom he labelled 'republicans' at a time when Alexandre Pétion, a 'coloured' King of Haiti, was aiding Simon Bolivar to overthrow slavery and colonialism in Venezuela, less than twenty kilometres from Trinidad.[129] In Trinidad, the press and influential planters of both episcopal churches initiated the persecution of the Methodists. A petition by 'respectable inhabitants' specifically mentioned that Talboys was violating 'the rules of our established religions' by 'profanely administering sacraments' to the 'free coloured inhabitants and slaves.'[130]

Had it not been for the intervention of the curate of the Anglican Church, Talboys would have been deported for his 'crimes.' The Council of Advice – there was no legislative or executive council – agreed with the curate that His Majesty's Instructions of 1801 protected dissenters' right of conscience. Yet, they ingeniously sought to circumvent the imperial Instructions by invoking Section 5 of the Toleration Act, 1689. They correctly claimed that Toleration preserved the Corporation and Test Acts, which prohibited dissenters from holding public office.[131] Hislop, however, must have been aware that public office had a more restricted application than claimed by his Council. Nevertheless, the governor did not wish for a political fight with the island's elites. Early in March 1811, when Talboys visited Government House, Hislop ordered him 'to close his chapel, stop preaching and join a militia.'[132] Two days later, the militia arrested and jailed him. Following his release, he had another audience with the governor who informed him that he did not recognise his license to preach and that he had 'disturbed the peace with his preaching.'[133]

The following month, Hislop issued a controversial, anti-conscience proclamation. Although he acknowledged that Methodist preaching was lawful, his proclamation required that dissenters' sermons adhere strictly to the *Bible*. It regulated the opening and closing hours of dissenters' chapels and prohibited them from performing marriages and burials, as well as administering baptism and the Lord's Supper.[134] Unable to function in that environment, Talboys was replaced by George Poole. To circumvent Hislop's proclamation, Poole broke up the Society into groups of twenty and continued expanding the base laid by his predecessor.[135] As highlighted earlier, the Places of Worship Act (1812) required registration of places of worship only when the congregation exceeded twenty, excluding the immediate members of a family, if the place of worship was a private home.

Hislop's successor, Ralph Woodford, had no greater liking for the free coloureds and no confidence in Sectarian proselytising. Nevertheless, to ensure strict adherence to the law, he sought advice from the secretary of state for the Colonies, Earl Bathurst. Based on his personal assessment, Bathurst directed that Woodford 'prohibit any Missionary from preaching to the slaves, unless he shall previously bind himself to a strict observance of it,' that is, Hislop's proclamation.[136] This ruling contradicted the mandate of the King in Council ten years earlier that all colonial legislation impinging on religious freedom must be submitted to the metropolitan government for vetting before implementation in the colonies. Hislop's decree had clearly violated that mandate.

With the weight of the Colonial Office behind it, the Council of Advice ordered the new missionary, Abraham Whitehouse, to sign a bond agreeing to abide by Hislop's proclamation.[137] Whitehouse declined. Methodist missionaries in the Caribbean were thoroughly schooled on their rights under the Toleration Act. Whitehouse was unequivocal that the bond 'disannuls the Act of Parliament which secures to him those privileges.'[138] The metropolitan Missionary Society were equally dismayed that the bond had the approbation of the imperial government, because it would lead to 'the final extinction of missionary labours in the West India Colonies.'[139]

The relentless battle of the Methodist Society led to a final resolution from the Judicial Officers of the King's Bench. In 1817, the legal luminaries overruled Bathurst's instruction to Woodford and annulled Hislop's Proclamation as a violation of the protection afforded to all dissenters or Nonconformists under Toleration Act 7th & 8th Wm.3rd c. 35; a violation of their rights to conduct burials and baptisms granted under Act 25 Geo. 3rd c. 75; and, a violation of their right to administer the Eucharist, which was protected by Act 13 Geo. 3rd c. 22.[140] By that time, however, based on the Trinity Act 1813, the only test any movement needed to entitle it to such protection was to be accepted as a religion.[141]

Post-slavery Persecution of Africans Intensifies

Africans in British Caribbean colonies became subjects of the English Crown from 1838 and constitutionally enjoyed the same rights as the working class of England. Indeed, Lord John Russell, secretary of state for the Colonies, appealed to the governor of British Guiana in a memorandum in 1840 to 'induce the African race to feel that wherever the British flag flies they have a friend and a protector;' Russell's guarantee of protection complemented his instruction that the government must 'let them partake of the blessings of Christianity.'[142] Devoid of racial prejudice, Lord Russell's promise of protection would naturally extend to African-Caribbean Christians including Revival Zion in Jamaica, Jordanites in British Guiana and Spiritual Baptists in the three southernmost island-colonies. These forms of Christianity evolved from imperatives of ethnocentrism like those of European denominational pioneers from the earliest centuries of Christianity and the Protestant Reformation.

Notwithstanding the Trinity Act and Lord Russell's memorandum, African-Christians in St Vincent were exclusively targeted for persecution in the post-emancipation era. The Methodists and Anglicans spearheaded the first wave when the sect was known as the Wilderness People. The common method was expulsion for non-conformity. Since expulsion led to expansion of the sect, it was not surprising that the state began paying attention to the Wilderness People in the early 1850s by which time the sect was already labelled 'Shakers,' a term first used by Revd Thomas Browne, son of Lt Thomas Brown.[143] Lt Governor John Campbell branded them 'a singular sect,'[144] implying that they successfully resisted integration into the Euro-Christian milieu. Motivated by such criticism, Chief Justice Sharpe condemned them as 'fanatics' and recommended that they be 'arrested and charged' if they persisted in remaining outside the fold of European Christianity.[145] Instigated by Sharpe, the Grand Jury, without any concrete evidence, accused the Penitents of being a potential conduit for 'immorality and crime.'[146]

The elitist propaganda unleashed against the Penitents in the 1850s bore fruit in 1862 when the government ordered the militia to destroy the Penitents' chapel on Mt Bentinck estate on the pretext that some of its members participated in the island-wide riots of that year.[147] By that time, many Afro-Barbadian immigrants had joined the faith and become 'leading members.'[148] The negative stereotyping and envy of Shakers' independence continued to fester for the rest of the century and became the major justification for proscription in the first decade of the twentieth century. Psychologically, it demonstrated, 'There's nothing so absurd that if you repeat it often enough, people will believe it.'[149]

In 1895, the arrest and incarceration of Alexander Bedward, Revivalist leader and patriarch of the Native Baptist Free Church in Jamaica, sent a clear message that the state had means of persecuting and subverting the right of conscience of African-Christians other than legislation. Bedward utterly rejected the quietism of European missionary Christianity. In one reported sermon preached in 1885, he overturned the age-old stereotypes of White supremacy, calling out 'White people' as 'hypocrites, liars, thieves.' He flipped the criminal label 'rogue and vagabond' with which Jamaican lawmakers had tarnished the reputation of 'unlicensed' and 'unauthorised' Black preachers earlier in the century and pinned it onto the clergy of the expanded oligarchy of 'recognised' churches. He aimed his knockout punch at the governor and his Council tagging them as the leaders of colonial 'oppressors of Black people.'[150] The state interpreted Bedward's exposure as a declaration of war. The large contingent of police despatched to arrest him in his sleep was a warning to future resistance theologians. Bedward was charged with preaching sedition. He was found not guilty by virtue of insanity and consigned to the lunatic asylum.[151] He was eventually released after his lawyer successfully argued that incarceration in an asylum was contrary to the law of sedition.

The Problematic of Defining 'Religion'

Although the criterion of 'religion' was the only test for relief under the PWRA, it was not a simple test. The term 'religion' is a relatively modern construct, grounded in European overseas colonialism. Religion lies beyond the scope of inductive science: just as the term 'racism' was debunked scientifically but religion remains an elusive concept. In the pre-colonised world, people expressed their beliefs and sacred practices in terms that cannot be properly translated as religion. In India, for example, Sanatana dharma expressed a way of life. British colonisers branded it Hinduism and Buddhism, which they recognised as different 'religions.' Similarly in Africa, people expressed their faiths as devotees of the gods; for example, in Yorubaland, the Omo Oduduwa lived in accordance with Odu Ifa (oral scripture in verse). Again, British colonisers deemed Ifa or Ifa divination a religion. They also imputed new meanings to some deities to suit a Euro-Christian worldview: to illustrate, they transliterated orisha Esu as the Devil, a concept previously alien to the Yoruba. Frances Henry affirms that there is no word for 'religion' in the Yoruba language. Separated from Africa before this colonialist imposition, most of the Yoruba diaspora in Trinidad identified as Shango devotees up to 1970. Since 1970, Yoruba Trinidadians have employed the term 'egbe' as in Egbe Orisha ile wa, which Henry translates as 'the religion of our land.'[152] The word egbe, however, simply means society or association.

Europeans understood the phenomenon of Euro-Christian 'religion' in such terms as Church, Catholicism, Lutheranism, Calvinism, or generically as denomination. 'The Fundamental Constitutions of Carolina,' issued in 1669, presented the clearest definition of religion before the PWRA. The primary consideration of a religious group was that it publicly worshipped 'a God' and that such a group must have a name distinguishing it from all other religious groups.[153] Authorship of 'The Fundamental Constitutions' is credited to John Locke.[154] The inclusion of the indefinite article before 'God' was deliberate: the authors of 'The Fundamental Constitutions' clearly intended that the God referred to was not to be perceived only as 'the God' of Christians and Jews and indeed, explicitly mentioned Native Americans and enslaved Africans. The acceptance of Locke's definition of religion in the Constitutions suggests a general understanding among the English intelligentsia. In their 'Declaration of Rights,' the Virginia Convention of 1776 formulated another useful concept of religion as 'the duty which we owe to our Creator and the manner of discharging it.'[155] Although the relevant Article affirms 'that it is a mutual duty of all to practice Christian forbearance, love and charity,' it also concedes, '[A]ll men are equally entitled to the free exercise of religion.' Religious issues remained high on the list of responsibilities of the Colonial Office well into the twentieth century. Of nineteen listed 'characteristics' of the Colonial Office, a former senior official who became a notable historian of imperial administration, had 'religions' as the first item.[156] It is noteworthy that religions is pluralised, an acknowledgement that the empire was a multi-confessional, multi-cosmological entity.

In Britain, the PWRA presented the first legal definition of religion in the evolution of toleration. Under this law, any organisation that revered a 'deity' was a true religion. This was a major advancement on the American Creator-exclusive definition. Had the secretary of state for the Colonies not conspired to keep the Shakers' Prohibition

Ordinance, 1912 away from the law officers of the King's Bench, British jurists could have advanced the definition of religion and the cause of freedom of conscience in the early twentieth century. Instead, there was no other major attempt to define 'religion' in English law until the Church of Scientology's case, 'R v Registrar General, ex parte Segerdal.' Scientologists first sued the Registrar General in 1970 to have a Scientology church recognised as a place of worship under the PWRA, the ultimate consideration for solemnising marriages. They lost the case. In delivering judgment, Lord Denning reasoned that the framers of the 1855 law must have meant 'worship of God' when they wrote 'place of worship;' he added, 'It need not be the God which Christians worship. It may be another God or an unknown God.' He viewed Scientology as 'a philosophy of the existence of man and life, rather than a religion.' He concluded, 'There may be belief in a spirit of man, but there is no belief in a spirit of God.'[157]

The Equality Act, 2010 was Britain's coming to terms with its rapid cosmopolitanising since the end of the Second World War. Section ten of the law addressed numerous 'characteristics' of human populations in order to end discrimination in the workplace. One of the nine listed characteristics was 'religion or belief.' Its inclusion must have given renewed hope to Scientologists; but even then, the definition is tautological and meaningless: 'Religion means any religion and a reference to religion includes a reference to a lack of religion;' 'Belief means any religious or philosophical belief and a reference to belief includes a reference to a lack of belief.'[158] It is doubtful that the Equality Act, 2010 would have prevented the prohibition of the Converted of St Vincent had it been enacted one hundred years earlier. The most progressive and final legal definition of religion came three years after the Equality Act as case law delivered by England's Supreme Court in a suit brought by the American Scientology movement for recognition of its churches under the PWRA.

The second application for recognition was made a few months after the proclamation of the Equality Act. Again, it was rejected by the registrar general on the ground that the 1970 judgment was *stare decisis* (stand by that which is decided), which compels subordinate courts to abide by precedent. The case was appealed in 2012 and the landmark judgment delivered in October 2013. In delivering the views of the Court, Lord Toulson mentioned the PWRA twenty-eight times. He traced the evolution of religious toleration in England from the seventeenth century, with the highlight on the PWRA. He explained, 'Religion could be defined more accurately as a "spiritual or non-secular system" which "claims to explain mankind's place in the universe and relationship with the infinite" and give people guidance on life.' He continued,

> Such a belief system may or may not involve belief in a supreme being, but it does involve a belief that there is more to be understood about mankind's nature and relationship to the universe than can be gained from the senses or from science.[159]

This judgement was delivered exactly one century after the Shakers' Prohibition Ordinance. Thus, it cannot be the test of the constitutionality of the prohibition ordinances passed against the Spiritual Baptists in 1912, 1917, and 1927. Accordingly, this study is guided by the progress of religious toleration up to The Places of Worship Registration Act and The Liberty of Religious Worship Act, both of 1855.

Notes

1. Asa J. Davis, 'The 16th Century Jihad in Ethiopia and the Impact on its Culture, Part ll: Implicit Factors Behind the Movement,' *Journal of the Historical Society of Nigeria* 3, no. 1 (December 1964), 116, https://www.jstor.org/stable/41856692.

2. Richard Pankurst, *A Social History of Ethiopia* (Trenton, NJ: Red Sea Press, 1992), 26.

3. See John G. Jackson, *Introduction to African Civilisations* (New York: Citadel, 2001), 206.

4. Jean Boyd, *The Caliph's Sister: Nana Asma'u 1793–1865 – Teacher, Poet and Islamic Leader* (London: Frank Cass, 2000), 126; Kenneth W. Harrow, 'Islamic Literature in Africa,' in *The History of Islam in Africa*, eds. Nehemia Levtzion and Randall L. Pouwels, 522–23 (Athens, Ohio: Ohio University Press, 2000).

5. Ahamad Faosiy Ogunbado, 'Impacts of Colonialism on Religions: An Experience of South-Western Nigeria,' *Journal of Humanities and*

Social Science 5, no. 6 (November-December 2012), 53, https://www.iosrjournals.org/iosr-jhss/papers/Vol5-issue6/10565157.pdf, accessed August 6, 2022.

6. The King of Fetu (in modern-day Ghana) was baptised in 1503; in 1457, the Mansa (King) of Numi (in The Gambia) 'was converted' to Christianity: see, J. O. Ijoma, 'Portuguese Activities in West Africa Before 1600: The Consequences,' Transafrican Journal of History 11 (1982), 143, https://www.jstor.org/stable/24328537.

7. John K. Thornton, '"I Am the Subject of the King of Congo": African Political Ideology and the Haitian Revolution,' *Journal of World History* 4, no 2 (Fall, 1993), 188–89, https://www.jstor.org/stable/20078560; Tsimba Mabiala, 'Afonso I,' *Dictionary of African Christian Biography*, https://www.dacb.org/stories/congo/afonso2/, accessed May 28, 2022; Richard Pankhurst, *History of Ethiopia: Teaching Notes for Secondary Schools* (Addis Ababa: Ministry of Education and Fine Arts, 1970), 34–38. Emperor Ezana was the first Coptic/Tawahedo King of Ethiopia.

8. Richard Gray, 'A Kongo Princess, the Kongo Ambassador and the Papacy,' *Journal on Religion in Africa* 29, no. 2 (May 1999), 141; 144–47, https://www.jstor.org/stable/1581869.

9. Ogunbado, 'Impacts of Colonialism on Religions,' 53.

10. A. F. C. Ryder, 'The Benin Missions,' *Journal of the Historical Society of Nigeria* 2, no. 2 (December 1961), 237, https://www.jstor.org/stable/41970980. 2022. Ijoma, 'Portuguese Activities,' 144.

11. Ijoma, 'Portuguese Activities," 144.

12. Ryder, 'Benin Missions,' 241–42.

13. Ijoma, 'Portuguese Activities,' 144.

14. Richard Pankhurst, *The Ethiopians: A History* (Malden, MA: Blackwell, 2001), 93–95.

15. Pankhurst, *The Ethiopians*, 103–08.

16. National Humanities Center, '*Requerimiento – 1510,*' https://nationalhumanitiescenter.org/pds/amerbegin/contact/text7/requirement.pdf, accessed March 2020. The Spanish-language version carries the date 1512. The declaration was a military farce because it was read in Spanish and therefore incomprehensible to the natives. *The Requerimiento* may have been a Christianised version of Muslims' declaration of jihad to which Iberians were historically familiar; see Sam Haselby, 'Muslims of Early America,' *Aeon Newsletter*, https://www.aeon.co/essays/muslims-lived-in-america-before-protestantism-ever-existed/, accessed May 1, 2023.

17. Andrew Lawler, 'Muslims were Banned from the Americas as Early as the 16th Century,' *Smithsonian Magazine* (Feb. 2017), https://www.smithsonianmag.com/history/muslims-were-banned-americas-early-16th-century-180962059/, accessed November 3, 2022.

18. John Coffey, 'European Multiconfessionalism and the English Toleration Controversy, 1640–1660,' in *A Companion to Multiculturalism in the Early*

Modern World, ed. Thomas Max Safley (Leiden: Brill, 2011), 340–64, https://brill.com.

19. Katharine J. Lualdi, 'Preserving the Faith: Catholic Worship and Communal Identity in the Wake of the Edict of Nantes,' *The Sixteenth Century Journal* 35, no. 3 (Fall 2004), 717–18, https://doi.org/10.2307/20477042.

20. Jonathan A. Bush, 'Free to Enslave: The Foundation of Colonial American Slave Law,' *Yale Journal of Law and Humanities* 5, no. 2 (January 1993), 421. Yale Law School, 'The Fundamental Constitutions of Carolina: March 1, 1669,' Clause 107, https://avalon.law.yale.edu/17th_century/nc05.asp.

21. See Douglas C. Sparkes, 'The Test Act of 1673 and its Aftermath,' *The Baptist Quarterly* 25 (1973), 75–76, https://biblicalstudies.org.uk/pdf/bq/25-2-074.pdf; 'Test Act,' *Britannica,* https://www.britannica.com/topic/test-act.

22. 'The Toleration Act 1689,' https://www.ssc.wisc.edu/~rkeyser/wp/wp-content/uploads/2015/06/TolerationAct1689.pdf, accessed April 25, 2020.

23. 'English Bill of Rights 1689,' https://avalon.law.yale.edu/17th_Century/england.asp, accessed July 6, 2022.

24. Bob Black, 'Ordination in the Wesleyan Tradition: Letting the Past Speak to the Present about the future,' https://www.resources.wesleyan.org/wp/content/, accessed May 20, 2023.

25. Cooperman, 'Legislating Christian Identity.'

26. Quoted by Nabil Matar, 'Islam in Britain, 1689–1750,' *Journal of British Studies* 47, no. 2 (April 2008), 284, https://www.jstor.org/stable/25482757, accessed 4 Sept. 2020. Matar is Professor of English.

27. 'Act of Toleration (1689),' https://www.encyclopediavirginia.org/entries/act-of-toleration-1689/, accessed March 20, 2022; Rachael Edmonston, 'John Locke—A Letter Concerning Toleration,' https://slaverylawpower.org/john-locke-leter-concerning-toleration/, accessed May 12, 2022.

28. Robert Hodgson, *The Life of the Reverend Beilby Porteus: Late Bishop of London* (London: 1812), 43.

29. Alfred Caldecott, *The Church in the West Indies* (New York: E. & J. B. Young, 1898), 83. Google Book.

30. Findlay and Holdsworth, *Methodist Missionary Society* 2, 78.

31. Ibid., 68

32. Hodgson, *Beilby Porteus,* 43.

33. Ibid., 44. Emphasis is original.

34. Ibid., 45.

35. Saunders, 'The State as Highwayman,' 244.

36. Ibid., 86.

37. *Select Parts of the Holy Bible for Use of the Negro Slaves in the British West India Islands,* https://archive.org/details/selectpartsholy00unkngoog/mode/2up.

38. See Jill Keeton, 'The "Slave Bible" is not What you Think' (June 2020), https://therevealer.org/the-slave-bible-is-not-what-you-think/.

39. Hodgson, *Beilby Porteus*, 87.

40. Stanley N. Katz, 'Introduction to Book 1,' in *Commentaries on the Laws of England 1*, William Blackstone (London: University of Chicago Press, 1979). Blackstone borrowed the words from French Enlightenment philosopher, Baron de Montesquieu.

41. William Curry, *The Commentaries of Sir William Blackstone, KNT, on the Laws and Constitution of England*, Bk. IV (London, 1796), 430.

42. Ibid.

43. 'Places of Worship Act 1812,' https://vlex.co.uk/vid/places-of-religious-worship-808464513, accessed July 29, 2022.

44. 23 *Parliamentary Debates* (1803), Lord Castlereagh, July 24,1812, 1105.

45. Ibid., Lord Liverpool, July 21,1812, 1111.

46. 138 *Parliamentary Debates* (1803), Earl of Shaftesbury, June 12, 1855, 1838.

47. Ibid., Shaftesbury, June 12, 1855, 1838.

48. Article 1, 'Liberty of Religious Worship Act, 1855,' https://www.irishstatutebook.ie/eli/1855/act/86/section/1/enacted/en/html, accessed December 12, 2022.

49. 'The Toleration Act 1689,' https://www.ssc.wisc.edu/~rkeyser/wp/wp-content/uploads/2015/06/TolerationAct1689.pdf, accessed April 25, 2020.

50. For the full Act see, 'Places of Worship Act 1855,' UK Public General Acts, https:///www.legislation.gov.uk, accessed June 20, 2020.

51. 'Places of Worship Act 1855,' UK Public General Acts, https:///www.legislation.gov.uk. Emphasis is not original.

52. 'Places of Worship Act 1855,' Schedule A (d), Article 2.

53. Rodney to Kernerhan, 14 July 1908 and Kernerhan to Cameron, July 16,1908, Encl. 6 in Cameron to Cork, August 25, 1908, BNA CO 321/243, 308–09.

54. 'Jews Relief Act 1858,' c. 49, UK Public General Acts, https://www.legislation.gov.uk.

55. 'Oaths Act 1888,' 51 & 52 Vict. c. 46, *Electronic Statute Book* (eBook), https://www.irishstatutebook.ie.

56. 'Criminal Justice and Immigration Act 2008,' c. 4 2008, *UK General Public Acts*, www.legislation.gov.uk. Paul Kearns, 'The End of Blasphemy Law,' https://www.sas-space.sas.ac.uk/20064/1/Amicus76_Kearns.pdf, accessed July 22, 2022.

57. End Blasphemy Laws Homepage, 'The Campaign to Abolish Blasphemy Laws, Worldwide: United Kingdom,' https://end-blasphemy-laws.org/countries/europe/united-kingdom/, accessed on August 6, 2022. Emma Park, 'Lessons from Britain's First Atheist MP,' *New Humanist* (Summer 2021), https://newhumanist.org.uk/articles/5814/lessons-from-britains-first-atheist-mp, accessed July 29, 2022.

58. Frey and Wood, *Come Shouting*, 126.

59. 'Toleration Act,' https://www.encyclopediavirginia.org, accessed April 25, 2020.

60. Noel Leo Erskine, 'George Liele: Liberated Slave and African American Baptist Missionary to Jamaica,' *Missiology: An International Review* 50, no. 1 (2022), 33, https://journals.sage.pub.com/doi/pdf/10.1177/00918296211043527; Ernest A. Payne, 'Baptist Work in Jamaica Before the Arrival of the Missionaries,' *The Baptist Quarterly* 7, no. 1 (1934), 21–22.

61. Liele et al., 'Letters,' 71–72.

62. Payne, 'Baptist Work,' 22.

63. Day, *Five Years Residence*, 78.

64. See Sylviane A. Diouf, *Servants of Allah: African Muslims Enslaved in the Americas* (New York: New York University Press, 1998), 107–08.

65. Joseph Gallagher, trans., Walter A. Abbott, gen. ed., *The Documents of Vatican 2* (New York: Guild, 1956), 492; 597. J. G. Davies, ed., *A Dictionary of Liturgy and Worship* (London: SCM, 1972), 60–61.

66. *The Baptist World* 20, no. 35 (26 Oct. 1916), 8, https://digitalcollections-baylor.quartexcollections.com/.

67. Findlay and Holdsworth, *Methodist Missionary Society* 2, 71: judgment of the Supreme Court of Jamaica, appeal of missionary David Campbell.

68. Edward Long, *History of Jamaica 3* (London: 1774), 463, https://ecda.northeastern.edu/item/neu:m04109796/. Tacky, a Coromanti or Akan, was the leader of uprising.

69. See Diana Paton, 'Obeah Histories,' https://obeahhistories.org/1760-jamaica-law/; accessed December 12, 2021.

70. 'An Act for the Punishment of Idle and Disorderly Persons, Rogues and Vagabonds, and Incorrigible Rogues,' cited in Sarah Nicolazzo, 'Vagrant Figures: Law, Labour and Refusal in the Eighteenth-Century Atlantic World' (PhD diss., University of Pennsylvania, 2014), 178, http://repository.upenn.edu/edissertations/1386, accessed August 6, 2022.

71. Nicolazzo, 'Vagrant Figures,' 178-79; Emphasis original.

72. Bryan Edwards, *The History Civil and Commercial of the British West Indies* (London: 1793), 107–08.

73. See Diana Paton, 'The Racist History of Jamaica's Obeah Laws,' *History Workshop, 4 July 2019*, https://www.historyworkshop.org.uk/the-racist-histories-of-jamaicas-obeah-laws/, accessed August 4, 2022.

74. *The Laws of Jamaica* (Kingston, Jamaica: 1898), Law 5 of 1898, 'The Obeah Law, 1898,' https://ecollections.law.fiu.edu/jamaica/60. The 1898 Act repealed several prior anti-obeah and anti-Myal laws including the 1856 law, 19 Vict. c. 30 for punishing 'Obeah and Myalism;' 21 Vict. c. 24 for punishing 'Obeah and Myalism;' Law 28 of 1892, 'The Obeah and Myalism Acts Amendment Law, 1892;' and Law 1 of 1893, 'The Obeah and Myalism Acts, Further Amendment law, 1893.'

75. C. L. R. James, *The Black Jacobins: Toussaint L'Ouverture and the San Domingo Revolution* (New York: Random House, 1963), 135; Mavis C. Campbell, *Maroons of Jamaica, 1665–1796: A History of Resistance, Collaboration, and Betrayal* (Granby, MA: Bergin & Garvey, 1988), 209.

76. Dr. Thomas Coke, *A History of the West Indies Containing the Natural, Civil, and Ecclesiastical History of Each Island: With an Account of the Missions 2* (London: 1810), 275. By comparison, it took the Moravian mission in Jamaica some fifty years to achieve a similar number of baptisms.

77. Coke, *History of the West Indies*, 274.

78. Ibid., 275.

79. Ibid., 274.

80. Ibid., 275.

81. Findlay and Holdsworth, *Wesleyan Methodist Missionary Society*, 55.

82. Coke, *History: of the West Indies*, 279.

83. Ibid., 276.

84. Ibid., 277; also see, St Vincent National Archives (hereinafter SVGNA). *St. Vincent Handbook 1912*, 11–12.

85. Findlay and Holdsworth, *Methodist Missionary Society 2*, 70.

86. Ibid., 68.

87. Ibid.

88. Coke called the law 'The Jamaica Act of the suppression of Methodism,' Findlay and Holdsworth, *Methodist Missionary Society*, 69. Keith Hunte, 'Protestantism and Slavery in the British Caribbean,' in *Christianity in the Caribbean*, ed. Armando Lampe, 104 (Barbados: University of the West Indies Press, 2001).

89. Findlay and Holdsworth, *Methodist Missionary Society 2*, 69.

90. Ibid.

91. Ibid.

92. Ibid., 70.

93. Ibid.

94. Ibid., 70–71.

95. Ibid., 71.

96. Ibid., 72.

97. Ibid., 15.

98. Ibid.

99. Ibid.

100. Ibid., 16–17.

101. Ibid., 19.

102. Ibid., 22.

103. Ibid.

104. Ibid., 21–23.

105. Ibid., 9–10.

106. Ibid., 10.

107. Ibid., 26.

108. Ibid., 30.

109. Findlay and Holdsworth, *Methodist Missionary Society* 2, 32. *The Baptist Magazine* 2 (1810), 41. Google Book.

110. Hunte, 'Protestantism and Slavery,' 104–05.

111. *Baptist Magazine* 2 (January 1810), 41; also, *Findlay and Holdsworth, Wesleyan Methodist Missionary Society,* 33.

112. *Baptist Magazine* 2 (January 1810), 41.

113. Ibid.

114. Ibid., Emphasis is original.

115. Fergus, *Revolutionary Emancipation,* 152.

116. Hunte, 'Protestantism and Slavery,' 105–06. Martin, *Caribbean History,* 185.

117. Smith, 'Slavery and Christianity,' 179–80.

118. Ibid., 180.

119. Ibid., 184.

120. Ibid., 180.

121. Catherine Hall, 'The Missionary Dream, 1820–1842,' 101, https://www.bllackwellpublishing.com/content/bpl_images/Content_Store/Sample_Chapter/0745618200/chapter1.pdf, accessed January 10, 2023, excerpt from Catherine Hall, *Civilising Subjects: Metropole and Colony in the English Imagination, 1830–1867* (Chichester, West Sussex, UK: Wiley, 2002).

122. Martin, *Caribbean History,* 185.

123. Jewel Fitila, 'The Realms of Absolute Power,' Facebook, accessed August 5, 2022.

124. Smith, 'Slavery and Christianity,' 181.

125. Martin, *Caribbean History, 185*; Baptist Missionary Society, 'World Mission: Jamaica,' https://www.bmsworldmission.org/heritage/jamaica/.

126. See Fergus, *Revolutionary Emancipation,* 134.

127. Vincent Leahy, *History of the Catholic Church in Trinidad, 1797–1820* (Arima, Trinidad: St. Dominic, 1980), 54.

128. See Fergus, *Revolutionary Emancipation,* 136–37.

129. Robin Blackburn, 'Haiti, Slavery, and the Age of the Democratic Revolution,' *William and Mary Quarterly,* Third Series 63, no. 4 (October 2006), 648

130. Fergus, *Revolutionary Emancipation,* 137.

131. Ibid.

132. 'Letter from [Thomas] Talboys, Trinidad, to Revd Dr [Thomas] Coke & the [Wesleyan Methodist] Committee,' London, March 29, 1811, [Wesleyan] Methodist Missionary Society Archive, School of Oriental and African Studies (SOAS) Archives, University of London, GB 102 MMS/17/03/03/06/03/48,' on the Archives Hub, http://archiveshub.jisc.ac.uk/data/gb102-mms/mms/17/03/03/06/03/48, accessed September 1,2023.

133. 'Letter from Talboys,' WMMS Archive on the Archives Hub.

134. Fergus, *Revolutionary Emancipation*, 138.

135. Ibid.

136. Bathurst to Woodford, 8 Nov. 1817, BNA CO 296/5.

137. WMMS Archive. Box 2, 9 May 1818, SOAS, mf. 66.

138. Ibid., Copy of original letter by Whitehouse to Murray, 2 May 1818.

139. WMMS Archive. Box 2, 9 May 1818, SOAS, mf. 66. Anthony Kewley to Richard Watson, 28 July 1818.

140. Bathurst to Woodford, 8 Nov. 1817, BNA CO 296/5.

141. 26 *Parliamentary Debates, 'Doctrine of the Trinity Bill,'* 20 July 1813, 1222.

142. Russell to Secretary Light, February 15, 1840, extracted from *Parliamentary Papers* (1849) 34, in *Select Documents on British Colonial Policy 1830–1860*, eds. Kenneth N. Bell and W. P. Morrell, 415 (Oxford: Clarendon Press, 1968).

143. Boa, 'Colour, Class and Gender,' 244, 262.

144. Ibid., 263.

145. Ibid., 264.

146. Ibid.

147. Ibid.

148. Ibid., 64.

149. Williams James, *AZ Quotes*, https://www.azquotes.com/quote/530410, accessed March 2, 2022.

150. Veront M. Satchell, 'Bedwardism,' in *The Encyclopedia of Caribbean Religions* 1, eds. Patrick Taylor and Frederick I. Case, 120 (Urbana, IL: University of Illinois Press, 2013); James, 'Pocomania,' 328.

151. Satchell, 'Bedwardism,' 120.

152. Frances Henry, *Reclaiming African Religions in Trinidad: The Socio Political Legitimation of the Orisha and Spiritual Baptist Faiths* (Barbados: University of the West Indies Press, 2003), 80. After 1970, Shango fell out of use for the more generic Orisha, meaning devotees of all the Orishas (deities) of Ifa.

153. 'The Fundamental Constitutions of Carolina: March 1, 1669 (1) (2),' https://avalon.law.yale.edu/17th_century/nc05.asp, accessed on July 29, 2022.

154. John Locke et al., *A Collection of Several Pieces of Mr. John Locke* (London: 1739): the document is part of John Adams Library at the Boston Public Library, https://www.ncpedia.org/fundamental-constitutions, accessed July 31, 2022.

155. 'Act of Toleration (1689),' *Encyclopedia Virginia*, https://www. encyclopediavirginia.org, accessed August 26, 2021; also see, 'Article 1, Virginia Constitution,' Ballotpedia, https://ballotpedia.org/Article_1,_ Virginia_Constitution, accessed July 31, 2022.

156. George Vandeleur Fiddes, *The Dominions and Colonial Offices* (London: Putnams, 1921), 43. Internet Archive.

157. Regina v Registrar General, Ex parte Segerdal: CA 1970, https://
      swarb.co.uk/regina-v-registrar-general-exparte-sergedal-ca-1970/.

158. Equality Act 2010, c. 10, *UK General Public Acts*, https://www.legislation.
      gov.uk/ukpga/2010/15/part2/chapter/1.   Equality   and   Human
      Rights Commission, 'Religion or Belief: a Guide to the Law,' 2016,
      https://www.equalityhumanrights.com/sites/default/files/religiom-
      or-belief-guide-to-the-law.pdf.

159. The Supreme Court (UK), 'Judgment,' https://www.supremecourt.uk/
      cases/docs/uksc-2013-0030-judgment.pdf; John Bingham, 'Scientology
      is a religion, rules the Supreme Court,' *The Telegraph*, December 11, 2013,
      http://www.telegraph.co.uk/news/religion/10510301/Scientology-
      is-a-religion-rules-Supreme-Court.html, accessed September 21, 2017.

CHAPTER 4

Prelude to Prohibition

'It is impossible to change the emotions of a people by legislation'

Prohibition of Dissenting Protestants in the British Caribbean was only marginally about the right of conscience but more particularly, the political and cultural hegemony of European and European-descended elites. This fact was evident as early as the first wave of prohibition from the late eighteenth to early nineteenth century. The joint petition of the 'Three Denominations of Protestant Dissenters' to the Board of Trade in 1808 prayed for relief from the Jamaica Prohibition Act of November 1807, which put them under the same 'spirit of domination' that denied Africans 'the common rights of humanity.'[1] Inherent in the plan of White domination in the Caribbean enterprise was the intellectual and cultural subjugation of Africans. Nothing was more threatening to the White-supremacy system than an African who rejected his or her assigned status to become an independent thinker and actor. The main reason for the imperial government's rapid deployment of formal education and Christianisation at the dawn of Emancipation was to achieve this objective. By the end of the nineteenth century the project had achieved only partial success.

Why Spiritual Baptists Were Specifically Targeted for Persecution

Spiritual Baptists became a force that colonial elites found the most difficult to reckon with because of two main reasons. The first

---

* Acting-Governor Philip Cork to Earl of Crewe, September 6, 1908, 276, BNA, CO 321/243.

was religious competition within small polities: the independence and rapid growth of Spiritual Baptists successfully challenged the cultural-cosmological dominance of the 'recognised' Churches. The African American Baptist Church in Trinidad was not targeted for proscription because it had grown little, if at all, since slavery. This denomination was not formally established in St Vincent. The most popular self-identification of Spiritual Baptists in St Vincent at the turn of the century was 'Converted' or 'Penitent.' Before prohibition, the Converted made no claims to be a Baptist denomination but they certainly claimed to be Christians. The same applied to Trinidad, even the term Converted being used. Colonial elites feared that the 'African form of worship' of the Converted would seriously undermine Europeanised norms, if it was not checkmated. This concern was explicitly addressed in the Legislative Council debate on Prohibition in St Vincent and Trinidad and Tobago.

The economic perspective preceded the rise of Spiritual Baptist. During his visit to the Montserrat hills in Trinidad in 1867, Charles Kingsley was fascinated with the Yoruba farmers whom he said contributed to a fund 'on which they may draw in case of illness or misfortune.'[2] This was the Yoruba/Igbo financial institution called *susu* or *esusu*, which they had reintroduced as indentured labourers. By the end of the nineteenth century, all sectors of the Black working class had adopted the *susu*, which remains a popular system of thrift regardless of social class. The *susu* complemented the Mutual Friendly Societies. Both institutions were popular among the Spiritual Baptists. Together they provided the financial wherewithal for the Spiritual Baptists to defeat the strategies of subservience that would otherwise have weakened their resolve to maintain religious independence. While scholars have adequately dealt with the issue of religious independence, they have generally failed to impart equal or any significance to Friendly Societies and *susu* as a factor in the heightened aggression against Spiritual Baptist at the turn of the nineteenth century.

There are two main types of Friendly Societies: the fraternal secret orders, the oldest and most iconic of which is Freemasonry, and the mutual-aid associations. Common to both types of societies is the Lodge, which refers to the meeting-place of the society as well as its members. Whereas secret orders promote charity to non-members, mutual-aid institutions provide financial benefits and psychological support in time of need, particularly in cases of sickness and the death of members or their kinfolk; they also make lump sum payments for capital projects.[3] Our primary interest in this study is the mutual-aid organisations generically labelled Mutual Friendly Societies.

Prior to emancipation in the British Caribbean colonies, Friendly Societies were almost exclusively of the secret Orders. Between 1738 and 1742, Freemasonry was established in all Britain's leading Caribbean plantation colonies, the first in Antigua.[4] Trinidad's oldest Lodge, *Les Frères Unis* (The United Brotherhood), was established in 1794 under the Grand Orient of France at Duncan Street, then called La Rue Trois Chantrelles (Three Candles Street) in Port of Spain.[5] Trinidad was then a Spanish colony dominated by French-speaking planters; in 1798, in the second year of British occupation, it was incorporated under the Grand Lodge of Pensylvannia.[6] From inception, Freemasonry became interwoven into the power structures of colonial societies no less so than in the imperial homelands. The most powerful slave owners, merchants, government officials and military officers were Masons.[7] On the other hand, the working class dominated the Mutual Friendly Societies but under the management of church authorities. Mutual Friendly Societies entered the British Caribbean via Jamaica during the waning years of slavery. The first lodge was founded in 1828.[8] For all other colonies, however, Friendly Societies were primarily a post-emancipation phenomenon.

Free Blacks within Caribbean slave colonies, Britain and the US eagerly joined secret societies, like Freemasons, whenever allowed.[9] Many separated from the parent bodies and formed independent lodges. One of the most significant independent societies of free Africans in Britain was the Sons of Africa, founded around 1787. Their activities included advocacy for abolition of the Atlantic slave trade and emancipation. On the other side of the Atlantic, several free Africans in North America also established associations with distinctive African labels. These included the Free African Society, a mutual-aid society for emancipated Africans, founded by Richard Allen and

Absalom Jones in Philadelphia in 1787. That same year, Prince Hall established African Lodge No. 1, affiliated to the White Freemasons. Hall was born into slavery, probably in Barbados, but enjoyed freedom in Boston, became a Congregationalist and joined the Freemasons. He also used his Lodge as a place of worship.[10] By 1800, many other lodges became the launch pad for Black churches and maintained close ties between the two.[11] African-American refugees from the Revolutionary War also pioneered independent Friendly Societies wherever they settled. By 1834, members of the Black Baptist Church in Nova Scotia had established the African Friendly Society and the African Abolition Society.[12]

Notwithstanding this early development, the imperial Churches maintained their dominance over these institutions for several decades of the post-emancipation Caribbean. Although the Anglican Church introduced the first Friendly Society in St Vincent, the Methodists quickly became the prime mover of these Societies. Not surprisingly, as early as 1841, the total number of Societies and the size of membership in that island almost doubled those of Trinidad, which were all owned by the Church of England up to that time.[13]

In the second half of the nineteenth century, independent Black Friendly Societies began to mushroom across the British-ruled Caribbean with Black Baptist churches in the lead. In the case of Trinidad, expansion followed immediately after the passage of the first regulatory law, the Friendly Societies Act of 1888.[14] The number of Societies rose from twenty-three in 1880 to fifty-seven in 1900 and two hundred and twelve in 1915, almost a ten-fold increase within thirty-five years. Correspondingly, membership rose from 4,624 in 1880 to 23,900 and forty-five in 2015, a six-fold increase. Cash balances also rose sharply from $7,000 to $135,000 in the same period.[15]

African-Caribbean and African-American Friendly Societies were existentially contiguous with ancient African secret societies or, as Michael Gomez prefers to call them, 'societies of secret.' Many founding members of the African-American societies were African-born and first-generation descendants of Native Africans.[16] Some of the better known African societies include the Ekpe (Egbo) of the

Efik and Ibibio; the Ogboni and Okonko of the Yoruba; the Poro (Purrah) and Sande (also known as Bundu) of the Mende (Mandinka) people of Senegambia. These societies still exist in West Africa.[17] The training in these institutions equipped Africans with skills of manhood and womanhood that prepared them for prominent roles in society. It also prepared many to respond to the worse terrors of enslavement in European colonies in ways that baffled their torturers. There is no shortage of accounts of Africans who remained stoically silent while being brutally flogged, disfigured, dismembered or burnt to death.[18] Such individuals were students and graduates of African secret societies. In many slave colonies, Africans in bondage re-established their secret-society culture. Where favourable demography allowed, some retained exclusive ethnic affiliations; others took on a Pan-African outlook. These societies were known to flourish in early nineteenth-century Trinidad where they had names such as 'Convois' and 'Regiments.'[19] In Cuba, the Abakua Society was an offshoot of enslaved Ekpe of southern Nigeria; the Cabildos were African secret societies that also operated with the sanction of the Cuban enslaver class.[20] The resettlement of Liberated Africans from Cuba to Trinidad may also have transferred practitioners of these societies. Although no direct evidence exists, it is quite likely that the Merikins would have had contact with, or membership in, Friendly Societies, either as soldiers in the British army or as sojourners in Canada and Bermuda. It is also likely that the experience of Nova Scotia refugees in Friendly Societies came to the Caribbean via Sierra Leone. In many of these scenarios, there are links with the Black Baptist Church.[21]

The earliest evidence for the marriage of Friendly Societies and Caribbean black Baptists in the Caribbean comes from testimonies of prohibitionists in St Vincent and Trinidad. The most outspoken was Anglican pastor, S. F. Branch, in a memorandum to the West India Royal Commission of 1897. Branch likened the Friendly Societies to a vehicle for economic and intellectual emancipation that would upset the post-emancipation status quo in St Vincent, if allowed to continue unabated. Writing as an advocate for the plantocracy, he expressed strong objection to any form of association that would afford labourers bargaining power over their employers. Reminiscent of Charles Day's sentiments on emancipation, Branch asserted,

> The [plantation] labourers in St Vincent have not yet been
> educated enough to combine for higher wages, but it would
> be wise if the employers in time, by a liberal policy, gave no
> occasion for combination.[22]

He seemed to begrudge labourers on sugar plantations the right to expect increased wages when export prices were high even though they were expected to endure patriotic suffering when prices fell. He was also against government's land-reform policy in breaking up estates to facilitate independent peasant farming. Only as a labouring class were Africans to be of value to the economic elites. Branch saw a connection between the fate of plantation labour and the popularity of progressive-thinking Black church leaders. He railed, 'We have an excitable, suspicious, and still ignorant labouring population, drifting away from the old clerical control, as shown in the numerous new friendly societies, all self-managed and not as heretofore directed by ministers of religion.'[23]

Denominational societies were affiliated to their respective Church organisations. Although there was a new influx of religious organisations toward the end of the nineteenth century, their venture into Friendly Societies was negligible; in any case, they had their own recognised clergy. Because Penitentism was not a 'recognised' religion, the government would not have pinned any society to their name in the official *Blue Books*. Branch leaves no doubt, however, that most of the patrons of 'the recent self-constituted religious societies' were the Penitents, when he wrote in his memo:

> The labourer, by his lay, friendly and religious societies
> and his revolt from the healthy control of the clergy of the
> Church and ministers of Wesleyan body shows he is testing
> the pleasure of thinking and determining for himself.[24]

As in North America, Spiritual Baptist lodges also served as places of worship. Herskovits and Herskovits noted, 'Participation of the shouters resembles that of a lodge.'[25] Any doubt about this conclusion is dispelled by St Vincent's Administrator Gideon Murray in his report to the governor immediately following the passage of his prohibition ordinance in 1912: 'Now that the Bill is law I expect that in a few weeks these lodges will likewise be closed down and that Shakerism in St Vincent will be as dead as mutton.'[26] One may logically assume a similar attack on the lodges in Trinidad as a strategy for eradicating the Shouters. Statistics point to a reversal in the pre-prohibition trend of expansion of Friendly Societies compared to the post-prohibition decade.[27] Field research conducted by Herskovits and Herskovits revealed that even if the Shouters' lodges in north-east Trinidad were closed as places of worship, the association of the Shouters as lodge people was still in vogue in the late 1930s, 'like the Rose of Sharon or other secret societies.'[28] Wallace Zane was more explicit: 'When the Shouters are compared to other groups in Toco, they are equated not so much with churches as with "orders," and they are often referred to as a lodge.'[29] Evidently, Spiritual Baptists' dominance in the second wave of expansion of Friendly Societies provided an economic rationale for prohibition that was closely intertwined with the challenge to White-controlled recognised denominations.

Gatekeeper of Religious Toleration Confront the First Shakerism Prohibition Bills

The government of St Vincent first seriously considered prohibition of the Penitents in late 1901. The administrator, Edward John Cameron, had arrived just a few months earlier. He was persuaded that the Penitents were enjoying a revival after an assumed weakening of the sect. Cameron considered bringing an Ordinance but the Executive Council had no law officer at the time; the catastrophic eruption of the Soufriere volcano in mid-1902 was the second pre-emptive factor but Cameron did not waste much time in refocusing on the Shakers.[30] In late 1903, he drafted his first prohibition bill 'to suppress any sort of religious meetings after sunset with the exemption of those "recognised religious denominations,"' which were identified in Section 2 of the bill as the Protestant Church of England, the Roman Catholic Church, the Church of Scotland, Wesleyan Methodist and 'any other religious denomination' recognised by government.[31] The bill did not specifically mention the Penitents or any of the newly arrived Euro-

American sects most of which had shared the corybantic style of liturgy with the Penitents and might even have been thought of as the objects of state prejudice under this ordinance. Nevertheless, the racist phrasing of the preamble left no doubt that it was an ordinance to outlaw Penitentism. The preamble affirmed that 'in the night time' many inhabitants in rural communities indulged in 'a practice of loud singing and praying ... and other pseudo religious practices at houses and places,' whenever those meetings were not presided over 'by the minister of any Christian religion.' Cameron also justified the ordinance because the alleged practices 'tend to exercise a pernicious and demoralising effect upon the said inhabitants.' The bill required the 'representative' applying for a licence to be 'the principal ordained minister or lay exponent' of a 'recognized religious denomination;' the bill delegated to the chief of police the right to determine an 'authorised Person' or his 'duly appointed servant' for this purpose. This was a new role for the police. Under this law, the Police could also invoke Article 6 to enter any meeting place suspected of having an unauthorised meeting without a warrant.[32] Because the PWRA recognised 'any other Body or Denomination of Persons' for equal enjoyment of the right of conscience, Cameron's concern that Penitentism was a threat to public health and safety was the sole selling point in the ordinance. The Legal Advisory Commission of the General Synod of the Church of England explained,

> A nuisance at common law consists of an unlawful interference with a person's use and enjoyment of his property. Making unreasonable noise is actionable as a nuisance and there are a number of earlier authorities which accept that the ringing of noisy church bells may constitute a nuisance.[33]

Coincidentally, the Jamaica government also introduced a public health bill in the Legislature in 1903 entitled, 'A Law to prohibit the holding of Noisy Assemblies,' a throwback to the days of slavery;[34] The ordinance was clearly intended to outlaw *Pukumina* and Revival Zion that the bill disparaged as 'Corybantic Christianity.' The pretext for prohibition was that Revival Zion had become a public nuisance, to wit, that 'in certain Towns and Districts hymns and noises kept up throughout the night make sleep impossible.' In 1884, Jamaica's representative system was partially restored. By 1901, the fourteen elected members in the Legislative Council were still outnumbered by officials and nominated members. The Select Committee of the Legislature rejected the Bill on the ground that it was 'too onerous' and inconsistent with the Toleration Acts.[35] In 1911, the attorney general introduced an alternative Bill, 'A Law to compel persons to desist in the night time from disturbing others,' otherwise known as 'The Noises (Night) Prevention Law,' which was carefully drafted 'to prevent frivolous and vexatious prosecutions,' by ensuring 'that the written consent of a clerk of the courts must be obtained before the law is put in motion.'[36] Liabilities for violating the Noises Prevention Act were considerably less onerous than those prescribed in Cameron's draft bill. *Pukumina* and Revival Zion were saved from prohibition because Jamaican authorities ultimately respected the Places of Worship Registration Act and religious toleration laws in general, which seasoned Governor Augustine Hemming respected as constitutional protection of Christian sects, however described, to which African-Jamaicans had given birth. Hemming had an extensive career in the Colonial Office rising through the ranks from assistant junior clerk in 1860 to chief clerk from 1879 to 1896 and private secretary to the permanent under-secretary for the Colonies. This was a time of radical advancements in laws of religious toleration, most of which impacted the colonies. Before his tenure in Jamaica, he was governor of British Guiana, one of the most religiously diversified British colonies in the Caribbean.

Although Jamaica's 1903 bill was presented as a nuisance law, the governor was compelled to withdraw it because the word 'Assemblies' implied religious gatherings. On the other hand, Administrator Cameron brazenly titled his Bill, 'An Ordinance to regulate the gathering of persons for religious purposes and to prohibit certain practices.'[37] Even its short title, the 'Religious meetings regulation ordinance 1903,' was bound to raise the red flag to imperial lawmakers. Cameron truthfully stated in the bill that its objective was to suppress 'religious meetings' of the Shakers, especially in the rural areas. Cameron was also no neophyte to colonial governance. He previous served as commissioner in the Turks and Caicos Islands from 1893 to 1899; he was a member of the Executive Council of the Leeward Islands from 1887 to 1893;[38] he ought to have known that the PWRA accorded all Christian sects the same religious protection in the colonies as in Britain. One valuable benefit of that experience was his awareness that proscription of any aspect of a religious sect was 'a thorny issue to legislate for.'[39]

Cameron's bill was clearly unconstitutional and discriminatory by freeing the first four categories of Churches from licensing conditionalities, while subjecting all others to the whim of the governor. Article 3 was the most controversial and most extreme departure from the toleration laws and the duties of governor. It sought to create a special power to the governor in Council 'to grant a licence to hold convene or organise meetings and services for religious purposes to the representative of any religious organisation not specified in section 2' of the ordinance. *The Colonial List*, an official publication of the Colonial Office, did not specify a religious role for governors beyond 'the power of granting licences for marriages.'[40] Article 4 of the bill stated,

> It shall be an offence against this ordinance for any person other than the representative or a duly appointed servant of a recognised religious denomination to hold after sunset or to convene organise or promote to be held at any house or place any meeting of persons at which any form of singing praying preaching or any religious or pseudo-religious practices rites or ceremonies are intended to be or are in fact carried on....

Article 5 deemed it an offence for a worshipper 'to commit or cause to be committed any act of indecency or immorality' at any meeting such as defined in Article 4 and made it an offence for anyone else 'at or in the vicinity' of a Shakers' meeting to commit 'any act of indecency or immorality.' The bill, however, did not identify any specific activities that could be legally deemed indecent or immoral.

English-born Chief Judge Percy Musgrave Sheriff provided the legal advice to Cameron that he would have needed to pursue his original plan of prohibition in 1901. Sheriff arrived in St Vincent in late 1902 to serve as acting-chief justice and provisional member of the Executive Council. In October 1903, he was re-appointed acting-chief justice.[41] He was confirmed as chief justice in December and would have been enjoying security of tenure when he commented on the bill in April 1904.[42] Sheriff was a seasoned colonial civil servant. He was first posted to British Honduras in 1893 shortly after being admitted to the bar. He spent his first ten years of colonial service in the Caribbean, including Jamaica, Belize, and Grenada. Based on his experience and knowledge of the Toleration Laws, Sheriff was apprehensive of the Colonial Office's reaction to Article 3 and noted, 'I fear the S. of S. may not like this.'[43] Sheriff realised that Article 4 was so sweeping that it had implications for all denominations in the island, particularly for leaders who might not find favour with a governor. He queried whether organisers of common events like the 'Sacred Concerts' of the Church of England might face liabilities under Article 4. His final advice left no doubt that the bill transgressed the fundamental right of Penitents to religious freedom: he reasoned, 'The secretary of state may think this Bill cuts at the religious liberty of the subject; it would also raise (here) a hornet's nest about your ears (probably).'[44] The implication of this caution is significant: it contradicts the administrator's presumption that the bill was his response to widespread concerns about the presence of Penitents in the colony. That is the only reasonable interpretation of the 'hornet's nest' metaphor. Cameron had explained to Governor Robert Llewelyn that he drafted the bill because of 'a considerable stir in the religious circles here about Shakerism.'[45] Yet, the only evidence from clerical elites that Cameron provided the governor was two sermons of Methodist minister, Wilfrid Lawson Broadbent. Secular advocacy was also sketchy: he believed 'the local paper' had published an article on the subject but provided no other details; his only testimonials came from the Inspector of Schools, J. Hardin, and two medical doctors, T. M. R. Leonard and Christian William Branch.

Dr Branch was born in St Kitts and trained in medicine at the University of Edinburgh.[46] He was a brilliant surgeon employed as the Medical Officer in the Colonial Hospital in Kingstown but his major contribution to Cameron's effort to proscribe the Penitents was 'an interesting memorandum of his observations' since his arrival in St Vincent in 1902; he would later upgrade the memorandum into the article, 'Endemic Religious Insanity of the Island of St Vincent,' published in 1907 in *The Monist* journal. The article would play a bigger role in Cameron's second prohibition bill in 1908.

Whatever had informed Cameron of a Penitent revival, he would have been further convinced by the report of the Inspector of Schools. European imperialists always targeted children as the best subjects for indoctrination in the values and behaviours of the colonised; so, it must have been particularly alarming for the government to learn from the Inspector's report that the Penitents 'had literally taken possession of St Vincent' and were subjecting school children in rural communities to the rite of mourning.[47]

Cameron forwarded two of Broadbent's sermons, the first delivered in September 1903 and the second in April 1904. Broadbent was stationed at Mt Coke in Stubbs. He confessed to spying on Penitent meetings. In at least two written sermons, he tried to woo members of the group away from the older 'recognised churches' to the Methodist fold. His first sermon, 'Earnest Address to the Shakers,' began with a racist indictment of their practices as being 'more fitting for the fetish worship of pagan Africa than for this Christian land.' He condemned their liturgy as an 'intoxication of bacchanalian mirth' and made the familiar prohibitionists' allusion to insanity and immorality. He condemned the Penitents for the high percentage of 'unlawful' births but presented no comparison for African members of the recognised churches. Nothing irked him more than their religious independence. Accordingly, he appealed to them to 'stop further acts of blasphemy [and] return to your churches.'[48]

Broadbent cited extensively from the Inspector of School's report on the case of a single pupil of Stubbs primary school who had gone 'on the knee,' an alternative term for mourning. He shared the Inspector's concern for the performance of that single pupil who became a Penitent but neither he nor Cameron expressed concern over the alarming statistic that of the 5,078 pupils enrolled only 2,435 had an 'average attendance.'[49] Cameron was also not perturbed by the frequency of the loss of labour resulting from other causes such as industrial injuries or personal illnesses; furthermore, his concern that mourning interfered with 'the due performance of work' on estates must be seen against the economic backdrop of massive unemployment resulting from the collapsing sugar industry. From 1880 to 1902, sugar estates declined from sixty-three to thirty-three, compounded by the destruction of 'most of the sugar mill works' by the Soufriere volcanic eruption.[50] Interestingly, Governor Llewelyn had recognised this economic disaster as one of the key reasons for the renewed vitality of Penitentism.

In the first half of a second sermon on the Penitents, some six months later, Broadbent tactically combined an imperious attitude of the frontier missionary with expediency as he sought to win the Penitents over to his church. He admonished imperiously, 'You are introducing into a Christian country African forms of worship and are practising them under the guise of Christianity.'[51] Such an emphatic indictment could only come from someone who was ignorant of the history of Christianity or too conceited to acknowledge the truth. Africa was Christian before Europe; African missionaries facilitated the expansion of Christianity into Europe. Coptic Christianity, the Christianity of the Lower Nile Valley and Ethiopia, is older than Roman Christianity or Roman Catholicism. The Athanasian Creed composed by Athanasius, a Coptic Patriarch, is the foundation of the Roman Catholic's Nicene Creed and the Church of England's Thirty-Nine Articles of Faith.[52]

Although Broadbent had come a long way in six months, he maintained the red flag over Penitents' 'rejoicing.' He revealed that his authority on the matter came from Cameron who 'knew only one thing like it, namely the fetish-dance of the wild savages of Africa round their sacred trees, which he witnessed.'[53] Available sources do not reveal Cameron's personal experience in Africa prior to his appointment as governor of The Gambia in 1914. Broadbent tried repeatedly to put a wedge between the Methodists and 'the older churches.' He surmised that Penitents would naturally be disenchanted with the Anglican and Roman Catholic Churches because their forms of worship were 'too tame;' he acknowledged that Penitents wanted 'a more excitable method of service, with more lively singing and more freedom in prayer and less restraint from staid and quiet ministers.'[54]

Broadbent lambasted the older Churches as historical enemies of the Penitents. He lamented, 'Only cold-blooded and formal Christians will object to your prayer-meetings, providing everything is done orderly and with profound reverence, and you pray and sing "with the spirit" and "with the understanding also" (I Cor. 14:15).' Broadbent's citation was an unusual but deliberate endorsement of Penitent liturgy, the essence of which would eventually see them identifying as Spiritual Baptist. Broadbent's most far-reaching compromise concerned the rite of mourning, which he correctly, but partially, interpreted as 'meditation and prayer.' He indicated a willingness to accede to it as canonical within his understanding of the Christian context, if the initiates 'really do meditate and pray, and do not think their seclusion is the same as conversion.' Methodists shared with other Protestants the theology of conversion as the pathway to salvation and a whole new way of living. 'In Christianity, there are few doctrines more important than salvation,' states Christopher Bounds in an essay on the subject.[55] Subjected to scrutiny, Broadbent's submission was superficial, condescending and imperialistic. He could not acquiesce to mourning as conversion because it would amount to capitulation to the perception of Penitentism as an autonomous denomination over which the Methodist Church had no spiritual claim. Indeed, Broadbent's realisation that European church leaders had to compromise on African Christian liturgy did not diminish his confidence that Europeans were the divinely appointed spiritual shepherds of Africans. In a small way, the concession was a well-deserved victory for Penitentism, but if the Penitents were to enter a covenant with Methodism, as proposed by Broadbent, their Leaders and Mothers would have had to surrender their constitutional right to denominational independence to white, foreign control. In this regard, Broadbent was deploying the same strategy used to persuade Maroons to surrender their arms for a life of limited emancipation under White political supervision.[56]

Broadbent continued to treat the Penitents as if they still operated 'prayer houses' of Methodism in the days of slavery. His indictment of rejoicing was viciously racist, consistent with his first 'Appeal' sermon. He pontificated, *'It is an insult to God*, and for your *"praise-house"* to be turned into a *dance-house* is a disgrace to religion, and to sing holy songs during the "jigging" and "whipping" and "jumping" savours of dreadful blasphemy.'[57] Broadbent personally resented the acclaimed spiritual powers of the Penitents. He raged, *'Your claims to prophesying* are most preposterous. Who made *you* the successors of the ancient Bible seers? Who gave *you* the *power to discern visions?* Who revealed the future to *you?'*[58] Abandoning his initial concessionary tone, Broadbent thundered, *'Your midnight meetings are said to promote immorality.'* After six months, it was obvious from this statement that Broadbent and other prohibitionists were still reliant on hearsay and there was not one shred of evidence of immoral practices during Penitent meetings.

Dr Leonard was the medical officer of District Four. His report confirmed that 'a large number' of Penitents were to be found in villages in his district, especially Lowmans, Chapman, Byera, Friendly and Biabou where the two most outstanding Shaker leaders, Robert Williams and Allan Merry, resided and were personally known to him.[59] Leonard's report, Broadbent's sermons and the report of the Inspector of Schools all influenced Cameron's decision to prioritise the occurrence of Shakerism in remote villages. Cameron combined these documents with a much larger collection from prohibitionists in support of his second prohibition bill.

Whites who personally witnessed Penitent meetings invariably operated as spies or claimed to have done so: Broadbent was one, Leonard another. Leonard claimed, 'I have personally attended one of these Meetings unknown to the people and obtained evidence from eyewitnesses of other meetings.'[60] The incognito 'attendance' of a White medical doctor, who was well known within his district, reeks with suspicion as to how close to the meeting he got. In any case, no White witness succeeded in getting close enough to provide information on a Praise House or Mourning Ground. Whatever his vantage point, Leonard's testimony is crucial to establishing the Penitents as an authentic Christian sect deeply rooted in all communities many of which were not served by any other denomination. He postulated, 'Shakerism appears to be a low type of Methodism with the worship of spirits, good and evil, chiefly the latter.'[61] If interpreted in the contemporary context of High Church and Low Church of the Anglican Communion, Leonard's description, though pejorative recognises 'Shakerism' as working-class Methodist reformism embedded in an African cultural milieu. Services were held every Sunday night beginning about nine o'clock and lasting some five to six hours.

Demonisation of Penitentism was integral to prohibitionists' strategy to delegitimise the religion. Leonard's allegation that the Penitents' spirituality was primarily evil was undermined by his own admissions about their exemplary lifestyle. He claimed to have seen worshippers 'in the height of the excitement tearing off their clothes and dancing in a state of nudity;' he surmised that after a meeting, Penitents were 'physically incapable of any work next day.'[62] Despite this damnation, he admitted,

> I am not in a position to state definitely whether any immoral practices are carried out, not having got any actual facts as yet but in my opinion, the initiation ceremony, which I hear is a very weird one and is carried out by two leaders alone, no one being allowed to witness it and the mental excitement produced in the Meetings resulting in the tearing off of their clothes must lead to such practices.[63]

Dr. Branch was better informed on the administration of the mourning rite, that the two 'leaders' were the Teacher and the Nurse, the latter being ever present to tend to the physical wellbeing of the mourner and to ensure that the Teacher behaved in the most ethical manner, especially toward female mourners.[64] Leonard, nevertheless, concluded on a positive note: 'I have not seen any drunkenness or its effects in any cases under my treatment at the various dispensaries.'[65]

Leonard's portrait of Penitent cosmology as 'chiefly evil' also featured in Broadbent's sermon and was embraced by later prohibitionists not merely to demonise the Penitents but, more so, to represent their practices as the antithesis of Christianity. Since both men claimed eyewitness status, their testimonies would have been compelling to those in search of a justification for government's intervention. Leonard's claim that 'in the height of the excitement' – which others acknowledged as 'rejoicing' – the congregants would tear off their clothes while 'dancing about in a state of nudity,' must be read with scepticism. Broadbent's account of rejoicing entailed similar scenes of jumping, shaking and 'wild frenzy of excitement' but he contradicted Leonard's allegation of nudity. Broadbent did not witness any nudity despite claiming to have witnessed intoxication during rejoicing and one case of psychotic effect of tobacco on a young man who dashed himself on the ground 'like a maniac.'[66] Transcending Leonard's concern about morality and lunacy was Broadbent's perception of the economic impact of Penitent meetings. Leonard most likely exaggerated when he declared the extended hours of rejoicing left the Penitents 'quite exhausted and physically incapable of any work next day.' There are numerous records of enslaved Africans who spent all night in merriment and turned out to work at the break of day, nonetheless. Leonard branded Penitent followers in all the Villages in his District as 'lazy' and who avoided all labour. Such a charge contradicts the image of self-reliance and growing prosperity drawn by R. F. Branch to the Royal Commission a few years earlier.

Cameron observed due process and did not seek to operationalise his ordinance before extensive scrutiny by competent and impartial jurists. Thus, he inserted in the final article that the ordinance

> shall not come into operation until the pleasure of His Majesty The King not to disallow the same shall have signified to the Governor by the Secretary of State for the Colonies and no notification thereof published in the *Government Gazette*.[67]

This decision was exemplary, being informed by the royal mandate of 1809 on religious ordinances, addressed in the previous chapter.

Also following established protocol, Governor Llewelyn forwarded Cameron's Ordinance to Chief Justice Sir Charles James Tarring in Grenada for advice. Tarring had been serving in that post since 1897.

In his memo, Llewelyn equivocated on the status of Penitentism: he disagreed with Cameron that Penitentism was a 'religion' and disparaged the movement as an 'epidemic,' which could be contained by deploying the 'recognised religious denominations;' if not, he wanted to know 'on what grounds could we stop the "Meetings;"'[68] nevertheless, he wanted to confirm 'if stopping the Meetings after dark and on private premises could be considered as interfering with the "Religious" liberty of the subject.' Llewelyn was a seasoned colonial administrator having served as governor of Tobago and administrator of St Vincent in the late 1880s, when Penitentism was commonly believed to be a dying sect. In 1900 when he was transferred from The Gambia to assume the post of governor of the Windward Islands there was no doubt that Penitentism was not only alive and well but the most entrenched denomination in the island. Llewelyn recognised that it would be easy to invoke the Public Nuisance law to curb Penitent meetings. Under the 'Summary Offences Act 1854,' persons keeping 'public or subscription dances' were to be arrested, if they continued beyond midnight, but only if the hosts failed to heed police warnings to stop. Invoking this law against meetings in rural communities posed a different challenge because villagers would hardly be expected to complain about such activities. In that event, the governor suggested that Cameron could invoke the laws against wakes, but acknowledged the limited potential of those laws. Violation of laws limiting the hours of wakes and dances were deemed 'petty offences.' The 1854 Act also punished persons attending wakes beyond 10:00 p.m. 'to the annoyance or disturbance of any inhabitant or neighbour.'[69] In desperation the governor asked Tarring, 'Can you refer me to any law in any other part of the world which might be adapted to check this degrading practice now I fear spreading in St Vincent.'[70]

Although Tarring personally favoured proscribing Penitentism, his role as legal advisor to the governor demanded that he privilege the law and not his own prejudices. In denouncing the proposed duty assigned to the governor in the highly contentious Article 3, Tarring warned that it was unlikely that the secretary of state for the Colonies would sanction 'any Ordinance for "regulating the gathering of persons for religious purposes;"'[71] furthermore, the British public might be incensed if the law were ever mentioned in Parliament. He counselled that it would be unlawful for the 'governor in Council to "grant a licence to hold convene or organise meetings and services for religious purposes to the representative of any religious denomination."' Knowing that he and the governor were on the same page of the prohibition playbook, Tarring suggested,

> It seems to me the line to take in any legislation is to strike at *the thing* not the name. I should carefully avoid the words 'religion', 'religious', 'services', 'denomination', 'representative', 'authorized person,' and other such expressions.

Tarring assured the governor that he was 'near the truth in refusing to consider Shakerism as a religion.' Seeing that to be the case, Tarring asked rhetorically, 'But why legislate as if you thought it was?'[72]

Tarring doubted that Penitentism could be legislated out of existence; but if the government should persist with legislation against the sect, he would agree that their practices should be treated 'as a nuisance or disorderly conduct.' He reminded the governor, 'even prostitution is not a crime by any English law, though keeping disorderly houses and affording opportunities for it are.' That was the position taken in Jamaica after the failure of the *Pukumina*/Revival Zion prohibition bill. In respect of Llewelyn's request for case law in other jurisdictions, Tarring replied, 'I do not at present call to mind any laws that might be adapted to check these practices.'[73] In actuality, Tarring did discover that some eastern European countries such as Austria and Russia still had 'plenty of laws against religious practices other than those of the established religion,' but he warned the governor, 'They are not models that could be followed in any British Colony.'[74] Governor Llewelyn agreed to the objections raised by Tarring and advised Cameron to withdraw the bill.

Cameron's Second Shakerism Prohibition Bill

Public enthusiasm for prohibition abated after Governor Llewelyn's veto because of the futility of continued effort so long as the same watchdogs were in office. Chief Justice Tarring demitted office in

1905; the following year, Llewelyn retired from the colonial service and returned to England; that same year, Chief Justice Sheriff left St Vincent to take up an appointment in St Lucia. With the departure of these gatekeepers of toleration, the political environment was once again conducive for prohibition. Immediately upon the departure of Llewelyn, Cameron commissioned Frank W. Griffith, the new chief of police, to produce a comprehensive intelligence report on Penitent places of worship throughout the colony. Because of the legally contentious objective of the mission, Cameron advised Griffith to maintain extreme discretion in order not to alert the Penitents. He urged, 'Caution should be used in this matter and the information gathered gradually in such a way as not to excite any curiosity or comment.'[75]

Llewelyn's successor, Welshman Sir Ralph Chamneys Williams, was a former colonial secretary in Barbados from 1897 to 1901 before assuming the post of resident commissioner in Bechuanaland (now Botswana) and Pretoria beginning 1901, under Lord Milner, high commissioner to South Africa.[76] Williams is the first of a long list of officials with links to South Africa, whose tenures overlapped with Cameron's successor as administrator, Charles Gideon Murray, the architect of the successful prohibition ordinance in 1912. The renewed advocacy for prohibition began under Williams' administration.

Methodist pastor, F. Ellis, arrived in the island in 1907 and immediately attributed the 'great evils' of the colony to the Penitents.[77] Of greater significance to Cameron's prohibition agenda was the publication that same year of Branch's scholarly article, 'Endemic Religious Insanity of the Island of St Vincent.' Branch began his article by affirming that Penitents' liturgy comprised 'a system of religious exercises.' He endorsed their religious character by acknowledging uncritically that they 'speak of themselves as the "Converted" or the "Penitents."'[78] He also acknowledged, 'The fundamental idea of their worship is the necessity for "Conversion" in the sense taught by Wesleyans, Salvation Army, Plymouth Brethren and other allied forms of Christianity.'[79] These sects were all present in St Vincent by that time adding dramatically to the marginalisation of the Spiritual Baptists.

To reinforce his judgement of Penitentism as authentic Christianity, he confirmed that their practices were 'a direct outcome of Wesleyan Methodism' and that there was nothing unusual about 'their extreme manifestation' because those practices were also associated with 'the revival meetings in Tortola in the Virgin Islands.'[80] Branch wrote from personal experience. Prior to his tenure in St Vincent, he had served as district medical officer in Tortola.[81]

Branch narrated an instance of a policeman who entered a 'penance house' or mourning ground and found several persons of both sexes asleep. The policeman's only conjecture was that they were worn out by their prayers.[82] This was the first claim by one of Cameron's informants to have entered the Penitents' sanctuary. It is therefore significant that the policeman debunked the allegations of white informants about scenes of copulation and other immoral behaviours. The article also debunked allegations of unethical and immoral conduct against Teachers during mourning. One woman, who had completed the mourning rite, assured Branch that whenever the Teacher who is in command of the mourning house enters the sanctuary at night to pray with the mourner, the Nurse is always present.[83]

Branch, however, demonised Penitentism as 'orgies of frenzied emotionalism,' which allegedly had a deleterious effect on the nervous system.[84] He also reduced the phenomenon of spirit possession during worship and the extraordinary discipline of mourners in the Penance House to 'hysteria and hypnotism,' which put too much power in the hands of Leaders and Mothers of the faith.[85] He concluded, 'A large proportion of those committed for lunacy in St Vincent have been Shakers;' nevertheless, he admitted, 'No statistics are available.'[86] Citing a 'Wesleyan Minister' – more likely than not, Broadbent – Branch iterated, 'Smoking is absolutely prohibited at meetings.'[87] On the impact of immorality, Branch again acknowledged, 'The writer has not been able to gather any evidence of immoral practices in connection with penitent services;' yet, he was able to 'arrive at the inevitable conclusion that the "rejoicings" of the penitents must very frequently end in episodes of sensuality.'[88] In the sixteenth century, the term orgy meant 'secret religious rites' but the documents relating to

Penitent prohibition carried two different meanings: it's eighteenth-century meaning, 'lacking legal or moral restraints especially disregarding sexual restraints;' or, its late-nineteenth-century meaning, 'a manifestation of extreme indulgence.'[89] Governor Llewelyn's reference to 'Shaker orgies in deserted spots in the country' might not have been a sexual reference, but rather one of 'extreme indulgence.'

Cameron discussed the Shaker question with Governor Williams during his first official visit to St Vincent in May 1908.[90] The timing was crucial. Shortly after, *The Times* newspaper made a strident call for prohibition of Penitentism. Its editorial began with a bigoted denunciation of the 'religious wave' of Euro-American sects that descended on the colony 'within the past decade.'[91] The Brethren established a presence in the colony in 1898, the Seventh Day Adventists in 1901 and the Salvation Army in 1905. *The Times's* description of their worship is noteworthy: 'The majority of the pastors of these organisations believe in an athletic style of worshipping God; they jump, dance, clap their hands, shout and gesticulate in a most unbecoming manner.' Without reference to the reverential title of Pastor, a reader might be forgiven for assuming that the object of editorial contempt was Penitentism.

The writer began by asserting that most of the increased numbers of lunatics were victims of this 'religious mania,' a claim that seriously challenged Branch's assumption. The writer also blamed the new missionaries for the revival of Penitentism. The writer acknowledged, 'Dwellers under the British flag boasts of religious toleration and freedom in serving God; this is a proud boast and one not to be despised.' Without reference to any toleration law, he concluded, 'But we cannot for a moment believe that Shakerism was intended.' He did not argue that 'Shakerism' was not a religion; only that it was 'more suited to savages than dwellers in a Christian land.' Interestingly, the reporter made no reference to immoral practices or substance abuse by Penitents at prayer meetings. Nevertheless, the report facilitated the mass circulation of the public health argument raised by the medical doctors, Leonard and Branch. He wrote,

> At these religious orgies some of the converts work
> themselves up to such a pitch of frenzy that they are for the

> moment oblivious of anything else and a frequent repetition
> of this state is in the end bound to result in madness.

As professed by the reporter, the only distinction between the liturgy of Penitents and that of the new Euro-American sects was the greater exuberance of the former. The newspaper called out the government 'to introduce an Ordinance giving the police power to break up all such meetings, prosecute the leaders and destroy the buildings devoted to the holding of these orgies.'[92]

The Times's report spread alarm among the Penitents. Immediately, one Penitent pastoral family demonstrated political acumen by applying to the land commissioner, J. B. Kernerhan, for a licence to construct a prayer house, located on the family's residential lot in New Adelphie. Rodney Allan's wife made the first application verbally to the land commissioner; her husband, Leader Rodney, followed up with a written application.[93] Kernerhan acknowledged the application was a direct reaction to *The Times's* publication and surmised that the Allans' strategy might have been designed 'to test the correctness of an impression … that the Government is about to stop Shakerism.'[94] Kernerhan confirmed, 'There is nothing in the Regulations to allow it or prevent it.' Under the PWRA, registration of houses of worship fell under the purview of the registrar, one of the many functions of the chief justice in St Vincent. Constitutional jurisdictions within the Empire that qualified for exemption from this law did not include Caribbean colonies.

The Times's report also impacted Griffith's investigation into the Shakers, which had been ongoing for a full year. As a result of *The Times's* advocacy, the administrator pressured Griffith to submit his report, which he did two months later. Griffith identified thirty-eight Praise Houses, of which thirty-three were purpose-built structures, the single largest number of specialised houses of worship of any denomination in the island.[95] Despite this evidence of growth and resilience, Griffith was hopeful that Shakerism would die out naturally on the return of better economic times and more aggressive proselytising by the recognised clergy. Griffith had called upon his trusted lieutenants in charge of various precincts to assist in the mission. At least one of these reports by Corporal Keane of the Barrouallie Station was deemed worthy of inclusion as a minority report to the secretary of state for the Colonies.

Keane reported on twelve Praise Houses personally known to him.[96] He affirmed that he was reporting on 'a form or practice of a religion … known as 'Converted or Shakerism.' Up to Prohibition, extempore was the characteristic mode of delivering sermons, prayers and hymns. The initiation 'Form' procured by Corporal Keane is, therefore, a crucial document, which affirms that the central tenet of Penitentism is salvation through faith in Christ and through credobaptism. According to Keane, Penitent meetings were extremely popular. 'Crowds of spectators' were always around the meetings.[97] They may well have been the most regular form of night-time socialising for rural folk. Although he reported that there were accusations of 'mischief by way of theft when returning home,' he was unable to say whether Penitents were at fault; nevertheless, he admitted that it was always Penitent members who bore the blame.[98] Most of the first part of Keane's report focussed on particulars of mourning. After the mourning period ended, members of the congregation formed a procession from the mourning house to accompany the spiritual pilgrims to the Praise House. Keane affirmed, 'The first part of the service is like the Wesleyan service' led by the Teacher; this was followed by exhorting after which the congregation joins with their own prayers.[99] He ridiculed 'rejoicing' in the second phase of worship as 'ridiculous to behold' but only described scenes of rejoicing which did not support allegations of immorality or indecency. Keane professed that Penitents were no different from members of other faiths: 'Smoking, drinking, swearing, stealing lieing (sic) and other immoral habits, though prevalent among them yet like other religions is quite contrary to the rule. The meeting always closed with the Doxology.'[100] Keane did not explicitly recommend banning Penitentism but branded it a lower-class religion whose 'form of worship is not tolerated by the upper and middle Classes.'[101]

Cameron's political candour in producing so many testimonies on the religious character of Penitentism was partly intended to prove former Governor Llewelyn wrong but in doing so, he made it impossible for his superiors to sanction his bill. Cameron categorically rejected Tarring's advice to omit all references to religion and religious organisations. After providing a brief history of his prohibition efforts, he stated hubristically, 'I think Sir R. Llewelyn took an erroneous view of the matter in regarding "Shakerism" as something apart from Religion.'[102] He contended, 'It is a distinctly religious manifestation, the outcome of the necessity inherent in the negro race of having an emotional outlet, and of propitiating the supernatural.'[103] To reinforce his opinion, he succinctly summarised the views of Broadbent, Keane and Branch:

> There is no dancing, postulating, or profanity whatever at the commencement of these meetings and thus no obvious reason for police interference such as Sir R. Llewelyn implied in his Minute of 21st April, 1904, on the subject of my Bill. It is just ordinary bible-reading and psalm-singing.[104]

Despite conceding that Penitents' prayer meetings deserved equal protection under law, Cameron sought to portray Penitentism as a public nuisance and a threat to public health requiring urgent government intervention. Leaning on Leonard's testimony, he argued,

> But it is in the later stage, that the element of white or other enlightened control being entirely absent the worshippers get worked up to the state described by those who have been onlookers and the degrading and demoralising practices take place.[105]

Without any concrete evidence of immorality from those onlookers, Acting-Governor Philip Cork would have been justifiably perplexed with Cameron's apparent afterthought: 'The actual immorality is the aftermath of the meeting.'[106] This accusation would have been worrisome to Colonial Office officials as well, after reading Corporal Keane's testimony that every Shaker meeting ended 'with the Doxology.' It is mindboggling that after many hours of prayers and rejoicing that culminated in doxology, worshippers would resort to immoral acts for the benefit of 'onlookers.'

Cameron was adamant that the Shakers must be controlled by legislation but realised that their rapid growth would make such a task extremely difficult. Taking a cue from Broadbent, he conceded that a syncretic compromise might be the only logical solution.[107] Thus, he adopted Sheriff's proposal that the episcopal churches aggressively extend their proselytising into the remote hills and valleys, enticing Shaker members with 'decent but less formal services' that would satisfy their 'emotional hunger' while keeping Shakerism 'under control.'[108] He iterated, 'If decent religions were well enough equipped and were sufficiently energetic and interested to fill that blank, the way would be a good deal smoothed.'[109]

If Cameron was comforted by Governor Williams' visit to revive his prohibition bill, he did not cater for the regency of Philip Cork as acting-governor of the Windward Islands when he finally submitted his bill for review. Cork was not a newcomer to Caribbean politics and administration: as the substantive administrator and colonial secretary of St Lucia, he was the second most senior administrator after the governor. Cork had acted as governor of the Windward Islands for three months after the departure of Llewelyn in 1906; moreover, he was acting-colonial secretary in Jamaica when the *Pukumina*/Revival Zion prohibition bill was presented to the House of Assembly in 1903 and rejected.[110] It was Cork as acting-governor of Jamaica in 1911 who assented to the 'Noises (Night) Prevention Law.'[111] St Vincent and Grenada enacted similar laws in 1911, which will be addressed in the next chapter. Cork described Shakerism as 'a local phase of emotional religious exaltation common to the negro race' and equivalent to the 'revivalism' of Bedwardism. He subscribed to Branch's view that the spiritual ecstasy manifested during rejoicing in the latter hours of worship was because of 'hysteria and hypnotism' but maintained, 'I do not believe that punishment by process of law would have any other effect than that of making martyrs of the so-called "Shakers."'[112]

Cork dismissed Branch's conclusion on the primary cause of lunacy in St Vincent and affirmed that the illness was much below the average for the three Windward Islands, St Lucia, St Vincent, and Grenada. He concluded, 'If Shakerism is the cause of lunacy in St Vincent other influences are quite as potent, or more so, in the other Islands.'[113] Cork similarly demolished Cameron's other justifications for prohibition by presenting figures to show that the rate of illegitimacy for St Vincent in 1907 had declined compared to that of the previous year. The marriage data also contradicted Cameron's alarm: the figure for 1907 showed 1.4 per cent increase in marriages over that of 1906. With the precedent of the failed *Pukumina*/Revival Zion bill as his point of reference, Cork assured his superiors in London: 'I do not recommend legislation as I think it would not be effective.'[114]

The Calm Before the Storm

Ultimately, the two primary targets of prohibitionists' assault on Penitents' freedom of conscience were the after-midnight rejoicing and the secrecy of mourning. Prohibitionists attached to rejoicing the most extreme expressions of immorality; and to mourning, the deleterious effects on sanity and the economy. Mourning and rejoicing were the cultural armour against which the 'recognised churches' had no effective weapon in their armoury, not even relentless demonising of Penitents. Their only hope was legislation and State oppression. The charge of immorality was mainly associated with dancing at the height of spiritual ecstasy. European colonials regarded the vivacious, energetic hip movements of women as sensuous or obscene and thus inappropriate for Euro-Christian church services. The accusation of the chief justice in 1850 that Converted had the potential 'to increase immorality' was substantiated solely on the African dance. About the same time, however, Methodist missionary William Fidler who had reported on the all-night prayer meetings of Wilderness People had praised them for their 'sexual morals.'[115] Fidler was aware of these dances accompanied by drumming both of which remained prohibited inside Methodist churches but he pragmatically acquiesced to the 'greater expressions of feelings of Africans during worship.[116] During slavery, African dance was feared more as a medium of communication and psychological preparation for war than its sensuousness. As allies of the plantocracy, missionaries played a major role in its suppression.[117] Consequently, African dance was woven into the colonial rhetoric of devilry. In general, missionaries demonised native dances around the world, but the Caribbean had a special marriage of dance and insurrection.

Of critical importance to the success of Gideon Murray's 1912 prohibition ordinance was the arrival and evaluation of Cameron's second bill in the Colonial Office when Murray was personal secretary to the under-secretary of state for the Colonies. Most of the key players involved in the conspiracy to sanction Murray's ordinance had access to Cameron's second bill with all its supporting enclosures. Keane was not the first to postulate Shaker worship as a dual phenomenon, but his testimony provided the clarity and text that Murray would weaponise against the Penitents and build a case for purging 'Shakerism' while preserving the right to prayer meetings. The reviews of Cameron's bill and enclosed testimonies provided valuable lessons for the evil machination of Gideon Murray to conceptualise two separate phenomena: Shakerism, to be eradicated; and Penitentism, to be tolerated.

Notes

1.   Findlay and Holdsworth, *Methodist Missionary Society 2*, 31.
2.   Charles Kingsley, *At Last: A Christmas in the West Indies* (London: MacMillan, 1871), 249.
3.   L. P. Fletcher, 'The Decline of Friendly Societies in Trinidad and Tobago,' *Caribbean Studies* 24, nos. 3 & 4 (1991), 60, https://www.jstor.org/stable/25612462.
4.   Dudley Wright ed., *Gould's History of Freemasonry Throughout the World 4* (New York: Charles Scribner, c. 1885), 150; 157, http://archive.org/details/GouldRFHistoryOfFreemasonryThroughoutTheWorldV41936Ed417p.
5.   Allison O. Ramsay, 'The Roots/Routes of the Ancient Order of Foresters in the Anglophone Caribbean with Special Emphasis on Barbados,' *History in Action* 2 no.1 (Apr. 2011), 3. *History in Action* is an online journal of the Department of History of the UWI, St Augustine Campus. The Lodge was brought to the island from St. Lucia.
6.   Wright, *History of Freemasonry*, 151.
7.   Darmon Richter, 'Freemasons of the Caribbean,' https://www.atlasobscura.com/articles/freemasons=of-the-caribbean, accessed August 19, 2014.
8.   Leonard Fletcher, 'The Friendly Societies in St Lucia and St Vincent,' *Caribbean Studies* 18, nos. 3 & 4 (October 1978–January 1979), 100, https://www.jstor.org/stable/25612842.
9.   Michael Bradshaw, 'True but Brief History of the Friendly Societies and Development of Black Bermudan Communities after Emancipation: Black People Seek Pride and Power in a Post-Slavery and Post-Emancipation World, the Bermudan Experience,' *Africology: The Journal of Pan-African Studies* 12, no. 1 (September 2018), 562; 566, https://www.jpanafrican.org/docs/vol12no1/12.1-34-Bradshaw%20(1).pdf.

10. Joanne Brooks, *American Lazarus: Religion and the Rise of African American and Native American Literatures* (New York, NY: Oxford University Press, 2003), 113.

11. Robert L. Harris, 'Early Black Benevolent Societies,' *The Massachusetts Review* 20, no. 3 (Autumn 1979), 619, https://www.jstor.org/stable/25088988.

12. Government of Canada, 'Significant Events in Black History in Canada,' https://www.canada.ca/en/canadian-heritage/campaigns/black-history-month/historic-black-communities.html.

13. Whereas St Vincent had nine societies with 1,128 members, Trinidad and Tobago had five with 656 members: see Fletcher, 'St Lucia and St Vincent,' 100; also, Fletcher, 'Trinidad and Tobago,' 60.

14. Fletcher, 'Trinidad and Tobago,' 60.

15. Ibid.' 62.

16. Michael Gomez, *Exchanging Our Country Marks: The Transformation of African Identities in The Colonial and Antebellum South* (Chapel Hill, SC: University of South Carolina Press, 1998), 94–101. He also referred to them simply as 'societies of men and women;' Harris, 'Early Black Benevolent Societies,' 611–12.

17. Claudius Fergus, 'African Secret Societies: Their Manifestations and Functions in West Atlantic Plantation Cultures,' in *Beyond Tradition: Reinterpreting the Caribbean Historical Experience*, ed. Heather Cateau and Rita Pemberton, 32–37 (Kingston, Jamaica: Ian Randle Publishers, 2006).

18. Fergus, *Revolutionary Emancipation*, 16–17.

19. Brereton, *History of Modern Trinidad*, 48–49.

20. Fernando Ortiz, 'The Afro-Cuban Festival 'Day of the Kings,' trans. Jean Stubbs, *Cuban Festivals: A Century of Afro-Cuban Culture*, ed. Judith Bettelheim (Kingston, Jamaica: Ian Randle Publication, 2001), 15–21; 44–45; also David H. Brown, 'The Afro-Cuban Festival "Day of the Kings": An Annotated Glossary' in *Cuban Festivals: A Century of Afro-Cuban Culture*, ed. Judith Bettelheim, 44–45 (Kingston, Jamaica: Ian Randle Publishers, 2001). Michael Barnett, trans. Christine Renata Ayorinde, *Afro-Cuban Religions* (Kingston, Jamaica: Ian Randle Publishers, 2001), 74–79.

21. Government of Canada, 'Significant Events in Black History in Canada.'

22. Tom Brass, *Toward a Comparative Political Economy of Unfree labour: Case Studies and Debates* (London: Frank Cass, 1999), n. 71, 178. Google Books.

23. Brass, *Unfree Labour*, 178.

24. Ibid.

25. Herskovits and Herskovits, *Trinidad Village*, 179.

26. Fraser, *From Shakers to Spiritual Baptists*, 36; Edward Cox, 'Religious Intolerance and Persecution: The Case of the Shakers in St Vincent,

1900–1934' (Unpublished paper), SVGNA, CR-RBC-179, 30; Cox's paper was presented to Annual Conference of the Caribbean Studies Association in 1993 and is available online.

27. Fletcher, 'Trinidad and Tobago,' 62, Table 1.

28. Herskovits and Herskovits, *Trinidad Village*, 179; 200.

29. Zane, *Spiritual Lands*, 246.

30. Cameron to Cork, Confidential, August 25 1908, BNA, CO 321/243.

31. Ibid.

32. Ibid.

33. Legal Advisory Commission of the General Synod, 'Ringing of Bells: Canon Law and the Potential Liability for Nuisance at Common Law and Under the Environmental Protection Act 1990,' *Legal Advisory Commission of the General Synod* (1992; updated 2008), https://www.churchofengland.org/sites/default/files/2017-12/bells.pdf.

34. *Jamaica 1911*, vol. 3 (June–August), BNA, CO 137/685, 140. Dana J. Epstein, *Sinful Tunes and Spirituals: Black Folk Music to the Civil War* (Chicago: University of Illinois Press, 2003), 59–60.

35. *Jamaica 1911*, vol. 3 (June–August), BNA, CO 137/685, 140.

36. *Jamaica Laws 1909–1913*, Law 31 of 1911, encl. in despatch 234 of 12 June 1911, BNA, CO 139/111.

37. Cameron to Cork, August 25, 1908, encl. in Cork to Crewe, 6 Sept. 1908, BNA, CO 321/243, 297.

38. Peoplepill, 'John Cameron,' https://peoplepill.com/people/edward-john-cameron, accessed June 2022.

39. Cameron to Llewelyn, April 11, 1904, encl. 5 in Cork to Crewe, September 5, 1904, BNA, CO 321/243, 293.

40. W. H. Mercer and A. E. Collins, comp., *The Colonial Office List 1905* (London: 1905), item 27, 419.

41. Mercer and Collins, *Colonial Office List 1905*, 574. *Government Gazette* 35, no. 211, December 1, 1902.

42. Cameron to Llewelyn, April 11, 1904, BNA, CO 321/243.

43. Cameron to Llewelyn, April 11, 1904, marginal note to Clause 3.1, BNA, CO 321/243.

44. Cameron to Llewelyn, April 11, 1904, BNA, CO 321/243, 301.

45. Ibid., 293.

46. Anon., 'Obituary,' *British Medical Journal* 2, no. 2537 (August 14, 1909), 427, https://doi.org/10.1136/bmj.2.2537.427-a accessed September 20, 2022.

47. Broadbent to Cameron, sermon no. 1, 'An Earnest Address to the Shakers of St Vincent, BWI,' September 21, 1903, encl. in Cork to Crewe, September 6, 1908, BNA, CO 321/243, 304.

48. Ibid.

49. W. H. Mercer and A. E. Collins, comp. *The Dominion Office and Colonial List* (London: 1908), 368.

50. Spinelli, 'Land Use,' 115.

51. Wilfrid Lawson Broadbent, 'A Second Address to the "Converted" or "Penitents" (so called "Shakers" or "Jumpers") of St Vincent, B.W.I.,' encl. in Cork to Crewe, September 6, 1908, BNA, CO 321/243, 306.

52. Article 8 of the 39 Articles of Faith includes all these creeds as fundamental truths; see 'Thirty-Nine Articles of Religion,' https://www.anglicancommunion.org, accessed March 20, 2020.

53. Broadbent, 'Second Address,' 306.

54. Ibid.

55. Christopher T. Bounds, 'How are people saved? The Major Views of Salvation with a focus on Wesleyan Perspectives and their Implications,' *Wesley and Methodist Studies* 3 (2011), 31, https://www.jstor.org/stable/42909800, accessed June 26, 2020.

56. The National Library of Jamaica, *'The Jamaican Maroons,'* Article 14 of The Leeward Treaty 1739, https://nlj.gov.jm/history-notes/The%20Maroons%20edited%20final.htm, accessed December 20, 2022.

57. Broadbent, 'An Earnest Address.' Emphasis is original.

58. Ibid.,' 307. Emphasis is original.

59. Leonard to Cameron, October 27, 1903, encl. in Cameron to Cork, August 25, 1908, BNA, CO 321/243, 302.

60. Leonard to Cameron, October 27, 1903, BNA, CO 321/243, 302.

61. Ibid.

62. Ibid.

63. Ibid.

64. Branch, 'Religious Insanity,' 307, BNA CO 321/243; Keane to Chief of Police, July 18, 1908, encl. in Griffith to Cameron, July 20, 1908, BNA, CO 321/243, 310.

65. Leonard to Cameron, October 27, 1903, BNA, CO 321/243, 303.

66. Broadbent, Sermon 1, 'An Earnest Address,' BNA, CO 321/243, 305.

67. Cameron to Cork, August 25, 1908, BNA, CO 321/243, 300.

68. Gov. Llewelyn to CJ Tarring, April 20, 1904, BNA, CO 321/243, 293.

69. Cap. LXIV & cap. LXV resp., *Laws of St. Vincent* (London: 1864), Google Books.

70. Llewelyn to Tarring, April 20, 1904, BNA, CO 321/243, 293.

71. Ibid.

72. Ibid., 295.

73. Ibid.

74. Cameron to Griffith, June 26, 1906, encl. 1 in Cameron to Governor, August 26, 1908, CO 321/243, 276.

75. See 'List of Colonial Secretaries of Barbados,' https://www.qudswiki.org/?querry=List_of_Colonial_Secretaries_of_CBarbados; also 'Lista de secretaries colonials de Barbados,' https://topkorae.com/wiki/es/List_of_Colonial_Secretaries_of_Barbados, accessed October 2, 2022.

76. Cameron to Cork, August 25, 1908, BNA, CO 321/243.

77. Branch, 'Religious Insanity,' 299.

78. Ibid. See also, Taylor and Case, *Caribbean Religions*, 244.

79. Branch, 'Religious Insanity,' 300.

80. Anon, 'Obituary.'

81. Branch, 'Religious Insanity,' 300.

82. Ibid., 302.

83. Ibid., 307.

84. Ibid., 304–05.

85. Ibid., 306

86. Ibid., 304.

87. Ibid., 308.

88. See 'Orgy,' Online Etymology Dictionary, https://www.etyonline.com/word/orgy, accessed August 16, 2022.

89. Cameron to Cork, August 25, 1908, BNA, CO 321/243.

90. *Times*, 25 June 1908, encl. 4 in Cameron to Crewe, August 25, 1908, BNA, CO 321/243, 292–93.

91. *Times*, June 25 ,1908, encl. 4 in Cameron to Crewe, BNA, CO 321/243, 292-93.

92. Allan to Kernerhan, 14 July 1908, encl. in Kernerhan to Cameron, July 16, 1908; encl. 6 in Cameron to Crewe, August 25, 1908, BNA, CO 321/243, 308-09.

93. Kernerhan to Cameron, July 16, 1908, BNA, CO 321/243, 308. Cameron did not enclose Kernerhan's response to Allan.

94. Griffith to Cameron, June 26, 2008, BNA, CO 321/243.

95. Keane to Chief of Police, July 18, 1908, encl. in Griffith to Cameron, July 20, 1908, BNA, CO 321/243, 313.

96. Keane to Chief of Police, July 20, 1908, BNA, CO 321/243, 312.

97. Ibid.

98. Ibid., 311–12.

99. Ibid., 312.

100. Ibid.

101. Cameron to Cork, August 25, 1908, par. 9, BNA, CO 321/243, 278–79.

102. Ibid., par. 9 BNA, CO 321/243, 279.

103. Ibid., par. 10 BNA, CO 321/243, 279.

104. Ibid.

105. Ibid.

106. Cameron to Cork, August 25,1908, par. 16 BNA, CO 321/243, 280–81.

107. Ibid., 281.

108. Cameron to Cork, August 25,908, par. 18, BNA, CO 321/243, 281.

109. See J. Scott-Keltie, ed. *The Statesman Year-Book 1909* (London: 1909), 266. Also, see *Jamaica Gleaner*, August 20, 2015.

110. Cork to Harcourt, Despatch No. 234, June 12, 1911, BNA, CO 139/111.

111. Cork to Crewe, 'Confidential,' September 6, 1908, BNA, CO 321/243, 276.
112. Cork to Crewe, September 6, 1908, BNA, CO 321/243, 276.
113. Cork to Crewe, 'Confidential,' September 6, 1909, BNA, CO 321/243, 276.
114. Boa, 'Colour, Class and Gender,' 265.
115. Ibid.
116. Fergus, *Revolutionary Emancipation*, 46.

CHAPTER 5

The Shakers' Prohibition Ordinance

*'We ease our national conscience by claiming that the development of Empire brings "the blessings of civilization." But we are not always clear as to what we really mean by the phrase.'**

After the departure of Administrator Edward John Cameron from St Vincent in 1909, there was a brief lull in legislative activities against the Penitents. The passage of Jamaica's 'Noises Assembly Act' in 1911 was an attack on the working class but a mark of respect for the right of conscience as enshrined in multiple toleration laws since 1689, especially the Places of Worship Registration Act, 1855. The Jamaican law provided the colonial precedent for the limits of the culture war with Africanised Christian sects. Spiritual Baptism was a nonconformist movement within Caribbean revivalism, no less so than Bedwardism, *Pukumina* and Revival Zion, which the Jamaican Act (Appendix A) implicitly acknowledged as constitutional and legal. Coincidentally, in 1911, Grenada and St Vincent also passed ordinances that targeted public, working-class behaviour deemed by the elites to be 'indecent,' 'obscene' or 'offensive.' Most likely, the new regime in St Vincent was responding to the widespread propaganda of immorality, obscenity and indecency of Penitent worshippers. Part Four of the Ordinance was titled 'Offences Against Public Order.' Under this Section, Article 87 sought to protect worshippers and pastors from molestation in a place of worship consistent with the PWRA (Places of Worship Registration Act)[1] Although no part of this Section referred to Penitents, Converted or Shakers, it curiously

---

* Bishop of Stepney, "The Empire and the Church," in *The Empire and the Century: A Series of Essays on Imperial Problems and Possibilities by Various Writers*, Comp. C. S. Goldman (London: 1905), 169–70.

preceded several Articles to punish working-class behaviour 'in any public place.' Headlined 'Offences Against Religion, Morality and Public Convenience,' there was no mention in this section of church, denomination, religion or any other term pertaining to religious worship. Article 96, however, is relevant to the debate on prohibition. It stated that it was an offence for any person who: 'Uses any indecent or obscene gesture; exposes his person in an indecent manner; Uses any indecent or obscene language; sings any indecent or obscene song or ballad.' A person found guilty of any of these offences would pay a fine of £5 or be imprisoned for one month.[2] Such laws did not directly violate the right of conscience, although they had the potential to do so, if abused.

Instead of staying the course of toleration, Cameron's successor, Charles Gideon Murray, decided to put toleration to another test with even more draconian legislation than his predecessor. Murray, a Scottish aristocrat, was a relatively young, but seasoned, colonial administrator and a 'staunch imperialist' by the time of his arrival in St Vincent in 1909.[3] He had served as private secretary to the governor of British New Guinea in 1898 and later, resident magistrate in that colony, leaving in 1900 for South Africa, where he took up several assignments over the next six years. He served as the private secretary to Sir Godfrey Lagden, the commissioner for Native Affairs in Transvaal; assistant native commissioner in Zoutpansberg in Northern Transvaal; and native commissioner in the Spelonken Ward in Limpopo by March 1902. He even saw active duty in the last months of the Anglo-Boer War.[4]

Except for his final year in South Africa, Murray was an official in the administration of Alfred Milner, a classic jingoist, who aggressively pursued a policy of English-race superiority. The South African War was a product of Milner's jingoism, but in the post-war reconstruction, the Boers (later called Afrikaners) recaptured power in their former republics and extended their influence to the Cape Province. On the contrary, Milner's policy toward indigenous South Africans, pursued through the Native Commission of which Murray was one of the highest officials, increasingly marginalised and disenfranchised them, including those who had supported the British campaigns.[5]

Murray's Machiavellian Politics of Prohibitionism

Murray's prior experience in South Africa accustomed him to acting impulsively and imperiously. He had also clearly developed the instincts of a professional politician and became a maverick administrator in St Vincent. Murray arrived in St Vincent with prohibition of the Penitents in his mind;[6] but a prohibition bill had to be perfectly timed, which finally came in mid-1912. The substantive governor and commander-in-chief of the Windward Islands, Sir James Hayes Sadler, was due to proceed on summer vacation from June to October 1912. Murray knew that, based on seniority, Edward Cameron, the commissioner for St Lucia, would be appointed acting-governor for the three months that Sadler would be away on vacation. Murray admitted that he had waited patiently for three years for such an opportunity to persecute the Penitents.[7] At the beginning of July, Murray drafted the new prohibition bill but decided to keep the governor in the dark about the pending legislation. Cameron met Murray at the end of July, three weeks after the introduction of the bill in the legislature, while the former was on his way to Grenada.[8]

On July 8, 1912, Murray introduced the bill, 'An Ordinance to render illegal the practices of Shakerism as indulged in in the colony of St Vincent,' known by the shortened title, 'The "Shakerism" Prohibition Ordinance, 1912.' As assistant private secretary to the permanent under-secretary of state for the Colonies immediately before his appointment as administrator, Murray would have been privy to the wealth of advice from colonial and metropolitan critics of Cameron's second prohibition bill. To reiterate, Chief Justice of the Windward Islands, Charles James Tarring, had advised governor Llewelyn, 'The line to take in any legislation is to strike at *the thing* and not the name.' He recommended that the legal draftsman should carefully avoid the words 'religion,' 'religious,' 'services,' 'denomination,' 'representative,' 'authorised persons' and 'other such expressions.'[9] Four years later, Cameron had persisted with the term 'religion' in his second prohibition bill, which was therefore bound to fail. Although Murray must have heeded Tarring's advice, he could not sanitise a bill on religion so completely as to leave no lexical traces to expose the deception. In his introductory remarks, the administrator assiduously avoided using religious terms to describe the Penitents and their practices: their Praise Houses were 'habitations of savages;' their liturgy was 'nuisance;' and their way of life 'a relic of barbarism, and appanage of paganism, a blot on our civilisation and a stain on the history of the colony.'[10] Acting-Chief Justice Robert E. Noble self-righteously thought, 'No one ... could accuse him of being opposed to the practice of other forms of worship but these meetings were often indecent and should be stopped.'[11] This was his first Freudian slip on the issue, admitting that Penitentism was one of many forms of religious worship.

The Legislative Council of the day was a product of 'pure' Crown Colony constitutionalism comprising four Officials, four Unofficials and no elected members. The Officials comprised the Administrator who was also the colonial secretary, the treasurer, the chief of police, and the chief justice; the four Unofficials were all nominated by the administrator.[12] The governor of St Vincent was the governor-in-chief of the Windward Islands with his seat of administration in Grenada. Whenever the governor visited St Vincent and sat in the Legislative Council, he did so as chairman of Council; otherwise, the administrator chaired the sessions as the Council's president. Although the administrator was responsible for legislation brought to the Legislative Council, it was the governor who was recognised under the constitution as the one who made and assented to legislation; the Legislative Council was officially an advisory body. The chief justice as magistrate of the Kingstown District had the power to appoint rural constables. He and the chief of police were Legislative Council members. Together they were largely responsible for policing, prosecuting and punishing the Penitents. This concentration of power was extreme even for the pure Crown Colony model. Nevertheless, whenever colonial legislation impinged on the rights of subjects, the Crown was the final arbiter. The Prohibition Ordinance trampled unambiguously on the rights of the Penitents. Instead of checking this abuse of power, the Crown explicitly condoned and sanctioned the violation of the constitution.

Murray adjourned the debate on the bill for a period of eight weeks after the first reading. He would later admit that he needed time to engage 'in regular electioneering campaign ... against Shakerism and its tenets all over the Colony.'[13] During the interval, he explained the impending legislation to the Penitents in the hope that they would voluntarily abandon 'Shakerism.' He also wished to create some distance between Sadler's departure and the passage of the ordinance in order to dampen suspicion of proceeding in haste or engaging in a legislative coup. He was equally concerned to justify his bill as a response to the desperate cry of the elites for action against the Penitents. For that reason, he also used the interval to mobilise the Churches, the media, the police, the schools and the big planters in his 'campaign against Shakerism.'[14] He appealed to Church leaders to provide intelligence on the location of Penitents' prayer houses. Pre-knowledge of those locations would facilitate prosecution immediately after promulgation of the law.[15]

The Times and *The Sentry* loyally regurgitated the racist propaganda of the principal politicians in the legislature. Three days after the bill was read for the first time, *The Times* claimed, 'Shakerism is not really a form of religion.' The article tried to legitimise prohibition because 'nearly every one' of the Penitents attended 'a recognised place of worship.'[16] *The Sentry* acknowledged that the Penitents enjoyed the right of independent worship under the British constitution but appealed to government to invoke the nuisance principle against them. It argued, 'The Shakers' camps are rather sources of vice' and it was the government's obligation under the British constitution 'to protect its subjects from self-destruction.'[17] *The Rambler* pulled off a unique stunt in publishing a letter to the editor from one Tony John, a working-class man from Lowmans Village. John's letter was written in authentic Vincentian creole in most of the content, except for suspiciously learned orthography for more difficult words, which betrays possible collaboration in its composition. John's letter was the sole textual support for prohibition originating from a purported Penitent. John admitted to stealing fruits after rejoicing and accused Leaders of preying on young female initiates.[18] Following Murray's rapport with

Penitent leaders, *The Sentry* reported that the administrator considered Shakerism and Penitence to be one and the same, to be 'put down with a firm hand.'[19] Murray did not refute this claim, which starkly contradicted his promise to the legislature. In a late publication, just two days prior to the resumption of the debate on the bill, *The Sentry* revisited Murray's introductory speech and reiterated that the main objective of legislation was to force the Penitents to 'return to worship in the different churches in which they were baptised.'[20]

The administrator toured the heartland of Penitentism to lay out an elaborate plan of deception and psychological war. He personally assured 'most of the Penitent leaders in the Colony ... that the Government had no intention of interfering with ordinary prayer meetings, that no British Government would take such a step.'[21] Chief of Police Francis Griffith was with the administrator in his office when the latter hosted the Penitent leaders and assured them that 'no Prayer Meeting or "Religious meeting" of any kind will be interfered with.'[22] Contrary to the legal posturing during debate on the bill, this assurance proves that Murray was under no illusion that Penitentism was a Christian sect protected under the toleration laws. He further assured the Penitents,

> All that the Government desired was to put a stop to the pernicious practices which were attendant on Shakerism as indulged in in this Colony and if they desired to hold their own prayer meetings they would not be interfered with so long as such meetings were conducted in a decent orderly manner and ceased at proper times.[23]

He was less than truthful; otherwise, he would have informed them of his intention to ensure strict enforcement of the 'Offences Against Public Order, 1911' or the 'Offences Against Religion, Morality and Public Convenience, 1911;' his bill would also have identified the 'pernicious practices,' warranting the imposition of a night curfew and not prohibition of worship. This, however, was not Murray's plan. Murray wanted nothing less than the obliteration of Shakerism. After three years in the colony, his reputation was well known. His personal communication with Penitent leaders was intended to scare them into voluntary recantation by informing them of the heavy fines and harsh imprisonment they faced if they failed to comply with the law. Like a true Machiavellian, he deployed the tried-and-tested imperial strategy of deceive-divide-and-rule. Accordingly, he sought out Black Christian members of the recognised Churches who were 'not mixed up with Shakerism.' He appealed for their assistance in helping to bring back the Penitents 'into the folds of the recognised Churches.' To these potential allies he also indicated that the measure that he was about to legislate would ultimately see 'the disappearance of Shakerism.'

When the legislature resumed on September 3, Acting-Chief Justice Robert E. Noble did the second reading of the bill in his capacity of Acting Attorney General. As mentioned earlier, the rapid departure of three key officials who had objected to Cameron's first prohibition bill had tempted him to make a second futile bid for prohibition. Murray was much more cunning than Cameron. In 1912, Murray calculatingly began to create an enabling political environment for prohibition by inserting hard-core prohibitionists in the Executive and Legislative Councils. Noble, a Vincentian, was the first. When Cameron drafted his second prohibition bill, Noble was the substantive Registrar of the Supreme Court, Assessor of Income Tax and Police Magistrate of the Second Division (Leeward). He often acted as chief justice when the substantive office holder, Rodney Sydney Shaw, went on vacation. Shaw, an English-born graduate of the Inns of Court, was chief justice from 1907 to 1912 and had therefore overseen the failure of Cameron's second prohibition bill.[24] When Shaw was granted leave to proceed on vacation in April 1912, Murray appointed Noble acting-chief justice.[25] As acting-attorney general, Noble was *ex-officio* member of the Executive Council and Legislative Council; as acting-chief justice, he became the second most powerful official in the colony after the Administrator. The second prohibitionist plant in the Legislature was Frank W. Griffith, another Vincentian. Griffith was in the public service since the 1890s; he was supervisor of customs in the early 1900s; Cameron appointed him chief of police and superintendent of prisons, among other posts, in 1904, but never nominated him to serve in the Legislative Council.[26] In February 1912, Murray appointed Griffith to the Legislative Council.[27]

Noble described himself as 'the Representative Catholic of the Colony.'[28] Ironically, since the seminal Toleration Act, every amending law had expressly excluded 'popish recusants' (Roman Catholics) from the benefits of Toleration, until the Catholic Emancipation Act, 1829, one hundred and forty years later. Even so, Catholics were still legally prohibited from holding public processions with Catholic iconography on display. Ironically, it was a Vincentian Catholic who piloted the bill to suppress the free conscience of a Protestant Christian sect because of racial prejudice. Noble alleged that he had consulted Father Busert who was 'strongly against Shakerism although objecting to nothing really religious.'[29] Busert's lukewarm advice to Nobel was given with full knowledge that the Catholic Church was the least likely to benefit from Penitent prohibition.

During the committee stage, Murray assured members of the legislature that he had the full backing of the 'recognised Churches,' having received resolutions of approval from the Wesleyans, Presbyterians, the Archdeacon of the Catholic Church and the Anglican Church.[30] The Presbyterian Church was Scottish, responding affirmatively to a Scottish Administrator. Although not specifically mentioned, it is to be expected that the Brethren, the Society of Friends and the Jews, whose pastors were recognised as marriage officers under the revised Marriage Act of 1908, would not have objected to Prohibition, even if they did not openly voice support for it. The Marriage Act had further isolated the Penitents, leaving them as the only religious organisation in the colony without the legal right to conduct their own marriage ceremonies.

Major Provisions of the Shakerism Prohibition Bill

Legislators rehashed the old charges of indecency, immorality, barbaric practices and insanity, but still provided no concrete evidence that could stand scrutiny in a British court of law. In recognising that subjectivity was a major flaw in the bill, Noble moved a motion to amend Section 6, the morality clause. His resolution proposed, 'In construing this section "the Magistrate's decision as to whether an act was or was not indecent or immoral or whether such an act of indecency or immorality was committed at or in the vicinity of any Shakers meeting shall be final" be deleted from section 6.' He affirmed that it was 'a question of fact which nobody could get behind.'[31] Ultimately, the clause was slightly modified to read:

> It shall be an offence against this Ordinance for any person at or in the vicinity of any Shakers meeting to commit or cause to be committed to induce or to persuade to be committed any act of indecency or immorality.

Although the absolute power of the magistrate in determining immorality and indecency was expunged from Section 6, it was not expunged from the bill. It is evident from the architecture of the Ordinance that it was simply relocated to Section 2, which stated, 'The decision of any Magistrate ... as to whether the customs and practices are Shakerism shall be final.' This was legal semantics that retained the arbitrary power of the lowest court against which there was no appeal. A critical reading of the Ordinance (Appendix B) reveals that it put the Penitents under Martial Law. Section 7 constituted the Constabulary into a moral police force. A raiding party was constrained only by the proviso that it must be led by a 'commissioned or non-commissioned officer' but such a party could enter any Penitent's abode, whether a private residence or place of worship, at any time of day or night, without a warrant. And even without an officer in charge an ordinary constable could arrest and detain anyone he suspected of being a Penitent or a participant in a suspected Penitent's outdoor or open-air meeting.

The allusion to customs and practices fitted Murray's diabolical scheme to avoid references common to religion, such as liturgy, prayers, belief and service. He had assured the Penitents that those would be protected. Acting-Chief Justice Noble also ensured this false promise was a major point of clarification in his official 'Report on the Ordinance.' Yet, the law carefully avoided an exception clause that would expressly protect the prayers and worship of the Penitents. The omission of such a clause further exposed the fact that the true objective of the law was to wipe out Penitentism and drive its followers back into the recognised churches. Ultimately, the police and magistrates would interpret customs and practices to encompass all matters concerning the Penitents as a sect.

The government adopted intelligence reports on Shaker religious meetings and concluded that there were two phenomena at play: one was Christian; the other, allegedly pagan and diabolic. Under Cameron's administration, Dr Leonard, a self-proclaimed spy to a Penitent meeting, had testified that Penitentism 'appears to be a very low type of Methodism.'[32] Murray, however, pivoted on Corporal Keane's Report of 1908 that discredited the link between Methodism and Penitentism and instead represented Penitentism as heathenish and demoniacal practices. Whereas Cameron had assiduously defended the movement as religious, Murray cleverly distinguished between 'Prayer meetings,' which were acceptable to government and 'Shakerism' or 'Shaker meetings,' which were reprehensible. Instead of two parts of a single night's service, the two phases were being represented as two distinct phenomena. Prayer meetings, when 'Wesleyan hymns' were sung, allegedly ended by midnight, after which Shakerism commenced. It was the after midnight phase that members of the faith called 'rejoicing,' which involved 'jumping' and the 'Shakers Dance,' but which the governing class equated with 'fetish practices' and 'an apanage of paganism.'[33] During the debate, Murray assured that 'people not mixed up with Shakerism' had nothing to fear from the Ordinance, yet, he repeated his promise that the law would bring about 'the disappearance of the Shakers.'[34]

If Griffith or Murray were genuine with their promise, prayer meetings would have received explicit protection in the ordinance, but it is evident that the promise of protection was mere political rhetoric contrary to the true objective of the government. Noble's Report on the ordinance was also silent on government's commitment to respect prayer meetings. Instead, it laboriously set out to convince the secretary of state for the Colonies that the Penitents were a threat to society and concluded emphatically, *Salus Populi suprema lex* ['The safety of the people shall be the supreme law'].[35] In omitting the centrality of prayers while insinuating 'that the meetings of Shakers take place late at night,' he reinforced the elites' portrayal of Shakerism as a diabolic cult, not a sect or denomination of Protestantism. His statement contradicted that of former Administrator Cameron who had assured

Acting-Governor Cork in 1908 that there was no need for police interference at a Penitents' meeting, because it was 'just ordinary bible-reading and psalm-singing.'[36] Noble's integrity as acting-chief justice and lawmaker was obviously compromised by being an advocate (pro bono) for the prohibitionists. His intention was clearly to sway the 'jury' of Colonial Office officials to believe the lie that 'their nocturnal orgies are attended to with indecency and immorality.'[37]

Magisterial adjudication on immorality was a weakness in Cameron's 1908 prohibition bill; it remained a weakness in Murray's bill. The Colonial Office had deemed Cameron's ordinance 'impossible' to sanction. They rejected the argument that the banning of wakes at midnight in the town was legal precedent for banning Penitents' 'orgies,' which allegedly took place in 'deserted spots in the country.' To Colonial Office officials the growing popularity of Penitentism was not a political issue but a failure of the recognised Churches to extend their reach into the rural communities, as the Penitents had done quite successfully.

The Failure of the First Guardrail of Conscience

The Legislative Council voted unanimously in support of the bill on its third and final reading on September 3. Acting-Governor Edward Cameron assented to it two weeks later. We should recall that in 1809, after the King in Council had disallowed Jamaica's prohibition Act of 1807, the secretary of state for the Colonies had instructed all colonial governors to 'refer all laws dealing with religious matters to Britain for royal scrutiny and assent.'[38] This protocol was the reason that Cameron had forwarded his draft ordinances to his superiors for scrutiny and advice. As a highly experienced official in colonial affairs, Murray should have been familiar with the common policy to await the assent and advice of the Colonial Office before a religious bill became law. Instead, Murray disregarded the protocol and gazetted the Ordinance on October 1, mere days before it was put in the transatlantic mail-boat to the Colonial Office. This maverick action by Murray put the reviewers on a spot because they were reviewing an Ordinance that was already aggressively being policed against a sector of the population that had no political influence and no recourse to legal representation. Yet, the imperial government had the power and duty to annul the Ordinance and instruct Murray to expunge all convictions under the Act and to reimburse all fines accordingly. Cameron is not without fault in facilitating this abuse of power. Murray's ordinance was substantively Cameron's second vetoed bill with only semantic modifications. As acting-governor, it was incumbent on Cameron to instruct Murray to hold his hand on implementation until he should receive the decision of the Colonial Office. Alternatively, he should have used the power of his office to veto the bill. Murray had no prerogative to overrule an acting-governor.

Significant Flaws in the Shakerism Prohibition Bill

The first defect in the statute arose from the imperative to portray Shakerism as 'anything apart from religion.' Thus, the Preamble to the Act defined Shakerism as 'meetings … where practices are indulged in and which tend to excite a pernicious and demoralizing effect' upon the inhabitants of the colony of St Vincent. The reduction of Shakerism to 'meetings' of members begged the question of what constituted the 'ism' in Shakerism. Furthermore, the law failed to define the 'customs and practices of Shakerism,' which it made illegal. The local lawmakers were aware that such vague definitions could apply to many activities not associated with the Penitents and not intended in the law. Legal scholar Wallwyn P. B. Shepheard's contemporary report on the legislation stated imperialistically, 'The "Shakerism" Prohibition Ordinance, 1912, prohibits under heavy penalty the practice of "Shakerism" as defined by the Ordinance.'[39] In reality, there was no definition of 'Shakerism' in the Ordinance.

Although equally deceptive, there was some attempt to define 'Shakers meeting' in Clause 1 and 'Shakers House' in Clause 2. These two clauses struck at the heart of Shakerism. A Shakers' meeting was defined as 'a meeting or gathering of two or more persons whether indoors or in the open air, at which the customs and practices of Shakerism are indulged in.' Open-air meetings or meetings of just two persons would invariably point to the traditional candlelight or wayside preachers with a long history dating back to the days of slavery in the Caribbean and North America. Those were essentially itinerant preachers responding to visions received in dreams to embark on evangelical missions. These meetings were never associated with anything but Bible exegesis and psalm-singing, yet they were equally subjected to the full burden of prohibition.

The law described a Shakers' House as 'any house or building or room in any house or building which is used for the purpose of initiating any person into the ceremonies of Shakerism.' The initiation rite of mourning was the ultimate pillar of Penitents' faith, and the most distinguishing feature of Shakerism. The Mourners' Room, commonly called the mourning ground in Trinidad, was so sacred to Penitentism that no members were allowed inside, except initiates or mourners and those administering to the needs of mourners. As mentioned earlier, Cameron's spies had admitted that it was the one place for which they had no personal information and had to rely on hearsay. Clause 4 did not only outlaw this pillar of faith but also aimed to desecrate the mourning ground by empowering the police to enter the sanctuary without a warrant to disturb the mourning rite and arrest all attendees, including the initiates at whatever the stage of their journey into the spiritual lands. The rude shock of such an invasion must have been infinitely more traumatic to a mourner than the potential insanity associated with mourning in government's specious allegations. All owners and managers of estates were obligated to report forthwith to the chief of police whenever they perceived that a Shakers' House was being erected on their lands or if they knew of any house that was being used for Shakers' meetings (Clause 5).

The Shakers Ordinance was not a public-order Act. It was full-scale religious persecution with economic implications. As previously discussed, Penitents' meetings were also held in lodges of Friendly Societies, which were legal entities. William Blackstone was of the firm opinion that whoever disturbed a congregation or abused anyone for whatever reason was liable to criminal prosecution under the Toleration Act, 1689.[40] According to Blackstone's tenet, it was the government that was engaged in illegal actions, not the Penitents. Blackstone's commentaries were reinforced by supplementary statute, particularly the PWRA, 1855 and the LRWA (Liberty of Religious Worship Act), 1855. Clause 5 of the Shakers' Prohibition Ordinance was a clear violation of the LRWA, Article 1, which stated unambiguously: 'No Person permitting any such Congregation to meet as herein mentioned in any Place occupied by him shall be liable to any Penalty for so doing.'

The meeting places listed included 'a private Dwelling House or on the Premises belonging thereto' and 'in any Building or Buildings not usually appropriated to Purposes of Religious Worship.'[41]

An examination of The Shakers' Prohibition Ordinance reveals a duplicity that was not cleverly disguised. The title of the Ordinance declared 'illegal the practices of "Shakerism,"' as defined by Murray. However, it's vague reference to 'customs and practices of Shakerism' without defining Shakerism was intended to bring the full weight of the law to erase the religion. There was no appeal against the decision of magistrates who were given arbitrary power in determining 'whether the customs and practices are Shakerism.' The legislation did not address the government's troubling claim of noisemaking late at night, which allegedly disturbed the sleep of inhabitants. It did not identify any specific immoral or indecent acts. Moreover, it did not make allowance for the contention, even by enemies of Penitentism, that up to midnight, these meetings were no different from Methodist services.

Wallwyn Shepheard had reported dispassionately that the Ordinance prescribed 'heavy penalty' on defiers.[42] At the time, the daily wage of a labourer was less than $2.00 per day. The Prohibition Ordinance's imposition of up to £50 (Clause 8) on any Penitent or associate deemed guilty of an offence could potentially cripple the Lodges and severely set back any individual financially: that fine is equivalent to £7,306 or XCD$25,991.00 in mid-2023.[43] In default of payment, a defier was liable to a maximum of six months imprisonment, with or without hard labour. It is no wonder that Penitent migration to Trinidad increased sharply after the passage of Prohibition.

Beyond British jurisprudence, the First Amendment to the Constitution of the United States of America is a useful guide for interpreting the logic of St Vincent's prohibition ordinance as well as the Colonial Office's sanction and persistent defence of it. The comparison is justified on the cultural and legal continuities between Britain and the US. The two relevant clauses are the 'Free Exercise Clause' and the 'Establishment Clause.' The Free Exercise Clause 'guarantees a person the right to practice a religion and propagate it without interference from government.' It further states, 'This right is a liberty interest and cannot be deprived except by due process of law;' and 'although the government cannot restrict a person's beliefs, it can limit the practice of faith when a substantial and compelling state interest exists.'[44] Although not explicitly stated, this reasoning could be applied to the preamble and debate on the Shakers' prohibition bill. The First Amendment prohibits a state from taking away 'the right to preach or to disseminate religious views' but it permits a state to criminalise certain religious practices 'in order to safeguard the peace, order, and comfort of the community.'[45] The framers of the American Constitution must have had in mind extreme 'practices' such as human sacrifice and the mass murders and suicides of fanatical doomsday prophets such as Charles Manson and James Warren Jones (Jim Jones) of the People's Temple, both American citizens. The Shakers' Prohibition Ordinance was premised on similar obligation to public safety, order and comfort, to wit, that Penitents frequently indulged in practices 'which tend to excite a pernicious and demoralizing effect upon the said inhabitants.' During the debate on the bill, Murray elaborated, 'There were common rights in a community and the orgies of the Shakers had such an effect upon their characters as to adversely affect their common rights.'[46] The preamble also presumed that the law would protect 'the best interest of the said Colony of St Vincent and its inhabitants' by not permitting such meetings and practices. Murray's law, however, was at variance with America's First Amendment in that the alleged practices of the Shakers were merely the dressing for prohibiting the religion. The title of the anti-Shakerism Ordinance announced that the government was seeking to criminalise certain 'practices,' which were explicated in the debate on the Bill. Certain sections of the law, however, criminalised the meetings, the places where meetings were held, and anyone who facilitated these meetings in any way, even if merely a bystander.[47] Methodist pastor Wilfrid Broadbent had preached against Penitent Leaders usurping the powers accorded to 'ancient Bible seers;' though he alleged that such 'prophesying' was 'preposterous,' he did not think it put believers in apocalyptic danger.

Acting-Governor Cameron's covering letter to the secretary of state for the Colonies affirms that the Colonial Office had communicated with him on Murray's ordinance during the month of September 1912, shortly after he had assented to it.[48] The vast majority of the enclosed documents provided to justify Penitentism as a menace to society and to demonstrate widespread support for prohibition were readily available prior to the passing of the bill. Of the five enclosures dated after the passing of the bill, the most significant were the Law Officer's report from Acting-Chief Justice Noble and two reports from the chief of police, Francis Griffith. One of Griffith's reports was dated three days after the passing of the bill; Noble's report, three days after Griffith's; but Griffith's other report was dated only the day before Murray mailed the prohibition package to Cameron for transmission to the Colonial Office.

Griffith's reports reveal the true intent of the prohibition law and the success of the authorities in bringing about a swift end to 'Shakerism.' Penitentism apparently went underground for a while, while some adherents of the faith chose exile mainly in Trinidad and the US. On June 30, 1912, there were forty Shaker Praise Houses or Shakers' lodges, an increase of two since Cameron's bill in 1908. Of the thirty-eight places of worship under Cameron, thirty-three were purpose built, while only two were described as 'casual meeting' places. A mere three days after the passage of the legislation, Griffith reported that 'Shaker meetings' were being held in only four locations. Based on Murray's assurance, 'nearly all the Shaker Leaders' from all districts, with whom he had met during the interval following the introduction of the bill in July, had 'expressed their satisfaction at being allowed to continue their Prayer Meetings.'[49] Yet, for twenty-five locations Griffith reported, 'No meetings of any kind are now being held;' they were 'entirely abandoned.' Murray had warned the deputations of

Penitent leaders that the government would permit prayer meetings only if they were 'conducted at proper times of day and evening and closing at a proper time in the evening.'[50] Griffith reported that Leaders of ten Praise Houses conducted 'prayer meetings only' and only on Sundays, 'up to 9.30 or 10:00 pm.'[51] Griffith attempted to reconcile the contradiction between his interpretation of the Leaders' reaction to Murray's assurance and the dramatic decline in prayer meetings by claiming that those who had completely shut down had reasoned 'that since they can't jump they are not going to bother with it again.'[52] If the Leaders were indeed satisfied with Murray's conditionality, as Griffith attested, the dramatic decline in prayer meetings raises questions of deep distrust in government, the aggressive policing of prohibition before the publication of the Ordinance, and the extent of migration of Penitent Leaders to the more hospitable environment of Trinidad.

A colonial Ordinance became law only after it was publicly proclaimed or published in the *Government Gazette*. No law existed to support the police intimidation of Penitent Leaders prior to publication of the Ordinance in the *Government Gazette* on October 1, 1912. There was at least one reported case of civil intimidation. Shortly after the passage of the bill but before the assent of the acting-governor, the manager of an estate at Owia Point Village ordered the demolition of the Praise House.[53] Cameron assented to the Ordinance on September 17. Whether the Leader was a paying tenant or tenant at will, the manager's action was illegal, according to William Blackstone, reconfirmed by the PWRA, 1855 and the LRWA, 1855.

Griffith's follow-up report, dated October 22, 1912, painted a grim picture of the state of Penitentism. The chief of police had ordered the posting of the published Ordinance at all police stations. The police also distributed copies of the Ordinance to all Penitent leaders known to them. The report stated that only one 'Shaker Meeting' was held since the publication of the Ordinance. According to Griffith, this meeting in Diamond Village in the Windward District occurred only because the Leader, Samuel Durant, had not been served with the ordinance. Nevertheless, Griffith boasted, 'Police reports from all the other districts are to the effect that Shaker practices have been entirely abandoned.'[54] Without providing a specific number or location, he affirmed, 'Prayer Meetings are being held at several of the former Shaker houses.'[55] The distinction between a 'Shaker Meeting' or 'Shaker practices' and 'Prayer Meeting' suggests that Penitents had abandoned 'rejoicing' or had adopted novel strategies that escaped police notice. Nevertheless, Griffith's two reports were remarkably silent on prosecutions.

Cameron received Murray's bundled despatches two days after mailing and immediately prepared his cover note to transmit them to the Colonial Office. Cameron's expeditious move contrasted sharply with Murray's procrastination and deviousness. Nevertheless, the acting-governor's covering letter to Secretary of State Lewis Harcourt was cleverly constructed to exonerate Murray from violating royal protocol, while sharing the credit for eradicating 'Shakerism.' Cameron informed the Colonial Office that Governor Sadler first learned of the prohibition bill through a newspaper report and sought Murray's confirmation. Murray had later stage-managed his response by ensuring that the governor receives it on the same day that he was due to sail on vacation.[56] Perhaps, just as Murray had hoped, Sadler did not address the matter further. Cameron, however, made a startling revelation that he and Murray had discussed the bill on the July 31, the same day that Sadler got wind of it in the newspaper. This meeting took place prior to Cameron assuming the acting-governorship. Nevertheless, in terms of colonial administration, and as Administrator of St Lucia, Cameron was senior to Murray. Instead of advising his junior colleague to submit his draft Bill for gubernatorial review, however belatedly, Cameron decided to endorse Murray's maverick action and advised the secretary of state for the Colonies, 'It would be inexpedient to do anything that might delay in any way the fulfilment of what he had laid out, as this might impair the vigour of the action and militate against its object.'[57] With this assurance Cameron deliberately inserted himself as an accessory to the violation of the right of Penitents to freedom of conscience. Perhaps he desperately wanted to share in the credit for eradicating Penitentism, which he had initiated but failed to accomplish during his tenure as administrator. He corrupted the legislative chain of command and directly compromised his role of the principal gatekeeper of conscience and religious freedom of the Windward Islands when he became acting-governor.

Notes

1. *Ordinances: Saint Vincent, 1926 Revision: Title 1, Administration of Justice* (London: 1927), Cap. 14, Article 87, SVGAG, 150.

2. *Ordinances: Saint Vincent, 1926 Revision*, Cap. 14, Article 96, SVGAG, 153.

3. Andrew Stewart succinctly described Murray during the Second World War as 'a Scottish aristocrat and staunch imperialist.' See, Andrew Stewart, *Empire Lost: Britain, the Dominions and the Second World War*, 53. Google Books.

4. Lindsay Frederick Braun, *Colonial Survey and Native Landscapes in Rural South Africa, 1850–1913: The Politics of Divided Space in the Cape and Transvaal* (Leiden, Neth: Brill, 2014), 319; e-book available at https://brill.com/view/title/25417, downloaded 10 July 2022; *Who's Who, 1935* (London: McMillan: December 2007), 1015, https://archive.org/details/whoswho1935001355mbp/page/1014/mode/2up, Internet Archive, accessed June 20 ,2022.

5. See Roger Beck, *The History of South Africa* (London, Greenwood Press, 2000), 94–95.

6. Fraser, *From Shakers to Spiritual Baptists*, 32–33.

7. Murray to Cameron, October 12, 1912, encl. in Cameron to Harcourt 24 Oct. 1912, BNA, CO 321/269.

8. Cameron to Harcourt, October 24,1912, BNA, CO 321/269.

9. Chief Justice Tarring to Governor Llewelyn, April 21,1904, encl. in Cork to Crewe, September 61908, BNA, CO 321/243, 295. Emphasis is original.

10. Minutes of the Legislative Council, July 8, 1912, SVGNA, 9.

11. Robert Noble, 'The Shakerism Prohibition Ordinance, 1912: Report,' October 12, 1912, encl. in Cameron to Harcourt, October 24, 1912, CO 321/269.

12. The nominated members who passed the prohibition bill were John George Windsor, D. A. MacDonald, F. A. Corea, and J. B. Kernerhan. See Minutes of Legislative Council, July 8, 1912, SVGNA.

13. Murray to Cameron, October 12, 1912, encl. in Cameron to Harcourt, October 24, 1912, BNA, CO 321/269.

14. *Minute Book 1912*, September 3, 1912, SVGNA, 72-73.

15. Fraser, *Shakers to Spiritual Baptists*, 4.

16. *The Times*, July 11, 1912, encl. in Cameron to Harcourt, October 24, 1912, BNA, CO 321/269.

17. *The Sentry*, July 12, 1912, encl. in Cameron to Harcourt, October 24, 1912, BNA, CO 321/269.

18. *The Rambler*, July 22, 1912, encl. in Cameron to Harcourt, October 24, 1912, BNA, CO 321/269.

19. *The Sentry*, August 2, 1912, encl. in Cameron to Harcourt, October 24, 1912, BNA, CO 321/269.

20. *The Sentry*, September 6, 1912, encl. in Cameron to Harcourt, October 24 1912, BNA, CO 321/269.

21. Minutes, September 3, 1912, BNA, CO 263/33.

22. Griffith to Murray, September 6, 1912, encl. in Cameron to Harcourt, October 24, 1912, BNA, CO 321/269.

23. Minutes, September 3, 1912, BNA, CO 263/33.

24. A. J. Harding and G. E. J. Gent, comp., *The Dominion Office and Colonial List, 1932* (London: 1932), 770. Internet Archive.

25. British West Indian Study Circle, *St Vincent Government Gazette*, No. 9, February 23, 1911, 53; *St Vincent Government Gazette*, No. 10, March 21, 1912, 65–66; *St Vincent Government Gazette*, No. 40, October 1912, 324, https://bwisc.org/wp-content/uploads/Reference/1964-1969_Research_StVincent_ColonialGazettes/1894-1969_Research_StVincent_ColonialGazettes.pdf, accessed on August 22, 2022. *St Vincent Blue Book, 1914*, 'List of Officers,' M-3, Google Books.

26. Mercer and Collins, *The Dominion Office*, 398; 512. Appointments other than ex-officio members were made by the Governor but obviously nominated by the Administrator.

27. *Government Gazette*, No. 7, February 22, 1912, 51. *Blue Book of St Vincent 1916*, 'Civil Establishment List,' M-3.

28. Minutes of the Legislative Council, September 3, 1912, SVGNA, 73.

29. Minutes of Leg. Co., September 3, 1912, SVGNA, 73. Fr. Busert may have been the Franz J. Busert who visited Trinidad in 1914. In 1915, the Archbishop of Caracas re-assigned him to serve the German colony there. Disillusioned by the 'spiritual neglect' of the German colonists, he disparaged them as "fallen Catholics" and demanded that they return to the Church and "avoid all contacts with Protestants:" see Holger H. Herwig, *Germany's Vision of Empire in Venezuela, 1871–1914* (Princeton, NJ: Princeton University Press, 1986), 76.

30. Minutes of Leg. Co., September 3, 1912, SVGNA, 72.

31. Ibid., BNA, CO 263/33, 73.

32. Dr. Leonard, October 27, 1903, encl. in Cameron's draft ordinance, BNA, CO 321/243, 302.

33. Chief of Police to Administrator, September 6, 1912, BNA, CO 321/269.

34. Murray, September 3, 1912 in *Minute Book 1906–1911*, Minute 15 Sept. 1912, SVGNA, 72–73.

35. Noble, 'Report,' BA 321/269.

36. Cameron to Cork, August 25, 1908, 'Confidential,' enclosed in Confidential, Cork to Crewe, September 5, 1908, BNA, CO 321/243, 276.

37. Noble, 'Report,' BNA, CO 321/269.
38. Keith Hunte, 'Protestantism and Slavery in the British Caribbean,' in *Christianity in the Caribbean: Essays on Church History*, ed. Armando Lampe (Barbados: University of the West Indies Press, 2001): 104–05.
39. Wallwyn P. B. Shepheard, 'St Vincent,' in Harcourt Malcolm, Wallwyn P. B. Shepheard, R. Escombe Willcocks and Charles J. Tarring, 'The West Indies,' *Journal of the Society of Comparative Legislation* 14, no. 1 (1914), 240, https://www.jstor.org/stable/752633.
40. Blackstone, *Commentaries* 4, 430.
41. 'Liberty of Religious Worship Act, 1855,' https://www.irishstatutebook. ie/.
42. Shepheard, 'St Vincent,' 240.
43. Official data, https:www.officialdata.org/uk/inflation/1912?amount =50, accessed July 2023; British pounds sterling to Caribbean dollars, https://wise.com/gb/currency-converter/gbp-to-xcd-rate,   accessed July 2023.
44. West's Encyclopedia of American law, edition 2, S.v., 'Religion,' http:// legal-dictionary.thefreedictionary.com/Religion, accessed September 10, 2017.
45. *West's Encyclopedia*, 'Religion.'
46. Minutes, September 3,1912, BNA, CO 263/33.
47. Law No. 13 of 1912, BNA, CO 262/26; Law No. 27 of 1917, BNA, CO 295/22.
48. The reference was to "Despatch No 65 of the 23rd ultimo" [September 3, 1912], Cameron to Harcourt, October 24, 1912, BNA, CO 321/269.
49. Chief of Police Griffith to Administrator, September 6, 1912, encl. in Murray to Cameron, October 12, 1912, BNA, CO 321/269.
50. Murray to Cameron, October 12, 1912, BNA, CO 321/269.
51. Griffith to Murray, September 6, 1912, encl. in Murray to Cameron, October 12, 1912, BNA, CO 321/269.
52. Ibid.
53. Ibid.
54. Griffith to Murray, October 22, 1912 encl. in Murray to Cameron, October 12, 1912, BNA, CO 321/269.
55. Ibid.
56. Cameron to Harcourt, October 24, 1912, BNA, CO 321/269.
57. Ibid.

CHAPTER 6

The Colonial Office Review: A Conundrum of Conscience and Expediency

*'The Secretary of State for the Colonies is the Colonial Office. Whatever is done there is done by him or under his authority, expressed or implied.'**

*C*olonial governors were viceroys with immense but not absolute power over policy and legislation. Even in self-governing colonies, that power resided in the Colonial Office, as stated by a former senior official in 1926 in the blurb to this chapter. Two decades before him, Frank Swettenham, another authority on imperial administration, shared the same perspective:

> The governor is subject to the authority of the Secretary of State for the Colonies, with whom he is in constant correspondence on every subject of importance, and sometimes on matters of apparently trifling detail. The ultimate authority, the final court of appeal, in executive matters, is Downing Street.[1]

Both writers failed to consider whether a colonial law that threatened the right of conscience was an 'executive matter' or imperial policy requiring a higher authority for final determination.

The Shakers' Prohibition Ordinance arrived at the Colonial Office on November 12, 1912; it would not be finally approved until twelve months later. By explicitly granting Murray's administration the right to enforce the law immediately and without modification, however, the Colonial Office had sanctioned it after a thorough review. This was not unprecedented. Some colonial laws were allowed to remain in force without royal assent for up to two years after which they

---

* Fiddes, *The Dominions and Colonial Offices*, 10. Emphasis is original. Fiddes was a reviewer of Murray's prohibition ordinance.

naturally expired.[2] It is for this reason that the royal Memorandum of 1809 was issued: to pre-empt persecution under unsanctioned laws. The Ordinance along with supporting documents were subjected to immediate and intense review by several officials, ranging from junior clerks to the permanent under-secretary of state for the Colonies before submission to the secretary of state for the Colonies, Lewis Harcourt. As Frank Swettenham unequivocally asserted, it was Harcourt who ultimately authorised the prohibition of Penitentism and the persecution of its adherents.

Murray's Network of Power and Influence and the South Africa Connections

Murray was personally familiar with the working of the Colonial Office and acquainted with many of the reviewers of his ordinance, having served as private secretary to fellow aristocrat, Sir Francis Stephens Hopwood, the permanent under-secretary of state for the Colonies in 1907, until his departure for St Vincent in 1909. A permanent under-secretary of state for the Colonies was the top civil servant in the Colonial Office, second in authority to the secretary of state for the Colonies. Murray was well connected to other senior officials at the centre of imperial governance. His older brother, Alexander William Murray, was a member of Parliament when he visited several constituencies in South Africa, including the Transvaal, shortly after the war. Gideon and many of his future Colonial Office colleagues were also in South Africa at that time. In 1905, the elder Murray joined the imperial government, serving as Comptroller of the House, a post he held until 1909. In late December 1911, after the prorogation of Parliament, Alexander was elevated to the Privy Council, the body that provided advice to the Monarch, and determined the merits of colonial legislation requiring the Monarch's sanction. When Gideon introduced his prohibition bill in the St Vincent legislature, Alexander was chief whip of the House of Commons doubling as parliamentary secretary to the Treasury, while his younger brother, Captain Arthur Cecil Murray, also an MP, was in another prestigious government position as parliamentary private secretary to Sir Edward Grey, the secretary of state for foreign affairs. In August 1912, the elder Murray became Baron Murray of Elibank and later served in the House of Lords.

Gideon Murray's relationship to Hopwood was pivotal to his career as a top civil servant in the Windward Islands for eight years. Murray became acquainted with Hopwood in South Africa. Hopwood was there as a legal expert to Milner's 'Kindergarten,' a group of young Oxford University graduates mandated to draft a new constitution for the Transvaal and Orange Free State, the two defeated Boer states.[3] Both Murray and Hopwood left South Africa for England in 1906. Hopwood was appointed permanent under-secretary of state for the Colonies in 1907; in that same year, Hopwood appointed Murray as his assistant private secretary. 'Sir F. Hopwood' is on the list of nine Colonial Office officials who reviewed Murray's prohibition Ordinance; he did not record his views. In 1912, Hopwood was elevated to the Privy Council, a decision that allowed Administrator Murray to retain the influence he would have lost with his brother's resignation from that body.

Another member of Murray's South African connection with considerable influence in the Colonial Office in 1912 was Sir George Vandeleur Fiddes who served as Assistant Under-Secretary in the Colonial Office from 1909 to 1916 and was one of the reviewers of the Shakers' prohibition ordinance. He was the principal clerk in the Colonial Office between 1902 and 1909, the latter part of which he was Murray's subordinate. The acquaintance of the two men preceded their stints in the Colonial Office. Between 1900 and 1902, Fiddes had served as Secretary to the Transvaal Administration under Sir Alfred Milner, which coincided with Murray's tenure as private secretary to the commissioner for Native Affairs and then Native Commissioner of the Transvaal. Fiddes departed South Africa in 1902 to take up the position of principal clerk in the Colonial Office. Between 1916 and 1921, Fiddes would occupy an even greater position of power in the Colonial Office as permanent under-secretary, when the Shouters Prohibition Ordinance arrived for review. He was the principal reviewer of that ordinance.[4]

Another reviewer of the Shakers' Prohibition Ordinance, Alfred Emmott, must have known Alexander Murray very well, both having served under Prime Minister Herbert Asquith. Emmott was chairman of Ways and Means in the House of Commons – a post equivalent to senior deputy speaker – from 1906 to 1911. He was created Baron of Oldham in November 1911 and joined the House of Lords, holding on to his post of under-secretary of state for the Colonies, to which he was appointed three months earlier, and in which he was still serving when he reviewed the prohibition ordinance.[5] Reviewer Sir John Anderson (1858–1918), a Scotsman like Murray, joined the Colonial Office in 1879, but went on to serve overseas from 1904. When Murray's Ordinance arrived, Anderson was the permanent under-secretary of state for the Colonies. Junior clerk, Gilbert E. A. Grindle, and senior clerks, Ernest Rowland Darnley and John Anderson (1882–1958) were all appointed to their respective position the same year that Murray entered the Colonial Office. Grindle was one of the reviewers of Cameron's bill in 1908, which was disallowed. There is no evidence that Gideon Murray had seen the draft Ordinance, although he was privileged to do so as private secretary to the permanent under-secretary of state for the Colonies.[6] Indeed, it stands to reason than if Sir John Anderson as permanent under-secretary of state for the Colonies in 1912 had reviewed Murray's prohibition ordinance, Murray, as private secretary to the permanent under-secretary of state for the Colonies in 1908, should also have seen Cameron's draft prohibition ordinance.

Winston Churchill, Britain's prime minister during the Second World War, was a media reporter and soldier in the Boer War, holding the rank of lieutenant. When Murray was appointed to the Colonial Office, Churchill was serving as parliamentary under-secretary to Lord Elgin, the secretary of state for the Colonies.[7] This put Churchill as another direct link between Murray and Parliament. It was said that Churchill was the most powerful man outside of the Cabinet.

It is not certain how all these connections played out in facilitating metropolitan sanction of the Shakers' Ordinance, but they certainly deserve consideration. There are too many fortuitous circumstances favouring Murray for the reader not to perceive either a conspiracy to cover up the Administrator's deviance from established protocol in formulating legislation that seriously impacted the rights of British subjects, or a bigger conspiracy that involved Murray and some officials in the Colonial Office to deny the Penitents the right of conscience guaranteed under the religious toleration laws of Britain. In any case, these relationships and acquaintances must have emboldened Murray and compromised the customary checks and balances of the imperial centre over colonial governors. According to Dudeney and Sheail writing in the period under study, 'The political heads of the department, namely the Secretary of State, Parliamentary Under-Secretary and Minister of State, wrote comparatively little' about the work they did.[8] Indeed, Lord Elgin informed Churchill, 'where the political element comes in the less *we* write the better.'[9] For this reason, the marginal notes and comments of the department's staff are critical to deconstructing the intrigues that went into the sanctioning of Murray's prohibition ordinance.

The Colonial Officers Review of Murray's Shakerism Ordinance

The two most significant analyses of the Ordinance and the enclosures were those of Darnley (Reviewer No. 1] and one Mr Corwell (Reviewer No. 2).[10] Darnley created the Minute to which other reviewers appended their comments. His affirmation that his department had requested the Ordinance 'in Bill form' confirms that knowledge of Murray's plan to legislate prohibition of the Shakers had somehow reached the Colonial Office before its sanction by the Acting governor.[11] Darnley acknowledged Cameron's explanation of Murray's 'independent action' but lamented, 'I am not however satisfied that a good case has been made out for the hastiness of the action taken.' Darnley clinically deconstructed the elaborate portrait painted by Murray and his allies concerning an alarming growth of the Penitents and corresponding data on the phenomenal rise in lunacy and illegitimate births. Cameron had provided similar data to justify his own prohibition bill of 1908, but the reviewers had rejected them as unreliable. The weakness of the data meant that it was impossible to apply the maxim '*Salus Populi suprema lex*,' which Chief Justice Noble had provided as the ultimate justification for prohibition. *The Times* newspaper had expressed the same sentiment in layman's terms, indicting the Penitents for 'demoralizing our country and undermining its moral structure.'[12] *The Sentry* newspaper went further in its editorial on the subject, claiming, 'It is the duty of a Government even to protect its subjects from self-destruction.'[13] First, Darnley concluded that an increase of only two Praise Houses from 1908 to June 1912 could not support the claim of an alarmingly rapid expansion, 'unless the membership of the lodges had materially increased,' which information was not provided. Furthermore, according to Murray's submission, lunacy should have been increasing, even in relation to the small increase in the number of lodges but this was not so. The number of new lunatic cases had declined from twelve in 1908 to ten in 1909 and six in 1910. Although the year 1911 showed an increase of 33 per cent over the previous year, it was still 25 per cent below that of 1908. In the same four-year period, 'illegitimate' births increased by just 1 per cent. Considering the increase in population over the same period, the illegitimacy rate was stable. Thus, Darnley correctly concluded, 'I cannot think that the figures shown above are sufficiently alarming to justify pushing the "Shaker" legislation through so rapidly & without any prior reference either to the Gov: or the S. of S.'[14]

Darnley was clearly more concerned with process, that is, Murray's haste in pushing the legislation, than with constitutionality. This legal spin set the tone for other reviewers, almost all of whom merely echoed Darnley's observation on due process. Not once did Darnley argue for the right of the Penitents to worship according to conscience. Instead, legality gave way to politics, as he observed, 'The Public Sentiment of the Community is in support of the action of the administration.' Darnley failed to point out that only one class of the public had vociferously supported prohibition. Accordingly, he concluded that the 'almost complete discontinuance of Shaker meetings, is perhaps a justification *ex post facto*.' He considered Murray's bill a superior piece of legislation to Cameron's because it had avoided the conundrum of describing Penitentism as 'a religious manifestation.' Nevertheless, he thought the ordinance would have been stronger if it had avoided mentioning Shakerism altogether. Although no concrete evidence was enclosed, Darnley implicitly acknowledged the unsubstantiated charge that Penitent prayer meetings invariably transitioned into 'demoralising orgies.' Despite the spurious charges and the absence of definitions, he believed it was 'safe to leave the decision in the hands of the magistrates.' Darnley began the slide of officials into the murky depth of complicity. It is inconceivable that the Colonial Office would expect magistrates to do anything other than to suppress the Penitents. The record of colonial magistracy is replete with judgements biased by race and social class. Many of the Stipendiary Magistrates sent from England to the colonies to oversee the administration of the Apprenticeship (1834–1838) were known to the Colonial Office to have sold their integrity completely to the plantocracy. The only safety net for subjects was the Colonial Office; but for this threat, its officials had no intention of protecting the targeted victims at the risk of embarrassing or infuriating the colonial governing class.

Corwell began with the same line of argument as Darnley: 'This Ordinance is in force; it has proved effective; it has the approval of the less corybantic religious bodies.'[15] Like Darnley, he concluded, 'On the whole then I think it has justified itself.' Darnley and Corwell fell right into Murray's trap by capitulating to well-orchestrated propaganda of colonial opinion-makers and agents of social control all of whom had vested interested in the eradication of the Penitents. Nevertheless, the logic of the two reviewers was tautological: they were justifying a law because it had been ruthlessly applied to achieve its objective. In effect, they were arguing that a law that violates the constitution ought not to be annulled if it satisfies the interests of the elites for whom the lawmakers are merely their political representatives. Claiming personal knowledge of 'a sect of "Holy Jumpers"' in the Cayman Islands, Corwell implied that its form of worship corresponded with Penitentism. His sole negative comment on the Holy Jumpers, written in parenthesis, was that it included 'amongst its votaries the ingenious Mr Mearus Coe, now in some disrepute in reaction to the practice of wrecking.'[16] Corwell's choice of parenthesis to comment on the

Holy Jumpers suggests that their existence had presented no perceived threat to warrant prohibition and thus it offered no precedent for the Colonial Office's response to Murray's Ordinance.

Corwell's acknowledgement that the Secretary of State for the Colonies wished to see Darnley's Minute with its appended comments indicated the gravity of the issue at stake that Murray, Noble and Cameron had tried to play down. Because of Harcourt's special interest in the process, Corwell proffered two critical suggestions that ultimately informed the Minister's official position on the ordinance. He suggested that Harcourt should call for a further report in a year's time; meanwhile, he should allow the ordinance to remain 'in operation without sending it to H.M.'[17]

In the opening paragraph of his official report on the ordinance, Noble assured the governor, 'It has no reference to "Shakerism" as a form of Religious worship.'[18] Noble was obviously signalling to Cameron that Murray's government had finally listened to the advice of Tarring and the Colonial Office on how to ban the Penitents. But by merely stating that Penitentism was not religious worship was itself an admission that it was so, indeed, as some Colonial Office officials realised. Like Noble, Murray made a Freudian slip in his memorandum to Acting-Governor Cameron by claiming that he had hosted deputations from Penitent leaders from all districts, 'from the Bishop downwards.' He further explained, 'the Bishop I may remark is a labouring man of the better type and a rural constable.'[19] One alert reviewer succinctly attached an exclamation mark after Murray's 'Bishop.' The reviewer had seen the emperor without his clothes but chose to close his eyes for the sake of political expediency.

Only two reviewers attempted to unmask Vincentian politics and expose the unconstitutionality and contradictions of the Ordinance. In responding to Noble's emphatic denial of suppressing a religious movement, Reviewer No. 3 stated,

> I confess I don't understand what the Report means by saying that this ordce has no reference to Shakerism as a form of religious worship. It must obviously apply to any act of religious worship which a magistrate finds to be a custom or practice of Shakerism.[20]

He also admitted, 'N's [Noble's] extreme generality and the wide powers given to magistrates are no doubt open to objections.' Nevertheless, he was not inclined to recommend disallowance. He did not wish to criticise the form of the ordinance, once there was a consensus that its principle was accepted. Thus, he concluded that despite the potential of magistrates to abuse their authority, 'it is difficult to see how else the ordinance could be made effective.'[21] The argument of Reviewer No. 4 was logical and showed some knowledge of the style of African worship:

> 'I agree that there was no need to be so hasty in this matter. With the exception of the jumping exercise the proceedings are such as might have been seen at the ordinary Revivalist meetings in this country not so many years ago.'[22]

Evangelical revivalism extended from late eighteenth into the mid-nineteenth century. It was spearheaded by Methodists but included members of the Church of England. One of the principal founders of the Salvation Army, William Booth, was a product of this movement. Interestingly, Salvationist missionaries to the Zulu in South Africa adopted strategies that would have greatly alarmed Vincentian prohibitionists. Recruited from the lower-middle and labouring classes of England, Salvation Army missionaries endorsed many Zulu cultural traditions, including polygamy. Rationalising that 'African culture could become a legitimate medium for biblical faith,' the London Society instructed them 'to become Zulus to the Zulus.'[23] In Britain and the Caribbean colonies, polygamy was both unchristian and a crime.

Reviewer No. 5 hit on the most salient weakness of the Ordinance: 'There is no definition of Shakerism.' Obviously, he rejected the prohibitionists' demonology as definition. Accordingly, he was certain that 'the power placed in the hands of magistrates and Policemen is far too great.' Falling back on the stereotypical perception of African religion advanced by Revd Broadbent during Cameron's time, the reviewer asserted, 'It is only "Emotional" religion that finds favour with the Negro. An orderly religious service does not appeal to the Negro, and the evidence of real evil from these proceedings is of the most tenuous order.'[24] Broadbent had admitted as much and sought a compromise that would allow the Penitents to maintain their corybantic fervour if they would be loyal to the Methodist Church. This reviewer dismissed the multiple newspaper reports orchestrated to lend credence to the charges of immorality. Although an official reviewer had considered *The Times'* article, 'Shakerism,' as specious, it nevertheless provided a snapshot of the racist attitude of the elites. Having identified the object of the prohibition bill as 'Shakerism or Penitentism,' the writer of the article proclaimed,

> We are proud of the liberty the subject enjoys under British Rule, we are more than thankful for the right to worship as we like, but when we see the disgusting, degrading and pernicious habit in the guise of Religion demoralizing our country and undermining its moral structure it is time to call it a halt.[25]

To such emotional journalism, Reviewer No. 5 said emphatically, 'We cannot justify legislation by the language of a "descriptive" reporter.' If he were in a court of law, he might have moved for a 'no-case' dismissal at that point. He concluded,

> Beyond ascriptions that there is an Evil no Evidence whatever is produced, and I would give a pretty broad hint that Mr Murray was a young man in a hurry in this case, and ask for the Evidence upon which he acted before deciding as to the fate of the Ordinance.

Murray had already marshalled all the 'evidence' he could conjure. Sadly, despite the reviewer's lucid and courageous arguments, by failing to recommend disallowance of the ordinance, he was surreptitiously toeing the line held by his colleagues who had critiqued the ordinance before him.

Lord Alfred Emmot (Reviewer No. 6) said nothing about the points raised. He candidly acknowledged that his concurrence with the soft criticism of the 'procedures' was that he would 'be sorry to see Ordinance disallowed now.'[26] At the time of Emmott's review he was the parliamentary under-secretary and a high-ranking member in the House of Lords. His suggestion that the Colonial Office 'should wait for an answer before sanctioning' lacked specificity. It is inconceivable that the suggestion to wait pertained to No. 5's request for evidence, which these experienced officials must have known did not exist. Evidence of the anticipated eradication arising from the suggestion of No. 3 to allow a trial run of the ordinance for one year would be *ex post facto* validation of an unconstitutional law.

Secretary Harcourt's comments came three days after Emmott's. He agreed with Cowell's suggestion to wait for a year before sanctioning the ordinance. He also agreed with the criticisms of the procedure and concluded, 'I have discussed this with Mr Murray & believe the suppression of Shakerism is necessary & will be successful.'[27] He did not reveal how and when he communicated with Murray on the subject; nevertheless, the meeting was also substantiated in the margins of a Cabinet note on the Shouters' Prohibition Ordinance, which stated that the Secretary of State for the Colonies allowed St Vincent's anti-Penitent ordinance only after discussions with Murray.[28] It is highly likely that the reviewers of the Ordinance would have known of Harcourt's conservation with Murray and his support for prohibition, which explains why no reviewer had proposed its disallowance.

One day after the completion of consultations on the Ordinance, Darnley drafted a memorandum addressed to Governor Sadler on behalf of the secretary of state for the Colonies. He wasted no time in scoring the primary point of the message:

> Before considering what advice to tender to His Majesty in
> the matter I propose to leave the Ordinance in operation
> for a year, at the end of which period you should furnish
> me with a further report as to its working and the extent to
> which its object has been obtained.[29]

Sanctioning a trial run was based on expediency, not policy. By not tendering Murray's ordinance to the King, Harcourt avoided the scrutiny of the distinguished law officers of the King's Bench and possibly that of Parliament.

Darnley's original draft of the official memorandum to Governor Sadler expressed strong approbation of Murray but only on the softer violation of protocol. He wanted Harcourt to say that despite the,

> peculiar difficulties surrounding any legislation on such
> a subject I am surprised that Mr Murray should have
> assumed the responsibility of independent action in the
> matter & I am unable to accept the consideration which

> he has put forward as justifying the haste with which this
> measure has been passed into law. I have to request that
> Mr. Murray be informed accordingly.[30]

In his comment on the draft communiqué, Reviewer No. 4 recognised that in making concessions for 'peculiar difficulties' the secretary of state for the Colonies would be providing colonial Administrators with 'covering sanctions' to circumvent the oversight of governors in the future. He wrote authoritatively, 'There is a right way and a wrong way of doing things & Mr Murray ought to receive a reproof for his procedure.'[31] Accordingly, Darnley modified that section of the draft to read,

> I consider that Mr Murray should have obtained your
> approval before taking action in the matter & I cannot
> regard the considerations which he has put forward as
> constituting an adequate justification for his omission to
> do so. I have to request that Mr Murray may be informed
> accordingly.[32]

No one directly addressed the constitutionality of the ordinance. Ultimately, the imperial government's reprimand of Murray was singular, unlike that of 1809, when it extended to all governors. For that reason, the government of Trinidad and Tobago was emboldened to replicate the ordinance to prohibit Penitentism just five years later.

Darnley's Memorandum became the official response of the secretary of state for the Colonies to the governor-in-chief of the Windward Islands. No reviewer had recommended or suggested that Acting-Governor Cameron be reprimanded for his advice to Murray to proceed with the ordinance. Like Brutus' dagger, Harcourt's memorandum was, however, the final nail in the coffin for Penitentism. His endorsement of Murray's suppression of the religion was politically expedient. His concealment of the ordinance from the King also indicts him as an active accomplice in denying freedom of conscience to the Penitents and supersedes Murray's culpability for violation of the constitution. It is historical farce that it was Harcourt who assumed the monumental role of guardian of morality of Vincentian Penitents. Their alleged orgies could not compare with Harcourt's immoral lifestyle. He was a well-known philanderer, paedophile, and sodomite.

One contemporary aristocrat described him as 'simply a sex maniac.'[33]

Corwell's advice to temporarily restrict the ordinance to the Colonial Office was boldly scripted at the top of the ordinance: 'before considering what advice to tender to H.M., proposes to leave Ordinance in operation for a year, when report is furnished on its working.' This note establishes that the ordinance was not an 'executive matter' on which the secretary of state for the Colonies had 'ultimate authority' to rule, as discussed in the opening of this chapter. Harcourt had usurped King's authority. The official stamp, 'SANCTIONED,' appears alongside the proposal: it was undated but the phrase '& Annual Report requested,' indicates that the Ordinance may have been formally sanctioned in order to legitimise Murray's 'operation' against the Penitents. Nevertheless, one could conclude that final authorisation was in November 1913, which was indicated in the words 'Report Supplied' immediately above the Colonial Office stamp.

Exposing the Irrelevance of 'Heathenism' and 'Paganism' in Asserting the Write of Conscience

In April 1813, one hundred years before the Colonial Office review of Murray's Shakerism ordinance, the House of Commons had tabled several petitions from denominations in many cities pleading for parliamentary authority to promote Christianity in India. The Petitioners of the synod of Fife considered the traditional beliefs and practices of 'the inhabitants of British India' as a hindrance to the advancement of Western civilisation: the natives were 'now sitting in darkness, practising horrid cruelties under the name of religious rites, and addicted to the most detestable usages.'[34] The petition from 'the inhabitants of Glasgow' also arrogantly deplored 'the ignorance in which that vast country is involved, and the prevalence in it of practices and customs abhorrent to every principle of humanity.'[35] Unlike the Fife petitioners, however, the Glaswegians respected 'the rights of conscience in the most ignorant and erring and are far from entertaining the thought that any mean (sic) should be employed which might disturb the inhabitants in the possession of their just privileges.'[36]

In conceding these rights, the Glaswegians specifically acknowledged that in India, 'Pagans and Mahometans are permitted to exercise their religion under every form.'[37] By pagans, the petitioners meant Hindus, Sikhs, Jains and other religions outside Christian-Judaic cosmology.

The distinction between India and the Caribbean was significant. In India, European colonisers were dealing with autochthonous populations that remained politically free, albeit disenfranchised, since the first encounters. In the Caribbean, the colonisers were dealing with transported populations whose chattel inductions to the region were only slightly modified since their emancipation. Racist intolerance of African cultures was always stronger than racist intolerance of Indian cultures. But, beyond racism, colonists generally believed that Caribbean colonies were Christian polities. English colonists grudgingly conceded toleration to non-Anglican denominations, Roman Catholics, and Jews. Non-Protestant concessions did not threaten White supremacy: Roman Catholics were predominantly Irish and French; Jews in the Caribbean were considered Caucasian, even if they were not originally counted in censuses as 'White.' Shakerism, however, was deemed 'more suited to savages than to dwellers in a Christian land.'[38]

In the Caribbean, colonists stood firmly against all non-White, non-Caucasian religious organisations as threats to their fragile hold on the 'recognised faiths' and control of the minds of the labouring class whose subjugation was necessary for maintaining White privilege and power. In 1835, education consultant, Revd John Sterling, proposed to the imperial government that it was imperative that the curriculum for the soon-to-be-emancipated Africans be designed to maintain 'power over their minds,' if the colonists were to retain the status quo ante-emancipation.[39] Sterling was a priest to the enslaver class in St Kitts before returning to England. His recommendations were based on submissions by Anglican clergy in the colonies. One of these clergymen was Revd Thomas Browne, son of Lt Thomas Brown of Bentinck estate in St Vincent. Revd Browne contended that the content of education of freed children should be 'consistent with their future prospects in life.'[40] Since he wished to employ child labour on his estate, it is evident what future he envisaged for them.

Colonial administrations, in collaboration with the imperial government, co-opted all Protestant denominations as the vanguard of psychological warfare against the emancipated class. Roman Catholics were not privileged with a share of the imperial education grant but no less aggressively pursued the emancipated with the support of colonial governments. African cultural retentions were the principal target of this relentless war. Although Thomas Buxton's only offer of compensation to enslaved Africans was to provide them with Bibles, the legacies of the African spiritual universe were not to be allowed to reincarnate within the worldview of Europeanised Christianity, and certainly, not to be accorded any degree of legitimacy. Toward the end of the nineteenth century, the resurgence of Penitentism as an alternative culture-system, with its own Friendly Societies and other financial securities, panicked the colonial elites. Dispensing with subtleties, the institutions of colonialist opinion-making (church, school, police, government and the press) were desperate for a final solution. This exigency could not be better expressed than in the editorial in *The Times* newspaper of June 25, 1908: by declaiming that Shakerism did 'more harm than good,' the author was presuming that the 'recognised churches' were doing better for the labouring classes. The author derided Penitents' 'athletic style of praising god; they jump, dance, clap their hands, shout and gesticulate in a most unbecoming manner.'[41] The writer presumed that the African-influenced liturgy was harmful to worshippers while European-styled non-corybantic worship was harmless. It cannot be overemphasised, however, that the form of worship was not a precondition for the enjoyment of protection under any toleration law.

The Beginning of the Police Crackdown on Penitent Worship

The first arrests under the prohibition ordinance occurred at Questelles on February 2, 1913, exactly four months after the passage of the legislation. They were directly related to Murray's strategy for endorsement from the Colonial Office. Murray submitted his first official report on the operation of prohibition, as demanded by the

Colonial Office, just three weeks after the convictions of the accused.[42] The timing of the arrests and submission of Murray's report give credence to the view that the arrests were politically motivated because without them he would not be able to satisfy the Colonial Office that legislation was necessary to resolve the threat allegedly posed by Penitentism.

The testimonies of the two arresting officers, Corporal DeShong and Constable Trumpet, were conveniently tailored to reflect Clause 7 (1) of the ordinance, which authorised any police officer without warrant to enter any place he had 'good ground to believe or suspect that a Shakers meeting is being held.' Penitents' prayer meetings continued to enjoy protection even under Murray's prohibition ordinance. Thus, the police could only make arrests based on the presumption that prayers would be followed by 'orgies.' This abuse of power, from the absence of definitions and broad powers given to the police and magistrates, was recognised by the reviewers of the ordinance. On this potential abuse alone the secretary of state for the Colonies should have disallowed the ordinance. That he failed to do so was consistent with his attitude to policymaking. According to De Marigny, 'Harcourt's influence on the formation of major policy was, if not minimal, definitely limited.'[43] As we have discussed above, Harcourt's memorandum to Sadler in December 1912 had no views of his own.

At least three policemen had gone on the raid of the Questelles Praise house. The two lower-ranked officers were deposed, that is, they gave sworn testimonies; the senior officer in charge of the raid, Sergeant-Major Gaffney, prosecuted the case in court.[44] The account of the raid as reported by the two subordinates differed in many respects, which would have provided fodder for a defence lawyer. Unfortunately, the accused were not represented by counsel. Corporal DeShong lived at Questelles. He swore that he was privy to several meetings at the Questelles Praise house that lasted until daylight. Thus, he deposed confidently, 'It was a Shakers Meeting. I know well what is so called in St Vincent.'[45] He contended, 'Acts of sexuality go on by the members who go outside.' He said he once saw worshippers collapse from exhaustion but did not state that he had personally witnessed immoral acts. If he had, he would have been derelict in the conduct of his duty;

as a police officer he was bound by other laws to arrest such persons. Yet, he affirmed, 'It was this kind of meeting that was going on the date on which the defendants are charged.' If he was being truthful in claiming that he was a regular visitor to Penitent meetings that lasted until the morning, it is inconceivable that no arrests were made after midnight, when the evidence would have been more credible, according to prohibitionists' narratives. DeShong's testimony did not rise to the minimum level of evidence necessary to indict a suspect, even under the generality of Murray's ordinance.

DeShong deposed that he arrived at the Praise House at about 10:20 p.m. and that the party waited outside for five minutes during which time he saw worshippers 'jumping and dancing, singing and clapping hands.' His description was nothing other than corybantic worship. According to his version of events, upon seeing the police, one worshipper shouted, 'This is Zion's water-wheel to-night,' the signal for all to flee. In all, there were approximately thirty worshipers. DeShong stated emphatically, 'We held 4 Patterson, Davis, McDowall and Shepherd.'

The most junior officer in the raiding party, Constable Trumpet, lived at Coulls Hill, several kilometres to North Leeward but claimed to 'know all the defendants' from the Questelles chapel.[46] Like DeShong, Trumpet claimed personal knowledge of Shakerism: 'I have often attended Shakers Meetings. This was one.' His knowledge of Shakerism might have come from Coulls Hill where Shakers' meetings were still being held. Trumpet asserted, when the lights go out 'the men and women have connexion' (sic) on the floor' of the Praise House at Coulls Hill. He also claimed, 'After the meeting I have seen the "Minister" remain and have one of the "Sisters" on the floor of the Shakers house.' Trumpet, however, did not explain why he had not arrested the Minister or any worshipper for immoral acts before February.

In describing the prayer scene on the night of the first arrests, Trumpet provided a different version of the alleged Zion water-wheel code. He claimed that the line, 'Zion water wheel is pouring down,' was being sung by all members, not by one man only, as DeShong had deposed and that the song was being sung during the five minutes that the officers were waiting outside; thus, it was not a coded warning of the police presence. Trumpet also deposed emphatically, 'We held three (3) but identified all the defendants except Davis.' In addition to the arrests, Trumpet testified, 'We took the names of Roberts Baptiste and Shephers (sic), Baptiste ran away.' He claimed that he caught Roberts and Patterson; DeShong did not include Roberts as being arrested that night. The Ordinance authorised the police to take the names of persons who escaped arrest, so that they might be held at a future time; but on the night of the raid, the combined names of the arrested worshippers amounted to only five, including Roberts, the disputed arrest. Baptiste must have been arrested after the raid, because six defendants faced the court, three women and three men: John Patterson, Joseph Roberts, Annie Davis, Robertha McDowall, Caroline Shepherd, and Alfred Baptiste, the apparent Leader.[47] According to DeShong, when the police stormed the Praise House, Baptiste was sitting at his desk with a book.[48] DeShong provided no reason for him not being immediately arrested. Trumpet, on the other hand, claimed that Baptiste was in the 'pulpit' with his book, but that he had run away.[49] As if to confirm that he had no concrete evidence to arrest the Shakers at Questelles, Trumpet concluded, 'What I saw at Questelles on the 2nd February instant was what I know from my experience to be a Shakers Meeting.' DeShong had made a similar appeal to his general knowledge of Shakerism.

The magistrate expressed no concern that the only raid on a Praise House occurred four months after the posting of the ordinance and during the Wesleyan-style prayer session. DeShong did not say where he had witnessed Penitents' orgies; Trumpet did not explain why the police did not arrest the Penitents of Coulls Hill. Furthermore, public acts of indecency did not require the Shakers' Prohibition Ordinance. It is not unfair to conclude that there was political or administrative pressure on the police to arrest penitents, even if the circumstantial evidence points to political or administrative pressure on the police to arrest Penitents, even if they were not in violation of the Ordinance so that Murray would have tangible evidence to present to the Colonial Office on the 'working' of the Ordinance. It should be recalled that Griffith's Report, dated September 6, 1912 had listed only four villages where Shakers' meetings were still being held. Both Questelles and Coulls Hill were designated as free of Shakerism: 'No meetings of any kind are now being held.' In his update of October 22, only in Diamond Village was there a Shakers' meeting. The evidence presented by the police involved in the raid on Questelles in February 1913 only supports a Prayer meeting, not a 'Shakers' meeting,' as dichotomised by the Murray administration. Baptiste and his congregation at the Questelles Praise House should have had no case to answer.

It would not have required much experience in the practice of law to unravel the police case. It was evident that they were reconstructing common allegations of Penitent meetings as if they had occurred at the Questelles Praise house. The arrested Penitents were all charged with 'taking part in and attending a "Shakers" meeting at Questelles Village within the First Police District on the 2nd instant contrary to Section 3 of "The Shakers Prohibition Ordinance 1912."' Prosecutor Gaffney's case was a rehash of the report of the other two police officers, except for two details: he changed the time of the raid to 10:15 p.m.; and Corporal DeShong was now Corporal DesChamps. If the prosecutor could not get his colleague's name right, the magistrate should have had less confidence in his testimony. Unfortunately, the accused had no legal representation and could not count on impartiality from the magistrate whose superior was a co-author of the ordinance.

The brief report of the case by Magistrate Robert Roden is no less convoluted than the evidence of DeShong and Trumpet. Roden stated that the defendants comprised four men and two women. The police, however, reportedly arrested three women. Roden stated that he dismissed the case against 'one woman,' presumably, Annie Davis, 'against whom there was no evidence.'[50] According to Edward Cox, the two other women, Robertha McDowell and Caroline Shepherd, pleaded 'guilty to attending;' the three men pleaded, 'Not guilty.'[51] The magistrate convicted the five, 'As there could be no doubt that the defendants had broken the law.'[52] A discerning reviewer of the evidence would definitely disagree. In the first case, Roden included only the evidence of the police for scrutiny. Although the ordinance deliberately avoided defining 'Shakers' meeting,' Noble's Report was specific about the elements of 'Shakerism,' the main congregational feature being trances or experiences of spirit possession and orgiastic scenes, neither of which the police had witnessed at Questelles. Magistrate Roden reprimanded the two women; he imposed a fine of £1 each on Patterson and Roberts with an alternative of fourteen days imprisonment with hard labour; and 30 shillings on Leader Baptiste, with an option of one month's imprisonment with hard labour.[53]

The exclusion of the evidence of the six defendants was a far cry from the amelioration period of slavery in Trinidad, St Lucia, and Demerara (1823–34) when the testimony of all witnesses, the accused and the litigants before the chambers of the Protector of Slaves and his Adjutants, was meticulously recorded.[54] Almost one hundred years later, justice had walked backward in St Vincent. Without a doubt, the Questelles Six were sacrificial lambs to attempt to convince the secretary of state for the Colonies that the Penitents remained a threat to society so that he might sanction the legislation retroactively. Even the inclusion of the exonerated woman fits the plot to send a message that the eradication of Shakerism was not a witch-hunt. Without legal counsel to challenge prohibition, many Penitents fled to Trinidad and other destinations, including the US in search of new provinces of religious freedom.

Murray's Apparent Blackmail of the British Government

One week after the trial of the six scapegoats, and three days after the magistrate submitted his written report, Murray's first report on the working of the Ordinance was in the hands of Governor Sadler for transmission to the secretary of state for the Colonies. Six weeks later, in early April 1913, Murray forwarded a copy of a lengthy column in *The Sentry*, 'Shakerism and Religion,' written by Everard Feilding, a lawyer, when he was Murray's guest at Government House.[55] The enclosure perplexed Darnley. It was the first official communication from Murray since transmitting the report of the first cases against the Shakers. No reason accompanied the article, but Murray was desperate enough to wield any weapon that would obfuscate the kangaroo judgements against the Questelles Six. Darnley's draft minutes was brief but scathing: 'I don't quite know why Mr. Murray expressly asks for this article to be transmitted to the S. of S.; I suppose *not* because of the passage which I have marked A towards the end.'[56] Several officials initialled the draft, but only two commented or rather, reacted. Both expressed a sense of humour; one quipped cynically, 'Shakerism regarded historically & psychologically!'

The highlighted text that aroused Darnley's suspicion of Murray's real intention read:

> The Burning Bush ultimately transplanted itself to the more grateful soil of Wales, where I hope it may make a convert of the Chancellor of the Exchequer, and assist him to cast off the burden of his sins against the Dukes and the Suffragettes in a pleasant and health-giving manner.[57]

The incumbent chancellor was David Lloyd George, a Welshman, Britain's second highest government minister and one of the most popular politicians of the day. George and several high-ranking government ministers, including Murray's elder brother, were accused of corruption in the scandal-ridden 'Marconi Affair' that became public in mid-1912. Murray's brother resigned as parliamentary secretary to the Treasury the following year; George successfully weathered the storm.[58] Feilding's jab, however, was obviously directed at George's 'notorious' extra-marital affairs, which were largely kept out of the media during and after his term as Chancellor.[59]

Darnley's dismay over Murray's potential complicity in Feilding's raunchy chastisement of the chancellor was underscored by his total lack of concern about any other detail in the article. There is a distinct probability of a subliminal link between Feilding's coded attack on the chancellor and Murray's anxiety to have the Colonial Office officially sanction his ordinance. No doubt, Feilding's reference to the Exchequer was political satire, but it was the only section of the article highlighted by anyone. Silence on the rest of the article suggests that officials chose not to entangle themselves in a private squabble or scandal. The article was not salutary to the Penitents; nevertheless, elements of it would have been valuable to a defence lawyer arguing against Penitentism as a danger to public order. By highlighting a satire with metropolitan value only, Darnley had consigned the bulk of the article to useless prohibition propaganda. Feilding acknowledged that he was merely 'jesting' about Penitentism while composing the column but 'only to the element in it which the government of the island has recently seen fit to prohibit.' Not wishing to project himself as a religious fanatic, he assured that he would 'make no allusion to such real religious element as Shakerism contains.' He did not clarify what those elements were; but even the general acknowledgement contradicted Noble's official Report that there was nothing religious about Shakerism. Feilding even had 'some personal regret' about the Shouters' Prohibition Ordinance, because 'there is a simplicity about jumping as a means to salvation which has always attracted me.'[60]

Feilding's article made a mockery of the prosecution of the Questelles Six by showcasing several similar movements around the world that governments did not move to stamp out. Indeed, the satire on Lloyd George was a mere sideswipe in a long paragraph on the Metropolitan Church Association or Metropolitan Methodist Mission commonly called 'Holy Jumpers' and 'Burning Bush,' a movement that emerged in Chicago in the late nineteenth century. The paragraph opened with a comment that absolved Penitentism from being a stain on European civilisation. The MCA had gone to Camberwell, a London Borough, to evangelise. Feilding's view of the sect is worthy of note. He wrote,

> For it isn't only in St Vincent that people still jump to Glory. Not long ago there appeared in London a small party of Americans who called themselves the Pentecostal Dancers of the Burning Bush, and hailed from Denver, Colorado. They had somehow been 'saved,' and the burden of their sins removed from them, with the result that they felt extremely light. And to show how light they felt, they took to jumping.[61]

This state of spiritual ecstasy is what the Spiritual Baptists call 'rejoicing.' While in Camberwell, the MCA taught attendees the joy of jumping. Feilding testified that he attended one such performance and described their style of worship, laced with humour rather than rancour: 'They pranced around the platform while they prayed, they bounded about with antic gestures while they preached.' He said sarcastically that during the singing of hymns, they performed 'a spirited Salvation Schottische … which should have lured many souls from the Pit.'[62]

The MCA did not completely escape civil and political persecution in the United States of America. Anti-Jumper sentiments peaked in the same decade as anti- Penitentism. Spectators sometimes physically attacked MCA preachers and cities brought charges against them for violating public-order laws.[63] The following case is instructive. At a street meeting in Waukesha in Wisconsin state, in June 1907, a female MCA exhorter proclaimed, 'All the Waukesha Methodists are going to hell.'[64] The spectators reacted with riotous hostility. The city of Waukesha arrested and charged six members of the MCA with 'disorderly conduct while holding a religious street meeting.' Since the city recognised them as a 'religious' group, the First Amendment protected their right to preach, just as Britian's PWRA protected the Penitents from Cameron. Unlike the Questelles-Six, however, the Waukesha-Six had competent legal counsel who demanded a trial by jury. Again, unlike St Vincent, some influential citizens of Waukesha 'offered to go as bondsmen' for the accused, although they were firmly against the beliefs of the MCA. They simply 'wished to see fair play.' And, unlike the case of the Questelles-Six, several witnesses testified for the accused. Defence lawyer, Joseph E. Waldish, argued 'that jumping and screaming was part of their religious belief and that the spectators and not his clients were guilty of disorderly conduct.' Of the four accused tried together, all were exonerated; of the other two tried separately, one was discharged on a no-case submission; the jury for the other was divided on conviction and a re-trial was ordered.[65]

Darnley extrapolated no lessons from Feilding's article to bring a measure of relief to the Penitents. He merely hoped that it was not the real intention of the writer to cast aspersions on the Chancellor's character. Having worked in the Colonial Office, Murray would have heard of the chancellor's philandering. The real purpose of the article appears to have been a veiled threat to expose the chancellor's scandal to the media. If so, it might have been political blackmail to facilitate final sanction of the ordinance, which was given in November 1913; exactly one year after the ordinance had arrived at the Colonial Office, thus faithfully adhering to the recommendation of Murray's friends and associates to the secretary of state for the Colonies.

Notes

1. Sir Frank Swettenham, *'The Administration of the Crown Colonies': The Empire and The Century: A Series of Essays on Imperial Problems and Possibilities by Various Writers* (London: John Murray, 1905), 885. Downing Street was both the geographical location and a metaphor for imperial Cabinet offices.
2. Leahy, *History of the Catholic Church*, 49.
3. Beck, *The History of South Africa*, 96.
4. *World Biographical Encyclopedia*, https://prabook.com/web/george. fiddes/2305992. 'george Vandeleur Fiddes,' *Alchetron: The Free Social Encyclopedia*, https://alchetron.com/George-Vandeleur-Fiddes, updated September 19, 2022.
5. 'Alfred Emmott, 1st and Last Baron Emmott,' last updated May 2011, https://www.thepeerage.com/p2214.htm, last updated May 2011. *Wikiwand*, https://www.wikiwand.com/en/Alfred_Emmott_1st_Baron _Emmott.
6. John Anderson (not to be confused with Sir John Anderson [1858–1918] both of whom were Colonial Office officials, since 1905. This author could not find any information on some the reviewers, including some listed in the Minute Book with the draft response to the Governor.
7. John Dudeney and John Sheail, *Claiming the Ice: Britain and the Antarctic 1900–1950* (New Castle Upon Tyne: Cambridge Scholars, 2019), 12.
8. Dudeney and Sheail, *Claiming the Ice*, 12.
9. Ibid., Emphasis is original.
10. The author assigned numbers to each reviewer because the identity behind some initials could not be ascertained.
11. E. R. Darnley (Reviewer No. 1), November 22, 1912; Cameron to Harcourt, October 24, 1912, file no. CO 35806, 'Ordinance 13, 1912, Shakerism Prohibition Submits,' BNA, CO 321/269. Darnley identified the request for the Bill with reference number '8883', which was also scribbled in the margin next to Cameron's affirmation of receipt of correspondence no. 65 of 3 September 3, 1912.
12. *The Times*, July 11, 1912; encl. in Murray to Cameron, 12 Oct. 1912, encl. in Cameron to Harcourt, October 24, 1912, BNA, CO 321/269.
13. *The Sentry*, July 12, 1912; encl. in Murray to Cameron, 12 Oct. 1912, encl. in Cameron to Harcourt, October 24, 1912, BNA, CO 321/269.
14. Reviewer No. 1, Darnley, November 22, 1912; Cameron to Harcourt, October 24, 1912, BNA, CO 321/269.
15. Roland Corwell (Reviewer No. 2), November 22, 1912, file CO 35806, BNA, CO 321/269.

16. Corwell, (Reviewer No. 2), November 27, 1912, file CO 35806, BNA, CO 321/269.

17. Corwell, 27 Nov. 1912, file CO 35806, BNA, CO 321/269.

18. Noble to Cameron, 'The Shakerism Prohibition Ordinance, 1912: Report,' September 7, 1912, encl. in Cameron to Harcourt, October 24, 1912, BNA, CO 321/269.

19. Murray to Cameron, October 12, 1912, encl. in Cameron to Harcourt, October 24, 1912, BNA, CO 321/269.

20. Reviewer No. 3 (initials not deciphered), November 26, 1912, file CO 35806, BNA, CO 321/269.

21. Review No. 3, file CO 35806, BNA, CO 321/269.

22. Review No. 4 (initials not deciphered), November 30, 1912, enclosed in Cameron to Harcourt, October 24, 1912, file CO 35806, BNA, CO 321/269.

23. Andrew M. Eason, '"All things to All People to Save Some": Salvation Army Missionary Work among the Zulus of Victoria Natal,' *Journal of South African Studies* 35, no. 1 (Mar. 2009): 9, https://www.jstor.org/stable/40283212.

24. Reviewer No. 5, November 30, 1912.

25. *The Times*, July 11, 1912, enclosed in Cameron to Harcourt, October 24, 1912, BNA, CO 321/269.

26. Review No. 6, (initial not deciphered), December 2, 1912, enclosed in Cameron to Harcourt, October 24, 1912, CO 321/269.

27. Review No. 7, Harcourt, December 5, 1912, enclosed in Cameron to Harcourt, October 24, 1912, CO 321/269.

28. Minutes, January 23, 1918, BNA, CO 295/513.

29. Darnley (Reviewer No. 1), BNA, CO 295/513.

30. Ibid.

31. Cameron to Harcourt, 24 Oct. 1912, Reviewer No. 4, November 30, 1912, BNA, CO 321/269.

32. Darnley (Reviewer No. 1), BNA, CO 321/269.

33. See Paul Frecker, 'Lewis Vernon Harcourt,' The Library of Nineteenth-Century Photography, www.19thcenturyphotos.com, accessed December 28, 2022. Obregon, 'Lewis Harcourt: The British Pedophile Port Harcourt was named after,' available at www.ng.opera.news, accessed September 20, 2020. 'Lewis Harcourt, 1st Viscount Harcourt,' https://peoplepill.com/people/lewis-vernon-harcourt-1st-viscount-harcourt, accessed December 20, 2022.

34. 'Petitions for Promoting the Christian Religion in India,' April 27, 1813, BL. *Parliamentary Debates* 25 (March 11–May 10, 1813), 1084.

35. 23 *Parliamentary Debates* 25, House of Commons, April 28, 1813, 1091.

36. 25 *Parliamentary Debates, 'Petitions,'* House of Commons, April 28, 1813, 1091.

37. Ibid., 1090. The 'Doctrine of the Trinity' Act was only passed months later: 26 *Parliamentary Debates, House of Lords,* July 20, 2013, *1222. Times,*

June 25, 1908, encl. in Cameron to Crewe, October 24, 1912, BNA, CO 321/243.

38. Shirley C. Gordon, *A Century of West Indian Education: A Sourcebook* (London: Longmans, 1963), 21.

39. Boa, 'Colour, Class and Gender,' 241.

40. *The Times*, June 25, 1908, encl. in Cameron to Crewe, October 24, 1912, BNA, CO 321/243.

41. Murray to Sadler, February 25, 1913, BNA, CO 321/273.

42. Guy Desvaux de Marigny, 'The Public Career of Lewis Harcourt (First Viscount) 1905 – 1916' (M.A. diss., University of Witwatersrand, Johannesburg, South Africa, 1987; v).

43. 'Report on Certain Convictions for "Shakerism,"' enclosed in Murray to Sadler, February 25, 1913, BNA, CO 321/273.

44. 'Evidence: Corporal DeShong,' enclosed in Murray to Sadler, February 25, 1913, BNA, CO 321/273.

45. 'Evidence: P. C. Trumpet,' enclosed in Murray to Sadler, February 25, 1913, BNA, CO 321/273.

46. Edward Cox, 'Religious Intolerance and Persecution: The Case of the Shakers in St Vincent, 1900–1934,' SVGNA, CR-RBC-179, 32–33. This is an unpublished paper with no date. A later version was published in the *Journal of Caribbean History* 28, no. 2 (1994): 208–43. In 1908 the Leader of the Praise House at Questelles was identified as Horatio MacDonald.

47. 'Evidence of Corporal DeShong.'

48. Ibid.,

49. For Davis as the exonerated accused, See Cox, 'Religious Intolerance,' 33.

50. Cox, 'Religious Intolerance,' 32–33.

51. Ibid, 33.

52. 'Report on Certain Convictions for "Shakerism."' Cox, 'Religious Intolerance,' 33.

53. Fergus, *Revolutionary Emancipation, 165-68; Claudius Fergus, 'Centring the City in the Amelioration of Slavery in Trinidad,' JCH* 40, 1 (2006), 128–33.

54. 'Shakerism and Religion,' *The Sentry*, 21 Mar. 1913, encl. in file 'St Vincent: Shakerism,' CO 14511, March 29, 1913, BNA, CO 321/273. Feilding was a lawyer and naval intelligence officer. Psychical research was a hobby.

55. Draft Minute, May 8, 1913; emphasis original, BNA CO 321/ 273.

56. 'Shakerism and Religion,' *The Sentry*, March 21, 1913, CO 321/273.

57. 'Marconi Scandal,' https://www.wikiwand.co.Marconi_scandal, accessed September 14, 2020. 167 *Journal of the House of Commons, 14 February 1912 to 7 Mar. 1913* (London, 1912), 349. Max Hastings, 'Corruption was ever a very British scandal,' *New York Times*, February 3, 2023.

58. Ben Johnson, 'Lloyd George,' *Historic UK: The History and Heritage Accommodation Guide*, https://www.historic-uk.com/HistoryUK/Historyof Britain/Lloyd-George/, September 14, 2020; Robert Norman William Blake, 'David Lloyd George,' Britannica, https://www.britannica.com/biography/David-Lloyd-George, accessed September 14, 2020].

59. Feilding, 'Shakerism and Religion,' *The Sentry*, March 21, 1913, BNA, CO 321/273.

60. Ibid.

61. The Schottische was a slow Bohemian country-dance characterised by its half steps; it was popular in nineteenth century England among the leisured class.

62. Susan 13202, Blog, posted April 12, 2008, excerpt from *Racine Journal* June 16, 1905, 10, https://www.city-data.com/forum/people-search/253236-leonard-ebenezer-wetherill-1883-1973-2.html, accessed September 12, 2020.

63. *The Waukesha Freeman*, October 10, 1907, 4, column 3, https://www.city-data.com/forum/people-search/253236-leonard-ebenezer-wetherill-1883-1973-2.html, accessed September 12, 2020. For a theology of this claim, see William Kostlevy, *Holy Jumpers: Evangelicals and Radicals in Progressive Era America* (New York: Oxford University Press, 2010), Google Books.

64. Susan130202, reports from *The Waukesha Freeman*, July 11, 1907, 7, column 3; *The Waukesha Freeman*, August 2, 1907, 5, column 5, *Racine Daily Journal*, 2, September 6, 1907, 4, column 3; *The La Crosse Tribune*, September 27, 1907, 4, column 3; *The Waukesha Freeman*, October 10, 1907, 6, column 5, https://www.city-data.com/forum/people-search/253236-leonard-ebenezer-wetherill-1883-1973-2.html, accessed September 12, 2020.

CHAPTER 7

The Shouters Prohibition Ordinance, with a Commentary on Grenada's Shakerism Ordinance

'Nuisance is a very old common law tort grounded in the idea that a property owner should be entitled to the peaceful enjoyment of his own property without reasonable interference from the use of their neighbouring properties.'

Much of the debate on the Shouters' Prohibition Ordinance was a rehash of the debate on St Vincent's Shakers' Ordinance. Nevertheless, it is important to consider some of these iterations as well as some of the key modulations to the Trinidad and Tobago case. The Colonial Office placed the colonies of Trinidad and Tobago under one government in 1889. The Shouters, however, remained a Trinidad movement within a predominantly Catholic-Anglican polity. Tobago was predominantly non-conformist Protestant; a BMS presence was established in mid-nineteenth century;[1] the island, however, did not have new African migrant labourers in the post-slavery era, the common element in the rise of Spiritual Baptist.

The pioneer BMS schoolteachers and missionaries to Trinidad arrived in 1843 and immediately sought out the African American Baptists in the Company Villages and Belmont.[2] Just as they did in The Bahamas and Jamaica, however, they could not reconcile with the unfamiliar brand of nonconformism of the Merikin Church. From first contact down to the end of the nineteenth century, the BMS maintained a cordial if tense relationship with Merikin clerics, but never invoked State prohibition. The BMS' attitude toward the Spiritual Baptists was radically different.

---

* Brett J. Haroldson, 'Saved by the Bells: A Look at Campanological Rights of U.S. Churches,' *Rutgers Journal of Law and Religion* 17 (2016): 92, https://lawandreligion. com/lawandreligion/wp-content/uploads/sites/4/2017/03/Saved-By-The-Bells/ Haroldson.pdf.

The Genesis of Shouterism Prohibition Propaganda

The first significant public attack on the Spiritual Baptists occurred in 1894, orchestrated by an anonymous writer in the *Port of Spain Gazette*. Interestingly, the object of attack was a group of Penitents from St Vincent. The title of the short article, 'The 'Shakers' in Town,' suggests a sudden awakening to a new religious phenomenon. The epithets that the writer hurled at the Penitents foreshadowed the virulent attacks on the movement in St Vincent. The writer labelled them 'an abominable nuisance' and 'a band of lunatics;' accused them of performing 'hideous incantations' at their meetings; and indicted male members for abducting teenaged girls 'for immoral purposes.'[3] One of the earliest public spotlights on the 'Shouters' as an object of law enforcement arose in 1898 from a report in the *Port of Spain Gazette* of a police case wherein two women were charged for disorderly conduct after a Shakers' meeting at the home of one Mr Primus in Tunapuna.[4] The newspaper report implied that the two women were part of a crowd that gathered in the road outside the improvised prayer house but did not confirm that they had attended the service. Significantly, the praise–house was filled 'every Sunday night … with a congregation of "Shouters."' The reporter concluded that the activities had 'gradually been approaching a public nuisance,' but did not call for police action or government's intervention.

Prohibitionism as a movement in Trinidad originated with two BMS ministers, Revd Joseph James Cooksey, stationed in Princes Town, and Revd B. E. Horlick, stationed in Belmont.[5] Cooksey arrived in Trinidad in 1902; he was not sent by the BMS, but was paid out of the colonial government's ecclesiastic fund. Cooksey resigned in 1906 in protestation against government's lack of political will to eradicate Shouterism.[6] This means that prohibitionism in Trinidad paralleled that of St Vincent, although there was yet no overt political mobilisation against the movement in Trinidad. It was *The Mirror*'s report of the Cooksey affair in 1906 and the reporter's own advocacy that set the parameters for the prohibition of Shouterism. The *Port of Spain Gazette* would eventually take the baton from *The Mirror* and lead the media attack on the Shouters. The allegation of *The Mirror* that rejoicing of the Merikin Baptists of Third Company disturbed the peace at night would become the focal point of political vendetta against Shouterism. Based only on the congregations observed in rural Merikin communities, the reporter inferred that the movement was a culturally marginal phenomenon; even so, it must have been enough of an enigma to cause 'a non-conformist minister' (Cooksey) to resign his post and abandon the island, shortly before the publication of the article.

The Mirror reporter betrayed a racial bias in selectively targeting Shouters' noises for special legislative action. As he approached Third Company Village, he could hear the 'distant booming' and 'blare of brass' of a Salvation Army meeting but he made no call for its prohibition or prosecution under the anti-nuisance laws. The Salvation Army began operations in Trinidad in 1901.[7] Two years after *The Mirror*'s report on the Merikins, the debate in the British Parliament on Roman Catholic right to publicly display religious symbols triggered a report in the local *Catholic News* berating the British as 'one of the most intolerant nations.'[8] The writer acknowledged, 'We tolerate the noisy nonsense of the Salvation Army, which very often disturb public worship as it passes by church or chapel with its odious din.' It could also be argued that the ringing of high-decibel bells of Roman Catholic and Anglican churches several times a day or the muezzin's call to Muslims to assemble for prayer five times a day also disturbed the peace of their respective communities. If Shouters were liable for 'common law tort' for rejoicing during worship, the same standard should have been applied to those religions. However, religious worship in the British Empire did not enter the boundaries of tort liability until the twentieth century, after prohibition.[9] Church bells and chimes from church clocks came under tort law regarding the Environment Protection Agency in the UK in the twenty-first century.[10] In this regard, the Spiritual Baptists were legal scapegoats.

The Mirror reporter did not randomly select the Third Company church for investigation. By 1906, only three African Baptist churches remained outside the Baptist Union, the Third Company church being one of them. The other two independent churches were St Julien's, established in 1890, and Momga, established in 1897.[11] The

Third Company church was a high cut above the purpose–built praise houses of St Vincent. The reporter was clearly astonished to see 'a big ecclesiastical sort of structure, with many windows flooded with light,' which comfortably accommodated a congregation of 'about 250 strong.' The unnamed pastor of the Third Company church was knowledgeable on the church's history and proudly acclaimed that the members of his congregation were 'Independent Baptists.' Interestingly, the pastor fingered Cooksey and Horlick as the first who 'tried to put down Shouterism.'[12] Independent Baptists were not 'Shouters' with a Baptist label. The Independents' retention of a Baptist identity well before the prohibition of the Penitents in St Vincent was a pre-emptive strike against the Trinidad and Tobago government making it impossible to include them in the prohibition ordinance of 1917; nevertheless, it did not completely immunise them from legal jeopardy vis-à-vis the Prohibition Ordinance, as addressed in the next chapter.

The *Port of Spain Gazette* notably shifted the politics of prohibition from the rural south to the suburban north. The paper was the oldest in the colony, with continuous publication since its debut in 1825. From inception, it had been the voice of the elite and official organ of government. In 1909, an anonymous writer with the unassuming pen name, 'A Resident,' wrote a lengthy letter to the editor making a case for 'the extermination' of the Shouters of East Dry River.[13] A major point in the letter was that the working class had no right to reform the European version of Christianity. But the two main charges of resident's indictment were summed up in the concluding paragraph: the 'profanity' displayed by women during prayer meetings and 'the nuisance created' in their daily lives. Resident's language was explicitly elitist, chauvinist, and racist, but not equal to the rabid demonology of the Vincentian media warriors.[14] Resident's letter did not betray influence of *The Mirror* report on the southern Shouters; nor did the writer reveal knowledge of advocacy against the Shakers of St Vincent. The call for action was specific to the Shouters in the East Dry River district. After presenting the case for immorality and disturbance of the peace of the community, the writer called upon the government to:

> ...institute such measures as would lead to the extermination of these individuals who profane all Christian doctrines by the pollution of the morals of the district and carry out all manner of lawlessness under the canopy of a licence granted to some of them as representatives of some religion.

This appeal suggests that some of the Shouter leaders, or church leaders that the authorities believed to be Shouters, were licenced preachers or teachers of other denominations, most likely under the Baptist Union or Independents.

In 1912, the passing of the Shakers' Prohibition Ordinance added fuel to prohibitionism in Trinidad that would burn for the next five years. The *Port of Spain Gazette* provided the spark. The paper praised the government of St Vincent for setting the example for Trinidad and Tobago to follow 'in dealing with those noisy and disorderly forms of so-called religious worship which have long been as great a nuisance in Trinidad as it would seem they have become in St Vincent.'[15] Although the expression 'so-called religious worship' was derogatory, it was still a recognition of Shouterism as a religious phenomenon, or a form of congregational worship that challenged traditional colonial Christianity. Nonetheless, up to that time, the Trinidad elites had not succumbed to the narrative of demonology that became prevalent among prohibitionists of St Vincent.

Distinguishing Features of the Legislature of Trinidad and Tobago

Trinidad and Tobago was a 'pure' Crown Colony but its population being much larger than that of St Vincent allowed for a much larger number of official and unofficial members in the legislative council and considerably reduced the concentration of power in a few officials. Notably, for example, the chief justice was not a member of the executive or legislative council, as in St Vincent. There were eleven officials and eleven unofficials: the governor was the president of the legislature; the other top three Executive Council members were ex-officio members of the legislative council; all other officials and all unofficials were 'personal appointments' of the governor.[16] Governor John Robert Chancellor, a soldier by profession, who had seen active duty in the Sudan, took up the post of governor of Trinidad and Tobago in 1916 after a five-year stint as governor of Mauritius, his first gubernatorial appointment. Mauritius was another pure Crown Colony from its capture by Britain in 1810; in 1885, a new constitution allowed for an elected minority. This means that chancellor was familiar with the culture of colonial opposition politics before assuming the governorship of Trinidad and Tobago. The social setting of Mauritius was not vastly different from that of Trinidad: the legacy of a plantation economy dependent of the enslavement of Africans; a strong Franco-colonial culture; a large Indian and Indian-descended population and a still vibrant indentured labour system.

There was a significant difference in the authority of the presiding officers in the two main prohibition colonies. In Trinidad the governor exercised much greater power than the administrator of St Vincent, who could not veto legislation if his casting vote was insufficient to give the government a majority; only the governor-in-chief based in Grenada had such power. In Trinidad and Tobago, the governor was the local apex authority for the colony: he had both an original and casting vote as well as veto power over legislation passed with a significant majority. As Trinidad was always ruled directly by the Crown since its capture in 1797, unofficial members had a long tradition of opposition to government on many issues, not unlike the elected members of the old representative colonies. Accordingly, in the debate on the Shouters' prohibition bill, some members of Council were expected to express independent views, which was customary for such a contentious piece of legislation that aimed to prohibit the practices of a religious sect.

Another high-ranking military officer in the legislative council was George Herbert May who served in the dual roles of commander of the local forces and inspector-general of constabulary from 1916 to 1930.[17] May previously served as a military police officer in British Guiana and Fiji,[18] which probably influenced his decision to militarise the police force in Trinidad and Tobago. May had gathered intelligence on the Shouters of Belmont and was a key on fficial in the debate on the prohibition bill. Attorney General Henry Cowper Gollan piloted the Shouters' prohibition bill in the legislative council on November 16, 1917. Whereas Murray was not a law graduate – although he was employed as a resident magistrate in British New Guinea prior to his appointment in St Vincent – Gollan was an accomplished lawyer who had practised in London before his venture into the colonial civil service. Before his appointment to Trinidad, he had served as private secretary to Frederick Lugard, High Commissioner to Northern Nigeria.[19] In the Caribbean he first served as chief justice of Bermuda and ex-officio president of the island's legislative council.[20] He was transferred to Trinidad in 1911, the same year that he was appointed a King's Council.[21] Any one at that level of jurisprudence would have been keenly following the unprecedented legal developments in a neighbouring British colony and the clamour in the local press for similar action against the Shouters. Although Gollan attempted to steer more in the direction of tort in so far as the allegations of Shakers meetings were public nuisance, he still got entangled with justifying the need for statute to regulate morality.

The First Reading of the Shouterism Prohibition Bill

In his introductory remarks Gollan claimed, 'The Bill was one which was exceptional in character.'[22] The allusion to exceptionalism was taken straight from the pages of St Vincent's prohibition playbook. Like Murray, Gollan was compelled to engage in political deception to make his case for prohibition; but unlike Murray, Gollan moved the bill through all its readings in one day. November 1917 was amidst the First World War, but the Shouters posed no threat to wartime security of the colony when they were suddenly targeted by the legislature for suppression. Yet, a government with a military governor and a military chief of police was an enabling political environment for Gollan to present his case for exceptionalism as if Shakerism represented a threat to peace and stability. He misleadingly informed the council that the Shouters had created 'a condition of affairs' that was so dire that the government was compelled to approach the legislature with 'proposals for interference with the practices.'[23] His allegation that the Shouters had had a 'stormy history' was not pertinent to Trinidad, but rather to St Vincent. Nevertheless, this distortion was critical to the execution of Gollan's prohibition scheme.

In reviewing Murray's prohibition ordinance, senior colonial office official E. R. Darnley had alluded to 'the peculiar difficulties surrounding any legislation' that proscribed selected practices of one sect that may be repugnant to so-called 'respected' denominations. He forewarned that colonial governments might adopt similar legalistic jargon as cover for interference with the individual's right of conscience. Like Murray, Gollan was acutely aware of the pitfall of legislating against an individual's right of conscience when he declared, 'It is very far indeed from the desire of the government to do anything which interfered with the liberty of the subject and the right of the individual to choose the way in which to worship.'[24] If Gollan was being truthful, the law would have addressed only the public order issues, mainly related to control of late-night noises in the town.

Gollan premised his case for prohibition on the presumption that the Shouters of Belmont were Penitent refugees who had fled to Trinidad following the passing of the Shakers' Prohibition Ordinance. He expected the colonial office to acknowledge that what was illegal in St Vincent should also be illegal in Trinidad and Tobago. Disregarding published evidence on the Shouters in Belmont prior to 1912, Gollan told the council that the Shouters had 'flourished exceedingly' in St Vincent; but after the passage of the Shakers' Prohibition Ordinance, 'they then came to Trinidad and continual complaints have been received by the government for some time past as to their practices.'[25] Modelling his argument on Murray's introduction of the Shakers Ordinance, Gollan excoriated Shouters' liturgical 'practices' as abhorrent to Euro-Christian sensibilities, as well as being a public nuisance. These grievances were not exclusive. While both grievances were tabled, the nuisance law was the main weapon for destroying the Shouters, to wit, that Shouters' rejoicing disturbed the peace and comfort of the community. Gollan explained, 'I understand that there is or was one meeting place in Belmont, at which their meetings were conducted with such fervour that the shouting and the singing and the noise generally could be heard somewhere about the Transfer Station.'[26] But even if the noises really made it 'almost impossible for rest and occupation,' Gollan realised that noise of itself did not require new legislation to prosecute offenders. Accordingly, he mischievously crossed the line into racialising and demonising the pillars of Shouterism: 'But it was not only the inconvenience they caused by their noise etc., which made legislation necessary, as it was the practices indulged in, which are such as should not be tolerated in a well conducted community.'[27]

The Structure and Salient Features of the Shouterism Prohibition Bill

The Shouters' Prohibition bill was much more intensely debated in plenary and more vigorously critiqued during the committee stage than its parent bill in St Vincent. Members exposed several flaws, some of which had already received royal sanction in the Shakers' Prohibition Ordinance. In both jurisdictions, Sections 2 (1), 6 and 7 were the most worrying, because they were the most likely to cause alarm among the legal watchdogs in the colonial Office. Section 2 (1) gave summary power to magistrates to determine whether certain 'customs and practices are those of the Shouters,' even if the practitioners went 'by any other name.' This broad sweep of the law anticipated a change of name from Shouters to Spiritual Baptists or Tubal Uriah Butler's Moravian Baptist Church; but the law also posed a potential threat to other African Baptist Churches, even those congregations that had assiduously distanced themselves from the Shouters

As in St Vincent, the Trinidad and Tobago lawmakers did not define indecent behaviour at Shouters' meetings; nor did it provide examples of such conduct. There was also no reference in the legislation to noise—making or other examples of public nuisance. Furthermore, the only complaints aired in the legislature concerned the Shakers of Belmont; yet the ordinance applied to the entire colony. Gollan did not attempt to split hairs over the distinction between Shouterism and Shouters' meeting, as Murray had done. In presenting the Bill, Gollan explained that Clause 6 'prohibits the committing of indecency or immorality in the neighbourhood of Shouters' meeting places.' The term 'neighbourhood' does not have fixed boundaries and should have no place in legislation unless the neighbouring places are identified. Gollan also pinned immorality and indecency to mourning, because 'certain of the initiatory ceremonies to be gone through before you can become a Shouter are of a kind to which the term "indecent" or "immoral" can alone be applied.'[28]

Section 7 of the Bill left no doubt that the Shouters' Prohibition Ordinance was not to be a nuisance law but a purge of Shouterism. By empowering the police to enter a Shouters' meeting place or suspected Shouters' meeting place or Mourning House without a warrant 'at any time of the day or night' and to arrest all persons present, Clause 7 of the Bill, like the parent law of St Vincent, directly contravened the Liberty of Religious Worship Act, 1855. Furthermore, all persons participating in, or simply observing, an open-air meeting believed by the police to be a Shouters' meeting were liable to arrest. Persons who refused to provide the police with their names and addresses were to be arrested and detained at a police station until their names could be ascertained. Section 2 (1) defined a 'Shouters meeting' as 'a meeting or gathering of two or more persons, whether indoors or in the open air, at which the customs and practices of the body known as Shouters … are indulged in.' Section 2 (3) equated a 'Shakers' house' to a mourning ground, as understood by practitioners of the faith, or a 'Mourners' House,' as understood by the inspector-general of constabulary. Article 3 made it a criminal offence 'to hold or to take part in or to attend any Shakers' meeting … in any part of the colony,' at any time of day or night. Article 4 similarly criminalised the erection or maintenance of a Shouters' house or keeping an initiate for mourning. Interestingly, it did not specifically impose criminal liability on mourners: Section 7 (1) only mandated the police to take the names of such persons.

Second Reading and Debate in Committee

In Committee, the unofficial members asked many pertinent questions of law, but no one spoke in defence of the Shouters' right to religious freedom. Dr Henrique Prada, a seasoned member, asked if the Shouters had a book describing their customs and practices.[29] Gollan ducked the question. The inspector general of constabulary responded that he was unaware of such a book but claimed that his own report was sufficient 'in describing the whole of the procedure.'[30] Prada was particularly concerned about the constitutionality of criminalising a prayer meeting or the mourning rite simply by deeming it an act of 'indecency or immorality.' Again, it was May who tried to justify the connection:

> There is a building in connection with the ceremony which is called the 'Mourners' House.' In this those being initiated are placed and not allowed to come out for a considerable time. They are not supposed to speak during this period, and when they do come out they, generally, are very emaciated. That is one of the practices.[31]

May's language was consistent with the Vincentian propaganda and betrayed knowledge of the testimonies from that colony. Prada was less than satisfied and responded, 'That is hardly indecent.'[32] Unable to defend his proposition, the inspector general of constabulary disingenuously shifted attention to Shouters' worship. Digging deeper into the Vincentian propaganda arsenal, he rambled on, 'At the meeting they take their clothes off and commit all sorts of indecent acts when they get shaking.'[33] The inspector general of constabulary offered no practical example of such acts and there is no record of a councillor requesting or offering any. John D. Hobson, another unofficial member of the council, offered a compromise: 'Take out the words "or immorality."'[34] Gollan concurred. In St Vincent, Acting-Chief Justice Noble had persuaded the administrator to disassociate the magistrate from determining 'indecent or immoral' acts committed at Shaker meeting in the same Clause (Section 6). This was done; but the Vincentian lawmakers merely yielded to Noble's legal semantics because they agreed to shift the same magisterial power to Section 2 to determine the commission of acts of 'indecency or immorality.'[35]

When Resident (the *Port of Spain Gazette* writer) had called for government's intervention against the Shouters in 1909, he had compared the 'vulgar antics' of female Shouters during worship to 'extortions seen only in the licence of our carnival season.'[36] The bacchanalian licence of Trinidad's carnival festivities may well have influenced the colony's legislators to omit the words 'or immorality,' while being faithful in every other respect to the phrasing of Section 6 of the Shakers' Ordinance.

The inspector general of constabulary described the Shouters as a formidable grassroots movement. In narrating his experience of a Shouters' meeting in Belmont he declared, 'There is a tremendous crowd there, and they shout and holla while they are getting "possessed of the spirit," as they call it.'[37] The mass attraction to Spiritual Baptists' prayer meetings was worrying to the status quo, as previously discussed. Although no one explicitly articulated the threat that a fast-growing, working-class religious movement posed to mainstream denominations, it was evident that one objective of the bill was the elimination of such a threat. However, the recently appointed unofficial, Dr Stephen M. Laurence, questioned the need for a law to treat an alleged nuisance for which laws already existed. He underscored this point, stating, 'What would be illegal everywhere it is hardly necessary, I suggest, to make especially illegal here.'[38] Like the inspector general constabulary, the attorney general was clearly engaged in shifting the goalpost when confronted with an indefensible query. Gollan acknowledged the validity of Laurence's intervention but was not prepared to abandon his mission to destroy the Shouters unless the governor so desired. Thus, he rebutted,

> In a sense that is quite true, but the idea was to make it more or less a little code on the subject. I have been informed that very indecent acts do occur in the course of these initiatory ceremonies, and I think it very advisable to have some clause of this kind, so that it might be dealt with.39

Besides Resident's letter to the editor in the *Port of Spain Gazette* there was no other claim that such acts occurred in the island. Hobson was an uncompromising prohibitionist and disagreed with Laurence, stating, 'I do not think the section is surplusage; on the contrary, I think it is necessary {hear, hear} because the general law only prohibits acts of indecency in public and this would prohibit them in a private house.'[40]

Despite Hobson's reassurance, his clarification revealed a serious flaw, which went beyond the boundary of English law in terms of its implications for the invasion of privacy for the wider society. Even with Victorian-era hype against prostitution as 'the Great Social Evil' of the age, the British parliament did not criminalise the practice or extend regulatory legislation into the private domain of prostitutes.[41] Gollan concluded that he would leave the clause as it stood in the draft Bill. To the governor's query whether there were any further objections, Hobson's final comment revealed that even he was aware of not only violating the right of the Shouters' freedom of conscience but also of the real possibility that the same clause could be invoked against other denominations. He affirmed, 'I do not suppose it will work any real harm although it is rather vague. We understand what is meant, but it must not be construed too widely.'[42] Largely because there was no pretence to protect Shouters engaged in prayer meetings, as in St Vincent, the Shouters' Prohibition Ordinance was more draconian. Unlike St Vincent's, the Trinidad and Tobago government did not engage the Spiritual Baptists in political propaganda and hastened the three readings and passage of the bill in one day. Hansard did not record any division in voting. The *Port of Spain Gazette* celebrated the day with large, bold headlines, 'SHOUTERS LEGISLATED OUT OF EXISTENCE;' the *Trinidad Guardian*'s heading was less dramatic but still euphoric, utilising the largest and boldest fonts in the column: 'Shouters Meetings Prohibited.'[43]

It is worthy of note that Governor John Chancellor actively participated in the prohibition debate. Later, in his capacity as viceroy, he would sanction the Ordinance (Appendix C). The decentralised power–structure in the Windward Islands allowed for more theoretical transparency in legislating against the Shakers. One could only speculate what Governor Sadler might have done had he been consulted by Murray prior to the drafting of the Shakers' bill or even if it had been transmitted to him for his assent.

Governor Chancellor received the ordinance ten days after it passed the legislature. Two days later it was on its way to London. This rapid transmission contrasted sharply with the Murray's procrastination in forwarding the St Vincent ordinance. Had Governor Chancellor refused to sanction the Shouters' Ordinance or if the colonial office disallowed it, it would have been embarrassing to Murray who was then commissioner for St Lucia and had acted as governor of the Windward Islands in 1916;[44] but it also would have delegitimised the St Vincent Ordinance. It is not known whether Murray and the Trinidad government communicated on prohibition.

Institutional Continuity in the Colonial Office

Neither Governor Chancellor nor Attorney General Gollan had the web of political connections in the metropolis that Murray enjoyed. But they must have been keenly aware that some of Murray's co-conspirators were still well positioned in the colonial office reviewing colonial legislation. These included E. R. Darnley who had drafted the conciliatory response to Murray's Bill, Sir George Fiddes who was promoted to ermanent under-secretary of state for the Colonies, and Gilbert E. A. Grindle, a junior clerk in 1912, promoted to assistant under-secretary of state for the Colonies.

In his report to the governor, Gollan repeated the error in identifying the Shouters as Shaker refugees operating under the name Shouters. The report extrapolated from the debate the two main reasons for the Ordinance: that the people called Shouters had suddenly gained 'considerable prominence;' and that they also became a public nuisance by indulging in 'practices of shouting and ringing of bells which are of very great annoyance to persons living in the neighbourhood of their meeting places.' He concluded, 'The existing law has been found insufficient to deal with them.'[45] The report acknowledged that the provision of Section 2 left 'a very considerable discretion to the magistrates.' It then went on to justify this flaw by asserting that 'the Shouters are largely illiterate and it would not be possible to say what their tenets are.' Nevertheless, the Report assured the reviewers, 'There is no practical difficulty in differentiating Shouters from other sects.' For this reason, it was 'safe to confer this considerable power to the magistrates.'[46] Even more important was Gollan's reminder to the stalwarts at the colonial office who had sullied their reputation recommending the persecution of the Shakers that the Trinidad and Tobago bill followed 'closely the provisions of the St Vincent

Ordinance No. 13 of 1912.' He, therefore, could not conceive any reason for royal disallowance.

One reviewer alerted the secretary of state for the Colonies to the opening statement in Gollan's Report concerning the ringing of bells and added, 'If their only offence is that of making a noise—that could have been dealt with very swiftly & without so drastic suppression.'[47] Interestingly, he also contested the Trinidad and Tobago government's claim that Shouters' meetings ended in orgies and drove mourners to lunacy. Comparing the Trinidad and Tobago Ordinance with St Vincent's, Darnley affirmed:

> The real charge against the Shouters, Shakers & Holy Jumpers is that they promote indecency & crazy excitement. Some exception was taken to the St. Vincent Ordinance on the ground that the charge was not fully proved. There is no evidence of it here either.[48]

He recalled that the only knowledge of the Shakers and Shouters within the colonial office emanated 'from common report' that they had roundly criticised. Despite his admission that the Ordinance was constitutionally flawed, he accepted that it 'seems to lend itself to the local legislature.'[49] This was clearly an attempt to avoid overturning the St Vincent Ordinance. Accordingly, he concluded, 'The St Vincent Ordinance was allowed, but periodic reports on its working were called for.' Without explaining the objective of those reports, he asked rhetorically, 'This might be sanctioned without calling for reports?'[50]

Only one other official, Gilbert Grindle, a former colleague of Murray at the Colonial Office, commented succinctly: 'This is taken from the St Vincent Ord-ce which was allowed by Harcourt, after discussion with the Administrator, Mr Murray as proposed?'[51] Other officials simply appended their initials without comments. Thus, the officials with institutional memory and direct involvement in influencing the sanctioning of the Shakers' Ordinance still ruled the day. Unlike the Shakers' Ordinance, the Shouters' Ordinance received the royal sanction without endorsements, except for the stamp acknowledging its receipt. One is astounded when considering that without evidence for the serious accusation of gross immorality; convinced that the legislation was unrealistically severe for the alleged offences; and acknowledging the Shakers and Shouters as religious sects different from the 'recognised' religions only because of the psychology of African peoples, the British government proceeded to sanction both pieces of legislation.

The Spread of Spiritual Baptist Prohibition to Grenada

The Grenada government under Governor Frederick Seaton James denied the Spiritual Baptists the right of conscience in 1927 under the disguise of a public morality ordinance. James was also the governor of St Vincent and thus responsible for the continuing persecution of the Penitents. The extended jurisdiction made it easier to extend prohibition to Grenada. At that time the indigenous Aladura Church of the Yoruba and other native Christian Churches in southern Nigeria were also facing increasing hostilities from the Anglican Church and colonial officials because of the phenomenal rise in their membership. Many new 'Independent' Christians had been converts of the Anglican and other European missionary Churches. One high-ranking official named Captain Ross proclaimed imperiously that these Africanised Christian faiths 'are not recognised Christian missions and they should be regarded as enemies.'[52] The weapon of 'recognition' first thrown at the converted of St Vincent continued to inform colonial officials as they confronted the challenge of the rapid growth and popularity of African–led Churches on both sides of the Atlantic Ocean. It is this fear of African corybantic Christianity draining resources and membership from European-led Churches that sustained resistance to repeal in the Caribbean up to the end of oligarchic governance. It is also this fear that drove Governor James to institute prohibition against the Spiritual Baptists.

The persecution of southern Nigerian Christians is relevant to the expansion of persecution in the Caribbean. Governor James was a product of Britain's racist 'civilising mission' and expansion of empire in Africa in the late-nineteenth and early-twentieth centuries. He debuted in the colonial service as an assistant district commissioner in 1896 in the British Niger Coast Protectorate, which was absorbed in the Southern Nigeria Protectorate in 1900 and Southern Nigeria from

1914. He served in many other influential positions over the southern principalities for the next twenty years. At the time, European–led Churches were still struggling to expand their missions in the region; Islam had penetrated only northern Yorubaland; so, the vast majority of the people were overwhelmingly practitioners of indigenous beliefs.[53] Many British officials researched these native religions in their cultural contexts, so James may well have been familiar with some of the cultural influences that fed directly into the making the Spiritual Baptist faith.

James' first post as governor was the Windward Islands, where he arrived in 1924. The following year the 'pure' Crown Colony constitution was modified to allow for a minority of elected officials, as occurred in St Vincent and Trinidad and Tobago that same year. Like St Vincent, Grenada was accorded five electoral constituencies. The following discussion, however, is limited to James' Ordinance entitled 'An Ordinance to render illegal certain practices indulged in at certain meetings in the Colony of Grenada.'[54]

The Structure and Character of the Grenada Prohibition Ordinance

Textually, Grenada' prohibition Ordinance departed sharply from those of St Vincent and Trinidad and Tobago, although most of its clauses indicate the neighbouring colonies provided the precedent for the Grenadian draftsman. The title recalls the advice of Chief Justice Tarring to Governor Llewelyn in reviewing Administrator Cameron's anti-Shakerism bill in 1904: that it should have avoided all references to the movement as a religion. Nevertheless, to ensure limited application of the law, Article 1 of the Grenada ordinance read, 'This Ordinance may be cited as The Public Meetings ("Shakerism") Prohibition Ordinance, 1927.' It is instructive that the word 'Shakerism' is not only in parenthesis but also enclosed in quotation marks. This was legalistic semantics to satisfy the Colonial Office that 'Shakerism' was not an organised religion but merely a convenient pseudonym for the danger threatening public morality. It was also a subtle message that the law was simply an extension of The Shakerism Prohibition

Ordinance, 1912. Tarring had advised Governor Llewelyn, 'It seems to me that the line to take in any legislation is to strike at *the thing* not the name.'[55] Tarring would have been proud of Governor James for taking his advice. Notably, two of the key imperial civil servants, Grindle and Darnley, who had succumbed to political expediency and supported prohibition in St Vincent and Trinidad and Tobago were still at the Colonial Office in 1927.[56] Interestingly, the Grenada Ordinance makes no mention of Shakerism in any other clause. If not for the title, the Ordinance could have applied to any person. On the other hand, the St Vincent Ordinance and the Trinidad and Tobago Ordinance each mentioned the name of the religion ('Shakers,' 'Shouters' respectively) in the first seven clauses; only the final clause under the heading 'Penalty' avoided mention of religion.

Most clauses of the Grenada legislation were more concise than the other prohibition ordinances. Nevertheless, the Grenada ordinance was more austere in its policing mandates. To illustrate, Clause 3 of the Shakers' Prohibition Ordinance stated, 'It shall be an offence against this Ordinance for any person to hold or to take part in or to attend any Shakers meetings or for any Shakers meeting to be held in any part of the Colony indoors or in the open air at any time of the day or night.' Clause 3 of the Shouters Prohibition Ordinance faithfully replicated the parent Ordinance, except for the substitution of Shouters for Shakers. This offence is combined with immorality and indecency in Clause 2 of the Grenada ordinance: 'No meeting or gathering of two or more persons, shall be held, whether indoors or in the open air, at which any obscene or immoral behaviour or practices are indulged in, or at which behaviour or practices are indulged in which tend to exercise a pernicious or demoralizing effect upon persons attending such meeting.' Clause 3 of the Grenada law added, 'No person shall hold, take part in, or attend any meeting prohibited by section two hereof.' In the previous prohibition ordinances, immorality and indecency are addressed in Clause 6, the original wording being,

> It shall be an offence against this Ordinance for any person at or in the vicinity of any Shakers meeting to commit or to cause to be committed or to induce or to persuade to be committed any act of indecency or immorality.

Here again, the Trinidad and Tobago Ordinance simply substituted 'Shouters' for 'Shakers.'

The second major difference between the first two Ordinances and the Grenada Ordinance is the policing of the law. The first two colonies restricted this responsibility to the police. A third major difference is the role of magistrates. Under the first two prohibition Ordinances, the magistrate is the final arbiter in determining the status of a meeting place. Clause 2 of these Ordinances stated, 'The decision of any Magistrate in any case brought under this Ordinance as to whether a house or building or room in any house or building is a Shaker's House shall be final.' In Grenada, however, these two roles were combined and expanded to 'any Peace Officer or any public officer' (Clause 4). Clause 6 (1) vested the same power in a peace officer as in the police to enter a suspected premise without warrant:

> It shall be lawful for any party of Police (of whom one at least shall be a Commissioned or Non-Commissioned Officer) or for any person acting upon the authority of a Justice of the Peace without a warrant to enter at any time of the day or night any house or place in which such Commissioned or Non-Commissioned Officer or such Justice of the Peace may have good ground to believe or suspect that a prohibited meeting is being held and to take the names and addresses of all persons present at such meeting or house.

Simply interpreted, the phrase 'any person acting upon the authority of a Justice of the Peace' suggests that the ordinance gave more power to a Grenada JP than the police who were not empowered to co-opt 'any person' – who might be a civilian – to exercise the power of police. Section 2 of this clause authorised a peace officer to take the names and addresses of persons taking part in these meetings, while Section 3 of the clause invested the peace officers with the power of arrest and detention of suspected Spiritual Baptists:

> Any person refusing to give his name and address to any Peace Officer when asked to do so under the authority of this section shall be liable to be arrested and to be detained at the nearest Police Station until his identity can be established.

The role of a JP in the administration of what in effect was a religious law had its immediate precedent in Jamaica's 'Noises (Night) Prevention Law, 1911.' In Jamaica, however, the JP's only role was that of magistrate; to minimise the risks from personal prejudices or incompetence, a complaint under this law could only be heard by two justices of the peace if a resident magistrate was not involved. Grenada's legislators went far beyond the limits set by Jamaica. The maximum fine remained at £50 but the maximum term of imprisonment was one month less than prescribed in the other Ordinances. With the Grenada prohibition Ordinance, the three southernmost colonies in the Caribbean basin would have fallen to racist prohibition laws sanctioned by the Colonial Office. This Ordinance remains on the statute books of Grenada.

Notes

1. *115th Annual Report of the BMS,* 110.
2. Through the *Methodist Magazine* they were familiar with the history and location of the two groups. Peter Brewer, 'The Baptist Churches of South Trinidad,' 82–83.
3. *Port of Spain Gazette, July 4,* 1894, TTNA, 2; print volume in very bad condition; only pieces of the article were available. In better condition at UWI/AJL (mfm).
4. *Port of Spain Gazette,* 'The "Shouters" at Tunapuna,' October 26, 1898, UWI/AJL, 4 (mfm).
5. Taylor and Case, *Encyclopedia of Caribbean Religions,* 246; *115th Annual Report of the Baptist Missionary Society,* 110.
6. Pastor of 3rd Company Church, *The Mirror,* April 23, 1906, enclosed in Cameron to Harcourt, October 24, 1912, BNA, CO 321/269.
7. Salvation Army, 'The Salvation Army in Trinidad,' February 28, 2014, https://salarmycentral.org/blog/2014/02/28/salvation-army-trinidad/, accessed on 22 September 2020; the denomination was incorporated in 1915. For St Vincent and Trinidad, see The Salvation Army International, 'Caribbean,' https://www.salvationarmy.org/ihq/caribbean, accessed September 22, 2020.
8. 'A Protestant Protest: Notes from the Catholic News of October 24,' *Port of Spain Gazette,* October 25, 1908, TTNA, 5. For a report on the debate in Parliament, see *Port of Spain Gazette,* October 16, 1908, 'Religious Controversy in the House of Commons,' TTNA, 3.
9. Basil S. Markesinis, 'Tort,' *Britannica, https://www.britannica.com/topic/tort,* accessed August 24, 2022.

10. See David Pocklington, 'Church Bells and the Law,' *Law & Religion UK*, https://lawandreligionuk/2018/02/13/church-bells-and-the-law/, accessed August 24, 2022.

11. *115th Annual Report of the BMS*, 110. Third Company had a proud history as the seat of the Baptist faith in Trinidad since the first generation of Merikins.

12. *The Mirror*, April 23, 1906, enclosed in Cameron to Harcourt, October 24, 1912, BNA, CO 321/269. In his M.A. dissertation Peter Brewer locates Hamilton at 5th Company; in a 1990 article, two years later, he locates Hamilton at Indian Walk, Third Company.

13. A Resident, 'A Growing Evil: Shouters in the East Dry River District,' *Port of Spain Gazette*, April 25, 1909, University of Florida, digital collection, 2, https://original-ufdc.uflib.uf.edu/.

14. 'A Growing Evil,' *Port of Spain Gazette*, April 25, 1909, 2.

15. 'Setting an Example,' *Port of Spain Gazette*, September 29, 1912, enclosed in Sadler to Harcourt, October 25, 1912, BNA, CO 321/269.

16. *Blue Book Trinidad and Tobago* 1914, UWI/AJL, Sections M1 & M2.

17. Ibid., 1921, UWI/AJL,124.

18. Ibid., 1916, UWI/AJL, Section M 2.

19. Ibid.

20. Ibid.

21. Ibid.

22. *Port of Spain Gazette*, September 17, 1917, UWI/AJL, October–December 1917, microfilm (mfm).

23. Ibid.

24. Ibid.

25. *Port of Spain Gazette*, November 17, 1917, 'The Legislature: Shouters Legislated out of Existence,' UWI/AJL (mfm). *Debates in the Legislative Council of Trinidad and Tobago (Hansard)* (January–December 1917), November 16, 1917, 349.

26. *Trinidad and Tobago Hansard*, January–December 1917, November 16, 1917, UWI/AJL, 349–50; *Port of Spain Gazette*, September 17, 1917, UWI/AJL, October–December 1917, (mfm).

27. *Port of Spain Gazette*, September 17, 1917, UWI/AJL, October–December 1917, (mfm).

28. T&T Hansard, January–December 1917, 350.

29. Ibid.

30. Ibid.

31. Ibid., 350–51.

32. Ibid., 351.

33. Ibid.

34. Ibid.

35. CO 262/26. 'The Shakerism Prohibition Ordinance, 1912.'

36. Resident, 'A Growing Evil,' April 25, 1909, 2.

37. *Hansard,* January–December 1917, 351.

38. Ibid.

39. Ibid.

40. Ibid., 352. The loud applause that accompanied Hobson's quip suggests that prohibitionists were in a strong majority.

41. See Fraser Joyce, 'Prostitution and the Nineteenth Century: In Search of the "Great Social Evil,"' *Reinvention: an International Journal of Undergraduate Research* 1, no. 1 (2008), http://www2.warwich.ac.uk/go/reinventionjournal/volume1issue1/joyce, accessed November 14, 2020.

42. *Hansard,* January–December 1917, 352.

43. *Port of Spain Gazette,* September 17, 1917, UWI/AJL, October–December 1917 (mfm). *Trinidad Guardian,* UWI/AJL, June–December 1917 (mfm).

44. *Blue Book St Lucia,* 1916, M-1, Google Books.

45. 'Attorney General's Report,' Attorney General's Report, November 27, 1917, enclosed no. 2, in Chancellor to Long, November 29, 1917, BNA, CO 295/513, 402.

46. Attorney General's Report, November 27, 1917, BNA, CO 295/513.

47. 'HGB,' Minute January 24, 1918, BNA, CO 295/513.

48. Darnley, Minute February 1, 1918, BNA, CO 295/513.

49. Ibid.

50. Ibid.

51. Grindle, February 1, 1918, BNA, CO 295/513.

52. Afe Adogame and Lizo Jafta, 'Zionists, Aladura and Roho: African Instituted Churches,' University of Pretoria, https://repository.up.ac.za/bitstream/handle/2263/21579/013_Chapter12_p309-330.pdf?sequence+14&Allowed=y.

53. C. K. Meek, 'The Religions of Nigeria,' *JIAI* 14, 3 (1943): 106, https://doi.org/10.2307/1155991.

54. Grenada, 'Act No. 11 of 1927,' BNA CO 103/26.

55. Tarring to Llewelyn, enclosed in Cork to Crew, September 6, 1908, BNA CO 321/243, 294.

56. See Louise Mathurin, 'The United Fruit Company and the St Lucia Banana Industry (1923–1942)', *History in Action* 2, no. 2 (September 2011): 19–27, https://journals.sta.uwi.edu/ojs/index.php/hia/article/download/1134/1046/2350.

CHAPTER 8

The Aftermath of Prohibition to the Second World War

'The purpose of repression is to create a climate of fear.'

After the passage of the Shakerism Prohibition Ordinance, Administrator Gideon Murray boasted, 'The suppression of Shakerism in this Colony will be as child's play compared with the difficulties attendant on the stamping out of illicit distillation in 1904–1906.'[1] Murray's hubris was directed at the colonial office as well as his predecessor, Cameron, who had overseen the campaign against illicit distillers but failed to rid the colony of Penitentism over a period of more than five years. But for over a half-century the Spiritual Baptist communion in St Vincent, Grenada and Trinidad and Tobago defied the machinations of rival denominations, police disruption of their prayer meetings, defilement of their mourning ground, police beatings, and harsh, punitive rulings of magistrates. In the true tradition of martyrs, they held on to their faith and continually expanded their membership such that by the Second World War they had founded umbrella organisations that proved the correctness of Governor Llewelyn's prognosis that statutory prohibition was more likely to harden resistance than destroy the faith.

Rationalising the Failure of Prohibition

Foremost among the factors facilitating survival and growth of the movement was the failure of government's objective to instil a climate

---

* Conway W. Henderson, 'Conditions Affecting the Use of Political Repression,' *The Journal of Conflict Resolution* 35, no. 1 (March 1991): 122. https://www.jstor.org/stable/174207.

of fear that would drive the persecuted fully into the fold of the recognised churches. The narrative of Shouters hiding in the forests to conduct prayer meetings does disservice to the resilience of the majority of Spiritual Baptists who courageously risked arrests, heavy fines, and imprisonment for openly declaring their fate during the prohibition. Partially feeding the narrative of fear was the confusion of identities between Shango (Orisha) and Shouter worshippers as well the intersection of the two, giving rise to the syncretic term, Shango–Baptist.[2] Shango feasts were often conducted in remote locations, because government and Euro-Christians frowned on animal sacrifice (ebo), which was central to Shango feasts. Drumming was also outlawed in the towns. Shouters, on the other hand, did not engage in animal sacrifice and depended on handclapping for musical accompaniment and communion with the spirit. Spiritual Baptists also established informal networks of communal security. The experience of Englishman Calder Hall in the hills of Laventille, Trinidad, is typical of several other communities where prohibition existed. Laventille became a natural refuge for Shouters because the villagers protected the chapels, prayer-houses, and members by not welcoming strangers, especially Whites, before informing the Mothers and Leaders of the faith. Every stranger was considered a police detective or spy.[3]

The ultra-sectarian structure of the Spiritual Baptists also facilitated resistance and survival. Sectarian communions were historically more resilient to state oppression than their Episcopalian counterparts. More than any other Sectarian denomination, Baptists flourished on fragmentation, as previously discussed. Furthermore, the leadership of Spiritual Baptist communions sprang from the local community. A member who had journeyed through the spiritual lands during mourning might emerge as Leader, Mother or Teacher; such offices equated with ordination, which authorised the office holders to form new congregations within their communities. Beyond this indirect ordination, the imperative of survival against oligarchic oppression motivated any gifted Spiritual Baptist member to assume the role of independent preacher to a micro-congregation. Calypsos of the 1930s provide anthropological insights into the retraction of Spiritual Baptism from lodges, community chapels, and praise-houses to units as small as one's own household. In comparing Shouterism and Shangoism, Neville Marcano aka 'Growling Tiger' extolled Shango devotees for bringing entire communities to their palais (shrine) to partake of their feasts, 'But the Shouters is [sic] a husband, children and wife.'[4] Nevertheless, even this small family unit was not safe from invasion by police, because the framers of the prohibition Ordinance had anticipated such a retreat and targeted 'any person' (Article 2) who held or attended a Spiritual Baptist meeting in 'any house or building or room in any house or building' (Article 3).

Another factor that sustained the Spiritual Baptists during the prohibition years was their delivery of specialised services to clients across denominational affiliations including faith–healing and spiritual empowerment or protection. The Roman Catholic Church long cherished such spiritual powers and bestows special status on priests as exorcists. Within recent times, Evangelical Christians have made spiritual healing a central feature of beliefs and worship, but Spiritual Baptists were the original faith–healers of modern Protestantism. Spiritual Baptists were both respected and feared as spiritual warriors. The public sought out Mothers and Leaders for their ability to identify pathologies beyond the realm of medical science as well as to restore the health of patients who manifested them. In Laventille, there was a well–known Spiritual Baptist healer popularly known as 'Scarlet Sister' and 'Scarlet Mother' because she was hardly seen without her scarlet cape across her shoulder. Calder Marshall acclaimed after meeting her: 'People like the Scarlet Sister to perform miracles. For this reason, she is hated by the police and persecuted.'[5]

This phenomenon was not unique to the diaspora. In Africa the social function of spirits of the pre-Christian era did not diminish with Christianisation. M. A. Adetunmibi sums up the view of many scholars of Yoruba spirituality in the proverb, 'Ile Aye ile ogun—The universe is a battle field.'[6] Adetunmibi succinctly explains the proverb less poetically: 'Spiritual forces can affect human destiny either positively or negatively.'[7] He maintains that the Yoruba–originated Aladura Church of south-western Nigeria, which bear striking resemblance to the Spiritual Baptist Church, have largely retained the belief that every misfortune is associated with the same evil spirits of the pre-Christian worldview.[8] Similarly, David Ihenacho affirms that Igbo descendants of several generations of Christians remain so fearful of retribution that certain big trees, such as the silk cotton, and patches of sacred forests in Igboland in south-eastern Nigeria have survived 'untouched for many centuries.'[9] To the Yoruba, the huge iroko (Milicia excelsa) tree featured in their creation cosmology was regarded as an orisha (deity).[10] In Trinidad, the closest resemblance to the iroko was the silk cotton tree (Ceiba pentandra) to which the native peoples also attributed some of the same qualities. The Yoruba and Igbo in Trinidad and Jamaica adopted the silk cotton as their iroko.[11]

Whether Christian or not, the daily lives of African descendants in Trinidad were defined by similar mythology-inspired fears of the spirit world mainly of the Igbo, Yoruba, and Congolese, the largest ethnic African populations of the nineteenth and early twentieth centuries. The selection of the silk cotton tree for esoteric rituals by diasporic Africans in Trinidad, and the associated fear of this tree, throughout the period of this study and beyond, although a shared multi-cultural experience, is just one legacy of ancestral African belief systems. There was widespread fear of bringing evil spirits into one's home at nights, which was resolved by walking backward to enter the house. Brooms were turned upside-down at night; parents believed envious persons could give their babies *maljo* [*mal yeux*/evil eye] – a condition with potentially fatal consequences – by merely looking at them enviously, jealously, or maliciously. There was also a fear of retribution for disturbing a place of spiritual power as well as for abusing a person acclaimed to wield spiritual power; associated with this was a fear of cemeteries and children were taught not to point directly at graves.[12]

Spiritual Baptist deployment of spiritual powers for physical wellbeing intersected with that of Shangoists (now Orisha), with implications for the society's dread of obeahmen and obeahwomen. Some Baptist paraphernalia also came to be associated with tools of obeah craft just as traditional African religions since the slavery period.[13] Unlike Shangoists, however, Spiritual Baptists found support for their powers of healing in both Old and New Testaments of the *Bible*: from Moses and the Pharaonic plagues to the disciples of Jesus. Most policemen were of African descent and had a shared legacy of African spiritism including the fear of Spiritual Baptists as spiritual warriors, which may have impacted the frequency of arrests.[14] Some police officers were Spiritual Baptists. Dr Henrique Prada's sarcastic suggestion, 'You will have to get a high-caste Shouter to become a police officer,'[15] may not have been oxymoronic and may have betrayed knowledge of Shouter policemen in Trinidad. At least one was mentioned by Noble in his report on the Shakerism ordinance.

The narrative of Spiritual Baptists' defiance of prohibition is often overshadowed by that of fear of the police and descent to underground to survive. The police report on the raid of the Questelles praise-house deliberately dramatised the scampering of worshippers in their bid to escape arrest. The more enduring narrative of the Spiritual Baptists during the prohibition, however, was less about persecution and escape and more about defiance of the law, an indomitable will to continue the practice of the faith and a concerted effort to restore numbers lost to migration. The Questelles praise-house, for example, had been revived within a few months of it officially been declared free of Shakerism. Running away from armed police is a hallmark of civil disobedience. Conscientious objectors run one day only to emerge the next, often in larger numbers as a demonstration of the commitment to their cause. Some Spiritual Baptists shared this experience, but the perspective is also validated by the continuous growth and expansion of the faith in St Vincent and Trinidad and Tobago from prohibition to repeal.

Select Case Studies and Summary Adjucation

Official police report of the abandonment of praise-houses in St Vincent in the wake of the passage of the prohibition ordinance had no parallel in Trinidad and Tobago, where the defiance to prohibition began more dramatically. On December 16, 1917, exactly one month after the passage of the Shouters' Prohibition Ordinance, twenty-seven year-old teacher Joseph Bailey and several of his congregation were arrested during their Sunday–night worship on the premises of John Brown of Cunupia in central Trinidad. The following night Bailey and several worshippers were arrested in Perseverance Village, near Couva in south-central Trinidad.[16] The second meeting-place was located within earshot of the police station. Three weeks later, on January 9, 1918, the accused in the second arrests appeared in the Chaguanas magistrates' court to answer the charge of keeping a Shouters' meeting. Others who were charged but failed to appear in court had their cases heard ex parte. Like the Questelles Six in St Vincent, they had no legal counsel. But this situation would soon change and affect the procedure and outcome of many cases, as discussed later in this chapter.

Probably because of the challenge of the defendants' vernacular and different reporting styles, the *Trinidad Guardian* and *Port of Spain Gazette* carried different versions of the case and should be read together to get a clearer picture of the defiance of the defendants and their witnesses. Caroline Frederick, an elderly woman, was separately charged for permitting the Spiritual Baptists to construct a 'meeting house' on her premises. In her defence, she claimed that she was not aware that her action was illegal; no one had told her of such a law, and she had not read of it anywhere; but if it was the law, she 'was compelled to plead guilty.'[17] Fourteen other worshipers who appeared in court were charged 'for having taken part in a shouters' meeting.' Twelve were female: Christine Frederick, Henrietta Bailey (probably Teacher Bailey's wife), Christiana George, Albertha Jack, Mary Farrell, Mary Joseph, Ethel Greenidge, Daisy Edwards, Margaret Fifle, Mrs John Hunt, Mary Brown, and Ann Brown, 'a little girl' (probably Mary Brown's daughter); the two men were Edgar George and Teacher Bailey. Three female defendants appeared in their signature white headgear. Bailey also appeared impressively dressed in regalia befitting the office of Teacher: a white head-tie; a bell under his left arm; in his right hand, a small wooden cross pressed against his chest; and a 'huge Bible' wrapped in red cloth.[18]

Sergeant A. Parris who laid the charges, testified that he was on station-duty on December 17, when he heard 'a great shouting' shortly after 10:00 p.m. and sent Rural Constable (RC) Moore to investigate. Moore subsequently accompanied him, Lance Corporal Archer, and another constable to Greaves Street in Perseverance Village where he 'saw a crowd' including the defendants 'and they were all taking part in the meeting.'[19] Disdainful of the police, Teacher Bailey allegedly told the Sergeant that 'he would shout in jail.' Other worshippers took their cue from Bailey: the vast majority chose not to run away; instead, to underscore their defiance, they 'shook themselves and gave off the sound 'hum; hum.'[20] This act of civil disobedience and display of self-confidence was corroborated by Moore and Archer. During Moore's testimony, Teacher Bailey interjected, accused him of falsehood and laid a curse on him saying, 'Christ going cut you down for lying.'[21] PC Phillips testified against the defendants who failed to appear in court.

The Prohibition Ordinance authorised the police to arrest all persons in attendance at a Shouters' meeting, whether worshipper or bystander; but apparently not all were arrested or charged in this instance. Some of the defendants called witnesses to testify on their behalf. The main witnesses were Wilfred Humphrey and Moses Jones. Humphrey also carried his Bible under his arm. He rejected the court's *Bible* and Magistrate Huggins allowed him to swear by his own *Bible*. Humphrey acknowledged his presence at the prayer meeting but submitted that the defendants were engaged in conventional worship and that 'the Gospel of Christ was being preached together with praying and singing.' He said defiantly that 'they were not making any noise;' he added, 'Nobody told them it was against the law to preach the gospel and the word of Christ.'[22] Jones declared, when the sergeant came, 'he met him singing Hymn 323 from the *Wesleyan Hymn Book*.'[23] Any lawyer would have been impressed by the witnesses' sagacity in claiming the right to freedom of conscience, while implicitly rejecting a law to prevent them from doing so as unconstitutional and unjust. Jones and Humphrey were obviously in the congregation; but the police did not explain why they were not charged for committing the same offence. After Cephas Rodney completed his testimony, the magistrate asked Teacher Bailer if he wished to call any more witnesses. Bailey lifted his cross, pointed it at the magistrate and said defiantly, 'Look me witness.'[24] Asked to plead 'guilty' or 'not guilty,' Bailey responded, 'I will only answer such a question if it comes from Christ, and not from any man.'[25]

Unlike the first cases in St Vincent, the Trinidad and Tobago police did not attempt to invoke negative stereotypes about Shouterism to influence the court and unlike the autocratic posture of magistrate Roden in the Questelles case, Huggins did not contest that Shakerism was a religion and was more inclined to let the rule of law prevail. He discharged Mary Joseph for improper identity; he also dismissed the charge against the little girl, Ann Brown. Ann's age was not revealed but young children in St Vincent were also found guilty of violating the Shakers' Prohibition Ordinance. The Shouters' Prohibition Ordinance permitted prayer meetings and the police presented no evidence of any other activity. Perhaps with this fact in mind the prosecutor, Inspector Paul, declared that he was unwilling to press the charges. Magistrate Huggins, however, discharged all the other defendants except Bailey, who, he said, was 'responsible for the whole thing.'[26] At that stage, Bailey was granted permission to address the court. He told the magistrate,

> My father is 58 years old, my mother is 49, and from the time I was born, 27 years ago, that is the religion I found my father and mother following—not shouting but praying in the name of the Lord.

Defiantly, he held up his cross and continued,

> I am prepared to go to jail every time; and to carry on these meetings. I will always do so. Christ was persecuted for religion, and if I go to jail for religion, it doesn't matter.[27]

The Guardian's report of the climax of Bailey's address shows the power of the vernacular that the *Port of Spain Gazette's* reporter lost in transcribing to standard English. According to *The Guardian*, Bailey drew his strength from the Old Testament. Having recounted his pedigree in the faith, he summarised a popular story among Spiritual Baptists: 'and as Nebuchadnezzar throw de tree Hebrew children in de fiery furnace, I make up me mine to tun a jail bud for Jesus.' In response, his followers shouted, 'Amen.'[28] Both reporters in their own way recognised the case as a showdown between Bailey and Huggins. According to the *Port of Spain Gazette*, 'This profession of Bailey's faith evoked considerable excitement in court amongst his followers, some of whom shouted from the well of the court, 'Alleluia, praise the Lord!' Magistrate Huggins, however, was determined to have his way and said to Bailey: 'You do what you like, but the law must be obeyed. I fine you 5s. and costs, and don't come back again, because you can be fined £50 or six months.'[29] Neither the fine nor the threat of a greater fine deterred Bailey who had obviously gone to court that day intent on being a hero for the cause of the Spiritual Baptists; paying a fine would be an act of surrender. Accordingly, Bailey interjected, 'I have no money, sir. I haven't had a biscuit since yesterday.' Bailey's supporters outside the courthouse numbered some two hundred. Some of them determined to deny him the experience of the harsh alternative of imprisonment by paying his fine.

Ten days later, Bailey was once more in court with several of his followers to answer the charges arising from the first arrests in Cunupia. Bailey was arrested in two different police precincts, but the presiding magistrate was the same Mr Huggins. Among the other defendants were eight women: Albertina Griffith, Rebecca Babb, Mary Joseph, Mabel Joseph, Isabella Jarvis, Elizabeth Mark, Sarah Callender, and Jane Jones; and five men: Nathaniel Walters, Richard Raymond, James Phillips, Henry Howard, and Abraham Mark. Again, the defendants had no counsel to represent them. This time, however, proceedings were less dramatic: Bailey, like all the women, simply wore a head scarf; he had no bell, cross or Bible. They all pled, 'Guilty.' As in the first case, the prosecutor, Sub-Inspector Darwent, was not anxious to press charges; nevertheless, as a police officer, it was not his responsibility to pronounce whether the law was unconstitutional or not; thus, he informed the defendants 'that they must not take part in these meetings.' Magistrate Huggins' demeanour was consistent with the prosecutor. He 'severely cautioned' the defendants but addressed Bailey separately: 'You seem to be the most active party in these meetings. That is why you were fined on the last occasion, but I advise you to obey the law.'[30] No punishment was handed down.

The attitude of Inspector Paul and Sub-Inspector Darwent is one aspect of the policing of prohibition that persisted throughout the period. As senior police officers they were bound to uphold the law, but they were not always anxious to punish people whose only offence was their insistence on worshipping the same Christian God but in their own way. Many officers seemed to have drawn a line between policing and persecuting and more evidently so after the Second World War.

To illustrate, C. M. Jacobs tells of a dramatic confrontation between Spiritual Baptists and police in Point Cumana in north-west Trinidad. A police contingent, led by Inspector Steele, went to arrest Archbishop Granville Williams around midnight during church service. Williams was a Barbadian who would establish the religion in that colony in the 1950s. The congregation was large, numbering some 150 worshippers. Steele and two plain-clothes officers entered the church. Williams commanded his followers to stand their ground and he continued with the service. The three officers stood listening to the sermon when suddenly, the inspector dramatically collapsed to the floor.[31] After his recovery, he was allowed to address the congregation and asked them to sing the hymn, 'She Only Touched the Hem of His Garment.' The inspector was moved to tears and told them that 'he did not see why Shouter Baptists had to be arrested at all.'[32] In Britain's Caribbean colonies all commissioned officers were White or passed for White. No Black man in the constabulary rose above the rank of sergeant. The Prohibition Ordinance mandated that one of the arresting officers must be 'a Commissioned or Non-Commissioned Officer.'[33] Many district police stations were headed by NCOs, a military ranking at the level of corporal and sergeant. In Trinidad and Tobago, lawyers made this proviso a point for challenging due process.[34]

Spiritual Baptists of St Vincent were not privileged with legal counsel until 1948, when Milton Cato represented a group of accused in Barrouallie. This was not the same in Trinidad. Even though magisterial prejudice sometimes prevailed, lawyers' cross-examination of police witnesses often brought to light violations of due process and raised issues of jurisprudence that would otherwise exonerate a defendant in a system where law was a function of justice rather than state oppression. In Trinidad, counsel for Spiritual Baptists called for the dismissal of charges, if the officer in charge of a raid was below the rank established by the Ordinance. The following two cases illustrate how broadly the police could spread the net of persecution under the Shouters' Prohibition Ordinance and how the fate of defendants depended on legal representation as well as the character of the presiding magistrate.

The first case resulted from a midnight raid led by Supt-Sergeant Dash from Besson Street Station on January 13, 1918, which saw the arrests of Teacher Archibald Forbes, popularly called 'Nosegay,' and fifteen members of his congregation of twenty-three or twenty-four who were engaged in Sunday worship on the ground floor of his home on Clifton Hill, Laventille.[35] Dash charged Forbes for holding a Shouters' meeting to which he pleaded not guilty. All the accused were represented by lawyer H. P. Wells. The cases were jointly tried at the City Magistrate's Court, but the reporter did not name the magistrate. Forbes was such a popular preacher in the community that he was known as 'the great Shouter.'[36] Following in Teacher Bailey's footsteps, Forbes appeared in court with his prayer book and distinctive Shouter's clerical garb although in his opening testimony, he declared that he was an Independent Baptist.

The case exposed how readily the law could be abused to silence any African Baptist denomination. Although Forbes lived a half-mile from the station, Dash claimed that he heard 'a great shouting noise and ringing of bells' emanating from Forbes' home. Dash claimed that upon his arrival at the prayer meeting he saw the worshippers 'jumping up, grunting, screaming, ringing bells, and in other ways making a great nuisance.'[37] Dash claimed that he knew Forbes as a Shouter Teacher for some fourteen years, but did not explain why Forbes' prayer meetings did not disturb him before. He testified that he did not go to arrest anyone but only to stop the meeting. Forbes, however, allegedly told the officer that 'he could not stop as long as the spirit was in the people; he would have to wait until it came out.' Forbes refuted Dash's version of the story and swore that 'no noise of any sort was being made;' rather, the congregation was praying 'singly, and everybody was answering "Amen."'[38]

When a constable from the raid testified that Forbes 'belonged to a sect known as the Independent Baptists,' his lawyer pounced on the admission saying, 'I am glad to hear you say that. That is just what I wanted.'[39] Indeed, had the magistrate accepted the constable's evidence as fact, Forbes would have had no case to answer. The *Port of Spain Gazette* reporter correctly stated, 'The Independent Baptists are recognised by the Government and marriages by them even allowed.' The judge had already shown by cynical comments that he was a biased adjudicator. This time he ruled, 'A rose by any other name smells just as sweet.' In taking the witness stand, Forbes assured the court that his church was 'praying for the Lord to have mercy upon King and Country.' The so-called Great War ended later that year but at the time of arrests there was yet no indication of the victors. Forbes' patriotism to the government of his oppressor, however, did not help his case especially when he admitted that the form of worship of his church 'is known as the Shouters.' Nevertheless, Forbes submitted under re-examination that his church was no different from that of John Herbert Poole's except that his was of the Independent Baptists and Poole's was of the London Baptists. Poole was pastor of St John's Baptist Church in Port of Spain, which was built by the Baptist Missionary Society in 1854.[40] Although the Baptist Missionary Society had abandoned Trinidad in 1892[41] and did not return till 1946, St John's retained its prestige as the headquarters of the London Baptists in the colony. St John's belonged to the Baptist Union and Poole was superintendent of the Baptist Churches in the South.[42]

The magistrate expressed his personal prejudice in describing the prayer meeting as 'a reversion to barbarism' before declaring Forbes guilty and imposing a fine of £5 with an alternative of six months' imprisonment with hard labour, the maximum allowed; the fifteen followers were 'bound over in £5 to be of good behaviour for six months' in violation of which they would be sentenced to seven days' simple imprisonment. Of the congregation, seven were women: Emily Joseph, Rosalina Hercules, Sarah Hunter, Annie Mac, Elizabeth Elliot, Caroline Stafford, and Virginia; the others were Alexander Edwards, Joseph Cosman, Sunga '(male East Indian),' George Shalow, John Morris, Jack Hercules, Vincent Brown, and Arthur Pilgrim.[43]

The second case study is that of Theophilus Ottley, 'an itinerant preacher,' of Laventille Road who was charged along with thirty-three of his congregants on Thursday July 4, 1918.[44] The case came before magistrate Victor Xavier de Verteuil with lawyer C. N. Scipio-Pollard appearing for all the defendants. De Verteuil served in the magistracy for Savanna Grande and Moruga, a densely populated Merikin-

Spiritual Baptist constituency for several years before his promotion to the magistracy of St Joseph, Tacarigua and Arima in St George East.[45]

The inspector who led the raid testified that he had put Ottley's residence under surveillance for two weeks. On two previous visits to Ottley's place, he 'heard they were preaching from the *Bible*.'[46] Finally the inspector knocked on the door, entered a room with about forty persons and observed a table with 'two lighted candles, chalk marks and two other books.' Ottley explained to him that the chalk marks 'were the spirit's interpretation of the text from the *Bible*.' He promptly arrested Ottley and charged him for keeping a Shouters' meeting. The magistrate cross-examined the Inspector because he wanted clarity on the customs and practices indulged in at the time of the raid. De Verteuil declared that Section 2 of the ordinance required,

> … that there must be a substantial number of customs and practices in the case to claim a conviction. The mere fact that a person has a lighted candle in his house would not justify him coming to the conclusion that it was a shouters meeting.

This was a rare instance of a magistrate ostensibly choosing altruism over class prejudice in a case under the prohibition ordinance. Section 2 did not explicitly quantify the forbidden actions, but de Verteuil decided to apply basic grammar to determine that 'customs and practices' amount to a plurality of each. He did not have to be so legally exacting because the ordinance empowered him as the ultimate authority on Shouters' customs and practices.

Pollard saw an opportunity to push the envelope: 'But there is not even any evidence of a custom or practice in this case.' De Verteuil disagreed, 'Only the chalk marks.' But Pollard would have none of it. He invoked the Biblical allegory of the woman who was accused of adultery and brought to Jesus who proceeded to draw a line in the sand. Pollard concluded, 'The complainant might as well say that because He wrote in the sand, Our Lord is a shouter.' The magistrate reminded the lawyer that the Inspector knew Ottley personally. Again, Pollard countered that he could not take the complainant at his word that he had never seen chalk marks in other parts of the island. The lawyer then dramatically drew the magistrate's attention to Section 7 of the prohibition ordinance to turn the tables on the police:

> I want to lay a charge against the police for false imprisonment and I am going to speak to him (complainant) about it. I want to show that the police were absolutely illegal in their proceedings. On any occasion upon which the police go into any shouters' house, they need to have a commissioned or non-commissioned officer. But two constables went to this man's (defendant's) house and brought him to the Besson Street Police Station.[47]

The magistrate's expectation of multiple customs and practices and the lawyer's charge of violation of due process did not help the police case. With his case slipping away, the Inspector sought to convince the court that he knew what Shouterism was, affirming that 'at a shouters' meeting there is generally shouting and the members go round a pole.' He also returned to his strongest evidence: 'Chalk marks are the chief parts of a shouters' meeting. They would not allow any other person than a "mourner" to make the marks.' Through cross-examination Pollard got the Inspector to admit that he never saw chalk marks on the ground and was never close enough to see if there were any marks; Pollard also got him to admit that the pole was not part of Ottley's prayer house. Since the police had no further evidence, de Verteuil ruled that 'under the circumstances he was not prepared to hold that as proved to him that this was a shouters' meeting.' Accordingly, he dismissed the case against Ottley and the thirty-three other worshippers.[48]

Tightening the Noose of Prohibition

It took more than a decade to close the loophole that Magistrate de Verteuil exposed, which gave defence lawyers an upper hand over the police. This was done by executive mandate. In 1936, the government amended the 'Trinidad Constabulary Manual' to include a sub-section entitled 'Shouters.' The section provided details of 'customs and practices' to include:

> (a) Binding the head with white cloth. (b) Holding of lighted candles in the hands. (c) Ringing of a bell at intervals during meetings. (d) Violent shaking of the body and limbs. (e) Shouting and grunting. (f) Flowers held in the hands of a person present. (g) White chalk marks about the floor.[49]

The preamble to the sub-section acknowledged that only a magistrate may decide 'whether the customs and practices complained of in any instance are those of the Shouters,' but it mandated that the provisions of the ordinance 'should be rigidly enforced by the Constabulary' based on the new guidelines.[50]

The spread of Garveyism across the Caribbean immediately after the First World War hardened the hostility of colonial governments against populist African-centred organisations. The end of the war saw returning servicemen leading mass protests over working conditions and against the colonial order on a whole. For many Africans the ideology that united them was Garveyism. Garveyism provided the strongest ideology of political, religious, and economic emancipation and empowerment through the Universal Negro Improvement Association and African Community League (UNIA-ACL) with networks across the African diaspora. The movement's flagship magazine, *Negro World*, gave them hope in an alternative future of genuine independence and Black empowerment. Garvey's repudiation of the God of the White man and his embrace of the God of the Ethiopians echoed the Spiritual Baptists' embrace of African spirituality.

In several colonies, the ruling class perceived Garveyism a major threat to the status quo. Reaction was swift and severe. In 1919, and 1920, the governors of the Windward Islands and Trinidad and Tobago issued executive orders or Orders in Council banning the importation of the *Negro World* from their respective territories; these orders were later reinforced by legislation.[51] In addition to banning the *Negro World*, Governor Hadden-Smith also targeted St Vincent's special Garveyite publication, *Greetings to the People of St Vincent*.[52] This environment of thought-suppression did not help the Spiritual Baptist cause. Instead of retreating or offering basic rights such as appeal upon conviction, the British government expanded its religious persecution to the Spiritual Baptists of Grenada under the 'Public Meetings ('Shakerism') Prohibition Ordinance, 1927.'[53]

In 1921, the St Vincent police arrested nineteen Shakers, the largest number in a single year since the start of prohibition. The court imposed fines totalling £210 or three years imprisonment with hard labour on the nine who were convicted.[54] The value of these fines at the beginning of 2023 was US$16,434; in Eastern Caribbean dollars (XCD) this sum amounts to $43,878.78.[55] Large fines were clearly intended to sap wealth from the Spiritual Baptist community and ensure that those who chose jail over payment would emerge with the stigma of ex-convict, thus diminishing their status as community leaders and their chances for employment or continuing employment with government. The cost of conscience, however, was not measured in currency or imprisonment alone. Although magistrates' verdicts invariably included the option of a fine or imprisonment, incarceration added considerable financial burdens on the unfortunate convicts and their dependants. Some convicted Penitents were peasant farmers; others, estate workers, craftsmen, and traders; a few were college graduates and professionals.[56] Many were sole breadwinners to their families. Since the law provided for the arrest of bystanders, the list of occupations destroyed by lengthy incarceration was extensive. Furthermore, imprisonment had a great potential to harm husband-wife relationships, including common–law and visiting arrangements.

Circumvention Strategies, Mass Petitions and the Radical Media

Spiritual Baptists were not privileged with ownership or editorial control of newspapers or with direct representation in Legislative Councils. Trinidad and Tobago made its first constitutional step out of pure Crown Colony at the same time as St Vincent and Grenada, with six electors held in check by government's command of a majority of nominated and ex-officio members. The property qualification of modified Crown–Colony representation still disenfranchised the working class. Nevertheless, the reformed constitution produced Captain Arthur Andrew Cipriani, a veteran of the First World War, who held his seat in the Legislative Council from 1925 to 1945 and served as mayor of Port of Spain several times in this period. Cipriani, the grandson of a wealthy enslaver of Corsican ancestry, became a pioneer trade unionist and held the unofficial title, 'Champion of the bare-foot man.' Cipriani was the first legislator to call for repeal of the Shouters' Prohibition Ordinance,[57] although he did not become a crusader for the cause, as George McIntosh in St Vincent.

Exclusion of the grassroots from the politics of Crown Colony propelled the Spiritual Baptists to become their own agency in the long struggle for legitimacy, equity and respectability. Several factors account for this transition including the emergence of more politically conscious, working-class leaders; circular migration of working-class leaders between colonies; a modicum of representation in the Legislative Councils via middle class champions, as the case in St Vincent; and popular uprisings across the Caribbean. Having failed to stop the ordinances, they adopted a combination of defiance and subterfuge, including changes of identity, the modification or elimination of 'shouting,' communal lookouts, isolation of rejoicing services, elimination of mid-night prayer meetings in some instances, and shortening the period of mourning. At this level, Spiritual Baptist leaders assumed the role of political vanguard of the repeal movement from the 1930s.

The struggle for freedom of conscience combined with the struggles for better living conditions and the reform of colonialism. One of the best examples of leadership embracing all these elements was Tubal Uriah 'Buzz' Butler who earns a high position on the list of political champions of repeal although his voice was not heard in the Legislative Council until 1951. Butler's father was a blacksmith and the sexton of the Anglican Church in St Georges, Grenada. Accordingly, the young Butler also grew up as an Anglican. He was a teen-soldier in the British West Indian Regiment during the First World War. Upon returning to Grenada after the war, he immediately plunged into anti-colonial politics, founding the Representative Government Movement and calling for universal adult suffrage.[58] He migrated to Trinidad in 1921, joined the Garveyite movement and submerged himself in trade unionism and political activism in Fyzabad, a pan-Caribbean constituency of migrants attracted to the higher wages of the petroleum industry.[59] Whether or not Butler was already a Spiritual Baptist in Grenada is uncertain, but he became an ardent advocate for repeal.

If Butler became a Spiritual Baptist after arriving in Trinidad, he would have done so under prohibition, but would have soon discovered a loophole in the ordinance to avoid prosecution. Accordingly, he founded the Moravian Baptist Church, which did not fall under the ordinance, and served as its chief pastor from 1931 by which time he was medically retired as an oil worker.[60] Official persecution of Butler's congregation would certainly have attracted attention and debate on the constitutionality of the prohibition ordinance. There was a First Baptist Church of Moravia since 1870; but there was no Moravian Baptist Church before Butler's. The Moravian Baptist Church of Fyzabad was a clever marriage of two of the most successful and oldest denominations in spreading the European model of Christianity out of England and the US. Both owed their Caribbean roots to African agency. The first Moravian mission in the Caribbean was established in 1732 in the Danish Virgin Islands.[61] Two decades later, they expanded to Jamaica and Antigua.[62]

Butler skilfully combined preaching with Garveyite activism and labour politics. He was the leader of the 'hunger march' from Fyzabad to Port of Spain in 1935 and one of the key instigators of the riots of 1937, which earned him the unenviable hostility of British authorities.[63] Thus, from being an active-duty soldier in the First World War, he spent the entirety of the Second World War as a prisoner-of-war in his own country. After his release in 1945, he immediately returned to the political battleground and founded the British Empire Citizens and Workers Home Rule Party, the most successful political party for the next decade. His party was the best organised to contest the first elections under universal adult franchise.

In the era of universal adult suffrage, Butler would clash with Gomes in electoral politics but in the 1930s they shared a common interest in anti-prohibition. Albert Maria Gomes, the son of a Portuguese immigrant shopkeeper, cut his political teeth in local politics in the Port of Spain City Council. He was the publisher and general editor of *The Beacon*, a magazine that featured progressive, young writers such as C.L.R. James and Alfred Mendes.[64] In the very first volume of the magazine, Gomes indicated his contempt for White supremacy, which he describes as 'the White man's superstition;' he appealed to the 'Black Man' of North America to keep his 'Beauty' and his 'spirituals', but put aside the law-abiding tradition … you must show a little resistance.'[65] The following month Gomes wrote an editorial under the headline, 'The Shouters' in which he questioned the logic and purpose of the prohibition ordinance as well as the judgements of magistrates. As lawyers for Spiritual Baptists had previously raised in court, Gomes zeroed in on the innocuous 'practices' that the ordinance criminalised. He railed,

> And what are those practices? We do not know. We never really know, it seems, until a Magistrate demands of us a sum of money not exceeding fifty pounds, or confines us for a term by the end of which our practices are calculated to be forgotten.[66]

He added, 'Why may not we be allowed to shout in peace?' It is not known if Gomes was a convert to the faith, but he spoke and wrote as one who was personally affected by the ordinance, not merely as an observer or spokesman for the denomination. Unfortunately, C. M. Jacobs misconstrued Gomes' sarcasm for cynicism when the latter wrote, 'But the shouters are regarded as a social evil; and the spirit that has sought to suppress gambling, brothels and the like has moved here.'[67] Gomes was unequivocally abolitionist and anti-colonialist.

The most iconic figure and Field Marshall of Spiritual Baptist resistance was Grenada–born Elton George Griffith. Like Butler, he grew up as an Anglican before converting to Pentecostalism in early adulthood, attaining the position of Elder. Griffith migrated to Trinidad and converted to the Spiritual Baptist faith becoming one of its most successful pioneer institution-builders. He founded the West Indian Evangelical Spiritual Baptist Faith (WIESBF), which petitioned the Legislative Council in 1940 'to repeal or modify' the Shouters Prohibition Ordinance. The petition was signed by Griffith, Pastor Brown, Richard Olivier Bobb, R. H. A. Phillips, A. G. Superville, S. Lovell, Granville Williams, B. Mathura, and the brothers, Robert, James and Medissa.[68] The petitioners identified themselves as 'African descendants' and boldly embraced Shakerism as 'our ancestral heritage.'[69] The Trinidad petitioners claimed that thirty thousand members of the faith were affected by prohibition, which they denounced as 'an annoyance' to the community. The allusion to this demographic was indicative of the rising consciousness of the Spiritual Baptists to a greater sense of the importance of politics to their continued persecution; it also alerted politicians who were to compete under universal suffrage that their fate in elections would depend on their interest in repeal. The petition was tabled in the legislature the following month. Nothing was done until years later when Albert Gomes successfully moved for a select committee to consider it, but the report was not made public until 1950.[70] Nevertheless, the pro-repeal decision of the committee may have influenced the legislative council in 1949 to incorporate Leo Sandiford's umbrella body, The West Indian United Baptist Sacred Order (WIUBSO), the first significant, constitutional victory for the Spiritual Baptists.

George McIntosh's Legislative Strategy in St Vincent

The reform of Crown Colony government in St Vincent and Trinidad and Tobago in 1925 allowed for elected representation. Although in neither colony could the elected representatives collectively command a majority vote, they wielded vastly greater power in St Vincent than in Trinidad and Tobago. Based on this premise, George Augustus McIntosh in St Vincent, emerged as a formidable force in the cause of the Spiritual Baptists, the first active politician to do so. McIntosh, son of a Scottish father and an African–Vincentian mother, was a pharmacist and shopkeeper in Kingstown. He made good use of his parental backgrounds to advance his professional and political careers. As an unofficial health consultant to the working poor, McIntosh enjoyed 'elder' status among the Penitents of the city and environs. In 1924, he became a member of the Kingstown Town Board, the equivalent of the Port of Spain City Corporation, where he remained for several decades. The Board was the only political arena permitted in the Crown Colony system up to 1925. The working–class uprisings of the 1930s provided the introduction for McIntosh's entry into political activism at a higher level. He gained unwarranted notoriety when a charge was levelled against him as instigator of the island-wide 'riots' of October 1935, which included an attack on the legislative council with the governor presiding.[71] Although a group of aggrieved persons had approached McIntosh to represent their cause to the governor during a special session of the legislative council, he may have had nothing to do with organising the attack on the courthouse, as widely believed. According to a columnist, Dr Kenneth John, ten days after the riots, McIntosh had moved a resolution in the Town Board congratulating the government 'on the stand taken in suppressing the disorder.'[72]

Nevertheless, taking advantage of the upsurge in popularity that came with victory in the courts, McIntosh immediately founded the St Vincent Working Men's Association (SVWMA), which won all five seats in the elections for the Legislative Council in 1937. Party politics transformed McIntosh into a champion for the rights of Shakers who were not yet a political force in the electorate. The franchise was still based on property qualifications designed to keep out the masses. Nevertheless, two years after his entry into the legislature, McIntosh made repeal of the prohibition ordinance his signature agenda. His main allies in the Legislative Council were Ebenezer Duncan and S. C. Bonadie.

For Spiritual Baptists in St Vincent, poor living conditions and suppression of wages combined with the suppression of religion. In 1933, two years prior to the riots, Hilton Fiffe, a Spiritual Baptist Leader of Barrouallie, who self-identified as a member of the United Penitential Faith, petitioned the King 'complaining about religious persecution' and pleading that he instruct the local authorities to allow the Penitents to worship in their own way.[73] Not surprisingly, McIntosh understood the prohibition issue from both the constitutional and class perspectives. His public life reflected this duality: inside the Legislative Council he fought relentlessly for Shaker freedom; outside, he pragmatically identified with the cause by facilitating the use of his home in Kingstown for Penitent prayer meetings.[74]

In March 1939, McIntosh gave Administrator William Bain Gray written notice of his intention to introduce a motion calling on the government to

> ...amend the Shakers' Ordinance to define what is
> Shakerism; secondly, to give the right of appeal and in

> every way to give freedom of the worship of God as is
> intended by the principles of right and justice under the
> British Constitution.[75]

Gray was a Major in the British army and a notable scholar. St Vincent was his first appointment as head of a colonial government.[76] When the executive council met in early April it decided that it was 'unwise to amend any of the provisions of the existing law' that would allow 'the practice of Shakerism.'[77] Dismayed by the Executive's obstinacy in denying the Penitents a modicum of equity, McIntosh decided that an unjust law ought not to be amended but repealed. Accordingly, he approached the clerk of the Legislative Council for permission to amend his motion to read,

> That government be requested to repeal the Shakerism
> Prohibition Ordinance, Chapter 172, of 1st October
> 1912, page 1091 of the Revised Edition of the Laws of St
> Vincent.[78]

Elected members revived the pre-Crown Colony tradition of opposition to the government and its nominated members. There were five elected members: P.S. Stevens, S. C. Bonadie, H.A. Davis, A. C. Allen, and McIntosh. There were also three nominated unofficial members, including Alexander Murdoch Fraser and W. A. Hadley, complementing two ex-officio officials and the Administrator as President.[79] The abolitionists appeared to be well informed on the freedom of conscience enshrined in the British constitution. In his opening arguments, McIntosh asserted that the Prohibition Ordinance 'would not have been passed by the present Council.'[80] He convincingly rebutted the oligarchy's propaganda that Shakerism induced lunacy in its followers. He expressed dismay over the class–race nexus, charging that 'because these people are poor, they were forbidden to worship God in the way they wished.' He affirmed, 'Under the British constitution, people had the right to serve God in whatever manner they pleased.'[81]

In chapter four, we showed how Friendly Societies run by Penitents represented a financial threat to the 'recognised' denominations. McIntosh revealed another equally sinister financial factor that exposed the naked materialism of prohibition. He accused the recognised denominations of supporting prohibition out of fear that recognition of Penitentism as a distinct religion would lead to a drastic decline in revenue. McIntosh concluded, 'Their support is a big factor in the upkeep of the church and the salary of Ministers of Christ;' he denounced the 'recognised' clergy's concern about saving the souls of the masses as merely a front for saving 'their collections and church dues;' thus, it was not spiritual conviction but political expediency that drove the clergy to pressure 'innocent' members of their congregation to sign a petition calling on the government to retain the ordinance.[82]

The abolitionists argued that the colonial oligarchy was a backward class and the ordinance a blot on the statute books of the colony. They claimed that Shakerism in St Vincent was an offshoot of Shakerism in England, which continued to enjoy the benefits of religious toleration in the metropolis.[83] Furthermore, the repealers drew parallels with marginalised Protestant sects in England, including devil worshippers, who were not burdened by discriminatory legislation.[84]

Bonadie, the councillor for South Windward, put on the record a recent case of extreme abuse of power against a devout Penitent. Sheltering under the ordinance, the police arrested a woman in the privacy of her home while praying alone for the recovery of her sick husband. Although the attorney general acknowledged that the woman was indeed engaged in an activity 'with the hope of making her sick husband better,' he arrogantly and tenaciously defended her conviction, because 'there was a certain amount of jumping up and noise.'[85] Jumping was not a crime, and she was not charged under any nuisance law. In the decade preceding the prohibition of Penitentism, Leaders and Mothers of the faith were labelled 'hypnotists' who could induce an entire congregation to perform unspecified acts of indecency and immorality during prayer meetings, while leaving many participants mentally deranged. Invariably, it was women's hip movements whilst 'shouting' that allegedly excited lascivious thoughts or disturbed the moral sensibilities of White male participants and onlookers. Men, particularly the Leaders, were mischievously accused of sexual congress with women during 'rejoicing' and mourning. The case highlighted by the councillor for South Windward was different. The woman was alone with her incapacitated husband; yet the attorney general postulated that by arresting her the police had saved her husband from 'mental demoralisation.' All elected members and one nominated member, Alexander Fraser, voted in favour of the motion, resulting in a six to four majority.[86]

Having heard of the majority vote in the Legislature, the St Vincent Clergymen's Fellowship wrote to the administrator expressing their regret and suggested that the ordinance be preserved in its original form and 'be rigidly enforced.'[87] The clergymen purported that the allegations justifying the passage of the Shakerism Prohibition Ordinance 'remains true today' and that repeal 'would be a retrograde step and most certainly not in the best interest of the community.' At the time, Administrator Gray was acting governor of the Windward Islands.

After six weeks of government's inaction on the successful repeal motion, McIntosh gave notice to the clerk of the legislature of his intention to introduce at the next meeting of the Council a private members' bill 'for an Ordinance to repeal the Shakerism Prohibition Ordinance.'[88] His action followed closely in the wake of the clergy's intervention, although most likely unaware of it. McIntosh made good his intention and delivered twelve copies of the proposed bill to the Clerk of the legislature. The official reason McIntosh provided for his Bill was the obligation of government to 'remove a hardship which is the source of discontent among a section of the population by having them free to the enjoyment of the right of religious freedom.'[89] This bold action was a new landmark in the struggle for justice for the Spiritual Baptists and a major challenge to the self-accredited moral elite. The Executive Council acted swiftly on McIntosh's Bill. Under the chairmanship of the acting administrator, the council noted the views of the clergymen's fellowship, but decided to table the Bill for debate at the next sitting of the legislature;[90] nevertheless, the Council took the position to oppose the Bill; but should it pass by a majority vote, the governor must not assent to it.

Shortly after resuming his substantive post of administrator toward the end of September, Gray brought the Bill once more before his executive council for final determination. The council stood firm on its earlier decision on the grounds that 'responsible public opinion' was against repeal of the Shakerism Ordinance. Nevertheless, the council also realised 'that under the present conditions the question might become one of considerable importance and it was necessary to consider what view would be taken of the Shakerism Ordinance by the imperial government.'[91] The council reconfirmed its position to oppose the bill in the legislature and to have the governor refuse his assent should it receive a majority vote.

McIntosh's Bill was on the order paper for introduction and first reading when the council met on October 3. In the meantime, McIntosh had lost the crucial support of Alexander Fraser who happened to be absent on leave when the administrator decided to bring the Bill to the legislature.[92] Strategically, the administrator had filled the temporary vacancy with a prohibitionist who committed to vote against the Bill. Accordingly, the administrator anticipated an even division of votes, which would guarantee defeat of the bill with his casting vote. McIntosh knew that he was outfoxed by government and asked for the bill to be deferred.

The deferral was not closure. Gray followed established protocol and duly consulted Governor Henry Popham on the proposed bill. Gray was not as systematic in mobilising dissent against Shakerism as Murray in 1912. His only evidence of public support of the government was the Clergymen's Fellowship's letter, which he imperiously claimed represented 'the majority of responsible public opinion in this Colony.'[93] This was gross disrespect for the five elected members who represented more authentic public opinion than clergymen who held their position without the consent of an electorate. Notwithstanding the clergy's endorsement, Gray anticipated that officials in the Colonial Office would be concerned about the government's hard-line on McIntosh's conservative original motion as well as his private bill. As a measure of compromise, and perhaps more so, to pre-empt negative criticism from London, he agreed to amend the ordinance to provide for the right of 'appeal from the decision of the Magistrate in regard to the customs and practices complained of are Shakerism (vide Section 2 of the "Shakerism" Prohibition Ordinance).'[94]

Popham concurred with the executive council on the question of repeal. He told Malcolm MacDonald, the secretary of state for the Colonies, 'I take the personal view that it would be a grave mistake to permit the repeal of Shakerism Prohibition Ordinance, 1912 which, even if it has not entirely eradicated, has at least controlled a demoralising and even dangerous cult.'[95] However, he was at variance with Gray's softening on the question of appeal against conviction. He assumed that the lack of definition of Shakerism tended to make such a proposal 'inadvisable.' Popham provided no material evidence to show what dangers could emanate from the Penitents, except to cite the report of Acting-Chief Justice Robert Noble in Gideon Murray's despatch of 1912, which contained evidence considered by Colonial Office officials as speculative journalism. Governor Popham was a military officer who saw active duty in the Anglo–Boer War in South Africa and was probably acquainted with Murray since that time; it was wartime again for England; Murray had risen to the peerage as Second Viscount Elibank and was an avid member of the House of Lords. Popham was keenly aware of Murray's new power and influence as well as his own situation as a rookie governor. In his memorandum to Malcolm McDonald, the secretary of state for the Colonies, Popham alluded to Murray as architect of prohibition in St Vincent and noted that the former administrator was now Lord Elibank.[96] The political strings that sealed Penitent prohibition had not yet disintegrated. Governor Popham concluded his correspondence by militaristically proclaiming, 'I am instructing the Administrator to suspend all action pending the receipt of your directions.'[97]

Secretary MacDonald, a Scotsman like Gideon Murray, also took a harder line on the proposed bill than the executive council. He rejected Gray's compromise on the right of appeal and advised him against amending any provision of the ordinance. He also instructed that in case of an equal division in the legislature the administrator must use his casting vote to reject the bill; but even if the Bill should pass with a significant majority, the governor must exercise his power of veto.[98] One may justifiably conclude that henceforth, prohibition was strictly imperial policy, with Britain having assumed the ultimate responsibility for continuing the persecution of the Spiritual Baptists.

The first month of the Second World War might have distracted the local government from social issues in the colony but the passage of McIntosh's repeal motion and his pending repeal bill emboldened the Penitents, while giving some legitimacy to their practices. The chief of police reported to Administrator Gray that on two consecutive Sundays – the last Sunday of September and the first Sunday of October – there were exuberant Penitent meetings in Paul's Lot in the capital city. One meeting was held 'in an open yard;' the other, on the compound of George McIntosh.[99] The police took no action because of anticipation of a moratorium on persecution after the passage of McIntosh's motion and his repeal bill, which had not yet been sent to the governor for review.[100]

Although McIntosh deferred his Bill indefinitely, he did not lose enthusiasm for repeal; he simply changed strategy. Because Administrator Gray's strongest reason for retention of the ordinance was public opinion, albeit from one section of the clergy, McIntosh launched a concerted propaganda war to change public opinion to a more progressive outlook. Two of his allies in the legislature were owners of influential newspapers: Bonadie, who owned *The Times* newspaper and Duncan, his chief political ally, who owned The Investigator. This strategy dealt a crippling blow to the hegemonic control that the validating elites enjoyed in early 1900s. McIntosh first published several articles in *The Times* toward the end of October 1939. Prioritising the unconstitutionality of prohibition, he labelled the law as 'unBritish' and its framers as 'despots' who had denied a select group of British subjects the right of conscience and the right of appeal, both of which were protected by the British constitution.[101] In November, Duncan added fuel to the pro-repeal *The Times's* articles by publishing several supporting editorials in *The Investigator.*[102]

After a brief lull, the police launched a massive crackdown of Penitent meetings. In a single case, forty Penitents appeared in court in Barrouallie to answer charges under the ordinance. The Shakers responded by deploying their faith as a weapon of civil disobedience. Instead of responding to the charges, the accused 'got the spirit' and 'indulged in some shaking' before the magistrate.[103] This incident was reminiscent of the first Shouters' case in the Chaguanas court in

Trinidad in 1918. The Barrouallie group could not have had a better defence. The magistrate simply cautioned them and dismissed all charges.[104] The defiance alone, however, does not explain the dismissal of the charges. Times had changed and the magistrate's decision was consistent with the mood of the day. Although arrests continued, the passage of McIntosh's motion was a watershed for the ordinance and the struggle for religious freedom. The successful motion and the government's initial willingness to concede the right of appeal almost produced a stalemate: the years following saw longer periods when no arrests were made. The favourable conditions also nurtured new organisational structures of Spiritual Baptists.

The Spiritual Baptist Diaspora in New York

Spiritual Baptist migrants from Trinidad and Tobago and St Vincent who settled in New York enjoyed religious freedom under the First Amendment. They built churches and contributed to the struggle for freedom to worship in their Caribbean homelands by remitting funds and engaging in advocacy through the performing arts, which served to legitimise the Spiritual Baptist and expose their plight to international audiences. Scholars have addressed the role of calypso from the 1920s.[105] A powerful art form never interrogated is dance. In 1945, Pearl Primus choreographed a new dance titled 'Shouters,' which she performed to a 'capacity audience' in Times Hall, New York City. The Second World War had just ended in Europe but the US was still at war in the Far East. Primus was born in Trinidad and migrated to the US with her parents at the age of two years. After graduating from university with a degree in biology, she became a civil rights revolutionary who used dance as a tool of protest and cultural identity against White supremacy. Dance critic, John Martin, had high praise for the concert. He described the 'Shouters' as 'a new primitive dance from Trinidad,' proclaiming that it was 'as exciting as it is strenuous.'[106] Primus's other Afrocentric dances performed alongside 'Shouters' were based on well-known themes, adding legitimacy to the vitality of Shouterism, the very elements that Caribbean oligarchs demonised to justify prohibition. One of those dances was 'The Negro

Speaks of Rivers,' choreographed from Langston Hughes's poem by the same name. Two of the rivers named were the largest in Africa, not only recalling Africans' achievements but also grimly reminding the reader of the Diasporas' greatest forced migration and the imperative to return to ancestral homelands: 'I built my hut near the Congo and it lulled me to sleep/ I looked upon the Nile and raised my pyramid above it.' Primus also received positive review for her choreography of the slavery-era Negro Spiritual, 'Sometimes I feel Like a Motherless Child.'

Notes

1. Murray to Cameron, October 12, 1912, BNA, CO 321/269.
2. Calypsos of the 1930s authenticate the perception that Shango and Spiritual Baptist were two distinct cosmogonies: see Claudius Fergus, 'From Slavery to Black Power: The Enigma of Africa in the Trinidad Calypso,' *Transactions of the Historical Society of Ghana*, New Series 16 (2014): 12.
3. Arthur Calder Marshall, *Glory Dead* (London: Michael Joseph, 1939), 135.
4. Growling Tiger, 'Yarraba Shango' (1936); see Fergus, 'From Slavery to Black Power,' 12.
5. Marshall, Glory Dead, 136–37; 142.
6. M. A. Adetunmibi, 'Yoruba Spiritual Heritage and its Implications for the Yoruba Indigenous Churches in Nigeria' (PhD disc., North-West University, 2017), 44.
7. Adetunmibi, 'Yoruba Spiritual Heritage,' 44.
8. Ibid, 68; 118; 142–43.
9. David Asonye Ihenacho, African Christianity Rises: A Critical Study of the Catholicism of the Igbo 1 (New York: iUniverse, 2004), 115–16.
10. Wande Abimbola, 'Ifa: A West African Cosmological System,' in Religion in Africa, edited by Thomas D. Blakely, Walter E. A. van Beck and Dennis L. Thompson,104 (London: James Curry, 1992).
11. Angelo Bissessarsingh, 'The Jumbie Tree,' July 6, 2014, Sunday Guardian, http://www.guardian.co.tt/article-6.2.384798.e3f7338027, accessed March 7, 2021. For Jamaica, see John Rashford, 'The Cotton Tree and the Spiritual Realm in Jamaica,' *Jamaica Journal* 18, no. 1 (February–April 1985), 49–51, https://socanth.cofc.edu/documents/Rashford_Jamaica%20Journal_18.1.pdf, accessed March 10, 2023.
12. Stella Bouville, personal interview; also, the personal experience of the author as a child.
13. See Cox, 'Religious Intolerance,' 13; 18.

14. Fergus, 'From Slavery to Black Power,' 9.

15. Debates in the Legislative Council of Trinidad and Tobago (Hansard) January–December 1917, November 16, 1917 (Port of Spain: T'dad, 1918), 350–51.

16. *Trinidad Guardian*, 'A "Shouters" Meeting: Batch of Defendants at Chaguanas—Obstinate Fellow Fined—First Case Under Prohibitive Ordinance,' January 9, 1918, 7, UWI/AJL (mfm); 'Shouters in Court: "Teacher Bailey" Before Mr Magistrate Huggins,' January 9, 1918, *Port of Spain Gazette*, 9, UWI/AJL (mfm). For a scholarly discussion of the case, see Jacobs, *Joy Comes in the Morning*, 137–43; also, James Ferguson, 'Defenders of the Faith: On This Day,' *Caribbean Beat* 148 (November–December 2017), https://www.caribbean-beat.com/issue-148/defenders-of-faith#axzz83QnbLN9c.

17. 'Shouters in Court: 'Teacher Bailey' Before Magistrate Mr Huggins,' *Port of Spain* Gazette, 9, UWI/AJL (mfm).

18. Ferguson, 'Defenders of the Faith.'

19. 'A "Shouters" Meeting,' January 9, 1918, 7, *Trinidad Guardian*, UWI/AJL (mfm).

20. Ibid.

21. Ibid.

22. Ibid, 'Shouters in Court,' *Port of Spain Gazette*, 9, UWI/AJL (mfm).

23. Ibid.

24. Ibid.

25. 'Shouters in Court,' *Port of Spain Gazette*, 9, UWI/AJL (mfm).

26. Ibid.

27. Ibid.

28. 'A "Shouters" Meeting,' January 9, 1918, *Trinidad Guardian*, 7.

29. 'Shouters in Court,' *Port of Spain Gazette*, 9, UWI/AJL (mfm).

30. 'Shouters Again in Court—Fourteen Persons Charged in Chaguanas—Leader Left off on Second Appearance,' January 19, 1918, *Trinidad Guardian*, 6, UWI/AJL (mfn).

31. Jacobs, *Joy Comes in the Morning*, 156.

32. Ibid.

33. Article 7 (1) of the Trinidad and Tobago and St Vincent ordinances; Article 6 (1) of the Grenada ordinance.

34. 'Keeping a Shouters' Meeting: Prosecution Collapses', July 15, 1918, *Port of Spain Gazette*, 13, UWI/AJL (mfm). NCO is a military rank of Corporal and Sergeant.

35. 'Shouters Meeting Interrupted by Police—"Nosegay" and Followers Prosecuted,' January 24, 1918, *Port of Spain Gazette*, UWI/AJL (mfm).

36. 'Prosecution Collapses,' July 15, 1918, *Port of Spain Gazette*, 13. Nosegay was mentioned although he had no interest in this case.

37. 'Shouters Meeting Interrupted by Police,' January 24, 1918, *Port of Spain Gazette*. The term grunting was used deliberately to connote barbarism,

but Spiritual Baptists call this unique sound 'doption,' which is made when worshippers are imbued with the Holy Spirit.

38. 'Shouters Meeting Interrupted by Police,' January 24, 1918, *Port of Spain Gazette*.

39. Ibid.

40. *Handbook of Trinidad and Tobago 1924*, 176; *Handbook of Trinidad and Tobago 1934*, 161. Taylor and Case, *Encyclopedia of Caribbean Religions*, 247.

41. Peter, Brewer, 'The Baptist Churches of South Trinidad and their Missionaries, 1815–1892' (MTheo. diss., University of Glasgow, 1988), 298; Peter Brewer, 'British Baptist Missionaries and Baptist Work in the Bahamas,' *The Baptist Quarterly* 32, no. 6, (1988): 299, https:// biblicalstudies.org.uk accessed May 25, 2022.

42. W. F. Webb, 'Reminisces of a Trinidadian Baptist,' *Missionary Herald*: The Monthly Magazine of the Baptist Missionary Society (January 1976): 8. Poole came to Trinidad in 1907 or 1909. He was honoured in 1940 in the King's birthday awards. Webb was a descendant of the Fourth Company settlers.

43. 'Shouters Meeting Interrupted by Police,' January 24, 1918, *Port of Spain Gazette*.

44. 'Prosecution Collapses,' July 15, 1918, *Port of Spain Gazette*, 13.

45. July 2, 1914, The Mirror, 9, https://www.simon-hurd-family-history. com/getperson.php?personID=17972&tree=Simon1; Trinidad and Tobago Blue Book 1920, 'Civil Establishment,' 158.

46. 'Prosecution Collapses,' July 15, 1918, *Port of Spain Gazette*, 13.

47. Ibid.

48. Ibid.

49. Herskovits and Herskovits, *Trinidad Village*, 345, Internet Archive.

50. Ibid, 344.

51. W. F. Elkins, 'Suppression of the "Negro World" in the British West Indies: 1919–1920,' *Science & Society* 35, no. 3 (Fall 1971): 346, https:// www.jstor.org/stable/40401583; W. F. Elkins, 'Marcus Garvey, the "Negro World," and the British West Indies,' *Science & Society* 36, no. 1 (Spring 1972), 69–70, https://www.jstor.org/stable/40401615.

52. See *St Vincent Ordinances for the Year* 1920 (Kingstown: 1920), SVGAG, 14; 15.

53. Act No. 11 of 1927, March 19, 1927, BNA, CO 103/126.

54. Cox, 'Religious Intolerance,' 40.

55. See Eric W. Nyle, *Pounds Sterling to Dollars: Historical Conversion of Currency*, https://www.uwyo.edu/numinage/currency.htm accessed 3 August 2023. For conversion of USD to XCD, the current standard rate of 1.00 USD to 2.67 XCD was applied.

56. The last category included men like Butler, E. T. Joshua and the Bishop in St Vincent who was a policeman, as mentioned by Acting-Chief Justice Noble.

57. *Port of Spain Gazette*, March 31, 1951, 5, UWI/AJL.

58. 'Butler, Uriah' Encyclopedia.com, https://www.enclopedia.com/history/enclopedias-almanacs-transcripts-and-maps/butler-uriah, accessed February 26, 2021; Gad Heuman, The Caribbean: A Brief History (London: Bloomsbury, 2014), 153, https://www.archive.org/details/caribbeanbriefhi0000heum_02ed/page/152/mode/2up, accessed February 26, 2021.

59. Henry, *Reclaiming African Religions*, 33.

60. Brereton, *Modern Trinidad*, 180; Heuman, *The Caribbean*, 159–60.

61. Oliver O. Furley, 'Moravian Missions and Slaves in the West Indies,' *Caribbean Studies* 5, no. 1 (1965), 4.

62. Fergus, *Revolutionary Emancipation*, 46.

63. O. Nigel Bolland, T*he Politics of Labour in the British Caribbean: The Social Origins of Authoritarianism and Democracy in the Labour Movement* (Kingston, Jamaica: Ian Randle Publishers, 2001), 254.

64. Bolland, *Politics of Labour,* 251.

65. Albert Gomes, 'Black Man,' *The Beacon* 1, no. 4 (July 1931), 1, UWI/AJL. The ellipsis is original.

66. Albert Gomes, 'Editorial Notes: The Shouters,' *The Beacon* 1, no. 5 (August 1931), 2, UWI/AJL.

67. Gomes, 'The Shouters,' 2. See Jacobs, *Joy Comes in the Morning*, 184.

68. Godfrey Gregg, 'Freedom for Shouters in 1951,' https://mysticalorderinc.org/2018/02/26/freedom-for-shouters-in-1951/ accessed November 20, 2022; Henry, *Reclaiming African Religions*, 35–36.

69. Henry, Reclaiming *African Religions*, 35–36.

70. Ibid, Godfrey Gregg, 'Freedom for Shouters in 1951,' https://mysticalorderinc.org/2018/02/26/freedom-for-shouters-in-1951/, accessed November 20, 2022.

71. Jomo Thomas, 'Sheriff Lewis is a National Hero,' *The Vincentian*, May 16, 2013, https://thevincentian.com/sheriff-lewis-is-a-national-hero-p2943-110.htm, accessed January 23, 2021.

72. Kenneth John, 'The Riot and Independence,' *The Vincentian* (October 2013), https://thevincentian.com/the-riot-and-independence-p4009-108.htm, accessed January 23, 2021; Jomo Thomas, 'Sheriff Lewis.' To Thomas, Lewis was the leader of the attack on the Court House/Legislative Council.

73. Fraser, *From Shakers to Spiritual Baptists*, 44. Fiffe had been fined under the ordinance as early as 1913 and prosecuted again in 1933: see Cox, 'Religious Intolerance and Persecution,' 19.

74. Chief of Police to Administrator, 'Confidential,' October 6, 1939, SVGNA, J 29, 1939, 10.

75. Minute No. 94, 'Motion by the Honourable Elected member for Kingstown,' April 3, 1939, SVGNA, J 29/1939, 2.

76. Gray obtained his M.A. and PhD from the University of Edinburg, British Guiana Blue Book 1929, Google Books, accessed July 10, 2022.

77. Executive Council No. 94, April 3, 1939, SVGNA, J 29/1939, 2.
78. Legislative Council Minutes, April 13, 1939, SVGNA, J 29/1939, 3.
79. Colonial Annual Report for St Vincent, 1948 (London: H.M. Stationery Office, 1950), 45. This report cites the 1936 Constitution. Some secondary sources refer to two nominated unofficials and three officials.
80. Fraser, *From Shakers to Spiritual Baptists*, 48.
81. Ibid, 47–48.
82. Ibid, 63.
83. Ibid, 49.
84. Ibid, 47–48.
85. Ibid, 50.
86. Gray to Popham, October 16, 1939, Confidential, SVGNA, J 29, 1939, 2.
87. Cole and Gantaume to Gray, June 19, 1939, SVGNA, J 29, 1939, 4. Revd Herbert H. Cole was President of the Fellowship and Revd Dom Placid Gantaume, Secretary.
88. Draft bill, 'An Ordinance to repeal the "Shakerism" Prohibition Ordinance,' June 23, 1939, SVGNA, J 29/1939, 5.
89. Appended to the draft 'Bill,' SVGNA, J 29/1939, 7.
90. June 24, 1939. Clerk of Council/ Minute 170, SVGNA, J 29/1939, 6.
91. Minute 263, September 29, 1939, SVGNA, J 29/1939, 9.
92. Fraser, *From Shakers to Spiritual Baptists*, 54.
93. Gray to Popham, October 16, 1939, enclosed in 'Confidential' Popham to MacDonald, October 21, 1939, SVGNA, J 29/1939, 11.
94. Ibid.
95. Popham to MacDonald, October 21, 1939, SVGNA, J 29/1939 11.
96. Gray to Popham, October 16, 1939, 'Confidential,' enclosed in Popham to MacDonald, October 21, 1939, paragraph 3, SVGNA, J 29/1939, 11.
97. Popham to MacDonald, 'Confidential,' October 21, 1939, SVGNA, J 29/ 1939, 11.
98. MacDonald to Popham, January 9, 1940, SVGNA, J 29/ 1939, 15.
99. Fraser, *From Shakers to Spiritual Baptists*, 55.
100. Bain had forwarded the draft bill to Gov. Popham only on October 16, 1939; see Fraser, *From Shakers to Spiritual Baptists*, 94, n. 76.
101. Fraser, *From Shakers to Spiritual Baptists*, 57.
102. Ibid., 57–58.
103. Ibid., 58.
104. Ibid.
105. For a summary of the relationship, see Henry, *Reclaiming African Religions*, 157–66.
106. John Martin, '4 Dancers Appear in New Group Fete,' *NYT*, June 16, 1945, 10.

CHAPTER 9

The Aftermath of Prohibition: Suffrage and Repeal

*'A law so vague that its application is arbitrary, breaches the rule of law.'**

Repeal of prohibition in St Vincent and Trinidad and Tobago occurred within the context of representative government when the plantation and merchant majority in the colonial legislatures were supplanted by representatives of the working class and local professionals who dared not ignore Spiritual Baptist constituents. The transition was gradual: it began with the incorporation of a minority of elected representatives in the legislature and culminated with a replacement of the majority unelected Executive members. The advent of adult suffrage in Trinidad and Tobago in 1946 and St Vincent in 1951 empowered the masses for the first time in colonial history to decide who would enter the Legislative Council and consequently, thrust the Spiritual Baptists centrestage in electoral politics in the two colonies.

The 1946 General Elections in Trinidad and Tobago

Arguably, Port of Spain North was the most hotly contested seat in the general elections of 1946, largely because the two most eminent political leaders, Albert Maria Gomes, a journalist and Tubal Uriah Butler, a trade unionist, locked horns for the right to represent the constituency whose suburb of Belmont famously featured in the

---

* Diana Paton, 'The Racist History of Jamaica's Obeah Laws,' June 16, 2019, *Jamaica Gleaner,* https://jamaica-gleaner.com/article/news/20190616/diana-paton-racist-history-jamaicas-obeah-act, accessed January 12, 2023. The quote is an excerpt from a 2018 ruling of the Caribbean Court of Justice condemning 'colonial-era laws.'

debate on the bill to proscribe the Spiritual Baptists. Gomes entered the Legislative Council in 1945 in a by-election and later founded the United Front (UF) party expressly to contest the 1946 elections. The UF's base was the merchant and planter elites who had no pretension to promoting the interests of the working class. Frances Henry claims that Gomes reactively courted the Spiritual Baptists because of Butler.[1] Gomes could not turn his back on them and win the seat against Butler, who professed the faith, was once a preacher in his own Spiritual Baptist Church, and unpretentiously spoke the language of the working class. But Gomes was also genuinely pro-conscience and had editorialised against prohibition of the Spiritual Baptists in *The Beacon* from the inception of the magazine in 1931. Henry's claim, therefore, is questionable. Ultimately, Butler lost the contest, although his three successful British Empire Citizens' and Workers' Home Rule Party candidates, Chanka Maharaj (St George), Timothy Roodal (St Patrick), and A. P. T. James (Tobago) must have benefited from the Spiritual Baptist being called out by two opposing party leaders[2]

Gomes aced Butler on one incontestable political advantage: he was born in the heart of the Belmont valley, a suburb within the constituency of Port of Spain North, which also included a substantial number of Shango/Orisha practitioners and other Christianised Yoruba descendants. Belmont was also home to the Rada, a Vodou sect of predominantly Ewe-Fon ethnic extraction. The devotees of Rada and Orisha (Shangoists) had shared communions and close familial ties with Spiritual Baptists and were naturally sympathetic to the struggle for repeal.[3] As a young boy of six years at the time of the Prohibition Ordinance, Gomes must have heard much more of the same sounds of Shouters' rejoicing as those living father away in the vicinity of the Transfer Station located at the corner of Frederick and Duke Streets, as mentioned by Attorney General Gollan when introducing the prohibition bill in the legislature. Like Butler, Gomes identified with the Spiritual Baptists as if he were a member of the faith.

Butler's decision to challenge Gomes for Port of Spain North in the 1946 elections, instead of running in a 'safe' seat closer to his industrial stumping ground in the south, robbed the Trinidad repeal party of the radicalism and flamboyance that McIntosh brought to the Legislative Council in St Vincent. Gomes faced a similar balance of power in the Legislative Council as McIntosh in 1937: there were nine elected members, six nominated and three ex-officio members in addition to the governor.[4] Unlike McIntosh, however, Gomes could not command the loyalty of most electors and would have had to navigate the treacherous terrain between grass-root and elite politics. Accordingly, Gomes' United Front could not sustain or even attempt to recreate the political drama for repeal that characterised Mcintosh's Working Men's Association for the entire life of their party as an elected unit in the legislature. Nevertheless, Gomes did not rest on his laurel. Following the reading of Elton Griffith's petition, Gomes called for a Select Committee to inquire into the question of repeal of the prohibition ordinance.[5] The report from that committee was withheld for 'several years,' thus lessening its impact on the legislature and the national community.[6]

Expansion of Spiritual Baptist Representatives, Disciples and Sympathisers in the Trinidad and Tobago Legislative and Executive Councils

Under Trinidad and Tobago's 1949 constitution, the number of electoral seats expanded to eighteen, which completely overwhelmed the five nominated Unofficials and three ex-officio members combined. The Executive Council was also reformed to include five elected members of a total of nine with ministerial portfolios. Thus, the general elections of September 1950 dramatically expanded the repeal party in the legislature. This was writing on the wall for Prohibition. Many successful candidates had contested seats in well-known Spiritual Baptist communities. More importantly, many of them 'had close and intensive relationships with the Shouter Baptist Church.'[7] Gomes had migrated to an upper-class enclave in Maraval in 1947 but still competed for the Port of Spain North seat.[8]

Butler was politically wiser in 1950 and opted for a safe seat in St Patrick West. His party romped home with six seats and 22 per cent of the total votes, by far the largest of all the parties, but still only one-third of the total elected seats.[9] Of the other twelve candidates, two Independents threw their support behind Butler.[10] Two Butlerites, Pope Mclean in Victoria North, and Ashford Sinanan in Victoria South, won with less than 350 votes combined. Within these constituencies were the Company Villages of Princes Town-Moruga, the oldest African Baptist enclaves in the country. If their constituents voted, they would have been the decisive factor in the elections.

All things being equal, Governor Hubert Rance might have asked Butler to lead the new government, but colonialism was not about equality. Butler, who was once charged with treason and became a war-time detainee, was still a marked man by imperial watchdogs. Rance considered him still too militant, too uncompromising, and too nationalistic to be entrusted with the new office of Chief Minister.[11] Furthermore, the appointment of Butler, a professed Spiritual Baptist, would have amounted to the governor's abrogation of the 1917 Ordinance. Accordingly, he selected Gomes, a political conservative, for that historic role. Gomes's new party, the Political Progress Group (PPG), had won only the two seats it contested, with 3.4 per cent of the total votes.[12] Rance completed Butler's humiliation by denying any member of his party a seat on the Executive Council.[13] Ironically, Gomes's appointment was a Trojan Horse for the repeal movement. It was not the governor's plan, but in appointing Gomes to slow the march toward independence, the governor had to reconcile with the fact that he was also appointing the former parliamentary leader of the repeal movement since 1946.

The Urgency of Repeal

The Repeal Bill, 'An Ordinance to remove the prohibition hitherto placed upon the Practices of the Body known as the Shouters,' was laid before the Council on March 16, 1951, just six months after the elections; the second reading and debate took place on March 30, two weeks later. Minister for education and social services, Roy Augustus Joseph, of Portuguese ethnicity, introduced the Bill. Joseph was born in Fifth Company, one of the birth places of the Merikin Baptist Church.[14] Joseph tried to shift responsibility for persecuting the Spiritual Baptists from Governor Chancellor to IGC May who was allegedly inspired by the St Vincent prohibition ordinance and prevailed on the government to prohibit the Shouters 'from practising their faith in the form in which they practised it.'[15] Joseph echoed Gollan and Murray when he assured the House, 'It is far indeed from the desire of the Government to do anything which interferes with the liberty of the subject and the right of the individual to choose the way in which he should worship.'[16] Although Joseph acknowledged the United Nations Charter on Human Rights that 'enshrined the principle of the freedom of worship,' which the colony had 'accepted,' he displayed some of the class and cultural biases that had bedevilled the attitude of Murray and Gollan toward the Spiritual Baptists:

> So long as these people practise their faith in the way it is practised in other parts of the World – and it is no new religion – they will have the freedom which this Government gives to all people who worship their God as they wish to do.

This was convoluted logic and unnecessary condescension. In acknowledging that Spiritual Baptism was not a new religion, Joseph should simply have acknowledged that government's prohibition was a gross violation of the constitutional guarantee to Spiritual Baptists' freedom of worship. Instead, he issued a veiled threat of continued government interference or punitive action against them for non-compliance with his unspecified world standard of worship.[17]

Butler seemed to understand that he was at the last major crossroads of religious toleration in the British Empire and wanted to ensure that history remembered him as a key agitator for the new dispensation. Pulling no punches, he described the Shouters' Prohibition Ordinance as a 'grave, serious and unchristian injustice which has been perpetrated on the Baptists of this Colony since 1917.'[18] The indictment provoked Speaker John Savary's admonishment: 'It is unparliamentary to refer to legislation passed by a previous legislature in that manner.'[19] McIntosh had engaged in more vitriolic condemnation of Murray's regime without attracting similar admonishment. Brushing aside the Speaker's intervention, Butler rejected the ascribed 'Shouter' label and insisted on the self-proclaimed 'Spiritual Baptist Faith' or simply

'Baptists' whom he recognised as 'spiritual teachers.'[20] He claimed to have agitated for repeal for fifteen years, which would coincide with the heyday of his crusade against the oil companies in the mid-1930s. He also claimed to have gone to England to speak to the government on their behalf. Challenging the popular notion of the Spiritual Baptist as an underground religion he countered, 'I have not known them to hide to practice their religion. I have never known them to practice their religion clandestinely although they have been made to suffer.'[21]

He affirmed, 'When the ban was put on them, rather than retreat or renounce their Creator they openly carried on the ancient practices of their religion and so it is not really true to say they went clandestinely about it.'[22] Butler's fight was also personal as a Spiritual Baptist: he referred to the God served by members of the faith as 'the God of Uriah Butler' and concluded, 'at long last they have come with the rest to enjoy one law as the Roman Catholics, Anglicans, Wesleyans and people of other denominations in Trinidad and Tobago.'[23]

Ashford Sinanan issued the strongest indictment of British lawmakers: 'I believe, Sir, that it would be extremely difficult for one to find in this island a piece of legislation which turns out to be a greater assault on the liberty and the freedom of the individual or a greater infringement of the religious rights and freedom of the people.'[24] Chanka Maharaj, another Butlerite, appealed directly to Chief Minister Albert Gomes to support his call for financial reparations. Maharaj recognised that without material reparations the Repeal Act would not erase the injustice of decades of persecution, stigmatisation and cultural stagnation. 'Grant the Baptist people money, as other denominations, to run their religion,' he pleaded.[25] Maharaj's call was directed at the colonial government. The metropolitan government, however, did not only assent to the original ordinance but reaffirmed the imperative for maintaining it when reviewed some years later. Raymond Quevedo, also known by his calypso sobriquet as Atilla the Hun, admitted that he had attended Spiritual Baptist meetings and took part in their ceremonies 'to bask in the glory of their spiritual enlightenment,' after which he became 'a much chastened man.'[26] He welcomed the Bill as 'the emancipation of a people from their thraldom.'

The bill passed unanimously at precisely noon on March 30, 1951.[27] Governor Hubert Rance assented to it on April 12, 1951; it was written into the statute book as law No. 20, 1951 to be referred to by its shortened title, 'The Shouters' Prohibition (Repeal) Ordinance, 1951.' The commencement date of the legislation was April 26, 1951.[28] As fate would have it, the architect of the first prohibition ordinance, Gideon Murray, died on March 12, 1951 in South Africa, where the roots and branches of the conspiracy originated. It is a curious coincidence that the repeal of the law was passed less than three weeks later and assented to by a governor exactly one month to the date of Murray's passing.

The results of the 1956 general elections strengthen the *prima facie* evidence of Spiritual Baptists as the post-war balance of power in Port of Spain North. Across the country, Spiritual Baptists threw their weight behind their new political Messiah, Dr Eric Williams, leader of the Peoples National Movement (PNM). So significant were the Spiritual Baptist women to PNM mobilisation that the public came to know them under a fetishised militarist terminology. With Williams contesting Port of Spain South and his party member, Ulric Lee, contesting against Gomes in the adjacent constituency, Port of Spain North, the incumbent did not have a ghost of a chance.

Cracks in the Unity of St Vincent's Prohibitionists

Although McIntosh's abolition Bill of 1939 did not see the light of day, the passage of the repeal motion coupled with his media advocacy disturbed the unity of the prohibitionists and haunted the Executive for several years. In 1945, Administrator Ronald Herbert Garvey solicited the opinion of English-born Anglican Bishop for the Windward Islands, Horace Norman Tonks, on the abolition of prohibition. Bishop Tonks was the spiritual leader of a diocese in which two of the three administrative units were persecuting one sector of the working class for religious rights guaranteed under the British constitution. The bishop was not opposed to government's effort to curb the alleged acts of unlawfulness of the Penitents but recommended that government should only be concerned with offences that fell 'within the orbit of the common law.'[29] His advice was consistent with the most eminent British and American jurists. An aggrieved person had the right to take an offender to court for tort if the actions of the offender were injurious to the wellbeing and liberty of the aggrieved. The bishop concluded, 'Repressive measures do more harm than good—as has been amply proved in this island. I never believe it does good to drive any practice under-ground if it can be avoided.'[30] Tonks was speaking from experience having been in St Vincent since 1936 after serving a short stint as Archdeacon in Grenada, another prohibition colony.[31] He had seen the sect grow under persecution. He held the view that no magistrate should be empowered to decide what is or is not Shakerism.[32] The Bishop's dissent from the canon of persecution was significant because of his physical proximity to the seat of government. Unlike the governorship of the Windward Islands, the seat of the Federation's Anglican diocese was Kingstown since 1927.[33]

Cane Garden Penitents Assert Leadership for Repeal

The legal battle for repeal might not be easily won, but the right of conscience might be advanced by a name–change of the movement and a title–change of its chief cleric from Leader to Pastor. This was obviously the strategy of the Penitents who convened a conference in 1949 at their chapel in Cane Garden, at which they repudiated the 'Shaker' identity and formally reconstituted the movement under a new name, 'Spiritual Baptists,' under the leadership of Pastor McDonald Williams.[34] Cane Garden has a special history in the prohibition of Penitentism. In his opening remarks on the Repeal Bill in 1965, E. T. Joshua, recounted that it was from the Cane Garden church that sounds of rejoicing and ringing of bells had purportedly panicked a governor's horse, which provided the pretext to treat Penitents' prayer meetings as public nuisance and ban Penitentism 'shortly afterwards.'[35] Although Joshua's anecdote was sketchy, it confirmed the Cane Garden church as a significant meeting place in the emergence and evolution of the Spiritual Baptist faith.

The Cane Garden conference adopted the government's mantra that a new religious organisation did not need government's permission or licence to operate. Acting swiftly under the new name, the Spiritual Baptists held a 'procession and feast' of between two thousand and four thousand persons in the streets of Georgetown in June 1949.[36] The lower estimate of the procession came from the police; the higher estimate from Revd Dunn of the Anglican Church at Calliaqua.[37] But even the lesser number was still a massive show of force, and a dramatic testimony to the resilience and indomitable spirit of the Spiritual Baptists. The choice of Georgetown was strategic. It was over thirty km from Kingstown, the capital city; moreover, it was the principal town of North Windward, the constituency of Ebenezer Duncan, who still served in the Legislative Council. To disarm detractors, the event was advertised as a celebration of their patron saint, John the Baptist. The organisers completely outfoxed the authorities who had no official knowledge of a group with the name Spiritual Baptists.

The organisers of the procession had clearly intended to make a political statement to affirm their legitimate status as a new Christian denomination and to demonstrate that the Spiritual Baptists were a well-organised, orderly, and peaceful community even when assembled *en masse*. The participants had come 'from all parts of the Colony.'[38] Many were dressed in distinctive uniforms demonstrating a show of force combined with military-like discipline of Garveyites. Although the Administrator disingenuously tried to downplay the impact of the parade by claiming that there was no way of knowing if all the participants were Spiritual Baptists, he admitted, nevertheless, that 'the majority wore some kind of uniform.'[39] He also acknowledged that the procession was orderly and peaceful. The procession dramatically destroyed the negative stereotype of immorality of Penitent worshippers and their meetings as havens for miscreants and petty criminals. Although the police maintained high visibility during the procession, they did not report a single incident that required their intervention. For the recognised churches the event was a rude awakening to the futility of persecution after almost four decades.

Panic and Desperation in the Ranks of the Recognised Clergy

The change of Administrator in 1948 and Anglican Patriarch in 1949 brought a change of attitude toward the Spiritual Baptists. Administrator Garvey's successor, Walter Coutts, was ambivalent about prohibition. He informed a trio of religious leaders that he harboured misgivings about the impolicy of 'persecuting a growing sect,' because it was likely to 'lead to unpleasant results and the strengthening of the present ties.'[40] The Georgetown parade had taken place shortly after his arrival. Coutts told the clerical heads, 'I have been concerned for some time regarding reports of the increase of Shakerism in the Island. My own view is that there appears to be little point in having an Ordinance which is unenforced, and to all intents and purposes a dead letter.'[41] Coutts, however, played on the clergy's fear of Penitent popularity. He intimated that 'the present growth of Shakerism must present a considerable challenge to the established Church.' He had no doubt that the leaders shared his concern and asked that they convene a meeting to make recommendations to government on how to tackle the 'ever-increasing problem of Shakerism in the Island.'[42]

One of those leaders was Archdeacon Roland Stanley Maxwell who succeeded Bishop Tonks upon the latter's return to England in 1949. Maxwell, a graduate of Cambridge and Oxford Universities, was appointed Archdeacon in St Vincent in 1947; previously, he was a military priest, having served as Chaplain in the Royal Air Force Volunteer Reserve from 1940 to 1946. St Vincent was his first civil assignment since his retirement from military service.

Not wishing to expose their naked prejudice and open violation of toleration laws, the committee of the clergy submitted a conservative report but hid behind a 'minority' report submitted by Revd J. R. Dunn of Calliaqua that 'savoured of persecution.'[43] Dunn, however, emphasised that his suggestions were personal. He boasted, 'I have had more contact with Shakerism, I believe, than any other clergyman here except Mr Pitt.'[44] He recommended, 'All outdoor meetings etc. in the streets & public places should require the written permission of the police.' He argued, 'I did not see injustice in this, as the roads are provided for travel not meetings (there is some such rule in Grenada).' He called on the police to make 'order & decency a strict condition of their permission.'[45] This was an explicit call for police intervention to pre-empt another demonstration of Spiritual Baptist power as occurred in Georgetown. Dunn tried to play down the impact of the Georgetown procession by alleging that people were attracted to 'the inducements of a free or nearly free outing.'[46] But he was also aware that some of his own congregation, including a member of his choir, were seduced by the inducements.[47] He alleged that the Spiritual Baptist procession was largely financed from contributions from the United States of America channelled through Trinidad.[48]

The Anglican clergy knew that the Spiritual Baptists had triumphed over the Ordinance, but instead of acknowledging defeat, it recommended a change in strategy: it called on the government to launch an investigation into penance–houses (mourning grounds) with a view to prosecuting Leaders and Mothers 'under the Sanitary Conditions and Disorderly Houses Regulations.' Unlike the Prohibition Ordinance, these regulations were constitutional though steeped in class prejudice. Nevertheless, such strategy was too late to stop a growing movement that was becoming more organised and internationally recognised. The official clerical report also recommended that the government 'withhold recognition of "this cult."'[49] This was in reference to applications for marriage licences, which the Christian Pilgrims had already successfully exploited to gain recognition in 1951.[50] Although it was not the official business of government to recognise religious bodies, the prerogative to grant or deny marriage licences to religious leaders had become a substitute for recognition and remained the most effective weapon deployed against the Spiritual Baptists.[51]

McIntosh Struggles to Maintain Relevance Amidst Changing Identity Strategies of the Penitents

It was not surprising that the police thwarted the plan of the Spiritual Baptists for an even grander show of force in Kingstown in 1950 by denying them permission for the procession. McIntosh challenged the police obstruction in the Legislative Council by way of a series of loaded questions intended to expose the government's bias toward a select religious denomination. A metropolitan law prohibiting Roman Catholics from publicly displaying religious paraphernalia had not been repealed. With this knowledge, McIntosh berated the police for allowing Catholics to march in the streets of the city with an image.[52] McIntosh also accused the government of allowing persons of unknown backgrounds from the US to set up religious organisations in the island, while denying 'the people' the right to do the same. These American organisations were mainly products of the nineteenth century, the same as the Spiritual Baptists.

Administrator Coutts continued to mobilise support for government intervention against the Spiritual Baptists well into the 1950s. Although resistance to prohibition never ceased, the unwillingness of the authorities to modify the law took a toll on adherents of the faith. Because the Spiritual Baptists had no written theology and had not been defined in law, the orthodoxy of some aspects of the religion had been contested or repudiated from time to time even by some leaders of the faith. For example, the delegation of Penitents who met with Murray in 1912 had allegedly promised to eliminate practices condemned by the elites, namely rejoicing and mourning. During his court case Trinidad's Teacher Bailey rejected the charge of 'shouting' and insisted that what he had inherited from his parents was 'praying in the name of the Lord.'[53] Bailey and other Shouter Leaders and Mothers were making the case for corybantic rejoicing as canonical to Spiritual Baptists while rejecting the connotation of unruliness, demagoguery or martial drills implied in the ordinary meaning of the word shouting. McIntosh took this repudiation to a new level and informed the Legislative Council that the Spiritual Baptists were 'prepared to help government strike out the pernicious practice of Shakerism.'[54] This revelation suggests that McIntosh was now representing the Cane Garden schism as the new orthodoxy. Unfortunately, as a strategy for legitimising the Spiritual Baptists as a new denomination, it also legitimised a posteriori persecution for 'Shakerism' under the Shakers' Prohibition Ordinance.

Apparently, not all the 'reformed' Penitents agreed with the new designation, Spiritual Baptist. In response to the police refusal to allow the Kingstown procession in 1950, the Spiritual Baptists convened another conference of leaders at the Cane Garden chapel to establish 'a clear distinction ... between our Religion and Shakerism.'[55] Accordingly, they abandoned the new Spiritual Baptist label and adopted yet another identity, 'Christian Pilgrims.' McIntosh also recalibrated his politics to align with the new identity and proposed to the government that it should recognise the Christian Pilgrims, which would 'help them to stop this practice of Shakerism and enable them to worship in a decent way.'[56] Ironically, McIntosh's proposal mirrored the colonialist thinking of the movement: that it was necessary to exorcise Shakerism from Penitentism, which would then qualify its followers for the right to worship according to conscience. The original exorcist was Administrator Gideon Murray who had made exorcism of Shakerism the official, principal object of his Prohibition Ordinance. Shakerism as defined by Murray was evil, unchristian, and anti-Christian. McIntosh was either overwhelmed by the schism or wearied by the struggle for repeal, because the acknowledgement of Shakerism as evil meant that he could no longer reconcile with the central tenets of the faith, rejoicing and the rite of mourning, the two elements clearly identified in the Prohibition Ordinance for eradication.

The Christian Pilgrims did not define Shakerism; nevertheless, by committing 'to worship in a decent way' they inadvertently endorsed the colonialist narrative of passivity of congregants as the ideal of religious decorum; moreover, the endorsement was a repudiation of after midnight 'rejoicing' or the so-called 'Shakers Dance,' which was 'objected to by every reasonable person in the community' as the injection of African 'paganism' into Europeanised christianity, according to Chief of Police Griffith.[57] The declaration, however, did not necessarily mean that the Church had repudiated the passion, vibrancy and ecstasy in its liturgy. In 1904, Revd Broadbent of the Methodist Church had proposed such a compromise to keep Penitents fully within the Methodist communion. Unfortunately, the conference did not leave a record of the tenets of the reformed movement.

To extract from government official recognition for Christian Pilgrims, McIntosh introduced a motion in July 1950 that supported the granting of marriage licence to the newly named Christian Pilgrims.[58] This time, elected members of the Council did not unanimously back McIntosh. The elected member for South Windward was opposed to universal toleration. He argued, 'As soon as you start to give recognition to bodies such as this, you will find hosts of applications coming in, and it may be from those who wish to indulge in practices.'[59] His words suggested that the Christian Pilgrims were a sect of reformed Penitents or that McIntosh and other spokespersons for the movement had successfully convinced members in political authority that they were a new denomination. Moreover, he did not agree that Christian Pilgrims should be recognised as marriage officers without prior investigation into the movement. Nominated members also strongly objected to the motion. E. A. C. Hughes, a nominated official, acknowledged that the Christian Pilgrims were worshippers at 'a church in Cane Garden.'[60] If they were indeed new on the religious landscape, he saw no problem with them 'marching through the streets.'[61]

McIntosh's frustration was typical of many seasoned politicians who had spent a long career in the shadows of opposition colonial politics. He became more belligerent than ever and even implicitly invoked violence: 'I tell you this much, if we don't get it one way we will get it another.'[62] He insulted the Commissioner of Police with the label 'lunatic' and crowned his attack on the Executive with the poetic words of militant, Jamaican-born, African American civil rights activist, Claude McKay: 'If we must die, Oh let us die nobly so that the very monsters we defy shall be constrained to honour us, though dead.'[63] McIntosh's motion was narrowly defeated 3 to 4 with one abstention.

The legal challenge for recognition as marriage officers did not end with the defeat of the motion in the legislature. In April 1951, McDonald Williams, who was elected Chief Pastor of the Christian Pilgrims at the Cane Garden conference, applied for a marriage officer's licence. The Executive Council's approval, although subject to periodic review, was a historic victory for the reformed Church.[64]

Nevertheless, the slow, incremental progress would have been more painful considering that the approval was coming a few weeks after the repeal of the Shouters Prohibition Ordinance in Trinidad and Tobago. Two years later, a new schism emerged in another attempt to probe for a loophole in the prohibition ordinance. Robert Barnwell of Lowmans Village in the Windward district, bearing the honorific title 'Spiritual Leader of the Christian Pilgrims,' applied for a marriage officer's licence under another identity, Wesleyan Baptists, a completely new name in Caribbean Christianity.[65] The idea of marrying two different 'recognised' denominations, however, was not new to the struggle of the Spiritual Baptists, as already observed with Butler's Moravian Baptist Church. A government official sent to interview Barnwell was impressed with the physical setting. Barnwell explained to him that the name-change was intended to bring greater respectability. However, he allegedly admitted that the members of the church were Shakers. Accordingly, the official reported that the law against Shakerism would preclude granting him a marriage officer's licence.[66] By then McIntosh's party had resoundingly lost the general elections, the first under universal adult suffrage.

General Elections of 1951, a Setback for Repeal in St Vincent

McIntosh and his political allies were all swept away in the general elections of 1951 by the new phenomenon of union-based political parties. The new behemoth was the Eight Army of Liberation (EAL), founded by Hamilton George Charles, with Ebenezer Joshua joining shortly afterward. Charles was one of many trade union and political leaders with experience in two or more regional territories. During the 1930s, he lived in Trinidad and learned militant trade unionism from Uriah Butler. He even won a local government seat in Diego Martin as a Butlerite.[67] After returning to St Vincent in 1950, Charles founded the United Workers and Rate Payers Union.[68] After many years as schoolteacher and law clerk, Ebenezer Joshua, a self-confessed Spiritual Baptist, migrated in search of greener pastures and lived in Trinidad from 1941 to 1943 and from 1945 to 1951. Like Charles, he was a Butlerite, and ran unsuccessfully for the San Fernando seat as a candidate for Butler's Home Rule Party in the general elections of 1950.[69] Shortly after returning to St Vincent in 1951, he joined the EAL and became its most charismatic orator. Joshua was the EAL's candidate for North Windward in the 1951 elections. The EAL was the only political party to contest the elections winning all eight seats, despite a good showing by Independents among whom were McIntosh and Duncan. The Spiritual Baptists of North Windward were fortunate to have a new, committed representative in the legislature to continue the activism of Duncan.

The repeal of the Trinidad and Tobago Ordinance should have led to a quick repeal of the same law in St Vincent and Grenada with instruction from the Colonial Office to do so, but there was no push for repeal by St Vincent's political class. George Charles' pre-eminence in the Legislative Council was fatal to the repeal movement. He failed to carry forward the repeal baton that McIntosh ceded to him. No one knows how Governor Edward Beetham might have responded to the passage of a bill for repeal under Charles' watch. Had the EAL leader accepted the challenge to walk in McIntosh's shoes in the wake of his electoral victory, he could have upheld the repeal of the Shouters' Prohibition Ordinance as precedent and moral catalyst to advance the case for prohibition in St Vincent.

Charles' silence on repeal was deeper than politics. Kenneth John unsympathetically describes him as 'a mere accident of history.'[70] John further alleges that Charles became 'a puppet of the planters' in the Legislative Council. As a young man, Charles had worked on the estate of one Willie Hadley, 'arguably the most backward of the planters.'[71] Most likely, it was Charles' elevation to the Executive Council that transformed him from a fiery advocate of the masses to an agent of 'the planter class and the colonial office.'[72] Joshua, on the other hand, sustained his Butlerite militancy in his new role of Vincentian politician. The split with Charles was predictable but it was the catalyst that revived the repeal question in the legislature. Joshua could not succeed in North Windward and ignore repeal. Although Charles was majority leader of the Legislative Council, it was Joshua who was the politician that other legislators truly respected and admired. From 1951 to 1954 the Legislative Council was filled with squabbles between the two leaders and their respective followers that undermined the quest for repeal.

Ebeneezer Joshua and the Restoration of Repeal

In 1953, following the breakup of the EAL, Joshua launched his own People's Political Party (PPP). He deliberately courted the Spiritual Baptists, recognising their value as union workers and voters.[73] The PPP was the only party to contest the 1954 elections but captured only three seats to the Independents' five. Notwithstanding the PPP's minority status in the Legislative Council, Joshua's resolution for repeal of the Ordinance in August 1955 passed unanimously, with only one abstention. The new governor of the Windward Islands, Sir Colville Montgomery Deverell, who arrived in January of that year, was unwilling to follow in the footsteps of Sir Hubert Rance who was also new to the governorship of Trinidad and Tobago when the successful motion for repeal was passed in 1951. Ironically, just a few months prior to Joshua's motion, Governor Beetham was transferred from the Windward Islands to the newly free religious environment of Trinidad and Tobago. Deverell's stunning move to veto the unanimous decision of the legislature set back repeal by a full decade, leaving St Vincent and Grenada as the only colonies in the Caribbean to subject a Christian denomination to state repression.

In 1956, Joshua became his country's first chief minister. As Head of government, he prioritised institutional, infrastructural, and economic policies and programmes, leaving repeal on the back burner. This was unlike the approach taken by Gomes; but the difference is understandable. Joshua became Chief Minister under Administrator Samuel Horatio Graham who took up office only the year before. It is not known why Joshua did not put Graham to the test, but it seems that the Chief Minister believed that once Deverell was governor, there was little chance of repeal getting on the statute books.

The Final Thrust for Repeal in St Vincent

The early 1960s was rife with civil-rights militancy in the US, rapid decolonisation in Africa and the Caribbean, beginning with Jamaica and Trinidad and Tobago. News of these events filtered into St Vincent via television, radio, and the press. Against this revolutionary backdrop, Joshua introduced a new Bill, 'An Ordinance to repeal the "Shouterism" Prohibition Ordinance' on March 22, 1965. The purpose was simply stated: 'To permit the exercise of the right of Freedom of Religion which is now universally acknowledged.'[74] There was greater urgency than attended the Shouters' Repeal Bill, as the first, second and third readings were completed in a single sitting. Joshua pulled no punches. He deftly reversed the stereotype imposed on the Penitents in 1912, calling the prohibitionists of the day 'a certain ignorant section of the inhabitants of the colony.'[75] Whereas McIntosh had disguised the race factor in prohibition under the rubric of the 'poor' working class, Joshua unequivocally identified racism as the primary motive of the framers of the prohibition ordinance of 1912. He asked rhetorically, 'Are we going to allow in this Golden Age that racial paragraph on our statute book when we are not only asking for independence but responsible government?'[76]

Joshua paid respect to George McIntosh for his long but futile struggle to emancipate the Shakers: 'McIntosh … tried his best but the age was not ripe when the iron heel of colonialism was still more rampant in these parts.'[77] He reminded the House that in 1955 his motion for repeal had passed unanimously but failed to free the Shakers because he was then in the Opposition. He noted that Jamaica and Barbados had 'all sorts of religions,' and asked rhetorically, 'Are we less tolerant than these people?'[78] Interestingly, he did not mention Trinidad and Tobago.

After decades of futile appeals to the colonial office and colonial governors to respect the constitutional guarantee of religious freedom and put an end to the persecution of the Spiritual Baptists – even after the example of the Trinidad and Tobago government – Joshua turned his moral gaze to the Atlantic Charter and the presidency of the US. He pontificated, 'We have a broad principle; from the very outset we endorsed and fully accepted the four freedoms of President Roosevelt and one of them is Freedom of Religion.'[79] He concluded, 'Therefore no religious body can approach this government and say they did not get full toleration from the government.'[80]

Joshua's address set the tone for many other legislators to vent the wrongs of slavery and colonialism and pay respect to the Spiritual Baptists for framing and leading the resistance to the culture war unleashed by European colonisers against the African race. Many speakers, like Joshua, identified closely with the Spiritual Baptists and expressed their gratitude to them for standing firm against state oppression that dated back to the days of slavery. While not admitting membership, many acknowledged that they frequently attended Spiritual Baptist prayer meetings for spiritual fulfilment, just as their counterparts in Trinidad and Tobago.

The Bill won favour with the Opposition, led by Robert Milton Cato. He announced in his opening statement: 'It is one of the rare occasions on which members of the Opposition side of the House are at one with the government.'[81] How rare, he did not say, because Trinidad was in a similar constitutional status in 1951 and the Opposition was also at one with the government on the question of repeal. Indeed, the debate on repeal in St Vincent reflected that of Trinidad. Just as Gomes and Butler had clashed over claims of championing the Spiritual Baptists, Cato poured cold water on Joshua's boast of his 1955 Repeal Motion. He expressed 'amazement' that although the motion had passed the legislature, 'no positive steps have yet been taken to have it erased from the statute books ... Let us hope, Mr. Speaker that we will not have another ten years to bring up another motion again.' He called on Joshua to be humbler and recognise that he was standing on the shoulders of McIntosh and that the success of Joshua's motion should be seen as 'the final steps' of McIntosh's Repeal Motion in 1939 and Marriage Motion in 1950.[82]

Cato was not a newcomer to the cause of Spiritual Baptist liberation. In the late 1940s, he had successfully defended a group of twenty-five Shakers charged under the 1912 ordinance. He recalled that his main defence was simply that 'there was no precise definition of the practices which they accused them of indulging in.'[83] The magistrate acquitted them all. This victory underscores the class and race prejudices that the law was founded upon and on which the government hoped to execute its plan of eradicating Shakerism. The government understood that legal counsel was not affordable to the masses and was not required in the magistrates' courts dispensing summary judgements. The significance of that case is its exposure of the unconstitutionality of the Prohibition Ordinance. Cato was a rookie lawyer fresh out of the Inns of Court in London to the court of Barrouallie, winning a stunning victory against the state by exposing the considerable flaws in the law, which was deliberately written that way to give liberty to the police and magistrates to oppress the Spiritual Baptists according to their own prejudices. It was a fitting tribute to him that he was in the Legislative Council at that crucial moment to marshal his forces to bring an end to more than a half–century of state persecution against the denomination.

In his contribution to the debate nominated member, R. F. Marksman, self-identified 'as a Black man, as a Negro.' He saw the case of the Spiritual Baptists as 'one of the trappings of slavery, one of the humbugs of colonialism in our country.'[84] He believed that when his ancestors were under the yoke of chattel slavery, 'It was their recourse to that religion that saved the race.'[85] He was proud of the resilience and conviction of the Spiritual Baptists under state oppression: 'I believe that although people were banned from worship in the way they chose to worship God, they worshipped even in the prisons, they worshipped in the Police Station, in the hands of the police....'[86] H. F. Young, the representative for South Leeward, was proud to have associated with the Spiritual Baptists: 'I have attended many of these meetings and when a man is spiritually taken and he has shaken hands with a man, he will feel the common touch, he is moved spiritually.' This admission made him more than an onlooker; he enjoyed active fellowship.

In his closing remarks, Joshua betrayed the hurt he felt from Cato's rebuke and descended into political banter. Perhaps it was why he felt compelled to enlighten the House that the emergence of Spiritual

Baptism was the African response to the racism and injustice in enslavers' religions. He said, 'The Cathedral where we go to worship now quite easily was built by slaves' but a slave would be flogged 'if he even attempted to look in the window.'[87] Joshua proudly announced that he was the first leader of a government to acknowledge allegiance to the Spiritual Baptist faith and to claim that his enslaved ancestors belonged to the same faith: 'In the early days of slavery this is my religion....People know that I belong to this faith, this is my faith, I am satisfied with this faith.'[88]

The Bill passed without amendment on March 22, 1965. Two months later Governor Graham gave his assent to the ordinance, which entered the statute books as Law No. 7 of 1965.

Notes

1. Henry, *Reclaiming African Religions*, 36.
2. The leaders of the three main parties all lost the general elections of 1946; see Brereton, *Modern Trinidad*, 195.
3. See Henry, *Reclaiming African Religions*, 138–141.
4. See Brinsley Samaroo, 'The Making of the 1946 Trinidad Constitution,' *Caribbean Studies* 15, no. 7 (January 1979), 12.
5. Henry, *Reclaiming African Religions*, 36.
6. Ibid.
7. Ibid.
8. Jeremy Taylor, 'Albert Gomes: Missing in Action,' *Caribbean Beat*, 68 (July–August 2004), https://www.caribbean-beat.com/issue-68/missing-action-albert-gomes#axzz7hGQ31Yh, accessed January 22, 2021.
9. Anon., 'Trinidad and Tobago General Election Results: September 18, 1950,' https://www.caribbeanelections.com/tt/elctions/tt_results_1950.asp; accessed February 2, 2022; Brereton, *Modern Trinidad*, 197-98.
10. Bolland, *Politics of Labour*, 527.
11. Following his release from detention Butler continued to be hounded by government and members of the legislature. See Daurius Figueira, *Tubal Uriah Butler of Trinidad and Tobago Kwame Nkrumah of Ghana: The Road to Independence 6ᵗʰ March 1957, 31ˢᵗ August 1962* (New York: iUniverse, 2007), Google Books.
12. 'Trinidad and Tobago General Election Results: September 18, 1950.'
13. Bolland, *Politics of Labour*, 527.
14. Lum, *Praising His Name in the Dance*, 33. The claim to birthplace of the Baptist is shared with Third Company: see Brewer, 'Baptist Churches of South Trinidad,' 82.

15. Hansard, Roy Joseph, March 30, 1951, UWI/AJL, 1369.

16. Ibid, 1370.

17. Ibid.

18. Hansard, Uriah Butler, March 30, 1951, 1373.

19. Hansard, Chamber Speaker, March 30, 1951, 1369.

20. Hansard, Butler, March 30, 1951, UWI/AJL, 1375.

21. Ibid, 1376.

22. Ibid. Gomes refuted Butler's claim that he represented the Shouters to the British government. The Attorney General also rejected Butler's claim that he presented Pastor Griffith's petition for repeal before the Legislative Council, Hansard, March 30, 1951, 1377; 1380.

23. Hansard, Butler, March 30, 1951, 1377.

24. Hansard, Ashford S. Sinanan, March 30, 1951, 1385-85.

25. Hansard, Chanka Maharaj, March 30, 1951, 1390.

26. Hansard, Raymond Quevedo, March 30, 1951, 1392.

27. Hansard, The Speaker, March 30, 1951, 1393.

28. The assented legislation is available at http://laws.gov.tt/ttdll-web/revision/download/63215?type=amendment, accessed October 19, 2022.

29. Bishop Tonks to Administrator Garvey, January 14, 1945, SVGNA, J 29/1939 (1).

30. Tonks to Garvey, January 14, 1945, SVGNA, J 29/1939 (1).

31. 'Tonks, Horace Norman Vincent, 1891-1959, Biographical Note,' https://dia.pitts.emory.edu/archives/text/miss120.html, accessed February 28, 2021; Tonks to Garvey, January 14, 1945, SVGNA, J 29/39 (1).

32. Tonks to Garvey, January 14, 1945, SVGNA, J 29/39 (1).

33. See 'Diocese of the Windward Island,' http://www.anglicanswi.org/about-us/ accessed February 28, 2021.

34. Revd V. Herbert & A. Eubanks of the Pilgrim Holiness Church to A. V. King, Acting-Government Secretary, November 29, 1950, SVGNA, CR-SMP-GA-62, Item 31.

35. E. T. Joshua recalled the event during the debate on the repeal of the ordinance in 1965: see *Hansard*, E. T. Joshua, March 22, 1965, SVGNA, CR-HOA-02, 14–15.

36. Revd Dunn to Coutts, September 28, 1949, SVGNA, J 29/1939 (18). Fraser, *Shakers to Spiritual Baptists*, 69–70. The recognised clergy had reported that there were at least thirty-five centres of Shakerism in 1949. This means that organisationally, the Shakers had almost recovered their pre-prohibition strength in terms of praise–houses and had probably gained in numerical strength. The procession was a strategic move to demonstrate that the Spiritual Baptists were a well-organised, orderly and peaceful community even when assembled *en masse*.

37. Dunn to Coutts, September 28, 1949, SVGNA, J 29/1939 (18).

38.   Fraser, *Shakers to Spiritual Baptists*, 71.

39.   Ibid.

40.   Coutts to Clergy (Archdeacon Maxwell, A. C; Father Van der Plas, R. C.; Revd E. Higman, Meth.), 'Strictly Confidential,' September 6, 1949, enclosed in Coutts to Governor, 'Secret,' December 16, 1949, SVGNA, J 29/1939 (17).

41.   Coutts to Clergy, 'Strictly Confidential,' September 6, 1949, SVGNA, J 29/1939 (17).

42.   Ibid.

43.   Dunn to Coutts, September 28, 1949 SVGNA, J 29/1939 (18).

44.   Ibid.

45.   Ibid.

46.   Ibid

47.   Ibid.

48.   Ibid.

49.   Fraser, *Shakers to Spiritual Baptists*, 82.

50.   Ibid, 81.

51.   Muslims in Trinidad and Tobago were denied marriage licences up to the early 1930s and Hindus up to 1945. Up to that time, this prejudice had successfully driven Hindus mainly into Presbyterianism; but most Hindus preserved their traditional marriage, rather than sacrifice cultural independence merely to escape the egregious stigma of concubinage and 'illegitimate' offspring.

52.   See Fraser, *Shakers to Spiritual Baptists*, 73. For an early debate on the perceived threat to public order by such processions, see Carol Devlin, 'The Eucharistic Procession of 1908: The Dilemma of the Liberal Government,' *Church History 63*, no. 3 (September 1994), 411-13.

53.   *Trinidad Guardian*, 'A "Shouters" Meeting: Batch of Defendants at Chaguanas—Obstinate Fellow Fined—First Case Under Prohibitive Ordinance,' January 9, 1918, 7, UWI/AJL (mfm).

54.   Fraser, *Shakers to Spiritual Baptists*, 75–76.

55.   Ibid, 76.

56.   Ibid.

57.   Chief of Police to Administrator, September 6, 1912, BNA, CO 321/269.

58.   Fraser, *Shakers to Spiritual Baptists*, 75.

59.   Ibid, 79.

60.   Ibid, 76.

61.   Ibid, 77.

62.   Ibid, 79.

63.   Ibid, 80. The poem, 'If We Must Die,' was published in 1919 during the Harlem Renaissance.

64.   Ibid, 81.

65.   Ibid.

66. Ibid, 82.
67. Cecil Ryan and Cecil A. Blazer Williams, *From Charles to Mitchell, Part 1* (n.p.: Projects Promotion, n.d.), 9, SVGNA, CR-RBS-78.
68. Dr Adrian Fraser, 'George Charles and the Eight Army of Liberation,' *Searchlight*, December 17, 2004, https://searchlight.vc/searchlight/dr-fraser/2004/12/17/george-charles-and-the-eight-army-of-liberation/, accessed January 28, 2021.
69. Ryan and Williams, *Charles to Mitchell*, 20; Karl Eklund, 'Saint Vincent and the Grenadines: Ebeneezer Theodore Joshua,' August 13, 2005, http://svgblog.blogspot.com/2005/08/ebeneezer-theodore-joshua.html?m=1, accessed on January 22, 2021; Kenneth John, 'Joshua, Ebeneezer,' https://www.encyclopedia.com/history/encyclopedias-almanacs-transcripts-and-maps/joshua-ebeneezer
70. Dr Kenneth John, 'Getting to Know the Real George Charles,' May 9, 2013, *Vincentian*, https://thevincentianonline.com/getting-to-know-the-real-george-charles-p2878-108.htm, accessed January 28, 2021.
71. John, 'Getting to Know the Real George Charles,' May 9, 2013, *Vincentian*.
72. Ryan and Williams, *Charles to Mitchell*, 14.
73. Ryan and Williams, *Charles to Mitchell*, 32-33.
74. Hansard, E. T. Joshua, March 22, 1965, SVGNA, CR-HOA-02, 11.
75. Hansard, Joshua, March 22, 1965, 16.
76. Ibid, 15.
77. Ibid, 14.
78. Ibid, 16.
79. Ibid, 11-12.
80. Ibid.
81. Hansard, R. M. Cato, March 22, 1965, 17.
82. Hansard, R.F. Marksman, March 22, 1965, 20.
83. Hansard, Marksman, March 22, 1965, 20.
84. Ibid, 21.
85. Ibid, 22.
86. Ibid.
87. Hansard, Joshua, March 22, 1965, 29.
88. Ibid.

Conclusion

*'Reparations – by which I mean the full acceptance of our collective biography and its consequences – is the price we must pay to see ourselves squarely.'**

Statutory prohibition and State persecution of Spiritual Baptists must be seen within a longer narrative of endemic religious intolerance in the Caribbean and the imperial homeland. For England the narrative begins before the start of colonisation and is yet to close its final chapter. The demonisation of the Spiritual Baptists by prohibitionists was without parallel in the Caribbean, making the politics of their suppression a unique chapter in this epic struggle for freedom of conscience by a Christian denomination. Spiritual Baptists worshipped the same God, preached from the same Scriptures, and sang the same hymns as those who persecuted them. Attorney General Henry Gollan's description of the Spiritual Baptists as a 'pseudo-religion' had no validity in statute or case law; neither is the term to be found in ecclesiastical laws of England.

This study locates the Spiritual Baptist faith as an offshoot of African American Baptist infused with new African cultural elements re-introduced into the Caribbean in the mid-nineteenth century. To ban the Spiritual Baptist, the colonial state had to prove that it was not a religion; that the meeting places of its members were not places of worship; that they did not worship a supreme being or that the protection of conscience under Britain's toleration laws did not apply to them. None of these conditions was met by the governments of

---

* 'Reparations Quotes,' https://www.goodreads.com/quotes/tag/reparations, from Ta-Nihisi Coates' anthology, *We Were Eight Years in Power: An American Tragedy.*

the persecuting colonies. While the law of England and the colonies allowed for the prohibition of practices deemed a threat to public order, such proscriptions could not constitutionally extend to the prohibition of prayer meetings or the prohibition of the religious denomination itself. If noise was an authentic reason for legislation, action against the Spiritual Baptists would have been initiated by the citizenry so disturbed. Instead, charges under the prohibition ordinances invariably resulted from police surveillance and intelligence gathering. William Blackstone had alluded to the immunity of congregations and pastors from the whims of political authorities.

Despite the State's requisition of information from the media, recognised clergy, scholars and police, the Administrator of St Vincent had no material evidence on which to build a *prima facie* case in a court of law that did not enjoy summary jurisdiction. The same could be said of Trinidad and Tobago. This study has demonstrated that the colonial elites, including the governing class, had targeted the Spiritual Baptists as political enemies. Instead of presenting a threat to public order, the Spiritual Baptists were increasingly becoming a highly disciplined community, less reliant on the colonial power–structure for guidance on matters relating to morality, self–empowerment and community–building.

When Administrator Gideon Murray brought his prohibition bill to the Legislative Council, he was keenly aware that his friend and former boss was influentially positioned in the Colonial Office and had a seat in the Privy Council. He was also keenly aware that his brothers were similarly positioned politically and that his departmental colleagues over whom he had wielded managerial authority for two years would oversee the review of his ordinance. Without these connections Murray could not have expected to have his unconstitutional ordinance sanctioned. Even so, its sanction exposes the British government to a historic crime that still screams for reparatory justice.

Historically state and ecclesiastical persecutors have often put revolutionary variations of Christianity to the test, and its advocates to the sword. The main difference with the Spiritual Baptist faith was that the British Empire within which it emerged had guaranteed it constitutional protection. Toleration Acts did not exclude syncretic or corybantic forms of Christianity. They failed to protect the Spiritual Baptists because of the evil genius of Gideon Murray in surgically separating the dominant African elements, particularly mourning and rejoicing, from the dominant Euro–Christian elements: Methodist-informed prayers and singing of hymns. The Doctrine of the Trinity Act, 1813 extended the full benefits of Toleration to Unitarians. Unitarians deny the divinity of Jesus. Spiritual Baptists, on the other hand, required a declaration from mourners that Jesus is God and Saviour.

The PWRA, 1855 did not exclude pagan or heathen practices. There were heathen Members of Parliament well before 1912. Thus, Murray's labelling of mourning and rejoicing as heathenism would not have qualified Penitentism for prohibition in England. To circumvent this roadblock, Murray's regime resorted to terms customarily associated with barbarism, Satanism, and cultism such as orgies, hypnotism, and incubators of lunacy. Since Murray could not successfully legislate against Penitentism as a movement based on these charges alone, he resorted to duplicity by purporting to legislate against certain practices, which would purge out Africanism from Penitents' prayer meetings without interfering with the right of its members to independent worship. The government of Trinidad and Tobago believed that if they stuck faithfully to the St Vincent script in all manner of speaking, they too might accomplish the impossible against the Spiritual Baptists. Grenada's Act No. 11 of 1927 could have been constitutionally framed had the government not included one word, 'Shakerism,' in its title. All three colonies, therefore, were equally contemptuous in their violation of numerous toleration statutes when they passed their prohibition laws to persecute and eradicate the Spiritual Baptists.

The fifteen-year period between the prohibition of 'Shakerism' in St Vincent and the prohibition of 'Shakerism' in Grenada was the height of the last stage of British imperialism that began with the Berlin Conference, 1884–85. Touted as a 'civilising mission,' culture was indeed central and indispensable to the success of the colonial enterprise. Colonial officials criss-crossed the empire. The resistance of the Spiritual Baptists was not new to them. Colonials had considered the Caribbean a Christian country fashioned by them in their own cosmological blueprint. They declared war against the Spiritual Baptist not because the latter practised a different religion but because they had fashioned it from a different blueprint. Yet, under Britain's toleration laws the Spiritual Baptist had no case to answer. The same could not, and still cannot, be said of the British government.

Appendix A
JAMAICA—LAW 31 OF 1911

A Law to compel persons to desist in the night time from disturbing others.

Be it enacted by the Governor and Legislative Council of Jamaica, as follows:—

1—This Law may be cited as the Noises (Night) Prevention Law.

Persons playing upon any musical or noisy instrument or singing or making any noise between 11 p.m. and 6 a.m. liable in certain circumstances to penalty not exceeding 40 shillings, and in default to imprisonment not exceeding one month.

2—Every person who shall between the hours of 11 p.m. and 6 a.m. sound or play upon any musical or noisy instrument, or sing or make any noise whatsoever in any town, village or district, after having been required by any person resident in such town, village or district, or by any police constable or district constable acting on the request of any person so resident, to desist from making such sounds or noises, either on account of the illness of any person, or because such sounds or noises are audible beyond a distance of two chains, or for any reasonable cause shall be liable on summary conviction before a Resident Magistrate or two Justices of the Peace to a penalty not exceeding forty shillings and in default of payment to imprisonment for any period not exceeding one month.

No prosecution to be commenced without written consent of Clerk of Court for the parish.

3—No prosecution under this Law shall be commenced against any person without written consent being first had and obtained of the Clerk of the Courts for the parish in which the offence is alleged to have been committed.

Passed in Council this 7th day of April, 1911.

Appendix B
The Shakers' Prohibition Ordinance
SAINT VINCENT

Ordinance No. 13 of 1912

AN ORDINANCE to render illegal the practices of "Shakerism" as indulged in in the Colony of St. Vincent.

[Commencement: *1st October, 1912.*]

WHEREAS there has grown up a custom amongst a certain ignorant section of the inhabitants of the Colony of St. Vincent of attending or frequenting meetings from time to time at houses and places where practices are indulged in which tend to exercise a pernicious and demoralizing effect upon the said inhabitants and which practices are commonly known as "Shakerism".

AND WHEREAS it is expedient in the best interests of the said Colony of St. Vincent and its inhabitants that such meetings and practices should not be permitted.

Be it enacted by the Governor with the advice and consent of the Legislative Council of St. Vincent as follows:

Short title.

1. This ordinance may be cited as 'The "Shakerism" Prohibition Ordinance, 1912.'

Definition of Shakers meeting.

2. (1) A "Shakers meeting" shall mean a meeting or gathering of two or more persons whether indoors or in the open air, at which the customs and the practices of Shakerism are indulged in. The decision of any Magistrate in any case brought under this ordinance as to whether the customs and the practices are Shakerism shall be final.

Definition of Shakers House.

(2) A "Shakers house" shall mean any house or building or room in any house or building which is used for the purpose of holding Shakers meetings or any house or building or room in any house or building which is used for the purpose of initiating any person into the ceremonies of Shakerism. The decision of any Magistrate in any case brought under this Ordinance as to whether a house or building or room in any house or building is a Shaker's House shall be final.

Definition of manager.

(3) The word "manager" shall include Town Wardens and any person having control over or charge of any land whatsoever in the Colony.

No person shall take part in Shaker's meeting.

3.   It shall be an offence against this Ordinance for any person to hold or to take part in or to attend any Shakers meetings or for any Shakers meeting to be held in any part of the Colony indoors or in the open air at any time of the day or night.

4.   It shall be an offence against this ordinance to erect or to maintain any Shakers house or to shut up any person in any Shakers house for the purpose of initiating such person into the ceremonies of Shakerism.

Owner or Manager of Estate or land shall inform Chief of Police of Shakers houses or meetings.

5.   (1) If it shall come to the knowledge of the owner or manager of any estate or land in the Colony that a Shakers house is being erected or maintained or that Shakers meetings are being held on the estate or land over which such owner or manager has control, he shall forthwith notify the Chief of Police of the erection or maintenance of such Shakers house or of the locality or place at which such Shakers meetings are being held.

(2) The manager or owner of any estate or land in the Colony who fails so to notify the Chief of Police or who knowingly permits the erection or maintenance of any Shakers house or the holding of Shakers meetings on any estate or land over which he has control, shall be guilty of an offense against this Ordinance.

No person to commit or to cause to be committed any act of indecency or immorality at or near Shakers meeting.

6. It shall be an offence against this Ordinance for any person at or in the vicinity of any Shakers meeting to commit or to cause to be committed or to induce or to persuade to be committed any act of indecency or immorality.

Police may enter without warrant house or place where Shakers meeting being held and take names and addresses.

7. (1) It shall be lawful for any party of Police of whom one shall be a Commissioned or Non-Commissioned Officer, without a warrant to enter at any time of the day or night any house or place in which such Commissioned or Non-Commissioned Officer may have good ground to believe or suspect that a Shakers meeting is being held or where he may have good ground to believe or suspect that any person or persons is or are being kept for the purpose of initiation into the ceremonies of Shakerism and to take the names and addresses of all persons present at such Shakers meeting or Shakers house.

(2) It shall also be lawful for any Commissioned or Non-Commissioned Officer of Police or for any Police or Rural Constable to demand the names and addresses of any persons taking part in any meeting in the open air which he has good reason to believe is a Shakers meeting.

Any person refusing to give name and address liable to arrest.

(3) Any person refusing to give his name and address to any Commissioned or Non-Commissioned Officer of Police or Police or Rural Constable when asked to do so under the authority of this section shall be liable to be arrested and to be detained at the nearest Police Station until his identity can be established.

Penalty for breach of Ordinance.

8. Any person guilty of an offence against this Ordinance shall be
    liable on summary conviction to a fine not exceeding £50, and in
    default of payment thereof to imprisonment with or without hard
    labour for a term not exceeding six months.

*Passed the Legislative Council the 3rd day of September, 1912, and published in the
Government Gazette this 1st day of October, 1912.*

PRESENTED BY THE GOVERNMENT PRINTER AT THE
GOVERNMENT PRINTING OFFICE KINGSTOWN, ST.
VINCENT, 1912.

Appendix C
The Shouters' Prohibition Ordinance
TRINIDAD and TOBAGO

AN ORDINANCE to render illegal indulgence in the practices of the body known as the Shouters.

Commencement [28 November 1917]

BE it enacted by the Governor of Trinidad and Tobago with the advice and consent of the Legislative Council thereof as follows:—

Short Title.

1. This Ordinance may be cited as the Shouters' Prohibition Ordinance, 1917.

Definition of 'Shouters meeting.'

2.—(1.) 'Shouters' meeting' means a meeting or gathering of two or more persons, whether indoors or in the open air, at which the customs and the practices of the body known as Shouters (hereafter in this Ordinance referred to as 'the Shouters') are indulged in. The decision of any Magistrate in any case brought under this Ordinance as to whether the customs and the practices are those of the Shouters shall be final, whether the persons indulging in such customs or practices call themselves Shouters or by any other name.

Definition of 'Shouters' house.'

(2.) A 'Shouters' house' means any house or building or room in any house or building which is used for the purpose of holding Shouters' meetings or any house or building or room in any house or building which is used for the purpose of initiating any person into the ceremonies of the Shouters. The decision of any Magistrate in any case brought under this Ordinance as to whether a house or building or room in any house or building is a Shouters' house shall be final.

(3.) The word 'manager' includes any person having control over or charge of any estate or land whatsoever in the Colony.

No person to take part in Shouters' meeting.

3.   It shall be an offence against this Ordinance for any person to hold or to take part in or to attend any Shouters' meeting or for any Shouters' meeting to be held in any part of the Colony indoors or in the open air at any time of the day or night.

No Shouters' house to be erected or maintained.

4.   It shall be an offence against this Ordinance to erect or to maintain any Shouters' house or to shut up any person in any Shouters' house for the purpose of initiating such person into the ceremonies of the Shouters.

Owner or manager of estate or land to inform Police of Shouters' house or meetings.

5.—(1.) If it shall come to the knowledge of the owner or manager of any estate or land in the colony that a Shouters' house is being erected or maintained or that Shouters' meetings are being held on the estate or land over which such owner or manager has control, he shall forthwith notify the non-commissioned officer in charge of the Constabulary station nearest to such house, estate or land of the erection or maintenance of such Shouters' house or of the locality or place at which such Shouters' meetings are being held.

(2.) The manager or owner of any estate or land in the Colony who fails to notify such non-commissioned officer as aforesaid, or who knowingly permits the erection or maintenance of any Shouters' house or the holding of Shouters' meetings on any estate or land over which he has control shall be guilty of an offence against this Ordinance.

Acts of indecency or immorality.

6. It shall be an offence against this Ordinance for any person at or in the vicinity of any Shouters' meeting to commit or cause to be committed or to induce or to persuade to be committed any act of indecency.

Police may enter without warrant house or place where Shouters meeting is being held.

7.—(1.) It shall be lawful for any party of members of the Constabulary Force, of whom one shall be a commissioned or non-commissioned officer, without a warrant to enter at any time of the day or night any house, estate, land or place in or on which such commissioned or non-commissioned officer may have good ground to believe or suspect that a Shouters' meeting is being held or where he may have good ground to believe or suspect that any person or persons is or are being kept for the purpose of initiation into the ceremonies of the Shouters' and to take the names and addresses of all persons present at such Shouters' meeting or Shouters' house.

(2.) It shall also be lawful for any member of the Constabulary Force to demand the names and addresses of any persons taking part in any meeting in the open air which he has good reason to believe is a Shouters' meeting.

(3.) Any person refusing to give his name and address to any member of the Constabulary Force when asked to do so under the authority of this section shall be liable to be arrested and to be detained at a Constabulary station until his identity can be established.

Penalties

8. Any person guilty of an offence against this Ordinance shall be liable on summary conviction before a Magistrate to a fine not exceeding £50 and in default of payment thereof to imprisonment with or without hard labour for a term not exceeding six months.

Passed in Council this Sixteenth Day of November in the year of Our Lord one thousand nine hundred and seventeen.

Appendix D
The Shakers' Prohibition Ordinance
GRENADA

No. 11 of 1927.

[Commencement: 19ᵗʰ March, 1927]

Be it enacted by the Governor with the advice and consent of the Legislative Council of

Grenada as follows:—

Short title.

1.   This Ordinance may be cited as The Public Meetings ("Shakerism") Prohibition Ordinance, 1927.

Meetings at which any immoral behaviour or practices are indulged in to be illegal.

2.   No meeting or gathering of two or more persons, shall be held, whether indoors or in the open air, at which any obscene or immoral behaviour or practices are indulged in, or at which behaviour or practices are indulged in which tend to exercise a pernicious or demoralizing effect upon persons attending such meeting.

No person to attend or take part in such meeting.

3.   No person shall hold, take part in, or attend any meeting prohibited by section two hereof.

Owner or occupier of any land or building and other persons having knowledge of such meetings shall inform Chief of Police.

4.—(1) If it shall come to the knowledge of any owner or occupier of any land or building, or of any person having control over or charge of any land or building, or of any Peace Officer or any public officer, that any meeting contemplated by Section 2 hereof has been held, or is being held, or is to be held, he shall forthwith inform the Chief of Police.

(2) Any person contemplated by the preceding subsection who fails so to inform the Chief of Police, or who knowingly permits the holding of any meeting on any land or in any house over which respectively he has control, or of which he is in charge, shall be guilty of an offense against this Ordinance.

No person to commit or to cause to be committed any act of indecency or immorality at or near prohibited meeting.

5. It shall be an offence against this Ordinance for any person at or in the vicinity of any prohibited meeting to commit or to cause to be committed or to induce or to persuade to be committed any act of indecency or immorality.

Police or Justice of Peace may enter without warrant house or place where prohibited meeting is being held and take names and addresses.

6.—(1) It shall be lawful for any party of Police (of whom one at least shall be a Commissioned or Non-Commissioned Officer) or for any person acting upon the authority of a Justice of the Peace without a warrant to enter at any time of the day or night any house or place in which such Commissioned or Non-Commissioned Officer or such Justice of the Peace may have good ground to believe or suspect that a prohibited meeting is being held and to take the names and addresses of all persons present at such meeting or house.

(2) It shall also be lawful for any Peace Officer to demand the names and addresses of any persons taking part in any meeting in the open air which he has good reason to believe is a prohibited meeting.

Any person refusing to give name and address liable to arrest.

(3) Any person refusing to give his name and address to any Peace Officer when asked to do so under the authority of this section shall be liable to be arrested and to be detained at the nearest Police Station until his identity can be established.

Penalty for breach of Ordinance.

7.   Any person guilty of an offence against this Ordinance shall be liable on summary conviction to a fine not exceeding fifty pounds, and in default of payment thereof to imprisonment with or without hard labour for a term not exceeding five months.

Passed this 14th day of March 1927.

Bibliography

Primary Sources

Manuscripts

Colonial Office. Public Record Office, National Archives, Kew Gardens, London. Several call numbers were consulted for Jamaica, St Vincent, Grenada and Trinidad and Tobago, all under class CO.

National Archives. Kingstown, St Vincent and the Grenadines. Manuscripts combined with printed pieces in the dossier, 'File on Shakerism.'

Printed-Archival

Alma Jordan Library, The University of the West Indies (UWI/AJL), Trinidad and Tobago. *Legislative Council Debates*, 1917; 1951.

Attorney General's Office. St. Vincent and the Grenadines. *Ordinances: Saint Vincent, 1926 Revision: Title 1, Administration of Justice* (London: 1927).

British Library. The *Parliamentary Debates from the Year 1803 to the Present*: several volumes consulted. Also, *Journal of the House of Commons*, 1908–1917, select volumes.

Colonial Office. Public Record Office, UK. All Prohibition Ordinances and other cited Acts.

National Archives. St Vincent and the Grenadines. *The Parliamentary Debates*, 1965.

National Archives. Trinidad and Tobago. Friendly Society constitutions. *Port of Spain Gazette* and *Trinidad Guardian*.

Printed-Online.

These include Google Books, Archive.org, JSTOR and other open access urls. *Archive.org* portal carries many Google Books but allows for reading of the full texts. JSTOR is a digital archive of scholarly works that allows public readers access to one hundred free items per month.

American Baptist Foreign Mission Society, *Baptist Missionary Society World Mission: Jamaica.* https://www.bmsworldmission.org/heritage/jamaica/.

Armitage, Thomas. *A History of the Baptists.* New York: Bryan, Taylor, 1890. https://archive.org/details/HistoryOfTheBaptists.

British Missionary Society. *The Baptist Magazine.* Several volumes consulted, from 1798 to 1905. Google Books. Inside these volumes are the volumes of *The Missionary Herald.*

Baptist Missionary Society, 115th Annual Report. London: 1907.

Blue Book of St Vincent, various volumes from 1900 to 1920. These were sourced from the SVGNA and Google Books.

Branch, C. W. 'The Endemic Religious Insanity of the Island of St Vincent,' *The Monist,* 17.2 (April 1907): 299–310, https://www.jstor.org/stable/27900040.

British West Indies Study Circle. *St Vincent Government Gazette,* multiple volumes consulted from 1894 to 1912. Available at https://bwisc.org/wp-content/uploads/References/1894–1969_Research_St-Vincent_ColonialGazettes.pdf.

Church, Mary. *Sierra Leone or The Liberated Africans in a Series of Letters from a Young Lady to her Sister in 1833 and 34.* London: 1835. http://www.sierra-leone.org/Books/Sierra%20Leone%20or%20the%20Liberated%20Africans.pdf.

Clarke, Robert. 'Sketches of the Colony of Serra Leone and its Inhabitants.' In *Transactions of the Ethnological Society of London ll.* London: 1863: 320–63.

Coke, Thomas. *A History of the West Indies Containing the Natural, Civil, and Ecclesiastical History of Each Island: With an Account of the Missions 2.* London: 1810.

Curry, William. *The Commentaries of Sir William Blackstone, KNT, on the Laws and Constitution of England,* Bk. IV. London: 1796.

Day, Charles William. *Five Years Residence in the West Indies.* London: 1852. (Google Book)

Dayrell, E[lphinstone]. 'Some Nsibidi Signs,' *Man* 10 (1910): 113–14. https://www.jstor.org/stable/2787339.

————. 'Further Notes on Nsibidi Signs with Their Meanings from the Ikom District of Southern Nigeria.' *The Journal of Royal Anthropological Institute of Great Britain and Ireland* 14 (July-December 1911): 521–40. https://www.jstor.org/stable/2843186.

Edwards, Bryan. *The History Civil and Commercial of the British West Indies*. London: 1793.

Fiddes, George Vandeleur. *The Dominions and Colonial Office*. London: Putnams, 1921.

Findlay, George G. and William W. Holdsworth, *The History of The Wesleyan Methodist Missionary Society* 2. London: Epsworth Press, 1921. Google Books.

Fyfe, Christopher. *'Our Children are Free and Happy:' Letters from Black Settlers in Africa in the 1790s*. Edinburgh: Edinburg University Press, 1991.

Gallagher, Joseph, ed. *The Documents of Vatican 2*. Translated by Walter A. Abbott. New York: Guild, 1956.

Handbook of Trinidad and Tobago. Select volumes from 1904 to 1934. These were sourced from the UWI/AJL and Google Books.

Hodgson, Robert. *The Life of the Reverend Beilby Porteus: Late Bishop of London*. London: 1812.

Hooke, Elyah. *The Year Book of Missions: Containing a Comprehensive Account of Missionary Societies, British, Continental and American With a Particular Survey of Stations in Geographical Order*. London: 1847. Google Book.

Kingsley, Charles. *At Last: A Christmas in the West Indies*. London: Macmillan, 1871. Google Books.

Liele, George, Stephen Cooke, Abraham Marshall, Jonathan Clarke and Thomas Nicholas Swigle. *'Letters Showing the Rise and Progress of the Early Negro Church of Georgia and the West Indies.' JNH* 1 no. 1 (Jan 1916): 69–92. https://jstor.org//stable/2713517.

Locke, John, Pierre Desmaizeaux and Pierre Coste. *A Collection of Several Pieces of Mr John Locke*. London: 1739. https://www.ncpedia.org/fundamental-constitutions.

Long, Edward. *History of Jamaica* 3. London: 1774.

Macgregor, J. K. 'Some Notes on Nsibidi.' *The Journal of Royal Anthropological Institute of Great Britain and Ireland* 39 (January–June 1909): 209–19. https://www.jstor.org/stable/2843292.

Mercer W. H. and A. E. Collins, comp. *The Colonial Office List.* Several editions consulted from 1902 to 1909.

————, comp. *The Dominion Office and Colonial Office List,* 1908 & 1932.

Scott-Keltie, J. ed. *The Statesman Year-Book,* 1909. London: 1909.

Select Parts of the Holy Bible for the Use of the Negro Slaves in the British West Indian Islands. London: 1807.

Shepheard, Wallwyn P. B. 'St Vincent.' In Harcourt Malcolm, Wallwyn P. B. Shepheard, R. Escombe Willcocks and Charles J. Tarring, 'The West Indies.' *Journal of the Society of Comparative Legislation* 14, no. 1 (1914): 224–43. https://www.jstor.org/stable/752633.

Swettenham, Frank. 'The Administration of the Crown Colonies.' In *The Empire and The Century: A Series of Essays on Imperial Problems and Possibilities by Various Writers.* London: John Murray, 1905. Google Book on Internet Archive.

The Supreme Court (UK). 'Judgment.' https://www.supremecourt.uk/cases/docs/uksc-2013-0030-judgment.pdf.

Trinidad and Tobago Blue Book. Select editions from 1914 to 1940. These were sourced from the PRO, the UWI/AJL and Google Books.

Secondary Sources

Many works were accessed on Questia Online Library, which ceased to operate from 2020.

Monographs

Adderley, Roseanne Marion. *'New Negroes from Africa': Slave Trade Abolition and Free African Settlement in the Nineteenth-Century Caribbean.* Bloomington, IN: Indiana University Press, 2006.

Bettelheim, Judith, ed. *Cuban Festivals: A Century of Afro-Cuban Culture.* Kingston, Jamaica: Ian Randle Publishers, 2001.

Bolland, Nigel O. *The Politics of Labour in the British Caribbean: The Social Origins of Authoritarianism and Democracy in the Labour Movement.* Kingston, Jamaica: Ian Randle Publishers, 2001.

Boyd, Jean. *The Caliph's Sister: Nana Asma'u 1793–1865 – Teacher, Poet and Islamic Leader.* London: Frank Cass, 2000.

Brass, Tom. *Toward a Comparative Political Economy of Unfree labour: Case Studies and Debates.* London: Frank Cass, 1999. Google Books.

Brereton, Bridget. *A History of Modern Trinidad 1783–1962.* Kingston, Jamaica: Heinemann, 1981.

Campbell, Mavis C. *Maroons of Jamaica, 1665–1796: A History of Resistance, Collaboration, and Betrayal.* Granby, MA: Bergin & Garvey, 1988.

Carmichael, Gertrude. *The History of the West Indian Islands of Trinidad and Tobago 1498-1900.* London: Alvin Redman, 1961.

Cox, Jeffrey. *The British Missionary Enterprise Since 1700.* London: Routledge, 2008. Google Books.

De Peza, Hazel Ann. *My Faith: Spiritual Baptist Christian.* Maitland, FL: Xulon Press, 2007.

De Verteuil, Anthony. *The Black Earth of South Naparima.* Port of Spain, Trinidad: Litho Press, 2009.

Diouf, Sylviane A. *Servants of Allah: African Muslims Enslaved in the Americas.* New York: New York University Press, 1998.

Epstein, Dana J. *Sinful Tunes and Spirituals: Black Folk Music to the Civil War.* Chicago: University of Illinois Press, 2003.

Fergus, Claudius. *Revolutionary Emancipation: Slavery and Abolitionism in the British West Indies.* Baton Rouge: Louisiana State University Press, 2013.

Figueira, Daurius. *Tubal Uriah Butler of Trinidad and Tobago Kwame Nkrumah of Ghana: The Road to Independence 6th March 1957, 31st August 1962.* New York: iUniverse, 2007. Google Books.

Fraser, Adrian. *From Shakers to Spiritual Baptists: The Struggle for Survival of the Shakers of St Vincent and the Grenadines.* Kingstown, St Vincent: Kings-SVG Publishers, 2011.

Frey Sylvia R. and Betty Wood. *Come Shouting to Zion: African American Protestantism in the American South and British Caribbean to 1830.* Chapel Hill, NC: University of North Carolina Press, 1998), 124–25. https://www.questia,com.

Fryer, Peter. *Staying Power: The History of Black People in Britain*. London, Pluto Press, 1984.

Glazier, Stephen D. *Marching the Pilgrims Home: A Study of the Spiritual Baptists of Trinidad*. Salem, WI: Sheffield, 1991.

Goldman, C. S., Comp. *The Empire and the Century: A Series of Essays on Imperial Problems and Possibilities by Various Writers*. London: 1905. Google Book, accessed at https://archive.org/details/empireandcentury00goldgoog.

Gomez, Michael. *Exchanging Our Country Marks: The Transformation of African Identities in The Colonial and Antebellum South*. Chapel Hill: University of South Carolina Press, 1998.

Gordon, Shirley C. *A Century of West Indian Education: A Sourcebook*. London: Longmans, 1963.

Hackshaw, John Milton. *The Baptist Denomination: A Concise History Commemorating One Hundred and Seventy-Five Years (1816–1991) of the Establishment of the 'Company Villages' and the BAPTIST FAITH in Trinidad and Tobago*. Trinidad: Amphy & Bashana Jackson Memorial Society, 1992.

Hart, Richard. *Slaves Who Abolished Slavery: Blacks in Rebellion*. Kingston, Jamaica: University of the West Indies Press, 2002.

Hastings, Adrian. *The Church in Africa, 1450–1950*. Oxford: Clarendon Press, 1996.

Henry, Frances. *Reclaiming African Religions in Trinidad: The Socio-Political Legitimation of the Orisha and Spiritual Baptist Faiths*. Barbados: University of the West Indies Press, 2003.

Herskovits, Melville J. and Frances S. Herskovits. *Trinidad Village*. New York: Alfred A. Knopf, 1947.

Hilton, Ann. *Kingdom of Kongo*. Oxford: Clarendon Press, 1985. Google Book.

Huggins, A. B. *The Saga of the Companies*. Princes Town, Trinidad: Twin Lock, 1978.

Ihenacho, David Asonye. *African Christianity Rises: A Critical Study of the Catholicism of the Igbo 1*. New York, NY: iUniverse, 2004. Google Book.

Jackson, John G. *Introduction to African Civilisations*. New York, NY: Citadel, 2001.

Jacobs, C. M. *Joy Comes in the Morning: Elton George Griffith and the Shouter Baptists*. Trinidad: Caribbean Historical Society, 1996.

James, C. L. R. *The Black Jacobins: Toussaint L'Ouverture and the San Domingo Revolution*. New York, NY: Random House, 1963.

Kostlevy, William. *Holy Jumpers: Evangelicals and Radicals in Progressive Era America*. New York: Oxford University Press, 2010. Google Book.

Laguerre, Michel S. *Voodoo and Politics in Haiti*. New York: St Martin Press, 1989.

Laitinen, Maarit. *Marching to Zion: Creolisation in Spiritual Baptist Rituals and Cosmology*. Helsinki: Helsinki University Printing Press, 2002

Lanning, Michael Lee. *African Americans in the Revolutionary War*. New York, NW: Kensington, 2000.

Leahy, Vincent. *History of the Catholic Church in Trinidad, 1797-1820*. Arima, Trinidad: St Dominic, 1980.

Lum, Kenneth Anthony. *Praising His Name in the Dance: Spirit Possession in the Spiritual Baptist Faith and Orisha Work in Trinidad, West Indies*. Amsterdam: Harwood Academic Publishers, 2000. Google Book.

Marshall, Arthur Calder. *Glory Dead*. London: Michael Joseph, 1939.

Martin, Tony. *Caribbean History: From Pre-Colonial Origins to the Present*. Boston, MA: Pearson, 2012.

Murphy, Joseph M. and Mei-Mei Sanford. *Osun Across the Waters: A Yoruba Goddess in Africa and the Americas*. Bloomington, IN: Indiana University Press, 2001.

Murrell, Nathaniel Samuel. *Afro-Caribbean Religions: An Introduction to the Historical, Cultural and Sacred Traditions*. Philadelphia, PA: Temple University Press, 2010.

Pankhurst, Richard. *A Social History of Ethiopia*. Trenton NJ: Red Sea Press, 1992.

———— Pankhurst, Richard. *The Ethiopians: A History*. Malden, MA: Blackwell, 2001.

Ryan, Cecil and Cecil A. Blazer Williams, *From Charles to Mitchell, Part 1* (n.p.: Projects Promotion, n.d.), SVGNA, CR-RBS-78

Simpson, George Eaton. *Black Religions in the New World*. New York, NY: Columbia University Press, 1978.

Stapleton, Ashram L. *The Birth and Growth of the Baptist Church in Trinidad and Tobago and the Caribbean*. Trinidad: A. L. Stapleton, 1983.

Stephens, Patricia. *The Spiritual Baptist Faith: African New World Religious History, Identity and Testimony*, London: Karnak House, 1999.

Warner-Lewis, Maureen. *Trinidad Yoruba: From Mother Tongue to Memory.* Kingston, Jamaica: University of the West Indies Press, 1997.

Weiss, John McNish. *The Merikens: Free Black American Settlers in Trinidad 1815–1816.* London: McNish & Weiss, 2008; 1995.

Woodson, Carter G. *The History of the Negro Church.* Washington, DC: Associated Press, 1921.

Wright, Dudley. Revision ed. *Gould's History of Freemasonry Throughout the World* 4. New York: Charles Scribner, 1936. Internet Archive.

Zane, Wallace W. *Journeys to the Spiritual Lands: The Natural History of a West Indian Religion.* New York: Oxford University Press, 1999.

Journal Articles and Book Chapters

Abimbola, Wande. 'Ifa: A West African Cosmological System.' In *Religion in Africa*, edited by Thomas D. Blakely, Walter E. A. van Beck and Dennis L. Thompson, 100–16. London: James Curry, 1992.

Besson, Jean and Barry Chevannes. 'The Continuity-Creativity Debate: The Case of Revival.' *New West Indian Guide* 70, no 3/4 (1996): 209–28. https://www.jstor.org/stable/41849777.

Blackburn, Robin. 'Haiti, Slavery, and the Age of the Democratic Revolution.' *William and Mary Quarterly, Third Series* 63, no. 4 (October 2006): 643–74. https://www.jstor.org/stable/4491574.

Bolland, O. Nigel. 'Systems of Domination after Slavery: The Control of Land and Labor in the British West Indies after 1838.' *Comparative Studies in Society and History* 23, no. 4 (1981): 591–619. https://www.jstor.org/stable/178395.

Bounds, Christopher T. 'How Are People Saved? The Major Views About Salvation with A Focus on Wesleyan Perspectives and Their Implications.' *Wesley and Methodist Studies* 3 (2011): 31–54. https://www.jstor.org/stable/42909800.

Bradshaw, Michael. 'True but Brief History of the Friendly Societies and Development of Black Bermudan Communities after Emancipation: Black People Seek Pride and Power in a Post–Slavery and Post–Emancipation World, the Bermudan Experience.' *Africology: The Journal of Pan–African Studies* 12, no.

1 (September 2018): 560–78. https://www.jpanafrican.org/docs/vol12no1/12.1–34–Bradshaw%20(1).pdf.

Brewer, Peter. 'Baptists of Trinidad (1815–1900).' *Missionary Herald: The Monthly Magazine of the Baptist Missionary Society* (January 1976): 5–7.

————. 1988. 'British Baptist Missionaries and Baptist Work in the Bahamas,' *The Baptist Quarterly* 32, no. 6, 295–301. https://biblicalstudies.org.uk.

Brooks, Walter H. 'The Evolution of the Negro Baptist Church.' *JNH* 7, no. 1 (January 1922): 11–22. https://www.jstor.org/stable/2713578.

————. 'The Silver Bluff Church: The History of Negro Baptist Churches in America,' *The Reformed Reader* (1910), https://www.reformedreader.org/history/negrobaptistchurches.htm.

Bush, Jonathan A. 'Free to Enslave: The Foundation of Colonial American Slave Law.' *Yale Journal of Law and Humanities* 5, no. 2 (January 1993): 417–70. https://openyls.law.yale.edu/bitstream/handle/20.500.13051/7629/24_5YaleJL_Human417_1993_.pdf?sequence=2.

Carr, Andrew. 'A Rada Community in Trinidad.' *Caribbean Quarterly* 3, no. 1 (1955): 36–54.

Christian, John T. 'A History of the Baptists.' Chap. 11, 'The Baptists of Virginia.' In *Baptist History: A History of the Baptist.* https://earnestlycontendingforthefaith.com/Books/JT%20Christian%20History%20of%20Baptists/BaptistHistoryJohnChristianV2S1c11.htm.

Coffey, John. 'European Multiconfessionalism and the English Toleration Controversy, 1640–1660.' In *A Companion to Multiculturalism in the Early Modern World*, edited by Thomas Max Safley. Leiden: Neth.: Brill, 2011. file:///C:C:/Users/kelfe/Downlaods/multiconfessionalismtoleration%20.pdf.

Cox, Edward. 'Religious Intolerance and Persecution: The Case of the Shakers in St. Vincent, 1900–1934,' SVGNA, file CR–RBC–179.

Cromwell, John W. 'First Negro Churches in the District of Columbia.' *JNN* 7, no. 1 (January 1922): 64–106.

Da Silva, Daniel Domingues, David Eltis, Philip Misevich and Olatunji Ojo, 'The Diaspora Liberated from Slave Ships in the Nineteenth Century.' *JAH*, 55, no. 3 (November 2014): 347–69. https://www.jstor.org/stable/43305212.

Davis, Asa J. 'The 16th Century Jihad in Ethiopia and the Impact on its Culture, Part ll: Implicit Factors Behind the Movement.' *Journal of the Historical Society of Nigeria* 3, no. 1 (December 1964): 113–28. https://www.jstor.org/stable/41856692.

Davis, John W. 'George Liele and Andrew Ryan, Pioneer Negro Baptist Preachers,' *JNH* 3, no. 2 (April 1918): 119–27. https://archive.org/details/jstor-2713485/page/n1/mode/2up.

Davy, Bandele Agyemang. 'Kumina in Rural Southeastern Jamaica: Beyond Resistance to Antithetical–Hegemonic–Subsumption.' *Africology: The Journal of Pan–African Studies*, 11, no. 7 (May 2018): 44–76.

Eason, Andrew M. '"All Things to All People to Save Some": Salvation Army Missionary Work Among the Zulus of Victoria Natal.' *Journal of South African Studies* 35, no. 1 (March 2009): 7–27. https://www.jstor.org/stable/40283212.

Elder, J. D. 'The Yoruba Ancestor Cult in Gasparillo: (Its Structure, Organisation and Function in Community Life).' *Caribbean Quarterly* 16, no. 3 (September 1970): 5–20.

Elkins, W. F. 'Suppression of the "Negro World" in the British West Indies.' *Science & Society* 35, no. 3 (Fall 1971): 344–47. https://www.jstor.org/stable/40401583.

Erskine, Noel Leo. 'George Liele: Liberated Slave and African American Baptist Missionary to Jamaica.' *Missiology: An International Review* 50, no. 1 (2022): 27–40. https://journals.sage.pub.com/doi/pdf/10.1177/00918296211043527.

Fatusi, Olayemi O.T. 'The Retransmission of Evangelical Christianity in Nigeria: The Legacy and Lessons from Bishop Samuel Ajayi Crowther's Life and Ministry (1810-1891),' *Southwestern Journal of Theology* (2019). https://swbtsv7.s3.amazonaws.com/media/Theology_Journal/61.2/61.2_The_Retransmission_of_Evangelical_Christianity_in_Nigeria_Fatusi.pdf.

Fergus, Claudius. 'African Secret Societies: Their Manifestations and Functions in West Atlantic Plantation Cultures.' In *Beyond Tradition: Reinterpreting the Caribbean Historical Experience*, edited by Heather Cateau and Rita Pemberton, 22–49. Kingston, Jamaica: Ian Randle Publishers, 2006.

————. 'From Slavery to Black Power: The Enigma of Africa in the Trinidad Calypso.' *Transactions of the Historical Society of Ghana, New Series* 16 (2014): 1–25.

Ferguson, James. 'Defenders of the Faith: On This Day.' *Caribbean Beat* 148 (November-December 2017). https://www.caribbean-beat.com/issue–148/defenders–of–faith#axzz83QnbLN9c.

Fletcher, L. P. 'The Decline of Friendly Societies in Trinidad and Tobago.' *Caribbean Studies* 24, no. 3/4 (1991): 59–78.

Forde, Maarit. 'The Spiritual Baptist Religion.' *Caribbean Quarterly: A Journal of Caribbean Culture* 65, no. 2 (2019): 212–240.

Furley, Oliver O. 'Moravian Missions and Slaves in the West Indies.' *Caribbean Studies* 5, no. 1 (1965): 3–16. https://www.jstor.org/stable/25611879.

Glazier, Stephen D. 'Adumbrations of Dread: Spiritual Baptists at the Dawn of the Millennium.' *Journal of Ritual Studies* 15, no. 1 (2001): 17–26. https://www.jstor.org/stable/44368584.

Gray, Richard. 'A Kongo Princess, the Kongo Ambassador and the Papacy.' *Journal on Religion in Africa* 29, no. 2 (May 1999): 140–54. https://www.jstor.org/stable/1581869.

Guano, Emanuela. 'Revival Zion: An Afro–Christian Religion in Jamaica.' *Anthropos* 89, no. 4–6 (1994): 517–28. https://www.jstor.org/stable/40463021.

Gullick, Charles. 'The Shakers of St. Vincent: A Symbolic Focus for Discourses.' In *New Trends and Developments in African Religions*, edited by Peter B. Clarke, 87–104. Westport, CT: 1998.

Harris, Robert L. 'Early Black Benevolent Societies.' *The Massachusetts Review* 20, no. 3 (Autumn 1979): 603–19. https://www.jstor.org/stable/25088988.

Harrow, Kenneth W. 'Islamic Literature in Africa.' In *The History of Islam in Africa*, edited by Nehemia Levtzion and Randall L. Pouwels, 519–44. Athens, Ohio: Ohio University Press, 2000.

Henderson, Conway W. 'Conditions Affecting the Use of Political Repression.' *The Journal of Conflict Resolution* 35, no. 1 (March 1991): 120–142. https://www.jstor.org/stable/174207.

Houk, James. 'The Role of the Kabbalah in Afro–Caribbean Religion in Trinidad.' *Caribbean Quarterly* 39, no. 3/4 (September–December 1993): 42–55. https://www.jstor.org/stable/40653859.

Hunte, Keith. 'Protestantism and Slavery in the British Caribbean.' In *Christianity in the Caribbean: Essays on Church History*, edited by Armando Lampe, 86–125. Barbados: University of the West Indies Press, 2001.

Ijoma, J. O. 'Portuguese Activities in West Africa Before 1600: The Consequences.' *Transafrican Journal of History* 11 (1982): 136–46. https://www.jstor.org/stable/24328537.

James, Harold R. 'Back to Africa.' In *African American Experience in World Missions: A Call Beyond Community*, edited by Vaughn J. Watson and Robert J. Stephens. Pasadena, CA: William Carey Library, 2002. Google Book.

Johnson, Kim. 'Born Again in Living Waters.' http://www.raceandhistory.com/historicalviews/africanspirit.htm. Accessed March 26, 2010.

Killingray, David. 'The Black Atlantic Missionary Movement and Africa, 1780s–1920s.' *Journal of Religion in Africa* 33, no. 1 (2003): 3–31.

Laurence, K. O. 'The Evolution of Long–Term Labour Contracts in Trinidad and British Guiana 1834–1863.' In *Caribbean Freedom: Society and Economy from Emancipation to the Present*, edited by Hilary Beckles and Verene Shepherd, 141–51. Kingston, Jamaica: Ian Randle Publishers, 1993.

Lualdi, Katharine J. 'Preserving the Faith: Catholic Worship and Communal Identity in the Wake of the Edict of Nantes.' *The Sixteenth Century Journal* 35, no. 3 (Fall 2004): 717–34, https://doi.org/10.2307/20477042.

Manuto, Ron. 'Historical Perspectives on Contemporary Freedom in America.' In *Religion, Law and Freedom: A Global Perspective*, edited by Joel Thierstein and Yahya R. Kamalipour. Westport, CT: Praeger, 2000.

Matar, Nabil. 'Islam in Britain, 1689–1750.' *Journal of British Studies* 47, no. 2 (April 2008): 284–300. https://www.jstor.org/stable/25482757.

Meek, C. K. 'The Religions of Nigeria,' *JIAI* 14, 3 (1943): 106–17, https://doi.org/10.2307/1155991.

Neal, John. '"In the Beginning": Gender, Ethnicity and the Missionary Enterprise.' https://www.methodistheritage.org.uk/missionary–history–neal–in–the–beginning–2011.pdf. Accessed January 3, 2020.

Newman, Albert H. 'Recent Changes in the Theology of Baptists.' *The American Journal of Theology* 10, no. 4 (October 1906): 587–609. https://www.jstor.org/stable/3154427.

Newman, Las. 'A West Indian Contribution to Christian Mission in Africa: The Career of Jackson Fuller (1845–1888).' *Transformation* 18, no. 4 (October 2001): 220–31. https://www.org/jstor/stable/43053953.

Ogunbado, Ahamad Faosiy. 'Impacts of Colonialism on Religions: An Experience of South–Western Nigeria.' *JHHS* 5, no. 6 (November–December 2012): 51–57. https://www.iosrjournals.org/iosr–jhss/papers/Vol5–issue6/10565157.pdf.

Payne, Ernest A. 'Baptist Work in Jamaica Before the Arrival of the Missionaries.' *The Baptist Quarterly* 7, no. 1 (1934): 20–26. https://doi:10.1080/0005576x.1934.11750306.

Pocklington, David. 'Church Bells and the Law.' *Law & Religion UK* (February 2018). https://lawandreligionuk/2018/02/13/church–bells–and–the–law/.

Porter, Arthur T. 'Religious Affiliation in Freetown, Sierra Leone.' *JIAI* 23, no. 1 (January 1953: 3–14.

Ramsay, Allison O. 'The Roots/Routes of the Ancient Order of Foresters in the Anglophone Caribbean with Special Emphasis on Barbados.' *History in Action* 2 no.1 (April 2011): 1–13.

Richter, Darmon. 'Freemasons of the Caribbean.' https://www.atlasobscura.com/articles/freemasons=of–the–caribbean. Accessed August 19, 2014.

Rocklin, Alexander. 'Imagining Religions in a Trinidad Village: The Africanity of the Spiritual Baptist Movement and the Politics of Comparing Religions.' *New West Indian Guide* 86, no. 1/2, (2012): 55–79. https://www.jstor.org/stable/41850694.

Ryder, A. F. C. 'The Benin Missions.' *Journal of the Historical Society of Nigeria* 2, no. 2 (December 1961): 231–269). https://www.jstor.org/stable/41970980.

Satchell, Veront M. 'Bedwardism.' In *The Encyclopedia of Caribbean Religions* 1, edited by Patrick Taylor & Frederick I: 117–22. Urbana, IL: University of Illinois, 2013.

Saunders, Alan. 'The State as Highwayman: From Candour to Rights.' In *Enlightenment and Religion: Rational Dissent in Eighteenth Century*

Britain, edited by Knud Haakonssen. Cambridge: Cambridge University Press, 2006.

Schuler, Monica, Mary Karasch, Richard Price and Edward Kamau Brathwaite, 'Afro–American Slave Culture [with commentary].' *Historical Reflections* 6, no. 1 (Summer 1979): 121–55. https://www.jstor.org/stable/41330420.

Simpson, George Eaton. 'Baptismal 'Mourning,' and 'Building' Ceremonies of the Shouters of Trinidad.' *The Journal of American Folklore* 79, no. 314 (October–December 1966): 537–50. https://www.jstor.org/stable/538219.

————. 'The Shango Cult in Nigeria and in Trinidad.' *American Anthropologist* 64, no. 6 (December 1962): 1204–219.

Smith, Gene Allen. '"Sons of Freedom": African Americans Fighting the War of 1812.' *Tennessee Historical Society* 71, no. 3 (Fall 2012): 206–27.

Smith, Robert Worthington. 'Slavery and Christianity in the British West Indies.' *Church History* 19, no. 3 (September 1950): 171–86. https://www.jstor.org/stable/3161292.

Sparkes, Douglas C. 'The Test Act of 1673 and its Aftermath.' *The Baptist Quarterly*, 25 (1973): 74–85. https://biblicalstudies.org.uk/pdf/bq/25–2–074.pdf.

'Test Act,' *Britannica*. https://www.britannica.com/topic/test–act.

Thornton, John K. '"I Am the Subject of the King of Congo": African Political Ideology and the Haitian Revolution.' *Journal of World History* 4, no 2 (Fall, 1993): 181–214. https://www.jstor.org/stable/20078560.

————. 'The Development of an African Catholic Church in the Kingdom of Kongo, 1491–1750.' *Journal of African History* 25, no. 2 (1984): 147–67. https://www.jstor.org/stable/181386.

Trotman, David. 'The Yoruba and Orisha Worship in Trinidad and British Guiana: 1838–1870.' *African Studies Review* 3 no. 2 (September 1976): 1–17. https://www.jstor.org/stable/523560.

Ukpuru. 'Igbo Water Divinities: Historical Images of the Igbo, their Neighbours and Beyond.' https://ukpuru.tumblr.com/post/157318196557/igbo–water–divinities. Accessed March 24, 2020.

Vansina, January 'Once Upon a Time: Oral Traditions as History in Africa.' *Daedalus* 100, no. 2 (Spring 1971): 442–468. https://www.jstor.org/stable/200224011.

Dissertations

Adetunmibi, M. A. 'Yoruba Spiritual Heritage and its Implications for the Yoruba Indigenous Churches in Nigeria.' PhD diss., North–West University, South Africa, 2017.

Boa, Sheena. 'Colour, Class and Gender in Post–Emancipation St Vincent, 1834–1884.' PhD diss., University of Warwick, 1998. https://wrap.warwick.ac.uk/39697/1/WRAP_THESIS_1998.pdf.

Brewer, Peter. 'The Baptist Churches of South Trinidad and their Missionaries, 1815–1892.' MTh diss., University of Glasgow, 1988.

De Marigny, Guy Desvaux. 'The Public Career of Lewis Harcourt (First Viscount) 1905–1916.' MA diss., University of Witwatersrand, Johannesburg, South Africa, 1987.

Knight, Charles William. 'A History of Expansion of Evangelical Christianity in Nigeria.' Louisville, KY: PhD diss., Southern Baptist Theological Seminary, 1951.

Roback, Judith. 'The White–Robed Army: Cultural Nationalism and a Religious Movement in Guyana.' PhD diss., McGill University, Montreal, 1973.

Spinelli, Joseph. 'Land Use and Population in St Vincent, 1763–1960: A Contribution to the Study of the Patterns and Demographic Change in a Small West Island.' PhD diss., Gainesville, FL: University of Florida, 1973.

Zane, Wallace Wayne. 'Journeys to the Spiritual Lands: Ritual Experience in Converted (Spiritual Baptist) Churches in St Vincent and Brooklyn.' PhD diss., University of California, 1987.

Index

www.ingramcontent.com/pod-product-compliance
Lightning Source LLC
Chambersburg PA
CBHW021939120726
47992CB00001B/56